PEGGY WEBLING AND THE STORY
BEHIND FRANKENSTEIN

Peggy Webling 1871–1949
Miniature by Ethel Webling (Webling Archive)

PEGGY WEBLING AND THE STORY BEHIND FRANKENSTEIN

THE MAKING OF A HOLLYWOOD MONSTER

Written and edited by
Bruce Graver and Dorian Gieseler Greenbaum

BLOOMSBURY ACADEMIC
LONDON · NEW YORK · OXFORD · NEW DELHI · SYDNEY

BLOOMSBURY ACADEMIC
Bloomsbury Publishing Plc
50 Bedford Square, London, WC1B 3DP, UK
1385 Broadway, New York, NY 10018, USA
29 Earlsfort Terrace, Dublin 2, Ireland

BLOOMSBURY, BLOOMSBURY ACADEMIC and the Diana logo are trademarks of Bloomsbury Publishing Plc

First published in Great Britain 2024

Copyright © Bruce Graver and Dorian Gieseler Greenbaum, 2024

Bruce Graver and Dorian Gieseler Greenbaum have asserted their right under the Copyright, Designs and Patents Act, 1988, to be identified as Authors of this work.

For legal purposes the Acknowledgements on p. ix constitute an extension of this copyright page.

Cover design: Bradford Louryk
Cover image of Peggy Webling by Ethel Webling

All rights reserved. No part of this publication may be reproduced or transmitted in any form or by any means, electronic or mechanical, including photocopying, recording, or any information storage or retrieval system, without prior permission in writing from the publishers.

Bloomsbury Publishing Plc does not have any control over, or responsibility for, any third-party websites referred to or in this book. All internet addresses given in this book were correct at the time of going to press. The author and publisher regret any inconvenience caused if addresses have changed or sites have ceased to exist, but can accept no responsibility for any such changes.

A catalogue record for this book is available from the British Library.

ISBN: HB: 978-1-3503-7164-4
PB: 978-1-3503-7165-1
ePDF: 978-1-3503-7166-8
eBook: 978-1-3503-7167-5

Typeset by Deanta Global Publishing Services, Chennai, India
Printed and bound in Great Britain

To find out more about our authors and books visit www.bloomsbury.com and sign up for our newsletters.

To the memory of Peggy, Josephine and Louis
Semper in corde meo

CONTENTS

List of illustrations	viii
Acknowledgements	ix
Introduction	1
Part I History and Commentary	7
1 Peggy Webling's story	9
2 The other woman who created Frankenstein	39
3 From Peake to Whale, and Webling's missing link	68
Part II Texts of Webling's *Frankenstein*	105
Frankenstein (1927)	109
Frankenstein (1928)	165
Prompt Script of *Frankenstein* (1930)	221
Appendix 1: Excerpts from Webling Letters Concerning Frankenstein	281
Appendix 2: Excerpt from *The Story of a Pen* by Peggy Webling, 1941	303
Appendix 3: Contracts	310
Bibliography	317
General bibliography	317
Sources from the Webling archive	322
Index	327

ILLUSTRATIONS

1.1	The Webling Family Tree, Miniatures by Ethel Webling	12
1.2	The Webling Sisters, *c.* 1884 Rosalind, Josephine, Peggy, Lucy	15
1.3	Programme cover, Steinway Hall, 29 October 1879	18
1.4	Left: 'A Sketch of John Ruskin' by Peggy Webling, 1914. Right: Frontispiece, silverpoint drawing of Ruskin by Ethel Webling	19
1.5	The Misses Webling, Lilliputian Fancy Fair 1882	21
1.6	Programme of Recital for their Royal Highnesses the Prince and Princess of Wales, 23 June 1882	22
1.7	Left: Lucy Webling as Little Lord Fauntleroy, 1888. Right: Peggy Webling as Dick the Bootlack and Lucy as Fauntleroy	23
1.8	Pauline Johnson and Friends, Brantford, Ontario, Canada, 1 July 1892	24
1.9	'Britannia', *c.* 1895: Peggy as Britain, Rosalind as Ireland, Lucy as Scotland	27
1.10	Postcard of the Women's Social and Political Union, *c.* 1912	31
1.11	'Peggy Webling, Novelist', 25 July 1920	34
2.1	Cover, yellowback copy of Mary Shelley's Frankenstein, G. Routledge and Sons, 1882	41
2.2	Title page of Webling's 1923 version of Frankenstein, registered on 16 January 1923	42
2.3	Peggy's letter to Josephine, 16 October 1927, p. 1	45
2.4	Programme for *The Only Way*, 19 June 1899	47
2.5	Hamilton Deane, Playbill for *Dracula*, 27 July 1931, Nottingham	48
2.6	Peggy's letter of 2 March 1928: 'another revolution in "F."!'	54
2.7	Frankenstein at the Theatre Royal, Nottingham, 11 June 1928	55
2.8	Playbill of *Frankenstein*, Little Theatre, London, 1930	60
2.9	Cartoon of *Frankenstein* in *Punch*, 19 February 1930, 219	62
3.1	Playbill of Frankenstein, The Lyceum Theatre, Sheffield, 27 October 1930	76
3.2	Scene from Act I of *Frankenstein*, Little Theatre, London, 1930	80
3.3	Scene from *Frankenstein*, Little Theatre, London, 1930	82
3.4	Scene from Act II of *Frankenstein*, Little Theatre, London, 1930	85
3.5	Scene from Act II of *Frankenstein*, Little Theatre, London, 1930	86
3.6	Scene from Act I of *Frankenstein*, Little Theatre, London, 1930	88
3.7	Scene from Act III of Frankenstein, Little Theatre, London, 1930	93

ACKNOWLEDGEMENTS

Bruce Graver:

I am grateful to the late Richard Gravil and Nick Roe for allowing us to debut our work on Webling's *Frankenstein* at the 2018 Wordsworth Summer Conference, on the 200th anniversary of the publication of Shelley's novel. Thanks also to Amelia Worsley, who invited us to Amherst College as part of their 2018 celebration of *Frankenstein*.

Without Anne McCullough's interest in the history of *Frankenstein* reception, and her fine senior thesis on the subject, I would not have heard of Peggy Webling. Thank you, Annie. And thanks also to Hannah Albright, who wrote her own senior thesis on the various versions of Webling's play, and convinced me of the value of Webling's achievement.

The Providence College Department of English sponsored a day-long celebration of *Frankenstein* on Halloween, 2018, including a student reading of the novel and a screening of Whale's film; Dorian Greenbaum presented an early version of her work on Webling's *Frankenstein* at that event.

Dorian Gieseler Greenbaum:

First, I thank Bruce Graver for a cordial collaboration, introducing me to the world of British Romantic literature and arranging for us to speak at the Wordsworth Summer Conference in 2018. (And I am grateful to Plato for writing the *Timaeus*, without which Bruce and I would not have met.) The organizers and participants of the Wordsworth Summer Conference 2018 supported us with their enthusiasm for our project and their hospitality.

David McLoughlin, executor of the will of Louis Drummond McRaye, arranged for me to have permission from the Library of Congress to receive a copy of the 1928 version of *Frankenstein* copyrighted there, and transferred the copyright to me. Bruce Kirby, librarian in the Manuscripts Division, Library of Congress, helped me to find the manuscript of Peggy Webling's *Frankenstein*, sent the pdf copy of the play to me and explained how to transfer copyright.

My Webling cousins, Tim French, the late Buzz French and the late Lindsay Dorney generously lent precious items from their family treasures so that they could be copied.

At the Westminster City Archives, Cecilia Alvik and Cliver Jones provided expert help and advice during my visit to the Archives on 25–26 May 2022. I thank Oliver Jones and Amanda House, senior archivist, for giving kind permission to use the text of the Prompt Copy of Peggy Webling's *Frankenstein*. Oliver also assisted me in obtaining quality scans for the book. The staff in the Newsroom, British Library, were expert and patient in assisting me during my visits, 28–30 December 2022. Stewart Gillies, News

Acknowledgements

Media Reference Team Leader, British Library, kindly found the page number of an obscure reference in *The Lady* magazine. Zoe Stansell, Manuscripts Reference Service, British Library, notified me of the British Library's kind permission to use the text of the 1927 version of *Frankenstein* in this book. Imaging Services and Karl Harris helped with hi-resolution scans of newspaper photographs of scenes from the play. The staff at the Billy Rose Theatre Division, New York Public Library, assisted me in examining the John L. Balderston material on *Frankenstein*.

David J. Skal, whose books were immensely helpful, took the time to go through his old notes to answer my questions about quotations from John Balderston concerning *Dracula* and *Frankenstein*. My dear friend Barbara Cronenberger gave useful advice and went above and beyond in proofreading. Bradford Louryk designed the cover and delighted me with his vast knowledge of Frankenstein *and* Peggy Webling.

Finally, my gratitude and love to Don, for everything he is and does.

INTRODUCTION
Bruce Graver and Dorian Gieseler Greenbaum

Peggy Webling's *Frankenstein* is the missing link between Mary Shelley's novel and James Whale's 1931 Universal film, which created the pop culture Frankenstein that we all know and fear. If you pick up a typical piece of scholarship on the reception history of *Frankenstein*, it's likely you will find nary a mention of Peggy Webling or, if you do, that the reference consists of a sentence or two about her (minor) contribution to the 1931 James Whale film. The starring roles will, instead, be given to Whale, to Boris Karloff and Colin Clive, to the adapter John Balderston, to Universal Studios or even, occasionally, to Mary Shelley, who at least deserves every bit of her fame. But Peggy Webling? Who's that?

This book will tell the story – ignored, forgotten and partly unknown – of a woman who ended up being nearly as important as Mary Shelley herself in the history of the Frankenstein legend and how we think about it today. It is our contention that the movie of Frankenstein released in 1931 by Universal Pictures would not have appeared in the form that it did without the success on the British stage of the play Webling wrote.

We present here, for the first time, the full text of Peggy Webling's *Frankenstein*, in three different versions that show the evolution of her thinking about the play. In addition, we provide a detailed biographical account of Webling herself, supported by crucial manuscript material from both public and private archives. We also place Webling's play in context with earlier stage and film adaptations of Shelley's novel, in order to show how (as one critic put it) Webling's 'treatment of the novel . . . is . . . central . . . to the reshaping of the Frankenstein tradition.'[1] As the first woman to adapt *Frankenstein* for the stage, Webling brings a feminist perspective to her play much closer to Mary Shelley's original vision than earlier adaptations, and one that clearly reflects her lifelong advocacy for women's rights. These playscripts, together with Webling's other unpublished writings, reveal the full story of her role in the history of the Frankenstein legend.

About the book and its contents[2]

The making of a Hollywood monster begins in Victorian London, where Peggy Webling was born in 1871, the next-to-youngest daughter of Robert James and Maria Webling. In Chapter 1, we present the story of her life, introducing Webling's world, her family and

---

[1] Audrey A. Fisch, *Frankenstein: Icon of Modern Culture* (Hastings, Sussex: Helm Information, 2009), 162.
[2] Information in this introduction comes from sources that will be fully cited in the chapters that follow.

the experiences that would influence the shape of her writing. She was one of six sisters, five of whom had talents that propelled them into the limelight of the theatre and art worlds of London as children and young adults. Fortunately for this family of daughters, their parents were unconstrained by the typical prejudices of the day regarding the abilities of women. They were intellectual and unconventional; they loved literature, art and the theatre, and encouraged their daughters in all their pursuits. Both parents were omnivorous readers, and the family read together nightly throughout their lives. Of the six, one became an artist, one a professional lecturer, one an actress and later novelist, and one a professional writer who one day wrote a *Frankenstein* play. All were activists for women's rights.

Webling became famous in her youth as one of the celebrated 'Webling Sisters', whose public career began when their mother, looking for ways to augment the family income, rented Steinway Hall in London and drew a crowd of six hundred to their first performance as dramatic reciters. Peggy was eight, Rosalind twelve and Josephine seventeen. With good notices in the London papers, and an admiring letter from John Ruskin (a lifelong influence on the three sisters), the girls were on their way. Soon they were receiving praise from the likes of Oscar Wilde, and performing for Lily Langtry and the future Edward VII and Queen Alexandra. They met people in the London theatre world such as Henry Irving, Ellen Terry and Herbert Beerbohm Tree. Their youngest sister, Lucy, joined them in 1885, and she toured England, Scotland and Ireland as 'Little Lord Fauntleroy' in 1888.

The sisters performed in the British Isles, United States and Canada for a total of eighteen years. In 1891, Webling published her first short story in Canada, and when she returned from their Canadian–US tour in 1897, began to write short stories for newspapers and magazines in London. She became a journalist for a theatrical newspaper in the early 1900s, but by 1910 was earning her living as a successful novelist. By 1921 she had had one play produced, and had published eleven novels, one non-fiction book, two booklets and numerous short stories.

Chapter 2 covers the writing and production of Webling's *Frankenstein*. In 1921 Webling wrote the first draft of her play based on Mary Shelley's *Frankenstein*. The idea had come to her more or less out of the blue in 1920, but it would be seven years before the play was produced. Most scholars writing about stage and film adaptations of *Frankenstein* claim that the actor Hamilton Deane was a friend who commissioned Webling's play as a companion piece for his successful stage version of *Dracula*. They are wrong: Webling did not know Deane when she wrote the play. She sent him the script unsolicited in 1927, at the suggestion of her sister Lucy, who had worked with Deane at the beginning of their acting careers.

Frankenstein, A Play in a Prologue and Three Acts (based upon Mrs Shelley's well-known book) by Peggy Webling was first performed on 7 December 1927 in Preston, Lancashire. It toured in the English provinces for more than two years, and was frequently revised before it arrived at London's Little Theatre on 10 February 1930, where it ran for seventy-two performances. By the time it came to London, the play was already being considered for an American run in New York, adapted by John L. Balderston, who had

Introduction

previously adapted Hamilton Deane's *Dracula* for the same purpose. Favourable reviews for the London production attracted the attention of Horace Liveright, who had also produced the New York *Dracula* in 1927, and Webling and Balderston signed a deal with him on 24 February 1930. That deal fell through, however, and on 8 April 1931, Webling and Balderston signed a contract with the Universal Picture Corporation, which allowed the film of 1931 to be produced. The play itself continued to be performed in provincial theatres for several years – according to Balderston, over 700 times.

Chapter 3 begins by placing Webling's *Frankenstein* in relation to the nineteenth-century stage adaptations written in the 1820s and produced with some regularity throughout the century. These include *Presumption* by Richard Brinsley Peake, first performed in 1823; *Le monstre et le magicien* by Merle and Béraud, produced in Paris in 1826, translated into English by John Kerr and produced in London that same year; and Henry Milner's *Frankenstein, or the Man and the Monster*, also produced in London in 1826. Attention will be given to the Edison film of 1910, written and directed by J. Searle Dawley, and starring Charles Ogle as the creature, as well as to a little regarded One-Act Frankenstein adaptation, *Aylmer's Secret* by Stephen Phillips. But the central focus will be on the four extant versions of Webling's play, beginning with the 1923 double-cast version, the 1927 version, which debuted in the Lancashire city of Preston in 1927, the 1928 version, performed in repertory with *Dracula* in provincial theatres between 1928 and 1930, and the 1930 prompt script, performed in London at the Little Theatre in 1930, as well as at various provincial theatres for the next several years. The first woman to adapt *Frankenstein* for the stage, Webling brings a distinctly different perspective to the story that is closer to Mary Shelley's original vision, and anticipates the feminist revaluations of the novel beginning in the 1970s. We will then consider John Balderston's revision of Webling's play for the New York stage, and conclude with a look at James Whale's borrowings from Webling in both the 1931 Universal *Frankenstein* and *Bride of Frankenstein* (1935). This will end Part I of our study.

Part II of the book consists of the full texts of three versions of Webling's play: the 1927 text, licensed by the Lord Chamberlain on 16 November 1927, and first performed at the Empire Theatre in Preston on 7 December of that same year;[3] the copyrighted 1928 text, revised during that year and deposited in the Library of Congress, Washington, DC, on 7 September, 1928; and the prompt script used in the 1930 London production of *Frankenstein*, held by the City of Westminster Archives. These are the versions that were performed on the English stage, and they trace the development of Webling's thought about her subject as she judged audience reaction and received various kinds of feedback and criticism from reviewers, as well as from the actors and producer she worked with. For instance, Webling and Deane almost immediately realized that Act III of the 1927 play was weak, and Webling set about revising it early in 1928, adding the creature's request for a mate. The 1928 script is the first *Frankenstein* script by any author

---

[3] This copy is on deposit in the British Library, #7975 in the Lord Chamberlain's list.

to incorporate this request, and is the version of the play sent to John Balderston, used as the basis for his revision of Webling's play for the New York stage. The 1928 text is similar to the 1930 script through the end of Act II. But she revised Act III for the London stage, probably at the urging of Hamilton Deane.

In addition to texts of the play, we include in the appendices excerpts from the correspondence between Webling and her sisters regarding the writing, production and performances of *Frankenstein*, including her negotiations with John Balderston. These are supplemented with copies of the various contracts she signed, both with Balderston and with Horace Liveright. (Webling and Balderston ultimately signed a contract with Universal Pictures for the 1931 film, directed by James Whale.) We also include the chapter about *Frankenstein* from her unpublished memoir, *The Story of a Pen*, written in 1941.

Sources

Our research is based on documents preserved in several public and private archives. Principally, we have consulted an archive of Webling documents owned by one of the authors, Dorian Gieseler Greenbaum, which we have designated the Webling Archive. This archive consists of letters and some playscripts, unpublished manuscripts, photographs, artwork (one of Webling's sisters, Ethel, was a professional artist), autograph birthday books, copies of Webling's published works, birth, marriage and death records and other memorabilia. The Webling Archive has been compiled from material left or given to Greenbaum by her immediate family and by her cousin, the late Louis Drummond McRaye (1915–2019), who inherited material from his aunt, Peggy Webling, and his mother, Lucy Webling McRaye. Some Webling documents have been made available in copies from some of Greenbaum's other Webling cousins.

We have also had access to several versions of Webling's *Frankenstein*, written and revised over a period of about a decade. These include the 1927 Preston, Lancashire version, the first to be performed on any stage, which is preserved as part of the Lord Chamberlain's Plays held by the British Library; the 1928 version copyrighted on 7 September 1928 and held by the US Library of Congress; and the prompt copy for the 1930 London production, part of the Hamilton Deane Papers at the City of Westminster Archives. The very first version of Frankenstein that Webling wrote in 1921 does not survive, but a previously unknown 1923 version – in which both the creator and his creature are played by the same actor – exists in the Webling Archive, and selections from this script will also appear in this volume.

In addition, we have consulted the John L. Balderston Papers at the New York Public Library.

How this book came to be

This is a tale of luck and serendipity on many fronts. For Peggy Webling, it was that she happened to be born into a family dominated by women, with parents who embraced

Introduction

eccentricity, at the height of the Victorian age; that she worked as a child in the English theatre world, and that these experiences led to her career as a novelist and dramatist. Born into a family of extraordinary people, her sisters' talents, as well as her own, gave her a well of experiences and contacts to draw on. For the owner of Peggy's unpublished writings (one of this book's authors), it was the chance of having a grandmother who saved the vital letters written to her mother-in-law; and a cousin, with his own raft of documents, whom she came to know because of them.

In 2017, the two authors of this book, Bruce Graver and Dorian Gieseler Greenbaum, met at a conference on Plato's *Timaeus* at Brown University. Graver, a Providence College professor of English literature specializing in British Romanticism, and Greenbaum, an ancient historian at the University of Wales, discovered a common interest in *Frankenstein* while chatting at a reception during the conference. Graver had directed senior theses on the composition of *Frankenstein* and the history of its adaptations. Greenbaum was the owner of a large collection of letters, manuscripts and photographs owned by the Webling sisters, one of whom was her great-grandmother Josephine, and another who was Peggy Webling, the author of the stage play *Frankenstein*, which was the basis for the 1931 Boris Karloff film. When Graver discovered that Greenbaum had unpublished manuscripts of *Frankenstein* written by her great-grand aunt, he asked to see a copy – and a collaboration was born.

PART I
HISTORY AND COMMENTARY

CHAPTER 1
PEGGY WEBLING'S STORY
Dorian Gieseler Greenbaum

'. . . a sweet little old lady with grey hair, a perfect lavender lady of a playwright, so mild in mien and so gentle in aspect . . .'

Herbert Farjeon, 'Seen on the Stage: The Mystery of the Woman Playwright', *Vogue*, 5 March 1930, 56

This impression of the author of *Frankenstein* after its London debut at the Little Theatre in 1930[1] evokes a life that was actually far more out of the ordinary than the 'sweet little old lady' image would suggest. This chapter will introduce you to Peggy Webling, her family and friends, and the life experiences that informed the playwright and her play. Much of this historical material has been unresearched or unknown until now. Before we begin, however, a note about the use of first names: since I grew up with family stories of Peggy and the Webling sisters, for reasons of familiarity and convenience I shall call them not by their surnames, but by the names I have heard throughout my life.

Peggy's story begins in London, where she was born in St Martin's Lane not long after midnight, on New Year's Day 1871.[2] She was the sixth of seven daughters (one died in infancy) born to Maria and Robert James Webling. Her given name was Margaret, but she was never called anything but 'Peggy'. She arrived into a family with four sisters and two parents who were unconventional in their views of child-raising and equality both within the family and outside of it. Peggy grew up in an environment that supported girls and their aspirations and talents, and in a setting well suited to the arts, books, theatre and conversations with interesting and sometimes noteworthy people. When Peggy was two, the family moved to Wellington Terrace on the Bayswater Road.[3] With the heart of London just outside her door, she used Kensington Palace Gardens as her playground

---

[1]Other reviews of *Frankenstein* in the same vein include the following. 'A Shelley Play', *The Star*, 8 February 1930: 'A charming, quiet voiced, white-haired woman . . .'; 'The Little. "Frankenstein"', *The Stage*, 13 February 1930, 16: 'as adapted by the now white-haired Miss Peggy Webling, years ago one of the celebrated Webling sisters'; 'Johanna', 'The Lady Looks On', *The Lady*, 20 February 1930, 240: 'Miss Peggy Webling herself came on the stage – a small, white-haired figure with a soft, sweet voice'; Hannen Swaffer, 'London as It Looks', *Variety*, 26 February 1930, 77: 'It was rather surprising, at the end, to find that this horrible play had been written by a dear old lady, for such Peggy Webling proved to be, . . . looking like a schoolmarm from a middle west main street.'
[2]Back of 1906 postcard belonging to Ethel Webling, in Maria Webling's hand (Webling Archive): 'P[eggy]. Jan 1.71, 1.20 AM'; Birth Certificate, Margaret Webling, General Record Office (UK), 1871, Strand District, No. 467, District of Long Acre, County of Middlesex, January–March Quarter, 3b 179, '92 St Martin's Lane'.
[3]Peggy Webling, *Peggy: The Story of One Score Years and Ten* (London: Hutchinson & Co., 1924), 20.

and was nurtured by her father's breadth of mind and omnivorous reading habits,[4] her mother's energy and intelligence,[5] and the loving circle of her sisters.

The ancestors

Robert James Webling and Maria Webling were first cousins, the eldest son and eldest daughter, respectively, of brothers Robert and Henry Webling. The Webling family had lived in Camberwell and Peckham, Surrey, since at least the 1770s,[6] though they claimed to have been Londoners since the 'Times of Old Queen Bess'.[7] They were a conventional family of dairymen, fruiterers, butchers and coachdrivers, decidedly middle-class tradespeople. Though the Weblings were not, as a rule, 'reg'lar church goers',[8] her great-grandfather, William Webling, was known to be exceedingly pious: when he went out he looked 'neither to the left or right, fearing – as he expressed it, "to lose the presence of the Lord"'.[9] Peggy's paternal grandmother called him 'Old Squire Square Toes' and her father dubbed him 'S. S. serious and staid'.[10] There were, however, streaks of eccentricity from time to time. William's son Robert eloped with Elizabeth Phillips, a beauty known as the 'nut brown maid of Peckham', whose family seems not to have approved of him.[11] But, as Peggy's father wrote in a letter to his daughter Josephine, 'people were much less

---

[4]Ibid., 18.
[5]Ibid., 16.
[6]Robert Webling married Elizabeth Smith in Camberwell St Giles on 9 November 1779 (Camberwell St Giles Parish Records: marriage record, 1779, no. 326, p. 109); from Church of England Parish Registers. London Metropolitan Archives, London, database online at ancestry.com (accessed 31 October 2022). They were the parents of Peggy's great-grandfather, William Webling.
[7]R. J. Webling to Herrick Torr, his grandson, 1 September 1912 (Webling Archive); Webling, *Peggy*, 20: 'I love with my whole heart the words of Spenser: "mery London, my most kyndly nurse / That to me gave this life's first native sourse"'; Josephine Webling Watts, 'Personal Recollections of the closing-in of the Victorian Era' (lecture given at Plandome, Long Island, NY, 1.00 pm, 7 October 1925) (Webling Archive): 'we have been Londoners for over 500 years, living and dying within the sound of Bow Bells'; Peggy Webling, *The Story of a Pen: A Book for Would-be Writers* (unpublished manuscript, 1941) (Webling Archive), MS page 60: 'I am a Londoner to my fingertips.' Weblings had arrived in England in the sixteenth century, probably from Groten Recken, near Coesfeld, Westphalia (research of D'Arcy Webling, with letter of 12 August 1993 from the Coesfeld Town Archivist, Ludwig Frohne, stating that men with surnames close to 'Webling' were living in the area in the fifteenth to seventeenth centuries) (Webling Archive). Returns of aliens in London for 1567 show a Nicholas Webling, Brewer (among others), arriving in 1553: R. E. G. Kirk and Ernest F. Kirk, eds, *Returns of Aliens dwelling in the City and Suburbs of London*, Part I, 1523–1571, vol. X, part 1 (Aberdeen: Publications of the Huguenot Society of London, 1900), 343. See also the 'Weblin of Barking' pedigree at the Essex Record Office, Sage Collection 105. It has not yet been possible to connect these Weblings to Robert Webling. Nevertheless, Robert James, Peggy and her sister Josephine all emphasized their deep London roots.
[8]Webling, *Peggy*, 24 (the phrase comes from Samuel Butler's *The Way of All Flesh*).
[9]R. J. Webling to Herrick Torr, 1 September 1912.
[10]Ibid.
[11]Webling, *Peggy*, 13–14; R. J. Webling to Josephine Webling Watts, undated (Webling Archive): 'Her folks objected to young Webling. Why? I dont [sic] know'. They married on 19 October 1823 at Upton-cum-Chalvey, Bucks: 'England Marriages, 1538–1973', database at familysearch.org https://www.familysearch.org/ark:/61903/1:1:N27Q-D5D (accessed 31 October 2022).

independent of public opinion than they now are'.[12] And the Weblings generally stayed in that vein.

Peggy's maternal grandparents, Henry Webling and Maria Astle, were equally conventional, though Maria had been known to throw off her married woman's cap and play with her children.[13] She also enjoyed taking them to the theatre with a food hamper to sustain them during the performance, and brought them to see Queen Victoria and Prince Albert when they stopped near their home in Chertsey, Surrey, to change horses on their way to Windsor.[14] Henry, on the other hand, resisted change and longed for the good old days.[15] When he signed Peggy's autograph birthday book,[16] he wrote, in a copperplate hand, the popular verse 'Henry Webling is my name / England is my nation / Peckham is my Birthplace / and Christ is my Salvation.'[17]

The parents

But Peggy's immediate family was anything but conventional. The marriage of Robert James and Maria, fittingly at the Free Church in Kentish Town in 1858,[18] united two eccentric members of their large families. Their educations would lead them to train their own daughters' sensibilities, interests and talents by combining a love of the fine arts, literature and music with practical ambitions. Robert James was essentially an autodidact, an idealist who loved ideas, and books, and beauty.[19] Maria's more traditional education was put to practical use as a governess and as the French correspondent for a firm of lace dealers in S. Audley Street, experiences that would serve her well later.[20] Both

---

[12] R. J. Webling to Josephine Webling Watts, undated.
[13] Webling, *Peggy*, 15.
[14] Ibid., 15–16.
[15] Ibid., 15.
[16] The autograph birthday book was popular in the nineteenth century: see Lauren O'Hagan, 'Guest Post: The birthday book: tracing an absent presence', 15 March 2017, Special Collections and Archives/ Casgliadau Arbennig ac Archifau, Showcasing Research Resources/Hyrwyddo Adnoddau Ymchwil, Cardiff University, https://scolarcardiff.wordpress.com/2017/03/15/birthday-book/ (accessed 31 October 2022). Peggy's contained quotations from Shakespeare opposite the date pages left blank for the signers.
[17] Peggy Webling's Birthday Book, 171, entry for August 12 (Webling Archive). The verse was used as early as 1765; see Pamphlet Wars, no. 4, 'Vox Populi, Vox Dei, A Providence Gazette Extraordinary. August 24, 1765', John Carter Brown Library, https://www.brown.edu/Facilities/John_Carter_Brown_Library/exhibitions/pamphletWars/pages/crisis.html (accessed 31 October 2022). It was popular on samplers from the eighteenth and nineteenth centuries, e.g. 'Esther Tincom's Sampler', National Museum of American History, Behring Institute, Smithsonian Institution, https://americanhistory.si.edu/collections/search/object/nmah_646290 (accessed 31 October 2022), and even appeared in Joyce's *Portrait of the Artist as a Young Man* (1916).
[18] Marriage Registration, General Record Office (UK), 1858, 1b 245, St Pancras District, No. 135 (Webling Archive). The Free Christian Church, Kentish Town, had broken away from the Congregationalists in 1853, led by its popular pastor, William Forster; see 'The Free Christian Church', *The British Millennial Harbinger*, vol. VI, Third Series (London: Arthur Hall and Co., 1853), 540–4. Forster married Robert James and Maria Webling.
[19] Webling, *Peggy*, 18–19.
[20] Ibid., 16.

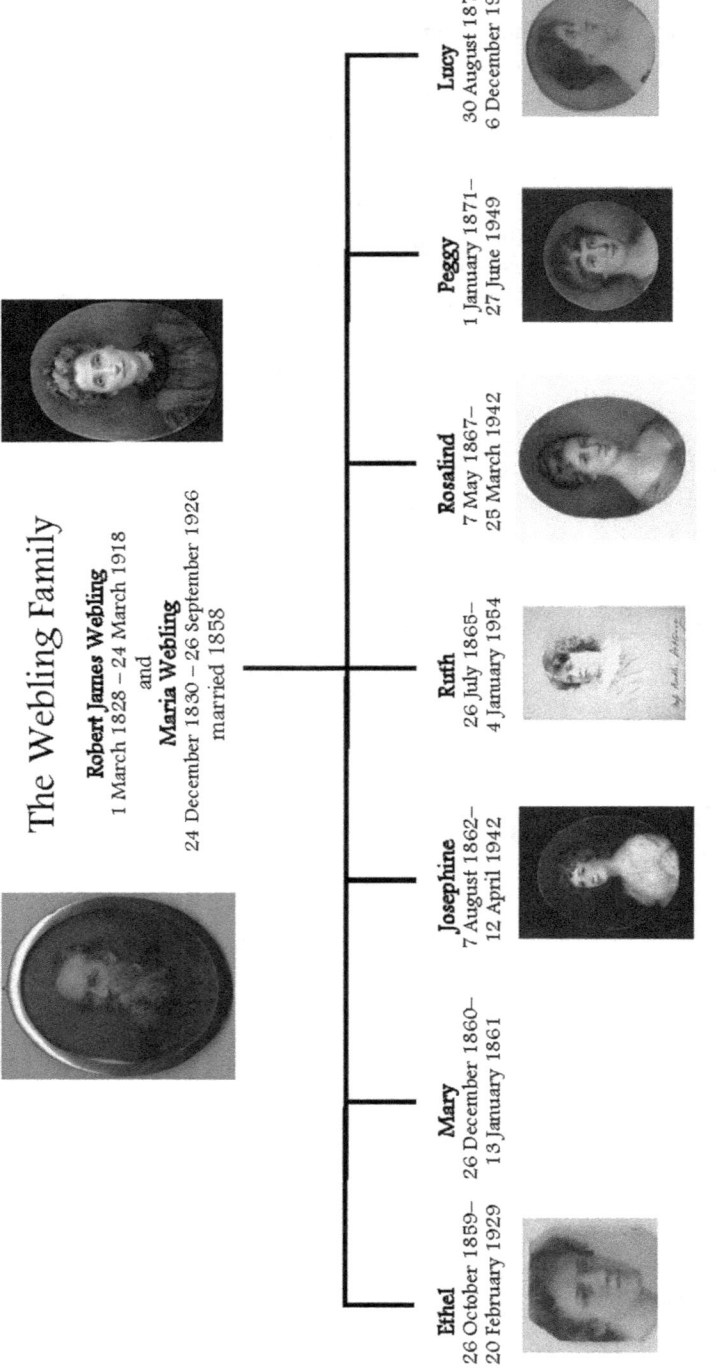

Figure 1.1 The Webling Family Tree, Miniatures by Ethel Webling (Webling Archive).

parents embraced the romanticism of the day, and prized cultural pursuits over worldly success. Theirs was a world of ideas, literature and the arts, a world where they met and chatted with Dickens in the street[21] and had Lewis Carroll for tea.[22]

The girls had some brief periods of schooling, but were mostly taught by their parents. Their mother read aloud to them every night, from the *Canterbury Tales*, Dickens and Shakespeare,[23] and Peggy was acting by the age of seven. Her first part, 'Moth', in *Love's Labour's Lost*, came about through her sister Ethel's friendship with Charlotte McCarthy, in an amateur production presented at the house of MP Justin McCarthy, 48 Gower Street, London, probably some time in 1878.[24] A family production of *Beauty and the Beast*, where Peggy played 'Silverstar, Queen of the Fairies', took place at the 'Theatre Royal', 78 Carlton Hill (actually the home of her uncle, Walter Webling), on 24 January 1879.[25] It seems that these events inspired their mother to consider a more professional, and income-producing, scheme. Later that year on the 5th of July, 'The Sisters Webling' (Josephine, Rosalind and Peggy) had their first paying gig, a 'Dramatic Recital' for a fee of three guineas, again at the house of Justin McCarthy.[26]

The sisters

This seems a good point at which to say something about Peggy's sisters, who were undoubtedly as large an influence on her life as her parents were. (Needless to say, without the voluminous correspondence among them over more than thirty years, much of the material shared in this book would not exist.) Theirs was a strong and loving relationship – Peggy called them 'the beloved five'.[27] There were six living sisters: Ethel, Josephine, Ruth, Rosalind, Peggy and Louisa Betty, known as Lucy (Mary, the second oldest, had died at the age of 18 days in January 1861). The anecdote shared by Peggy in her autobiography, *Peggy: The Story of One Score Years and Ten*, is worth repeating here:

> Only girls? Yes. No brothers? No. (One is generally asked both questions, as if the second was an original improvement on the first.) When Stopford Brooke put it

---

[21]Josephine Webling Watts, 'Personal Recollections of the closing-in of the Victorian Era'. In an anecdote described as 'hearsay', she wrote that she and her parents met Dickens in St Martin's Lane a few months before his death in June 1870.
[22]Webling, *Peggy*, 36–7. Peggy was unimpressed with the Reverend Charles Dodgson, who subjected her to frustrating puzzles she was unable to solve.
[23]Ibid., 24.
[24]Ibid., 26–30.
[25]Programme, *Beauty and the Beast*, dated 24 January 1879 (Webling Archive). In the 1875 *London Post Office Directory*, 2250, Walter Webling was at that address (London Metropolitan Archives; London City Directories 1736–1943, database online at ancestry.com); see also Webling, *Peggy*, 31.
[26]Programme, 'Dramatic Recital' by 'The Sisters Webling', 5 July 1879 (Webling Archive); Webling, *Peggy*, 32.
[27]Webling, *Story of a Pen*, MS page 40; Webling, *Peggy*, 85. In 1910 she wrote in her copy of *A Spirit of Mirth*, 'To the Beloved Five: Ethel, Josephine, Ruth, Rosalind and Lucy' (Webling Archive).

to my Mother, he added: 'Bad stock, Mrs. Webling, bad stock!' 'We don't want brothers,' said Josephine. 'We shall be quite happy to have other people's.'[28]

Josephine, Rosalind, Peggy and Lucy were the major players in the dramatic recitals that gave the Webling sisters their dose of fame in the 1880s and 1890s. Ethel, their artist sister, was instrumental in the inauguration of this career and was the sister Peggy lived with from 1897 on, as they cared for their ageing parents. It was especially through Ethel and Lucy that Peggy's connections with the theatrical world were forged.

Josephine (7 August 1862–12 April 1942), called 'Jossie', was the rock on which the other reciting and acting sisters leaned. She 'feared nobody on earth and could fight her own battles when she was five years old.'[29] With her fierce intellect, skill at reciting and acting and her ability to coach her other sisters, she was the mainstay of their troupe. She coached her sister Lucy when the latter was cast as Little Lord Fauntleroy.[30] She was an expert in English literature, and made her living as a lecturer on books, plays, the Victorian age and women's rights. During a voyage to England on the RMS *Adriatic* in 1915, Josephine took the pro side in a debate on women's suffrage.[31] Peggy's correspondence with her sister, which Josephine saved, is what gives us vital insights into Peggy's writing, her sensibilities and the history of her Frankenstein play.

Ruth (26 July 1865–4 January 1954), whose talents were musical, not dramatic, rarely performed with the sisters, and after her marriage in 1889 was not involved with their careers. Her contribution to this story comes through her daughter, Ruthie, some of whose memorabilia, including Peggy's Birthday Book, came to me through Louis McRaye, her first cousin (Lucy's son).

Rosalind (7 May 1867–25 March 1942) possessed a pre-Raphaelite beauty, and, of all the sisters,[32] became John Ruskin's favourite.[33] She performed with Josephine and Peggy from the beginning as one of the 'Sisters Webling' and continued reciting until her marriage in 1898 to Canadian George W. Edwards, a photographer in Vancouver, BC.

---

[28] Webling, *Peggy*, 7. Stopford Brooke was an Irish clergyman and author who lived in London at the same time as the Weblings, and was 'greatly influenced by [John] Ruskin': James Quinn, 'Brooke, Stopford Augustus', in *Dictionary of Irish Biography*, https://doi.org/10.3318/dib.000993.v1. Originally published October 2009 as part of the *Dictionary of Irish Biography*, last revised October 2009 (accessed 10 January 2023). Stephen Gill, *Wordsworth and the Victorians* (London: Oxford University Press, 2001), 235–46, emphasizes Brooke's important role in Wordsworth studies: a founding member of the Wordsworth Society, as was John Ruskin (1881), Brooke spearheaded the effort to purchase Dove Cottage (1890) and became a co-founder of the Dove Cottage Trust.
[29] Webling, *Peggy*, 42.
[30] 'Little Lord Fauntleroy', *The Era*, 15 December 1888, 9.
[31] Programme from the RMS *Adriatic*, 26 March 1915, 'a Debate on "Should Women Vote" . . . Suffrage, Mrs. A. A. Watts; Anti, Mr. P. B. Millar' (Webling Archive).
[32] A miniature portrait of Rosalind by her sister Ethel (see it in Figure 1.1 above), painted in a pre-Raphaelite style, shows her beauty (miniature in the collection of Lindsay Dorney).
[33] Webling, *Peggy*, 52.

Peggy Webling's Story

Figure 1.2 The Webling Sisters, *c.* 1884 Rosalind, Josephine, Peggy, Lucy (Webling Archive).

Lucy (30 August 1877–6 December 1952), the youngest sister, and the most dramatically talented, was known as 'the prettiest child in England'[34] after she was discovered by the London photographers Elliott and Fry. At seven, she joined her older sisters in recitals,[35] and at eleven became 'The Real Little Lord Fauntleroy',[36] playing the part around 500 times throughout England, Scotland and Ireland in 1888 and 1889. Interviews with the family during the run of *Little Lord Fauntleroy* emphasize the talents of the sisters and Lucy's in particular ('she has gained three prizes for original writing in "Atalanta"');[37] she began writing poetry from an early age. Lucy was the only sister to have a professional acting career as an adult; among other engagements, she played in George Alexander's *The Ambassador* (1898)

---

[34] 'They are the Fad Now: The Misses Webling Very Popular in New York Society', *The Gloucester County Democrat*, 17 December 1891 (vol. XIV, no. 18), 4; the same article in numerous other newspapers (see n. 77).
[35] Programme, 'The Misses Webling's Dramatic Recital', Steinway Hall, 30 June 1885 (Webling Archive): 'On this occasion Miss LUCY WEBLING (Aged Seven) will make her first appearance.'
[36] Programme for *The Real Little Lord Fauntleroy* (Horace Lingard's Company), first performance 30 August 1888 (Lucy's eleventh birthday) at New Cross Public Hall (Webling Archive); 'Review, The Real Little Lord Fauntleroy', *The Era*, 1 September 1888, 8.
[37] 'Little Lord Fauntleroy', *The Era*, 15 December 1888, 9. *Atalanta* was a monthly magazine for girls, which ran from 1887 to 1898: see COVE (Collaborative Organization for Virtual Education, a scholar-driven open access platform), https://editions.covecollective.org/chronologies/launch-atalanta (accessed 14 September 2022).

15

and William Haviland's *The Only Way*, a drama based on *A Tale of Two Cities* (1899).[38] In 1909 she married Walter McRaye, the stage and business partner of the renowned Canadian poet Pauline Johnson (Tekahionwake).[39] She also published two novels.

Ethel, the eldest sister (26 October 1859–12 February 1929), was a professional artist specializing in portraits and miniature painting, though she painted landscapes as well. She exhibited at the Royal Academy and became known especially for her theatrical illustrations of actors and plays produced by the likes of Henry Irving and Beerbohm Tree.[40] She must have shown a talent for art very early. Her father was impressed enough to show one of her drawings to George Boughton, R. A.,[41] who told him 'You must send that child to an art school. Send that child to an art school if you have to sell your boots!'[42] So Ethel went to the Slade School, University College London, which had just opened in 1871.[43] Ethel was in one of the first cohorts of students: her teacher was Sir Edward Poynter, the first Slade professor in London.[44] It was a joyous day for her when he noted on one of her drawings that she could go into the 'Life' (the studio with live models).[45] It was Ethel's friend at the Slade, Charlotte McCarthy, who had arranged for Peggy to play Moth, and the Slade also provided an opportunity for Peggy to stand on a model table and recite poetry as the students worked.[46]

The Slade was also indirectly responsible for the introduction of the Weblings to John Ruskin. Ethel and Peggy were invited to tea by the wife of Marcus Huish, director of the Fine Art Society,[47] to which Ruskin had also been invited. Peggy was asked to recite.

---

[38] Programme for *The Ambassador*, 2 June 1898 (Webling Archive); two programmes for *The Only Way*, 19 June 1899 at the Prince's Theatre, Bristol and 17 July 1899 at the Theatre Royal Merthyr (Webling Archive).

[39] See more on Johnson's partnership with Walter McRaye in Betty Keller, *Pauline: A Biography of Pauline Johnson* (Vancouver: Douglas & McIntyre, 1981).

[40] The Folger Shakespeare Library in Washington, DC holds a script of *Twelfth Night* as performed by Henry Irving and Ellen Terry, with illustrations by Ethel in the margins. The Shakespeare Birthplace Trust recently publicized Ethel's illustrated renditions of *Julius Caesar*: Ella Hawkins, 'Solving Mysteries in the SBT Archives: Ethel Webling and Herbert Beerbohm Tree', https://www.shakespeare.org.uk/explore-shakespeare/blogs/solving-mysteries-sbt-archives-ethel-webling-and-herbert-beerbohm-tree/ (accessed 31 October 2022); 'Julius Caesar, Ethel Webling and Herbert Beerbohm Tree', YouTube video, https://www.youtube.com/watch?v=QNBuImo3CY0 (accessed 31 October 2022). The Garrick Club in London has a portrait of Tree by Ethel, given to them by Lucy Webling McRaye in 1951: https://garrick.ssl.co.uk/object-g0819 (accessed 31 October 2022).

[41] George Boughton, R. A. (1833–1905), was an American-raised, British-born painter and illustrator who spent his career in London. Originally self-taught (perhaps why he was adamant for Ethel to go to an art school?), he was known for peasant scenes ('Sketching Rambles in Holland') and New England historical subjects; he illustrated *Rip Van Winkle* and *The Scarlet Letter*: see Martin Hardie, 'George Henry Boughton', in *Dictionary of National Biography*, ed. Sidney Lee, Supplement II, vol. 1 (London: Oxford University Press, 1912), 197–8.

[42] Webling, *Peggy*, 7–8.

[43] The Slade School of Fine Art (part of University College London) was created from the legacy of Felix Slade to endow three chairs in Fine Art: one in Oxford, one in Cambridge and one in London. See the history of the school at https://www.ucl.ac.uk/slade/about/history#1868-1899 (accessed 31 October 2022).

[44] She probably enrolled *c.* 1875, because Poynter left sometime during that year.

[45] Webling, *Peggy*, 7.

[46] Ibid., 31–2. Another friend of Ethel's from the Slade was Evelyn Pickering De Morgan, a pre-Raphaelite artist who married the novelist William De Morgan. In 1914, Peggy and her father visited the De Morgans' house in Chelsea, where they toured Evelyn's gallery (Letter from R. J. Webling to Josephine, 17 January 1914, Webling Archive).

[47] Anne Helmreich, 'Forum: Eminent Victorians, Marcus Huish (1843–1921)', *Victorian Review* 37, no. 1 (2011): 27.

Peggy Webling's Story

After reciting some of Lear's 'Nonsense Verses' and 'On a day (alack the day!)' from *Love's Labour's Lost* for him, Ruskin told his cousin Joan Severn that 'We are not going back to Brantwood just yet, Joanie. We're going to stay in London to hear Peggy at Steinway Hall.'[48]

The misses Webling give dramatic recitals

This story brings us back to the beginning of the Webling Sisters' reciting career, which began when their mother rented Steinway Hall after the small success of their three-guinea performance at Gower Street. By sheer grit and determination, Maria Webling organized the recital, publicized it and ended up with an audience of 600 on 29 October 1879 at Steinway Hall, Portman Square.[49] The recital was favourably reviewed.[50] It was repeated, with some changes of material, on 4 December.[51] John Ruskin attended one of the Steinway Hall performances, and endorsed the sisters' reciting skills in a letter written to their father on 16 February 1880; this was later used as a testimonial in attracting public audiences and private engagements.[52] Tom Taylor, the dramatist and art critic,[53] also may have seen the 4 December recital, since he wrote a letter on 19 February 1880, at the request of the Webling parents, to assess the girls' skills, citing some performance pieces from that date. He said of Peggy:

> I seem to see in Josephine & Peggy unusual aptitude & ability – i.e. beyond the *average* of children, in many of whom the mimetic or acting & reciting power, is very strong.... Peggy has uncommon humour & intelligence, & in a form likely to receive even fuller & readier appreciation than her elder sister's qualities, because humour, the power that causes laughter is always the quickest to be applauded & the most generally liked.... I feel less confident in pronouncing an opinion as to vocation – she is too young as yet, to afford safe ground for conclusions, as to

---

[48]Story related in Webling, *Peggy*, 45–6. The same anecdote in Peggy Webling, *A Sketch of John Ruskin* (London: self-published, 1914), 12–14.
[49]Webling, *Peggy*, 33: 'an audience of over six hundred.'
[50]H. Savile Clarke, 'The Examiner of Plays', *The Examiner*, 8 November 1879, 1438: '[the Webling sisters] recite well-known pieces with wonderful elocutionary power and admirable expression.'
[51]Review in *The Era*, 7 December 1879, 6, 'The Misses Webling's Recitals', mentions the performance on 'Thursday evening at Steinway Hall'.
[52]Webling, *Peggy*, 43–4, 46; Letter reprinted in John Ruskin, *Arrows of the Chace: Being a Collection of Scattered Letters Published Chiefly in the Daily Newspapers, 1840–1880*, vol. 2 (Boston: Dana Estes & Company, no date [c. 1900]), 357–8 . The letter was reprinted in the *Daily News*, 18 February 1880, 6, col. 6: 'Mr. Ruskin on the Misses Weblings' Recitations.'
[53]Charles Kent, 'Taylor, Tom', in *Dictionary of National Biography*, ed. Sidney Lee, vol. 55, Stow–Taylor (London: Smith, Elder & Co., 1898), 472–4: Taylor (1817–80) was born in Sunderland, educated at Cambridge and was a professor of English at London University (two years), a lawyer (briefly) and a public health professional until 1871. He is best known, though, for his journalism (art critic for the *Times* and *Graphic*, and editor of *Punch*) and his work as a dramatist, starting in 1844 and writing over 100 plays, including 'The Ticket-of-Leave Man' and 'Our American Cousin'. He died suddenly at his home, Lavender Sweep, Wandsworth, on 12 July 1880.

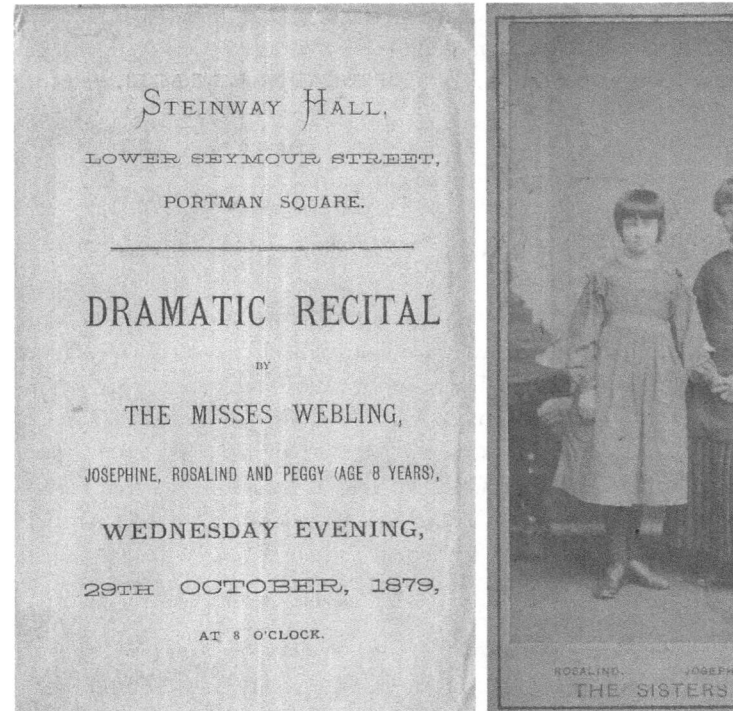

Figure 1.3 Programme cover, Steinway Hall, 29 October 1879: Dramatic Recital by the Misses Webling; and The Sisters Webling, c. 1880: Rosalind, Josephine, Peggy (Webling Archive).

either her powers or her bent – though all seems to promise fairly for the first, &, if so, she too should have a future open to her on the stage.[54]

The sisters probably had no further contact with Taylor, since he died on 12 July 1880. His assessment seems apt – though the Weblings did not eliminate the Shakespeare scenes from their recitals as Taylor advised them to do![55]

They did have more contact with John Ruskin, and he became an influence and inspiration, at least to the three sisters who saw and wrote to him the most – Josephine, Rosalind and Peggy, whom Ruskin nicknamed 'Fate' (the sisters called him 'the Professor' and 'Fidelity'). Much of Ruskin's correspondence with them can be viewed at the Ruskin Museum, Coniston, Lancashire.[56] Peggy devoted an entire chapter of her autobiography

---

[54] Tom Taylor (Lavender Sweep, Wandsworth) to Mrs Webling, 19 February 1880 (Webling Archive).
[55] Ibid. Taylor letter, sheet 1, p. 4 'My advice is to omit the scenes of Lysander, Hermia & Helena & not to give them anything Shaksperian to read in public at present.'
[56] Most of the letters were written between 1881 and 1888. There are twenty-two letters to Peggy in the Coniston collection. Two of Ruskin's letters to Josephine were given to Patricia and Pamela Watts by their grandmother,

Figure 1.4 Left: 'A Sketch of John Ruskin' by Peggy Webling, 1914. Right: Frontispiece, silverpoint drawing of Ruskin by Ethel Webling (Webling Archive).

to Ruskin, and also wrote a short, self-published appreciation of him, with a frontispiece life-drawing by Ethel.[57] Peggy and Rosalind made two trips to Brantwood to stay with Ruskin, in August of 1880 and sometime in the autumn of 1881 (Josephine and their mother joined them in the latter visit). Josephine lectured on Ruskin,[58] and both Josephine and Rosalind named sons after him.

The recitals continued – both in public venues and private homes – throughout the 1880s. They were a means for meeting London literati and others. Josephine became friends with Emily Davis Pfeiffer, the Welsh poet known for her sonnets and feminist leanings,[59] who gave garden parties at her house in Putney. Here the sisters met Oliver Wendell Holmes and Mark Twain when they were in London, and Robert Browning,[60]

Josephine Webling Watts, now held respectively by Dorian Gieseler Greenbaum and Kathryn Kiningham Donovan.
[57]Webling, *A Sketch of John Ruskin*.
[58]'John Ruskin', Radio Lecture by Josephine Webling Watts, 30 April 1929 (Webling Archive).
[59]See Jessica Hinings, 'Pfeiffer [née Davis], Emily Jane', *Oxford Dictionary of National Biography*, https://doi-org.ezproxy.uwtsd.ac.uk/10.1093/ref:odnb/22084 (accessed 30 October 2022).
[60]Ethel made a miniature of his wife Elizabeth Barrett Browning and her son 'Pen' from a Fratelli d'Alessandri 1860 photograph (miniature in the Webling Archive). See the original photograph in the National Portrait Gallery,

who misquoted Shelley's 'To a Skylark' (Josephine noticed this instantly because 'Skylark' was one of her recital poems).[61] They recited for Lily Langtry and Patsy Cornwallis-West.[62] Highlights of their performances included a Fancy Fair in Knightsbridge, where they dressed entirely in peacock feathers and acted with the sons of Henry Irving.[63] They also performed for the then-Prince and Princess of Wales (later Edward VII and Queen Alexandra), at Milner Field, Saltaire, the home of businessman and philanthropist Titus Salt, Jr near Bradford, on 23 June 1882.[64] The fame of the Webling sisters began to spread, and they gained admirers like Oscar Wilde ('Is not Peggy Webling a wave of delight from God?' he remarked to John Ruskin).[65] Ellen Terry, whose luminous presence stayed with Peggy all her life, lent them her box at the Lyceum when she and Henry Irving were performing in *Faust* in 1885[66] and *Becket* in 1893.[67]

Their friends were not limited to those they met from recitals. One in particular, a frequent presence at Wellington Terrace, was Henry Page, an artist[68] who introduced her to books she loved (*Alice in Wonderland*, Lear's *Nonsense Verses*, Charles Kingsley's *Heroes*), drew pictures for the sisters and showed Peggy how to 'love all that was beautiful, and the truth that underlies beauty'.[69] He was the reason she put a character named 'Henry' in all her stories, 'for I made a promise to myself always to use it in memory of a beloved friend of my youth.'[70]

In 1888, Lucy was asked to play 'Little Lord Fauntleroy' in the touring company of *The Real Little Lord Fauntleroy*, with the special approval of Frances Hodgson Burnett. After a three-week rehearsal period[71] the tour began, with Peggy also cast in the small role of Dick, the Bootblack. Lucy's success in this tour of *Fauntleroy* led to her being offered the role of

---

https://www.npg.org.uk/collections/search/portrait/mw111433/Robert-Wiedemann-Barrett-Browning-Elizabeth-Barrett-Browning?LinkID=mp83905&role=art&rNo=1 (accessed 30 October 2022).

[61] Webling, *Peggy*, 68.

[62] Ibid., 83. Mrs. Cornwallis-West was a mistress of the future Edward VII.

[63] Ibid., 71–2; 'A Lilliputian Fair', *Daily News*, 1 July 1882, 6: 'One young lady, who presided at a magic well, was attired literally from head to foot in a . . . costume, composed solely of peacock feathers.' See also Austin Brereton, *The Life of Henry Irving*, vol. 1 (London: Longmans, Green and Co., 1908), 361.

[64] 'Programme of Recital given in presence of Their Royal Highnesses The Prince and Princess of Wales (by the kind invitation of Mrs. Titus Salt) at Milner Field On Friday, June 23rd, 1882, by The Misses Webling, (Josephine, Rosalind and Peggy)' (Webling Archive); Webling, *Peggy*, 72–3.

[65] Webling, *Peggy*, 71.

[66] Ibid., 79.

[67] Ellen Terry to 'Miss Lucy Webling', 25 May 1893; programme for *Becket*, 29 May 1893 (Collection of Lindsay Dorney; copies in Webling Archive). See also Webling, *Peggy*, 78–80.

[68] Unknown today, Page exhibited 'Nereid', a watercolour, at the Dudley Gallery in 1881 ('Mr. Henry Page, whom we seem to meet for the first time—paints with admirable glow of colour and richness of tone a "Nereid"', *The Standard*, 7 March 1881, 2); and ten bronze portrait medallions at the Royal Academy from 1889 to 1892, including Sir Richard Burton *The Exhibition of the Royal Academy, 1892. The 124th*, https://w`ww.royalacademy.org.uk/art-artists/exhibition-catalogue/ra-sec-vol124-1892, 59; 'Royal Academy', *Nottingham Evening Post*, 9 May 1892, 2) and Jerome K. Jerome (*The Exhibition of the Royal Academy, 1889. The 121st*, https://www.royalacademy.org.uk/art-artists/exhibition-catalogue/ra-sec-vol121-1889, 63) (accessed 30 January 2023).

[69] Webling, *Peggy*, 36, 42, 201.

[70] Webling, *Story of a Pen*, MS page 94.

[71] 'Little Lord Fauntleroy', *The Era*, 15 December 1888, 9.

Figure 1.5 The Misses Webling, Lilliputian Fancy Fair 1882 (Webling Archive).

'Nixie', in a play version of Burnett's *Editha's Burglar*, written especially for her by Burnett and her future husband, Stephen Townsend. The Weblings were persuaded to invest in and produce the play, but on the opening night (7 April 1890), the reviews were not kind to Burnett and Townsend, though they praised Helen Forsyth as Kitty and Lucy as Nixie.[72] The failure of *Nixie* was a financial blow to the Weblings, and so Josephine and Peggy were sent to Brantford, Ontario, to live for a time with their paternal uncle Ted and his family, with perhaps a hope to augment the family income by giving recitals in Canada.[73]

The years in Canada were formative for material that Peggy would use in her writing career. They would also introduce her to Pauline Johnson, the revered national poet of Canada, who wrote a poem for her in that first languid summer of 1890.[74] Peggy and

---

[72] E.g., 'The Theatres. Terry's', *The Morning Post*, 8 April 1890, 5; 'Stage and Song. "Nixie"', *Pall Mall Gazette*, 8 April 1890, 1.

[73] They left on 12 June 1890 with their cousins Walter and Emilie Webling (Ted's children) and Hastings Webling (son of their paternal uncle Charles Frederick Webling). Ship Manifest, SS *Vancouver*, arriving Montreal 21 June 1890 (Library and Archives Canada, Passenger Lists, 1865–1922, Microfilm Reel Number: C-4537, List Number 27, page 9 of 12, Reference RG 76, Item Number: 2868).

[74] Webling, *Peggy*, 148–9. Johnson (1861–1913) was born and raised near Brantford, ON, Canada. The daughter of Chief George Johnson and Emily Howells, she was educated in both European and Mohawk culture. She began her career as a poet, adding recital and performance; her performances were partly done in Mohawk dress, where she used the name Tekahionwake. She toured Canada and the United States (from 1901 to 1909 her partner was Walter McRaye, who would marry Lucy Webling), and performed in London, where her first book, *The White Wampum*, was published. She died in 1913 in Vancouver (see Marilyn J. Rose, 'Johnson, Emily

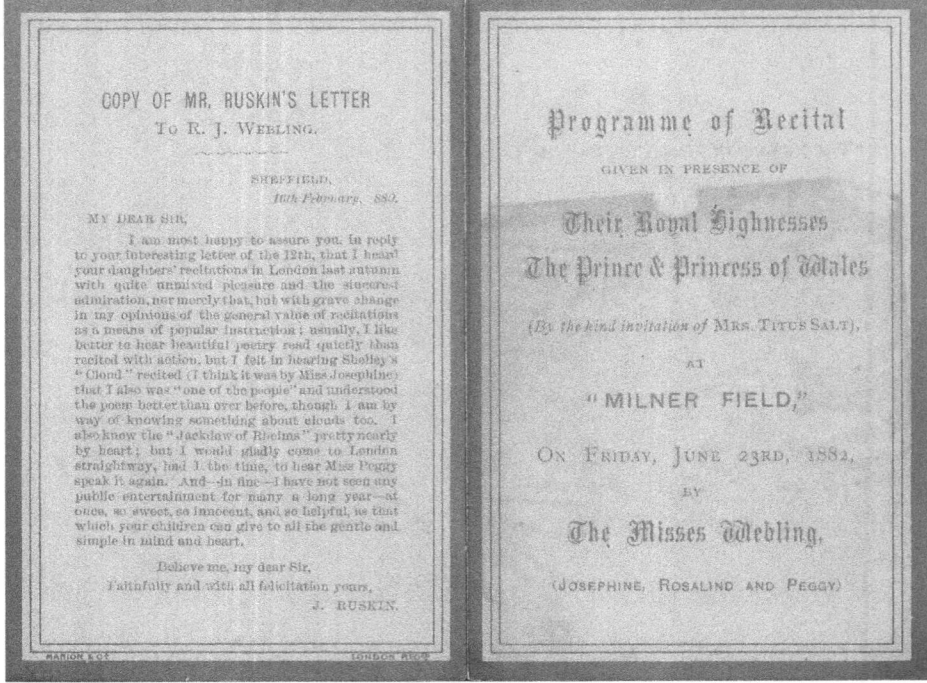

Figure 1.6 Programme of Recital for their Royal Highnesses the Prince and Princess of Wales, 23 June 1882 (Webling Archive).

Josephine went canoeing with Pauline out on the Grand River; later, Josephine would meet her husband, Alfred Allen Watts, through her, at the Brantford Fair in May 1891.[75] A photograph taken by the river in Brantford on 1 July 1892 shows Pauline, Rosalind, Peggy, Josephine and Lucy Webling, Emilie Webling and A. A. Watts shortly before Josephine and A. A.'s marriage. The Brantford Fair also provided Peggy with her first view of the 'show people' she would use as characters in short stories and novels. Pauline gave advice to the sisters when they began to give recitals in Canada, and persuaded them to go on a Canadian tour in the mid-1890s.

Peggy wrote her first published story in Brantford. 'An English Actor's Ghost Story' appeared in the *Brantford Expositor* and earned her $C3.[76] (There is a strange coincidental connection here between Peggy's 'ghost story' and Mary Shelley's 'ghost story' that was *Frankenstein*, their first published works.) Peggy's utter absorption and delight in writing it showed her that she had found her métier, though years would pass before its realization.

Pauline', in *Dictionary of Canadian Biography*, vol. 14 (University of Toronto/Université Laval, 2003–), http://www.biographi.ca/en/bio/johnson_emily_pauline_14E.html (accessed 12 January 2023).
[75]Webling, *Peggy*, 169–70.
[76]Ibid., 150–1; *Brantford Expositor*, 2 January 1891, 7.

Figure 1.7 Left: Lucy Webling as Little Lord Fauntleroy, 1888. Right: Peggy Webling as Dick the Bootblack and Lucy as Fauntleroy (Webling Archive).

The year 1891 saw Peggy and Josephine leaving Brantford for New York, to join their mother and sisters arriving from London in a bid to find an American audience for their performances. Their reputation followed them: articles from Yonkers, New York to Los Angeles spoke of their success in London.[77] Maria Webling brought letters of introduction with her to a well-known entertainment agent and New York Society hostesses to get things rolling.[78] The reciting engagements were few, but the girls did attend and perform at the salons of Mrs Frank Leslie (new bride of Oscar's brother, Willie Wilde),[79] and Lucy acted at a

---

[77] At least fifteen newspapers in the United States printed 'They are the Fad Now: The Misses Webling Very Popular in New York Society' between 25 November 1891 and 7 January 1892, including the *Yonkers Daily Herald*, 28 November 1891, 3 and the *Los Angeles Herald*, 7 January 1892, 10.

[78] Webling, *Peggy*, 171, 174. The agent was Major J. B. Pond, manager of the American Lecture Bureau, a premier booking agent whose clients included Charles Dickens, Ellen Terry, Mark Twain and many others; see 'Biography', found in the description of the James B. Pond papers (1863–c. 1940s), Clements Library, University of Michigan, https://quod.lib.umich.edu/c/clementsead/umich-wcl-M-3073pon?id=navbarbrowselink;view=text (accessed 26 September 2022).

[79] Webling, *Peggy*, 181–2; Peggy called her 'an amazing woman!' She married Wilde on 4 October 1891 in New York. 'Mrs Frank Leslie' was the legal name of Miriam Follin Leslie, who took over her husband's bankrupt business (and his name) and made it a media success; she also left her fortune to Carrie Chapman Catt, thus invigorating the American women's suffrage movement. See Gillian Brockell, 'Mrs. Frank Leslie ran a media empire and bankrolled the suffragist movement', *The Washington Post*, 28 March 2022, https://

Figure 1.8 Pauline Johnson and Friends, Brantford, Ontario, Canada, 1 July 1892. Front row, Pauline holding paddle; second row, l. to r. Rosalind, Peggy, Josephine, Lucy; back row behind Josephine, Alfred Allen Watts (Webling Archive).

charity matinée.[80] For Peggy, the eight months (October 1891–June 1892) spent in New York were fruitful only for glimpsing Edwin Booth at the New York Fair, and entering a writing contest put on by the *New York Herald* – she didn't win, but afterwards received helpful literary advice from the winner, a Mrs Lucius Whitney.[81] The sisters and their mother went to Canada in June 1892 for Josephine's wedding, but in August they departed for England.

'I always wanted to write stories'[82]

They returned, still hard up, to a small house in Shepherd's Bush at 2 Camden Gardens. Ethel was painting Herbert Beerbohm Tree and illustrating his acting edition of *Hamlet*.[83]

---

www.washingtonpost.com/history/2022/03/28/mrs-frank-leslie/ (accessed 26 September 2022); for a full biography, Betsy Prioleau, *Diamonds and Deadlines: A Tale of Greed, Deceit, and a Female Tycoon in the Gilded Age* (New York: Abrams Press, 2022).
[80]Webling, *Peggy*, 181–2; 'Children Aid the Fair', *The World*, 8 May 1892, 16.
[81]Webling, *Peggy*, 179–81.
[82]Webling, *Story of a Pen*, MS page 11.
[83]Webling, *Peggy*, 191. Ethel's portrait of Tree was given to The Garrick Club in London by her sister Lucy McRaye in 1951. A black and white image is here: https://garrick.ssl.co.uk/object-g0819 (accessed 11 October 2022).

Peggy Webling's Story

The other girls needed to contribute, if they could. Peggy wrote story after rejected story, until finally 'Go!', about a trotting race (based on her time in Canada with her uncle Ted, a trotting enthusiast), was accepted by the *Sun*, edited by T. P. O'Connor.[84] Her aim, Peggy said, 'was to suggest the sound of trotters on a hard track, the trip-clip-clop of their hoofs pounding along, and this could only be done by clear, sharp words.'[85] 'Go!' ended up on the first page of the paper.[86]

Her next creation, a comedietta (billed as a sketch), was called 'An April Jest', about a woman who had been made the April Fool of her sweetheart, and turned the tables on him by having her sister take her place in disguise to deliver her own 'jest' to the lover. She wrote it under a pseudonym, Arthur Weston, for fun but also out of trepidation about its reception. She worried for nothing. First performed at a charity matinée at Terry's Theatre on 26 July 1893, it was very well received, to Peggy's surprise, with laughs in all the right places.[87] Later, it became one of the staples in Peggy, Rosalind and Lucy's tour of Canada from late 1894 to mid-1897.

Oh, Canada!

And what about this Canadian tour? It came about through Pauline Johnson, who was visiting London to promote her book *The White Wampum*. She encouraged the sisters to try the touring circuit again, but this time in Canada. She set them up with an agent in Toronto, and they left in late September of 1894 to try their luck again across the pond.[88] Meant to last six months, the tour ended up being almost three years. *An April Jest* and *Britannia*, another of Peggy's sketches, became highlights of the show. The latter featured Rosalind and Lucy representing Ireland and Scotland, with Peggy as 'Mrs. Brit', complete with helmet, shield and flag. During the tour they travelled twice from Ontario to British

---

[84]Webling, *Peggy*, 196; Webling, *Story of a Pen*, MS page 12. T. P. O'Connor was a well-known editor, critic and MP, whose bust stands today in 72–78 Fleet Street; see 'Father of the House', *Time Magazine*, 28 May 1923, https://content.time.com/time/subscriber/article/0,33009,715538,00.html (accessed 1 November 2022); see also Francis Fytton, 'The Legacy of T. P. O'Connor', *The Irish Monthly*, 1954, 83, 169–73.
[85]Webling, *Story of a Pen*, MS page 13.
[86]Peggy Webling, 'GO! A Canadian Trotting Tale', *The Sun*, 1 August 1893, 1; Webling, *Story of a Pen*, MS page 13; Webling, *Peggy*, 196 . 'Go!' is also in Lucy and Peggy Webling, *Poems and Stories* (Toronto: R. G. McLean, 1896), 150–6.
[87]Webling, *Peggy*, 204; J. P. Wearing, *The London Stage, 1890–1899: A Calendar of Productions, Performers and Personnel*, 2nd edn (Lanham, MD/Plymouth: Rowman & Littlefield, 2014), 182; *The Theatre*, 1 September 1893, 169, reviewing a performance at the Bijou Theatre, Bayswater: 'Mr. Arthur Weston has displayed a pretty fancy in the treatment of his little sketch, and it ought to meet with a measure of popularity.'
[88]Webling, *Peggy*, 205; SS Berlin, leaving 22 September, arriving 1 October 1894 (UK and Ireland, Outward Passenger Lists, 1890-1960, database online at ancestry.com; The National Archives; Kew, Surrey, England; BT27 Board of Trade: Commercial and Statistical Department and Successors: Outwards Passenger Lists; Reference Number: Series BT27; New York, U.S., Arriving Passenger and Crew Lists [including Castle Garden and Ellis Island], 1820–1957, database online at ancestry.com; Records of the US Customs Service, Record Group 36: National Archives at Washington, D.C., Passenger Lists of Vessels Arriving at New York, New York, 1820–1897, Year: 1894, Arrival: New York, New York, USA, Microfilm Serial: M237, 1820–1897, Line: 31).

Peggy Webling and the Story behind Frankenstein

Columbia and back, the second time also touring through the western United States. In 1896 in Toronto, Peggy and Lucy published *Poems and Stories* (poems by Lucy and stories by Peggy).[89]

Their experiences in 'the wild and woolly west', chronicled in seven chapters of *Peggy*, gave Peggy much grist for her writer's mill, including being offered a bear cub as a gift, driving their touring cart through water up to the horses' manes in the Bow River, riding a cowcatcher for a day and climbing 350 feet down a ladder to tour the Le Roi gold mine in British Columbia.[90] During their time in Vancouver, Rosalind met G. W. Edwards, a photographer whom she would marry in 1898. Her engagement prompted the winding up of the tour, and in June of 1897 they returned to London, coincidentally on the same ship as Major J. B. Pond, the agent they had hoped would book their New York engagements in 1891.[91]

'When I began to write I meant to make my living at it'[92]

Peggy's goal when they returned to London was to be a professional writer. She had lost the desire to act professionally, and the need to make money was foremost in her mind. She began writing stories about Canada and offered them to two weekly papers called *Stories* and *Longbow*, which went out of business shortly after they were accepted (but, luckily, paid for).[93] Other publications began to accept her work, too, which she turned out at a rate of one story every other day for the first few years.[94] She also began to write newspaper articles for the *Morning Leader*, *To-Day* and others.[95] T. P. O'Connor (who had accepted 'Go!' for *The Sun*) had begun the weekly *M. A. P.* (*Mainly About People*) in 1898, so Peggy decided to send him a sketch on Franklin McLeay, a Canadian actor who was having success in London. The assistant editor, John Hannon, responded by asking that she write some 'personal paragraphs' about Vesta Tilley, a male impersonator. She impressed him by managing to get Tilley's address and do the interview by the following day.[96] Thus began her fruitful association with *M. A. P.* She progressed to doing six or

---

[89]The published book, printed by R. G. McLean in Toronto, is undated, but an inscription on the inside cover dedicating the book to their parents is signed 'Peggy Lucy Toronto August 1896'. (Collection of Lindsay Dorney; copy of the inscription page in Webling Archive.)
[90]Webling, *Peggy*, 220–1, 226, 227–9, 253–5. Chapter 7 of *Peggy* was called '"The Wild and Woolly West"'. The phrase dates from the late nineteenth century: see Christine Ammer, *The Facts on File Dictionary of Clichés*, 2nd edn (New York: Facts on File Inc., 2006), 480.
[91]Incoming Passenger List of SS *Mongolian*, arriving Glasgow 9 June 1897, 3–4 (UK and Ireland, Incoming Passenger Lists, 1878–1960, database online at ancestry.com; The National Archives of the UK; Kew, Surrey, England; Board of Trade: Commercial and Statistical Department and successors: Inwards Passenger Lists.; Class: BT26; Piece: 100; Item: 35).
[92]Webling, *Story of a Pen*, MS page 20.
[93]Ibid., MS pages 20–1.
[94]Ibid., MS page 22; Webling, *Peggy*, 282.
[95]Webling, *Story of a Pen*, MS page 23. See also Webling, *Peggy*, 295–6.
[96]Webling, *Peggy*, 288; Webling, *Story of a Pen*, MS pages 25–6.

Figure 1.9 'Britannia', *c.* 1895: Peggy as Britain, Rosalind as Ireland, Lucy as Scotland (Webling Archive).

seven interviews a week, covering all the theatrical news including first nights, and also writing stories for them.[97] The interviews were the most difficult for her, but they were invaluable training for learning 'the art of omission'.[98] She became friends with some of her subjects: an American comic entertainer, 'Happy Fanny Fields', 'a bright, flashing star of the old halls';[99] and Dicky Douglas, a British comedian, who introduced her to a contortionist who ended up as a character in one of her books.[100] The interviews were also critical for meeting the London theatre people who would be invaluable as she moved into playwriting.

She began her first novel, *Blue Jay*, about a Canadian circus performer, while working for *M. A. P.*[101] It was inspired not only by her experiences in Canada, but also by her many interviews of 'show people', all those performers who worked in places like the Hippodrome and the Alhambra.[102] Published by Heinemann on Valentine's Day 1906,[103] with the cover illustration by her sister Ethel, she received good reviews but the book did not sell well, earning her a mere £28.[104]

Still, she was on her way. She continued working for *M. A. P.*, the *Morning Leader* and *The Era* but found time to begin her second novel. She improved her dialogue writing through one-column dialogues in the *Morning Leader* and received advice from John Hannon at *M. A. P.* and Bertram Christian, assistant editor at the *Morning Leader*.[105] *The Story of Virginia Perfect* sold much better, had fine reviews and resulted in a contract from Methuen for five books.[106] Notably, Sir Algernon Methuen, besides immediately accepting the book, also remembered Peggy and her sisters from their reciting at Sir Algernon's old school – 'I think it was "The Jackdaw of Rheims" that particularly charmed me', he told her.[107]

Her growing career, and income, as a novelist allowed her to drop her newspaper jobs, for journalism, she realized, was not her calling.[108] She began to produce novels at

---

[97] Webling, *Story of a Pen*, MS pages 28–9.
[98] Ibid., MS page 29.
[99] Ibid., MS page 33; see also Webling, *Peggy*, 293.
[100] Webling, *Story of a Pen*, MS page 34. This was *A Spirit of Mirth* (1910).
[101] Webling, *Story of a Pen*, MS pages 37, 39. The working title was 'Brother of the Birds', later changed to 'Blue Jay'.
[102] Ibid., MS page 38.
[103] Ibid., MS page 44; Webling, *Peggy*, 300.
[104] E.g. in the *Daily Telegraph* (2 March 1906, 4), *The Bookman* (April 1906, 38) and *Manchester Courier* (22 March 1906, 10). See also Webling, *Story of a Pen*, MS pages 40, 44.
[105] Webling, *Story of a Pen*, MS pages 44–5. For more on Hannon and Christian, and the topic of advice-giving, see Webling, *Peggy*, 296: she noted wryly that 'All men like to instruct women who are clever enough not to appear *too* stupid'.
[106] Webling, *Story of a Pen*, MS page 53, mentioning the *Daily Telegraph*, *Morning Post*, *Westminster Gazette*, the *Standard*, the *Weeklies* and *Punch*.
[107] Ibid., MS pages 53–4.
[108] Ibid., MS page 55. This despite her creation of 'Peggy's Paper or Unch and Udy' in 1887. One issue exists in the Webling Archive, filled with quips, puns and advice from the Editor, 'Percy Vane'.

the rate of about one a year, completing her five novels with Methuen in 1915.[109] During this time she also set her hand to playwriting, which leads to another tale.

Westward Ho!

Charles Kingsley's story of Amyas Leigh and the Spanish Main had been one of Peggy's childhood favourites. She finished a dramatization, which she called *Men of Devon*, by the autumn of 1908, and thought about a venue to present it. The Lyceum (previously Henry Irving's theatre) now specialized in popular melodramas for big audiences. One of the principal players there was Matheson Lang (1879–1948), whom she had interviewed for *M. A. P.* when he was playing in *Tristan and Iseult* [sic] at the Adelphi in July of 1906.[110] When she saw that Lang was at the Lyceum playing in *Pete*, Hall Caine's drama, she wrote to him to say she had written a play.[111] Lang asked her to call on him at the theatre. The minute he heard the words 'Westward Ho!' he said, 'Amyas Leigh is a part I've always wanted to play. Of course I should like to read your play.'[112] After making some alterations that Lang suggested, the Lyceum accepted it immediately, but the production foundered after the death of its theatrical manager, Ernest Carpenter, on 23 December 1909.[113] And that, Peggy thought, was the end of *Westward Ho!*.

It wasn't. Lang took a copy of the play with him on his world tour, though he had only made 'a vague promise' of production; Peggy was therefore astonished to hear from him, in 1912, that he was going to produce it in Johannesburg, South Africa.[114] Terms were quickly agreed, and *Westward Ho!* was performed ninety-two times, in South Africa (sixteen performances in September 1912), Manchester (Gaiety Theatre, 24 February 1913, for two weeks), London (Palladium, March and April 1913) and suburban theatres (the last performance in Hammersmith). The rehearsals before opening night in Manchester, which Peggy witnessed, were harrowing: 'I left them at the theatre struggling through the third act, Matheson Lang hoarse . . . and no prospect of the weary company and staff being dismissed until daybreak.'[115] But a bad dress rehearsal makes for a good performance, as theatre people say: '[Matheson Lang as Amyas] had a magnificent reception, and directly he was there I felt safe' and at the end 'there were

---

[109]*Virginia Perfect* (1909), *A Spirit of Mirth* (1910), *Felix Christie* (1912), *The Pearl Stringer* (1913), *Edgar Chirrup* (1915).
[110]Webling, *Story of a Pen*, MS page 59. The actual name of the play was *Tristram and Iseult*.
[111]Ibid. *Pete* ran at the Lyceum between September and December 1908 according to advertisements in the *Times*.
[112]Webling, *Story of a Pen*, MS pages 59–60.
[113]'Obituary. Mr. Ernest Carpenter', *Times*, London, 25 December 1909, 9; Death Notice, *Liverpool Daily Post and Mercury*, 25 December 1909, 6.
[114]Webling, *Story of a Pen*, MS page 62.
[115]Ibid., 67.

shouts of "Speech! Speech!" . . .' 'The most important paper (the *Guardian*) gave us a good notice.'[116] All told, *Westward Ho!* earned Peggy £306 8s. 9d.[117]

Westward Ho! was critical for Peggy's development as a playwright, especially in adapting a play from another's novel. She learned, first, how to shorten a book for the stage – which parts to cut and which parts were essential. She was mostly successful, as the *Guardian*'s reviewer noted: 'there is much skill in the choice of incidents and in the stringing of them together.'[118] She cut what she considered the 'best Chapter in the book, "Spanish Bloodhounds and English Mastiffs"'. She also had to determine the parts that needed adjustments – Rose Salterne does not go willingly with Don Guzman de Soto as in the book, 'the tragic ending of Frank Leigh has to be entirely changed' and Amyas Leigh was not blinded at the end.[119] She also enlarged the part of the 'wild and passionate Ayacanora', to accommodate Hutin Britton, Matheson Lang's wife and a fine actress in her own right.[120] Peggy was proudest of two scenes that were solely hers, untouched by the tinkerings of actors or producers: the 'Leigh Brothers and their friends swearing fealty to The Brotherhood of the Rose', and the recognition of Ayacanora by the old sailor Salvation Yeo[121] (played by Peggy's paternal first cousin, Harry Ashford). With a successful play under her belt, and the novels flowing smoothly, she also found time for some political and social pursuits.

Sister suffragettes

I grew up with family stories about the Webling sisters' support of feminism and the right to vote. We had mementoes – a grosgrain sash with 'Votes for Women' on it, in the purple, white and green of the Women's Social and Political Union; a button in purple, green and white proclaiming 'Votes for Women New Jersey 1914'; Ethel Urlin's pamphlet 'The Return of the Matriarchate' – that my great-grandmother Josephine had saved. It thrilled me to have suffragists in the family, and I imagined her marching for women's rights while I sang 'Sister Suffragettes' from the movie version of Mary Poppins.

We have already seen Josephine taking the suffrage side in a debate on the SS *Adriatic* in 1915. Peggy, now established as an author, joined the Writers' Club, strictly for women professional writers, in 1909,[122] and then the Women Writers' Suffrage League (WWSL),

---

[116]Peggy to Josephine, 7 February 1913, 6; A. S. W., 'Gaiety Theatre. "Westward Ho!"', *Guardian*, 3 February 1913, 8.
[117]Webling, *Story of a Pen*, MS pages 62–3.
[118]'Gaiety Theatre', *Guardian*, 3 February 1913, 8.
[119]Information in this paragraph from Webling, *Story of a Pen*, MS page 64.
[120]Ibid., MS page 65. Britton played Portia to Lang's Shylock, and Kate to Lang's Pete, among other parts.
[121]Ibid.
[122]The Writers' Club was founded in 1892, with headquarters in Hastings House, Norfolk Street, Strand. The Club was a constant in her life and she became its chair in the late 1920s (Webling, *Story of a Pen*, MS page 108).

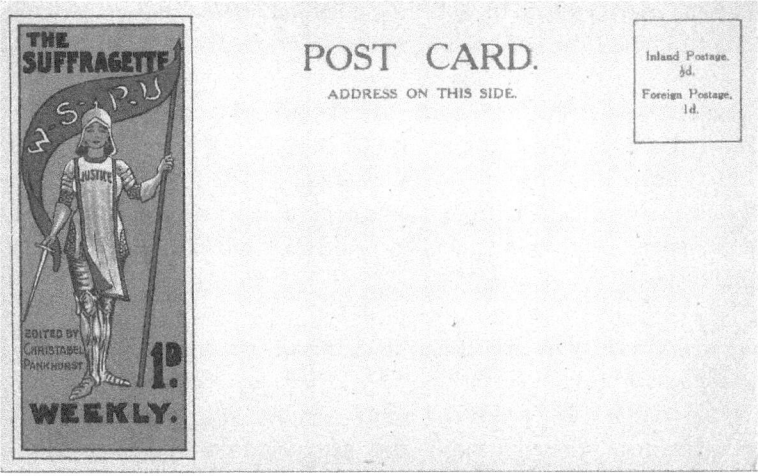

Figure 1.10 Postcard of the Women's Social and Political Union, c. 1912 (Webling Archive).

founded in 1908.[123] She assiduously followed the actions of the Women's Social and Political Union (WSPU), and discussed pertinent events with her sister in America. In a letter to Josephine written nine days after Emily Davison's death at the Epsom Derby, she wrote:

> The death of Miss Davison on the Derby course sent a shudder through every thoughtful person in this country. I never saw her, but of course I knew all about her career – its heroism, its following of an ideal, its dauntless courage. I *have* seen and heard Mrs Pankhurst many times and felt the wonder of her personality, although I have never joined the Union. . . . There never was a more sane, gentle, loving little being, but with a great force of character, an absolutely fearless heart, that no abuse, no cruelty, no brutal ridicule can daunt.[124]

Though she did not join the WSPU, she was a committed member of the Women Writers Suffrage League, serving on the Committee and at the end of 1917 becoming its

---

She was mentioned as 'President' of the Club in newspaper articles: 'Miss Webling's Thriller', *The Somerset Standard*, 6 July 1928, 3; 'A Woman's Shocker', *Derby Daily Telegraph*, 18 December 1929, 8.

[123]The League was founded by playwright Cicely Hamilton and journalist/playwright Bessie Hatton; Hamilton was also chair of committee, with Elizabeth Robins as the first president: see Sowon Park, 'The First Professional: The Women Writers' Suffrage League', *Modern Language Quarterly* 57, no. 2 (1997): 186–7. When Peggy joined the WWSL, Flora Annie Steele was president and Elizabeth Robins vice-president (see Peggy to Josephine, 13 June 1913, 3). Steele was president from 1912 to 1917: see Sowon Park, 'Women Writers' Suffrage League', *The Literary Encyclopedia*, 2002, https://escholarship.org/content/qt9rg5g6t3/qt9rg5g6t3_noSplash_ac8968ef86f d89b8017e3f7730021bd7.pdf (accessed 18 October 2022).

[124]Peggy to Josephine, 13 June 1913, 3–4.

chair.[125] She had marched with them from the Embankment to Albert Hall in the Great Procession of 18 June 1910, later writing in *The Story of a Pen*,

> Our League possessed, and carried in the great London processions, a very beautifully embroidered banner – a golden pen on a black and white ground – and a number of pennons bearing the names of famous women writers of the past. . . . When [the crowds] saw 'Jane Austen' not a few people greeted the woman carrying it as 'Good old Jane' . . . and an indignant anti-suffragist said 'George Eliot ought to be ashamed of "imself".[126]

Peggy was well informed on rebutting the claims of the anti-Suffragists, as she wrote to Josephine for her birthday letter in 1913, and was especially passionate on changing government laws that privileged men's rights – 'in our Insurance Act, for instance, all the amendments relate to men's affairs (they are even debating whether the Maternity benefit ought to go to the husband or the wife!!!!!)'. She was equally fervent about wage inequalities, calling women the forced '"blacklegs" of the labour world':[127]

> they are the worst paid and the worst put upon beings in the country. The conditions are simply shocking, and for men to talk (as some of the Antis do) about chivalry is absolute nonsense while thousands of women are working for – say – fourteen shillings a week, ten or twelve hours a day, and many of them for less – for half that sum, at the hardest and most dirty and unfit work, while thousands more are always on the starvation line, and more than one dares to say [they] are living lives that are more terrible than death.[128]

Instead of the public going on about white slave traffic, she added,

> it is more to the purpose to think about the Wage Slave traffic – it is that that drives girls to destruction. . . . I mean, by introducing that ill-used word chivalry, that a new chivalry is springing up and we have the suffragists to thank for it – a chivalry that will not stop at a man's own wife or daughter, but include all women – that's the *real* thing![129]

---

[125]'Women Writers' League', *Votes for Women*, 7 December 1917, 319: 'Miss Elizabeth Robins has become President of the Women Writers' Suffrage League, and Miss Peggy Webling Chairman of Committee'. She succeeded Elizabeth Robins as chair (Webling, *Story of a Pen*, MS page 108); see also Peggy to Josephine, 25 May 1918, 3.
[126]*Story of a Pen*, MS pages 108–9; 'The Great Procession', *The Vote*, 25 June 1910, 101: 'With the Women Writers walked many well-known women. . . . [including] Miss Peggy Webling, author of "Virginia Perfect"....'
[127]Peggy to Josephine, 29 July 1913, 1–2. She explained, 'Why are women "blacklegs"? Because they are compelled to work for lower wages than men – not because they like it!'
[128]Peggy to Josephine, 29 July 1913, 2.
[129]Ibid.

Peggy Webling, Novelist[130]

Peggy's published writing eventually grew to include eighteen novels, four works of non-fiction, two books of poetry, 200 short stories, two playlets and three plays (and *Poems and Stories* with her sister Lucy) (see Bibliography, list of Webling's works). Her fiction is very much of its time, although it clearly appealed to the public enough to keep good reviews and sales fairly constant. Peggy herself had no illusions about her writing style. When she was asked to become a candidate for the Committee of the Writers' Club, one of the Committee members (who supported her!) remarked, "'Now, we all know Peggy Webling's style of work and" – here the lady paused and concluded emphatically – "and it must be admitted that *some people* like her books!'"[131] Though her characters could be finely drawn, and her descriptions well crafted, many of her novels tended toward the formulaic, with trite plot devices and stock characters.[132]

Nonetheless, reviews praised her 1915 novel, *Edgar Chirrup*, with more than one paper remarking on its Dickensian sensibility and atmosphere[133] (one character notably resembled Uriah Heep). *The Bookman* proclaimed it 'the best novel Miss Peggy Webling has given us' and 'steeped in that spirit of sympathy and genial humour that we have come to look upon as essentially Dickensian'.[134] It remained one of Peggy's favourites and, as a lifelong lover of Dickens and member of the Dickens Society, it must have pleased her to read this comparison. Some of her novels dealt with odd professions like pearl-stringing, amber-selling and scent-making.[135] Others tackled occult or psychic subjects.[136] Her 1916 novel, *Boundary House*, was made into a silent film in 1918 by Cecil M. Hepworth (distributed by Moss Empires, Ltd). It was, according to publicity, 'a big production', receiving good reviews, and Peggy was 'thoroughly delighted' with it.[137] The last novel she published was *Young Laetitia*, in 1939.

---

[130]Written in Peggy's hand on the back of a photograph of her, Hulton & Co., Ltd., dated '25.7.20' (Webling Archive).
[131]Webling, *Story of a Pen*, MS page 108: evidence of Peggy's wry sense of humour.
[132]Jeanie Grant Moore, 'Lucy Webling and Peggy Webling', in *The Dictionary of Literary Biography*, vol. 240 (Late Victorian and Edwardian Women Poets) (Detroit: Gale Group, 2001), 324.
[133]Including the *Times*, *Daily Telegraph*, *Daily News and Leader* and *Yorkshire Daily Post* (of thirteen reviews in toto).
[134]'Martinus Scriblerus', 'About Books', *The Bookman* 48, no. 283 (April 1915): 16.
[135]*The Pearl Stringer* (1913), *The Amber Merchant* (1925), *The Scent Shop* (1919).
[136]*In Our Street* (1918), *Opal Screens* (1937), *Strange Enchantment* (1929). This last was written after the sudden death of her beloved artist sister Ethel, who in many ways was the rock of their household. Ethel had long been interested in the occult; she belonged to the Society for Psychical Research and the Theosophical Society, where she also learned astrology. Though Peggy remained mostly sceptical, after Ethel's death she spent two sessions with a medium at the Psychic College. In a thirteen-page report sent to Josephine, she outlined evidence that convinced her Ethel was communicating with her (Letter to Josephine, 10 December 1929, with reports of 8 March 1929 and April 1929).
[137]'big production': Peggy to Josephine, 16 November 1918; 'thoroughly delighted': in Fred Dangerfield, 'Editorial', *Pictures and the Picturegoer*, vol. xv, 14–21, December 1918, 613; see also Alan Goble, ed. *The Complete Index to Literary Sources in Film* (London/Melbourne/Munich/New Providence, NJ: Bowker–Saur, 1999), 493. Stills can be found on YouTube, https://www.youtube.com/watch?v=rgW64k-tPBs (accessed 25 October 2022).

Figure 1.11 'Peggy Webling, Novelist', 25 July 1920 (Webling Archive).

Peggy Webling's Story

Reality and rhyme

Peggy also wrote non-fiction and poetry. As noted above (p. 19), her self-published *A Sketch of John Ruskin* appeared in 1914.[138] It was a gauzy yet tender memoir of her recollections of Ruskin when she and her sisters knew him in the 1880s, including some of his letters and poetry to them.[139] Various sections were later transferred to the chapter on Ruskin in her autobiography, *Peggy*. Her 1917 booklet of essays on personified virtues and vices, the mawkish *Guests of the Heart*, was also self-published as a Christmas gift.[140] *Saints and Their Stories*, published for children in 1919, was a commission from Nisbet & Co.[141] The request was somewhat perplexing, for Peggy was the first to admit she knew little about the saints, and had to be talked into accepting the (low) offer of £50 at publication plus £25 after 3,000 copies.[142] Simply and engagingly written, its popularity lasted.[143] Peggy's 1924 autobiography *Peggy: The Story of One Score Years and Ten* was glowingly reviewed in *The Bookman* and the *Daily Telegraph*.[144] Save for *Guests of the Heart*, Peggy's non-fiction is far more engaging for a modern reader than her novels. (The same goes for her unpublished letters and literary memoir.)

She self-published two quite different works of poetry. *The Rhyme of Little Mark*, a forgettable and trite piece of children's doggerel, was published in time for Christmas 1936. The other was the clever, satirical and humorous *Verses to Men*, which appeared in 1919 (she had three books published that year – the others being *The Scent Shop* and *Saints and Their Stories*). *Verses* was favourably reviewed in *The Bookman* and by Arthur St John Adcock in the *Sunday Sun*.[145] The first copy was inscribed to editor W. H. Spence of the *Daily Telegraph*, 'One of my first editors, and very good friend'.[146] Begun during the year 1918, when women finally obtained (partially) the right to vote, *Verses* shows Peggy's sense of humour, and her feminism.[147] To wit, a verse from the sixteen-stanza 'Ode to a Husband (An Attempt to Write when Inspired by His Presence)':

---

[138] She printed 1,000 copies, selling over 700 herself and the rest to a publisher (Webling, *Story of a Pen*, MS page 104). A signed copy at abebooks.com can be had for $475 (accessed 27 October 2022).
[139] Arthur St John Adcock called it 'charming' and 'a thing to buy and keep' in *The Bookman*, December 1914, 124.
[140] Circular advertising the 'book for Christmas' enclosed with letter to Josephine, 25 November 1917 (Webling Archive).
[141] Bertram Christian, her former editor at the *Morning Leader*, was then the managing director at Nisbets (Peggy to Josephine, 12 March 1918).
[142] Webling, *Story of a Pen*, MS pages 96–7.
[143] *Saints* continued to show up on children's booklists for years (e.g. Wilfrid F. P. Ellis, 'Saints and Their Stories', *Birmingham Post*, 19 November 1943, 3). It had a brief afterlife when William Bennett, Ronald Reagan's Secretary of Education, used it in his book *The Moral Compass* in 1995.
[144] '"This is one of the happiest books of recollections, I think, I have ever read. . .", A. R., 'How I Began', *The Bookman*, November 1924, 124; 'their happy story, so sympathetically told, reminds the world that there is still faëry gold for those who know where to look for it,' 'Books of the Day', *Daily Telegraph*, 24 October 1924, 16; (perhaps over the top!) 'every paragraph quivers . . . with an indefinable genius', 'Peggy. The Story of One Score [sic] and Ten', *The Western Daily Press*, 24 January 1924, 10.
[145] *The Bookman*, December 1919, 34; the *Sunday Sun*, 9 November 1919, 6.
[146] Flyleaf of *Verses to Men*, copy no. 1 (Webling Archive) (never delivered?)
[147] See an extensive examination of the book in Moore, 'Lucy Webling and Peggy Webling', 325–8.

> 'O, struggle on, my king of men
> And work as ne'er before –'
> (You reached the office after ten,
> And left at half-past four.
> But found the time to go through *Punch*?
> I'm glad you had a ripping lunch).[148]

The metre recalls a satirical verse the sisters made up as children, based on a saccharine rhyme in one of their despised 'goody-goody' books:

> 'Mother guide my little steps
> Gently while you can,
> Guide me up the hill of life
> Till I grow a man.
> Mother, when I grow a man,
> Good, and strong, and brave,
> I'll lead my Mother down the hill
> Kindly to the grave.'[149]

Their version ran:

> 'Mother guide my little steps
> Harshly while you can
> Kick me up the hill of life
> Till I wed a man.
> Mother, when I wed a man,
> Stout, and rich, and brave,
> I'll trot my Mother down the hill
> Quickly to the grave.'[150]

Peggy's irreverent streak began early.

The play's the thing

We have seen Peggy's *Westward Ho!* produced by Matheson Lang in 1912–13. Chapter 2 will cover the production of *Frankenstein* in extensive detail. But Peggy also had another play produced. This was *Reprieve*, based on the novel by Halbert J. Boyd, and produced in

---

[148] Webling, *Verses to Men*, 27. Note the sardonic capitalization of 'His' in the poem's title.
[149] Webling, *Peggy*, 93.
[150] Ibid., 94.

1931 by Hamilton Deane. As Peggy said on the day after *Frankenstein* closed in London (12 April 1930), 'I shan't be happy till I get another play out!'[151] As early as 4 April, while *Frankenstein* was still running at the Little Theatre, Hamilton Deane told Peggy about Boyd's novel and asked her to dramatize it.[152] The story concerns the return of a soul to life in an attempt to make amends for its previous existence. Although the first two acts were finished by 27 April, she found it rough going: 'this book is even thinner and less satisfactory than I thought at first – poor in fact, and I have completely altered the plot (if one can be said to alter a thing that did not exist).'[153] She persevered, however, finishing the play by 13 May;[154] the play was first performed on 20 July 1931 at the Theatre Royal, Nottingham (programme in the Webling Archive) and went into repertory until the 6th of November, receiving generally good reviews.

Though only three of Peggy's plays were produced, we know of eleven other plays she wrote or co-wrote, for which six manuscripts exist (see Bibliography, Sources from the Webling Archive). Most were written after 1931. (Her earliest full-length play, *The Stream*, was written before *Westward Ho!* but later revised.[155]) Of these, probably the closest to being produced were *Rossetti's Wife* and *Abominable Snowmen*.[156] She got the idea for writing the story of Dante Gabriel Rossetti and Elizabeth Siddal from P. W. Chaple, a family friend, so he was listed as the co-author of *Rossetti's Wife*, but Peggy did the actual writing.[157] It seemed as though the play would be produced by Kenelm Foss in 1935, but difficulties arose in casting the chief parts.[158]

Abominable Snowmen came about through Hamilton Deane, who wrote to Peggy in 1939 to 'collaborate with him in writing a drama on a most original idea that has occurred to him'.[159] The play was set in London and Tibet. Its tale of the abominable snowmen, the Mi-Go of Tibet, pits an Englishman and his arrogance against the Lamas of Tibet and their knowledge of the human monsters roaming the Mountains of the Eternal Snows. The Mi-Go are immensely tall and strong, able to live in the vicious high mountain weather where they rip the throats out of regular humans and, the Tibetans say, steal their souls. Of course the Englishman, who persists in going into the mountains with his unwilling but loyal Indian companion, comes to grief and sees his friend murdered

---

[151] Peggy to Josephine, 13 April 1930.
[152] Peggy to Josephine, 4 April 1930.
[153] Peggy to Josephine, 27 April 1930.
[154] Peggy to Josephine, 13 May 1930.
[155] Webling, *Story of a Pen*, MS pages 57–8.
[156] They were both registered with the Incorporated Society of Authors, Playwrights and Composers, League of British Dramatists, *Rossetti's Wife* on 26 July 1934, and *Abominable Snowmen* on 15 January 1941.
[157] Peggy to Josephine, 13 January 1934.
[158] Lucy McRaye to Josephine, 23 November 1935 (Webling Archive). However, in May of 1935, another play about Rossetti, by R. L. Mégroz and Herbert de Hamel, was denied a licence based on objections from the grandson of William Rossetti, the poet/artist's brother; this may have warned off any other producers on that topic (see, e.g. '"Rossetti" Play Abandoned', *The Manchester Guardian*, 21 May 1935, 10).
[159] Peggy to Josephine, 11 August 1939.

before his eyes.¹⁶⁰ In an eerie echo of past plays, Webling and Deane refer to themselves on the title page of *Abominable Snowmen* as 'Authors of Frankenstein and Dracula', thus combining in the Mi-Go the blood-thirstiness of Dracula with the monstrous qualities of Frankenstein. The play was written in forty-seven scenes arranged like a film script; apparently both Peggy and Deane came to the conclusion that it would be a better film than a play, for Deane ended up sending it to California.¹⁶¹

Peggy's last piece of writing, done while she was living at West Malvern, Worcestershire, during the Second World War, was not a play but a literary memoir, *The Story of a Pen: A Book for Would-be Writers*, written in the spring of 1941. After the war Peggy returned to London, where she remained until her death, from heart failure, on 27 June 1949.¹⁵² Her will left the bulk of her estate (£1180, plus her copyrights, books, etc.) to her sister Lucy Betty McRaye, with bequests of her letters from John Ruskin to the Ruskin Museum in Coniston, and 'my old edition of Johnson's dictionary given to me by John Ruskin to Louis Drummond McRaye'.¹⁶³ Her invaluable legacy, however, was her letters, papers and memoirs – and, of course, her conception of Frankenstein.

> Have I told you of my latest literary effort? It is nearly finished – the first rough copy – and is in sixteen chapters. The title is 'The Story of a Pen', with the subtitle 'Book for Would-be Writers'. You see I've written 200 short stories, 18 novels, 5 other books, three plays and had two films founded on my 'works', 'Frankenstein' and 'Boundary House'. So I *ought* to know something about it – whether I do or not is another matter!¹⁶⁴

---

¹⁶⁰This synopsis was gathered from the script.
¹⁶¹Peggy to Josephine, 25 June 1940: 'It is really more suited to the screen than the stage.' On 20 August 1940: 'No news yet of my "thriller." Mr Deane has written about it to the people who did "Frankenstein."' On 7 October 1940: 'Mr Deane has sent it to California and received no reply as yet.'
¹⁶²Death Certificate, 'Peggy otherwise Margaret Webling', General Record Office (UK), 1949, Camberwell, No. 158, Jul–Sep Quarter, 5c 174: 'twenty-seventh June 1949, Peckham House' (Webling Archive). The *New York Times*, 'Hollywood Report', 24 May 1953, X5, reported that she died in 1947. The error was repeated in Donald F. Glut, *The Frankenstein Legend: A Tribute to Mary Shelley* (Metuchen, NJ: The Scarecrow Press, 1973), 45; Gregory William Mank, *It's Alive: The Classic Cinema Saga of Frankenstein* (San Diego/New York: A. S. Barnes and Company, Inc., 1981), 13n; and John T. Soister, *Of Gods and Monsters: A Critical Guide to Universal Studios Science Fiction, Horror and Mystery Films, 1929–1939* (Jefferson, NC/London: McFarland and Co., 1999, repr. 2005), 115.
¹⁶³Will of Margaret Webling, proved London 15 September 1949 (Webling Archive). Louis Drummond McRaye (1915–2019) was Lucy's son.
¹⁶⁴Peggy Webling to Josephine Webling Watts, 16 March 1941 (Webling Archive).

CHAPTER 2
THE OTHER WOMAN WHO CREATED FRANKENSTEIN
Dorian Gieseler Greenbaum

A New Play

In October 1920 Peggy published her ninth novel, *Comedy Corner*. Sydney Blow (1878–1961), a playwright and actor, had proposed the idea for it to her, with the eventual goal of collaboration on a play[1] and a possible production for the screen as well as the stage.[2] For Peggy, the book was ultimately unsatisfactory: 'I do not care for *Comedy Corner*. . . . The plot . . . was like a feeble fairy tale, pretty, and improbable.'[3] Though she added, 'it sold very well. That's all I can say about it.'[4]

Peggy now found herself in the gap between works. She had struggled with her writing since her sister Ethel's mental breakdown and slow recovery in the summer and autumn of 1919. Though she had signed a new contract with Hutchinson's for three novels in October of that year, she told Josephine that 'that seems just at present about as easy as flying to the moon in an aeroplane!'[5] In the autumn of 1920, after the unavoidable sprint of writing *Comedy Corner* so quickly that spring and summer,[6] she had been unable to find space to rest and come up with new ideas. As she hoped for motivation at the end of the year, she was cheered by a visit from Josephine, who arrived on 24 September 1920 and stayed until the end of January 1921.[7]

We do not know exactly when it happened, but sometime during those months Peggy finally got the inspiration to write – not a novel this time, but another play.[8] She must

---

[1] Webling, *Story of a Pen*, MS page 82; Peggy to Josephine, 7 January, 1 February and 13 February 1920.
[2] Peggy to Josephine, 1 February 1920: 'I have a *very* good agreement with him, and if he makes his usual hit with the play I shall probably make a good sum. I also get a share of the film rights.'
[3] Webling, *Story of a Pen*, MS page 82. Reviewers agreed. *Punch*, 29 December 1920, 516, wrote: 'Webling has quite a remarkable talent for making ordinary places and people seem improbable.' And *The Athenaeum*, 10 December 1920, 813 called it a 'bright, pretty, unreal trifle'.
[4] Webling, *Story of a Pen*, MS page 82.
[5] Peggy to Josephine, 21 October 1919.
[6] Although the contract with Blow had been signed in February 1920, she only began to write it in April, and finished the 85,000-word manuscript at the end of July; see Peggy to Josephine, 2 July 1920, 'It has to be finished (if I can possibly manage it) by the end of this month, and you have no idea how difficult it is to do it at such a pace'; and Peggy to Josephine, 28 July 1920, 'this one is about 85,000 words'.
[7] Passenger Lists, RMS *Adriatic*, for 'Josephine Watts': arrival in Southampton, England 24 September 1920; arrival in New York 2 February 1921.
[8] The play of *Comedy Corner* was still hanging fire, though Sydney Blow claimed to be working on it in February 1921, and anticipated film rights (Peggy to Josephine, 18 February 1921). No play or film was ever produced.

have talked about it with her sister, because shortly after Josephine returned to her New Jersey home, Peggy wrote her on the 27th of February 1921 to say: 'I went to see Mr Lang at the theatre on Tuesday last (22 February), and was much encouraged by his still keen interest in the Frankenstein idea; he says certainly to go on with it & remembered all about the prologue. So I'm longing to get on with it.'[9] This is the first mention of Frankenstein in Peggy's letters to Josephine, and the wording clearly shows her sister would already have been familiar with the idea. It is unclear whether she had written any of the play at this point, since she mentions only the 'idea' of Frankenstein, but she appears to have discussed the prologue with Matheson Lang.

The Weblings had had a fourpence ha'penny copy of *Frankenstein* on their bookshelves for years, but Peggy did not read it until she was grown. She then found it absorbing but 'somewhat wearisome', with 'stilted language'.[10] She had not thought of it for years, but one day, when she was walking home and trying to think of topics for a play, Mary Shelley's novel *Frankenstein*[11] popped into her head. She shared her moment of inspiration with the *Daily News and Westminster Gazette* after the successful opening of *Frankenstein* in London in 1930: 'it came to me in a flash. I was walking down a street turning over in my mind the possible subject for a good play and suddenly I thought of Mary Wollstonecraft Shelley's book, "Frankenstein."'[12] Her literary memoir of 1941 gives a similar account: 'One day I was walking along High Holborn, meditating (as I so often do) on the possibility of writing another play. Suddenly Frankenstein flashed into my mind.'[13] Her immediate impulse was to dismiss the book as impossible to adapt for the stage,[14] but after she had walked from Oxford Street to Marble Arch and turned into Hyde Park,[15] 'the idea came to me again and so I really considered whether it could be done. Before I realised it I had arrived at my doorstep and the plot and various details were all worked out in my mind.'[16]

It appears that Peggy wrote the first full draft of the play at a scorching pace, in about five weeks. By the middle of October 1921 she was immersed in writing:[17]

> I am so absorbed in Frankenstein I can hardly think of anything else. I have written the Prologue & first act, and all the rest is in my head ready to be written down. It is much more difficult than I imagined and perhaps I shall not be able to pull it off.[18]

---

[9] Matheson Lang had produced *Westward Ho!* from Peggy's playscript, as we saw in Chapter 1.
[10] Webling, *Story of a Pen* (MS page 110), 303 in this volume.
[11] Peggy would probably have known the 1831 edition.
[12] 'Women Love Thrillers', interview with Peggy Webling, *The Daily News and Westminster Gazette*, 27 February 1930, 2.
[13] Webling, *Story of a Pen* (MS page 110), 303.
[14] 'Women Love Thrillers', 2.
[15] Webling, *Story of a Pen* (MS pages 110–11), 303.
[16] 'Women Love Thrillers', 2.
[17] In the spring, summer and early autumn of 1921 she had to work on her tenth novel, *The Fruitless Orchard*, which was finished and galleys proofed by the end of September.
[18] Peggy to Josephine, 17 October 1921.

The Other Woman who Created Frankenstein

Figure 2.1 Cover, yellowback copy of Mary Shelley's Frankenstein, G. Routledge and Sons, 1882. Courtesy of the Thomas Fisher Rare Book Library, University of Toronto.

On the 30th of October she wrote to Josephine:

> I have finished the prologue and first two acts of 'Frankenstein'; of course I may be wrong, but *I* think it is very strong; it was much more difficult to write than I imagined, but I had thought it out so thoroughly that on the last day I worked at the second act – the longest and most important in the play – I could not write the words down fast enough and when it was done I was shaking from head to foot and (as they say in novels) gave way to a burst of emotion![19]

She finished the play on 8 November 1921, and after she read it to her sisters Rosalind and Ethel, Ethel wrote to Jossie: 'it is very fine – it made Rs [sic] eyes fill with tears. . . . F is a great play – original & deep & strong.'[20]

Selling *Frankenstein*

So, play in hand, Peggy began the rounds of London producers. Her first stop may have been Matheson Lang;[21] she also mentions writing to 'several leading London actors whom I knew.'[22] None were interested, 'and the play, like a curse, came home to roost.'[23] With less enthusiasm than before, she rewrote the play and sent it out again. This prompted a request from 'a certain young actor, then on the crest of the wave', to rewrite it so that creator and creature were played by the same actor 'on the lines of The

---

[19] Peggy to Josephine, 30 October 1921. In Webling, *Story of a Pen* (MS page 112), 304, she says this was precipitated by the scene of the drowning of a character called Katrine (not in Shelley's book) at the end of Act II.
[20] Ethel Webling to Josephine, 9 and 11 November 1921.
[21] Ibid.: 'I long for P to go & see Lang.'
[22] Webling, *Story of a Pen* (MS page 112), 304.
[23] Ibid.

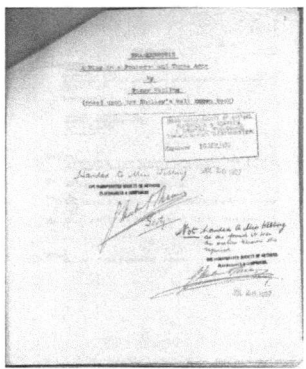

Figure 2.2 Title page of Webling's 1923 version of Frankenstein, registered on 16 January 1923 (Webling Archive).

Corsican Brothers, The Lyons Mail, and other old successes.'[24] This double-cast version was registered with the Society of Authors, Composers and Playwrights on 16 January 1923. Peggy realized the difficulties in staging such a version, and it eventually went into a drawer.[25] And time, as she said, 'rolled on.'[26]

During the next couple of years, *Frankenstein* receded into the background. It would not emerge until 1925. Only a few letters to Josephine exist between 1922 and 1924, but one long letter from 1923 informs us that Peggy had begun 'the "Life" at last; one chapter is finished and I am well into the second.'[27] This was an autobiography she first thought of writing in 1920,[28] and would eventually result in *Peggy: The Story of One Score Years and Ten*. Written 'on spec', she spent the rest of 1923 and the beginning of 1924 on it.[29] Happily, it was accepted and published by Hutchinson's in October 1924.

The first part of 1925 was spent on her thirteenth novel, *The Amber Merchant*, and by July it was finished and proofed. She was now free to turn to other things, including the dormant *Frankenstein* script. She considered sending it to the well-known American producer Edgar Selwyn (1875–1944),[30] an idea suggested by her sister Lucy, who had come to England in May. Peggy had 'met him years ago, and I think of writing to him

---

[24]Ibid., (MS page 113), 304.
[25]Now preserved in the Webling Archive, this version was later sent to Josephine's son Ruskin, as we shall see.
[26]Webling, *Story of a Pen* (MS page 113), 304.
[27]Peggy to Josephine, 2 September 1923.
[28]Peggy to Josephine, 26 March 1920: 'I have quite decided to write an autobiography some day and I will do justice to the subject!!'
[29]Peggy to Josephine, 2 September 1923: 'Of course it is a "spec," for I'm sure Hutchinson's will not take a book like this into our contract.'
[30]Edgar Selwyn, born Edgar Simon in 1875 in Cincinnati, Ohio, was an actor, playwright, theatre owner and producer. He took the name of Selwyn when he began work as an actor. According to his biography on the Internet Movie Database (IMDb) https://www.imdb.com/name/nm0783629/bio (accessed 16 November 2022), Edgar Selwyn and his brother Archibald formed the Goldwyn Pictures Corporation with Samuel Goldfish (later Goldwyn), which in 1924, after mergers with Lowe's Metro Pictures and Louis B. Mayer, became Metro-Goldwyn-Mayer. See also his obituary, *Los Angeles Times*, 14 February 1944, 13.

The Other Woman who Created Frankenstein

about Frankenstein'.[31] Hoping her nephew, Ruskin Watts (this writer's grandfather), would be a go-between, she sent him the script via her agent, John Farquharson, along with a letter about Edgar Selwyn and Frankenstein. But Watts, though a businessman, was a novice (and probably uninterested) in the ways of the theatrical world, and botched the possibility of a meeting with the producer. He apparently sent the letter about Selwyn and Frankenstein to Selwyn *before* he had arranged a meeting in person; as Peggy remarked, 'I am not surprised at any discourtesy on the part of Edgar Selwyn. I am sorry Ruskin did not do as I suggested – not give up the letter until he had a reasonable chance of seeing the man.'[32] In the end, no meeting took place. And that was the end of *that* attempt.

While she waited in vain to hear about Selwyn, she also approached Nigel Playfair (1874–1934), an actor-manager associated with the Lyric Theatre, Hammersmith.[33] Peggy had been living at 124 The Grove, Hammersmith, since she returned from Canada in 1897, so perhaps that is why she thought of him. But no dice. The chances of a production of *Frankenstein* seemed more and more bleak. By the autumn she had decided to tackle her own play version of *Comedy Corner*, since Sydney Blow had returned her dramatic rights after failing to write his own version.[34] She began working on that in November.[35]

The year 1926 brought no rewards for *Frankenstein* either, complicated as it was by the illness of her sister Lucy at the beginning of the year and then care and grief for the slow decline and death of her beloved 95-year-old mother Maria in September. Peggy did manage to get an article done, 'Some Queer Trades of London', for St John Adcock, who was editing a book about the city;[36] and finished all but two and a half chapters of her next novel, *Anna Maria* (published in 1927).[37] She also won a competition given by the Dickens Fellowship with a satirical essay entitled 'The Real Pumblechook'.[38] *Frankenstein* remained in suspended animation. But her luck was about to change.

'I always have a feeling that some day I shall pull off a play that will be produced and – perhaps – make a hit'[39]

We don't know the exact date, but sometime before March of 1927, an urgent plea from Peggy arrived in Josephine's mailbox, asking her to *'send me the copy you have of "Frankenstein" as soon as you conveniently can*. It is the only correct one I have & I

---

[31] Peggy to Josephine, 30 July 1925.
[32] Peggy to Josephine, 7 November 1925.
[33] Peggy to Josephine, 10 December 1925. See Robert Sharp, 'Playfair, Sir Nigel Ross', *Oxford Dictionary of National Biography*, https://doi-org.ezproxy.uwtsd.ac.uk/10.1093/ref:odnb/35740 (accessed 8 June 2023).
[34] Peggy to Josephine, 23 September 1925.
[35] Ethel to Josephine, 3 November 1925.
[36] Peggy Webling, 'Some Queer Trades of London', in *Wonderful London*, ed. Arthur St John Adcock, vol. 2 (London: Fleetway House, 1926), 598.
[37] Peggy to Josephine, 12 November 1926.
[38] Peggy to Josephine, 25 April 1926; the essay was published in *The Dickensian* 22, no. 3 (July–September 1926): 157–8. Peggy was a lifelong fan of Dickens and described herself in that issue (157) as 'an original and deep student of the famous Victorian novelist'.
[39] Peggy to Josephine, 23 September 1925.

want to show it to somebody over here.'[40] This was the manuscript sent to Ruskin Watts via Peggy's agent John Farquharson back in July of 1925, the version with one actor playing the two main parts (the registered 1923 version) – a concept which apparently was not yet completely off the table.[41] But the manuscript had somehow been mislaid in New Jersey, and by April it had still not turned up. No letters mention it again until September, when the manuscript at last was found and mailed.[42] In the meantime, Peggy had retyped the play and sent it to Stanley Drewitt (1878–1964), an actor and producer well known in the London theatre scene;[43] and, again as a suggestion from Lucy,[44] 'a man named Hamilton Deane, who knew Lucy in the old Haviland days. He has lately written & produced in London a version of Bram Stoker's vampire book "Dracula"'[45] Previous writers, among them Steven Forry, David Skal (following Forry), Lester Friedman and Allison Kavey, have erroneously stated that Peggy was 'a friend of Hamilton Deane' and that *Frankenstein* was 'originally composed as a companion piece' (or 'commissioned') for Deane's *Dracula* – but Peggy had not known him before she sent him her manuscript.[46] In sending the script to Deane, at last – at last! – she had hit pay dirt:

> We must not hope too much – there's many a slip, etc. – but I am writing a hasty note to tell you that the second man to whom I sent 'F.' is simply delighted with it & wants to know terms at once, with talk of giving it a provincial production to be followed by London! . . . I have now to see Mr Farquharson [her agent], as I think of putting the business into his hands. You can imagine how excited I feel. . . . This morning I have been to the Author's Society, making some enquiries about copyright, but all is satisfactory on that score. The book ('F') was published in 1818 & Mrs Shelley died in 1851, so the rights are free. Mr Hamilton Deane says it is [a] 'deep & moving tragedy' & he has not read any play for years that has 'impressed him so much.' He wants 'the film & world rights.' Oh, if 'F.' comes out – wot larks![47]

---

[40] The first page of this letter is missing, but the date is probably some time in February, as Peggy's March 1st 1927 letter covers the same topic of the *Frankenstein* manuscript in New Jersey.
[41] We know it was that version because Peggy says so in her letter of 16 October 1927: 'But, after all, it is not that version Mr Deane has accepted, but the one in which "Henry" and "F." are played by different actors.'
[42] Peggy to Josephine, 24 September 1927.
[43] An actor since the late 1890s (see *The Era*'s listings 1897–9), Drewitt became the head of his own company in 1904 (see the *Dover Express*, 12 August 1904, 2).
[44] Webling, *Story of a Pen* (MS page 113), 304.
[45] Peggy to Josephine, 20 September 1927.
[46] See Steven Earl Forry, '"The Foulest Toadstool": Reviving Frankenstein in the Twentieth Century', in *The Fantastic in World Literature and the Arts: Selected Essays from the Fifth International Conference on the Fantastic in the Arts*, ed. Donald E. Morse (New York/Westport, CT/London: Greenwood, 1987), 192–3; Forry, *Hideous Progenies: Dramatizations of Frankenstein from Mary Shelley to the Present* (Philadelphia: University of Pennsylvania Press, 1990), 90–1; repeated in David J. Skal, *The Monster Show: A Cultural History of Horror* (New York: Farrar, Straus and Giroux, 1993, rev. 2001), 100; Skal, *Screams of Reason: Mad Science and Modern Culture* (New York: W. W. Norton and Company, 1998), 113; and ('commissioned') Lester D. Friedman and Allison B. Kavey, *Monstrous Progeny: A History of the Frankenstein Narratives* (New Brunswick, NJ Rutgers University Press, 2016), 86.
[47] Peggy to Josephine, 28 September 1927. 'Wot larks' comes from Dickens' *Great Expectations*.

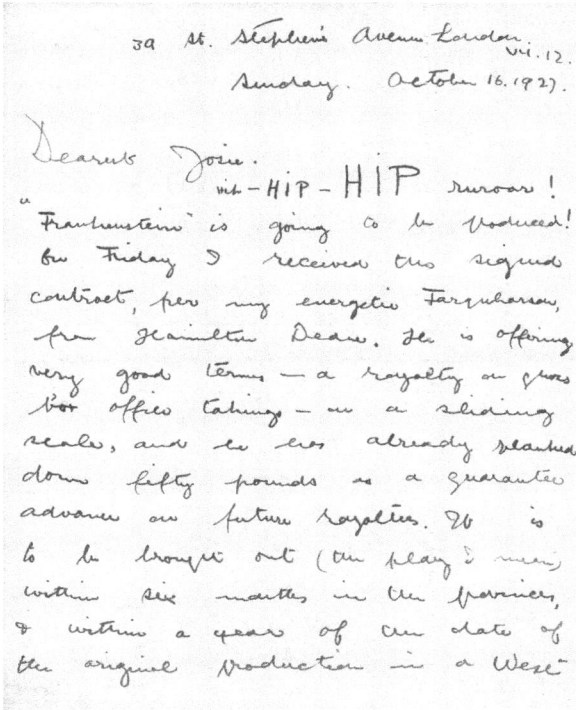

Figure 2.3 Peggy's letter to Josephine, 16 October 1927, p. 1 (Webling Archive).

'Wot larks' indeed. Her October 16th letter began:

> Hip – HIP – HIP huroar! 'Frankenstein' is going to be produced! On Friday I received the signed contract, per my energetic Farquharson, from Hamilton Deane. He is offering very good terms – a royalty on gross box office takings – on a sliding scale, and he has already planked down fifty pounds as a guarantee advance on future royalties. . . . I couldn't sleep on Friday night with excitement.[48]

Apparently Deane was shown both versions of the play, but preferred the one where Henry and Frankenstein (as Peggy called the 'Monster') were played by different actors, which of course would be much easier to stage. Deane also told Peggy he considered the play 'quite wonderful.' She added, 'He wants a few slight alterations, chiefly to stress the moral point of the absurdity of man trying to assume the powers of God.' The seven-year slog 'of waiting, and typing, & rewriting, and disappointments, & hopes' had finally been given its happy ending. She signed the letter 'Your devoted P(laywright).'[49]

---

[48] Peggy to Josephine, 16 October 1927.
[49] All quotations in this paragraph are from the 16 October letter.

Peggy Webling and the Story behind Frankenstein

Enter Hamilton Deane (1879–1958)

When Peggy mentioned that Lucy knew Deane from 'the old Haviland days', she referred to the theatrical company they both belonged to. One of Deane's first engagements as an actor was with the Haviland-Coleridge Company in 1899, performing in *The Only Way*, an adaptation of Dickens' *A Tale of Two Cities* by Freeman Wills and Frederick Langbridge.[50] During the tour, Deane seems to have alternated between the roles of the Vicomte de St Evremonde and the Marquis de Boulanvilliers.[51] Lucy, coming off George Alexander's production of *The Ambassador* at St James's Theatre, London,[52] played the critically praised supporting role of Mimi, a French serving girl who convinces Carton 'to renounce his dissolute life'.[53]

Hamilton Deane was born Hamilton Knudson Deane Roe on 2 December 1879 in Knockmullin, New Ross, Wexford, Ireland.[54] Deane was his mother's name.[55] Following his stint in *The Only Way*, he was a member of various repertory companies touring mostly in the provinces.[56] Between 1900 and 1911 he began to make a name for himself, at first in smaller parts, then villains, and then more leading roles; he was often noticed in reviews.[57] In the autumn of 1911 he decided to tour the United States and Canada

---

[50]The first mention of Deane as an actor in any UK paper was for *The Only Way*, in *The Era*, 28 October 1899, 15. Langbridge was not acknowledged as a co-author until 1926: see Joss Marsh, 'Mimi and the Matinée Idol: Martin-Harvey, Sydney Carton and the Staging of *A Tale of Two Cities*, 1860–1939', in *Charles Dickens, A Tale of Two Cities and the French Revolution*, eds C. Jones, J. McDonagh and J. Mee (Basingstoke: Palgrave Macmillan, 2009), 142, n. 3. *The Only Way*, originally produced in London by John Martin-Harvey, was a hugely popular adaptation, not only on stage but also in the silent film adaptation of 1925 (see 'London Film Reviews', *Variety*, 23 September 1925, 40: 'Never in the history of a picture shown in this country has an audience deliberately refused to leave a theatre and called insistently for the leading actor and producer as they did in this case.'); Marsh called it 'a cultural phenomenon' ('Mimi and the Matinée Idol', 126).
[51]Hamilton Deane was listed as the Marquis de Boulanvilliers in the opening night programme for *The Only Way*, Bristol, 19 June 1899; the Vicomte was played by Henry G. Shaw. But for the performances of the week of 17 July 1899, Deane was the Vicomte and Shaw the Marquis at the Theatre Royal, Merthyr, Wales (both programmes in the Webling Archive).
[52]Programme for *The Ambassador*, Thursday, 2 June [1898] (Webling Archive); review in *The Era*, 4 June 1898, 13.
[53]'"The Only Way" at the Prince's Theatre', *Bristol Western Daily Press*, 20 June 1899, 5. 'Mimi' was not in the book, but was created and expanded from the brief character of a lowly seamstress who accompanies Sydney Carton to the guillotine. In the provincial tour authorized by John Martin-Harvey (producer of the London production), Lucy took over the role of Mimi from Nina de Silva, Martin-Harvey's wife.
[54]Ireland, Select Births and Baptisms, 1620–1911, database online at ancestry.com: Hamilton Knudson Deane Roe, born 2 December 1879, parents Henry Joseph Deane Roe and Cecilia Catherine Deane. The 1939 England Register (a kind of census), database online at ancestry.com, gives a birthdate of 2/12/1879 [2 December 1879], profession Theatrical Manager.
[55]Ireland, Civil Registration Marriages Index, database online at ancestry.com, July–September Quarter 1878, Dublin South, vol. 2, p. 527 (marriage to Henry Joseph Deane Roe): 'Cecilia Catherine Deane'.
[56]In the 1901 and 1911 British censuses, he is an actor, living with other actors, in Sheffield, Yorkshire and Carlisle, Cumberland, respectively. In the 1921 Census, he is in Redditch, Bromsgrove, Worcestershire (born 1880 New Ross, Wexford, Ireland).
[57]E.g. 'Amusements in Hastings', *The Era*, 19 May 1900, 7: [in *The Octoroon*] 'Jacob M'Closky is strongly enacted by Mr Hamilton Deane'; 'Sentenced for Life at the Imperial', *Birmingham Daily Gazette*, 1 October 1901, 5:

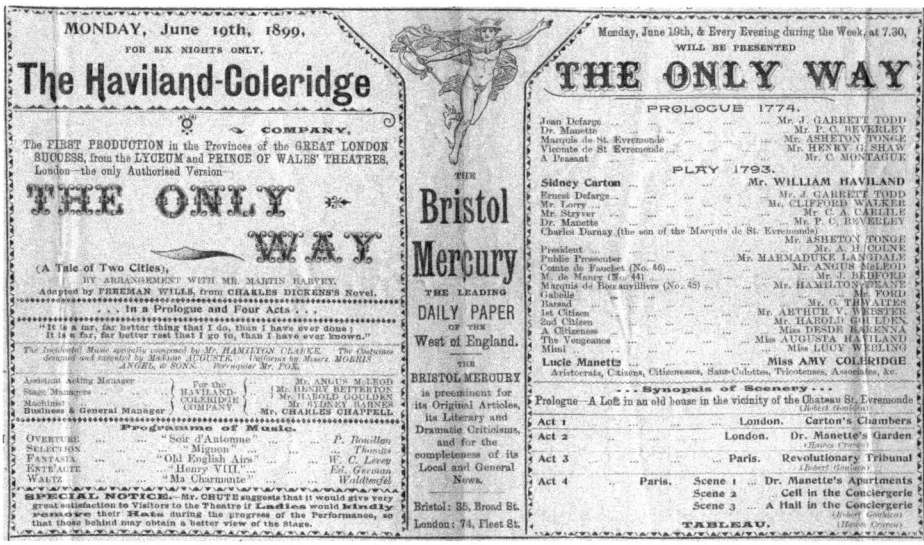

Figure 2.4 Programme for *The Only Way*, 19 June 1899, Prince's Theatre, Bristol (Webling Archive).

as a member of companies performing plays popular in England, making trips back and forth between England, the United States and Canada between 1911 and 1915, listing his occupation as 'actor' and his reason for travel as 'touring'.[58] In January 1916 he signed on as 'Lord Haggett' for a more than year-long US tour of *Fixing Sister*, a vehicle for the comedian William Hodge, which included a run in New York from October to December, and continued into the middle of 1917.[59]

By the time he returned to England in 1918,[60] he was an accomplished actor who had played leading roles in dramas, melodramas and even a 'mammoth stage spectacular'. This last was *The Whip*, where he played the 'hero' in a production that required a special boxcar to transport its horses, used real trains and automobiles, and contained scenes of trainwrecks and horse races.[61] *Fixing Sister* and *The Whip*, both commercial successes,

---

'Derrick is another villain ... whose proclivities ... are presented with much effect by Mr. Hamilton Deane'; 'David Garrick at Exeter', *Devon and Exeter Daily Gazette*, 29 May 1906, 8: 'In the role of David Garrick Mr. Hamilton Deane was seen at his best'.

[58] E.g. Passenger Lists, SS *Philadelphia*, arriving New York 25 August 1912 Hamilton Deane, actor, in US 1911 – twelve months touring; RMS *Olympic*, arriving New York 20 August 1913, Hamilton Deane, actor, in US two years touring. The plays included *With Edged Tools*, *Leah Kleschna*, *A Butterfly on the Wheel*, *The Blindness of Virtue* and *The Whip*.

[59] As 'Fixing Sister', *The News Journal*, Wilmington Delaware, 17 January 1916, 12 reported: Hodge was 'able to secure the release from other engagements of that notable portrayer of English lords, Hamilton Deane, to enact Lord Haggett'.

[60] Passenger List, RMS *Carmania*, arriving 13 September 1918 Liverpool, Hamilton K. D. Roe, aged thirty-eight, actor.

[61] '"The Whip" Arrives Packed with Thrills', *Marysville Evening Democrat* [California], 19 October 1914, 5.

Figure 2.5 Hamilton Deane, Playbill for *Dracula*, 27 July 1931, Nottingham (Webling Archive).

allowed Deane the experience of popular theatre, which would influence his later choices as an actor-manager. Back in England, he joined the Armitage and Leigh Company as one of its principals, and by 1921 was producing his own shows. He was described as a 'matinée idol' and 'brilliant actor'.[62] As 1923 began, his company (which now included Dora Patrick and Stuart Lomath, both actors in *Frankenstein*) was nicely established in provincial repertory. And then came *Dracula*.

Bram Stoker, who served as Henry Irving's Acting Manager at the Lyceum Theatre for twenty-seven years, had written a hurried dramatization of *Dracula* in 1897, mainly to keep control of the dramatic rights.[63] When he died in 1912, the rights to *Dracula* passed to his widow, Florence Balcombe Stoker. How the idea of dramatizing *Dracula* occurred to Hamilton Deane is not clear. He claimed to have thought about it for at least twenty years;[64] previous newspaper and biographical accounts of his connections with Bram Stoker have been examined and credibly dismissed by Paul Murray.[65] In the end, he approached Florence Stoker sometime in 1923, asking for permission to turn her late husband's novel into a play. The widow Stoker was, at the time, embroiled in a case she brought against the German film company that had produced *Nosferatu*, which had clearly copied *Dracula*.[66] Pleased at having her own copyright control, she made a deal giving Deane the dramatic rights.[67]

---

[62]Respectively, the *Derby Daily Telegraph*, 10 October 1922, 4 and *Walsall Observer and South Staffordshire Chronicle*, 17 February 1923, 8.

[63]Paul Murray, 'Hamilton Deane (1879–1958)', *The Green Book: Writings on Irish Gothic, Supernatural and Fantastic Literature*, no. 20 (Samhain 2022): 91.

[64]'I carried "Dracula" round with me for twenty years before I made a play of it', Deane's interview with 'R. C.', 'The Technique of Terror', *The Era*, 19 February 1930, 9; see also Harry Ludlam, *A Biography of Dracula: The Life Story of Bram Stoker* (London: The Fireside Press, 1962), 153.

[65]Murray, 'Hamilton Deane', 89–90.

[66]Murray, 'Hamilton Deane', 91; see also David J. Skal, *Hollywood Gothic: The Tangled Web of Dracula from Novel to Stage to Screen* (New York: W. W. Norton & Co., 1991), 56–61.

[67]Murray, 'Hamilton Deane', 91.

Deane worked on the script 'all through the winter' of 1923–4,[68] and by March of that year he had submitted it to the Lord Chamberlain's Office for approval.[69] The censor, George Street, wanted to ban it, but relented after Deane made some amendments, and granted the licence on 6 May 1924.[70] *Dracula*'s first performance, with Deane as Van Helsing and Edmund Blake as Dracula, was at the Grand Theatre, Derby, on 15 May 1924. The review was also grand: 'For sheer thrills, "Dracula" not only has "The Bat" absolutely "skinned to death" (as our American friends would say), but it is also a polished example of the playwright's craft, revealing the talent of Mr Deane in a new light.'[71] The play toured in repertory and alone for the next three years, until London beckoned Deane at last. *Dracula* opened on 14 February 1927, at the Little Theatre, known for being José Levy's Grand Guignol theatre in London between 1920 and 1922.[72] The play received generally negative reviews, but that did not deter the audiences who flocked to see it. There was even a nurse on hand for patrons who were overcome during the performances.[73]

On 25 March 1927, the American publisher Horace Liveright (1883–1933), co-founder of the Modern Library and would-be producer, arrived in England.[74] *Dracula* was going strong at the Little Theatre, and Liveright went to see it with John Balderston[75] (both men will play roles in the history of Peggy Webling's *Frankenstein*). Liveright realized the possibilities of the play, despite its flaws, and eventually would bring it to Broadway on 5 October 1927, with Balderston, who had already co-authored the hit *Berkeley Square* with John Squire, reworking Hamilton Deane's script (this version would be noted as 'by Hamilton Deane and John L. Balderston').[76] While the Balderston–Deane script played

---

[68]'Dora's Doggie', interview with Dora Patrick about *Dracula*, *Derby Daily Telegraph*, 7 May 1924, 2. Patrick had joined Deane's company around 1921, and was playing Mina Harker in *Dracula* when she gave the interview. She continued to play leading and important supporting roles for Deane throughout the twenties. That theirs was also a romantic relationship is borne out by Patrick's and Deane's eventual marriage in 1938: England General Register Office, Marriages, October–December Quarter 1938, Brentford, vol. 3a, p. 842, Dora M. P. Thompson, spouse Deane Roe.
[69]Murray, 'Hamilton Deane', 92.
[70]Ibid.
[71]'Satanic "Dracula." Noteworthy Production at the Grand Theatre', *Derby Daily Telegraph*, 16 May 1924, 2.
[72]See Richard J. Hand and Michael Wilson, *London's Grand Guignol and the Theatre of Horror* (Exeter: University of Exeter Press, 2007); N. M. Bligh, 'The Little Theatre', *Theatre World* 58, no. 446 (1962): 45–9. Levy still held the lease for the Little when both *Dracula* and *Frankenstein* were produced there; see *The Star*, 22 February 1930, 8.
[73]Skal, *Hollywood Gothic*, 67. See also A. T. Borthwick, 'A hospital nurse', *Daily News*, 20 February 1930, 4: 'The same nurse had "95 authentic cases" during the London run of "Dracula"'; and '"Little" Thrills: Nurse to be on duty in the "Frankenstein" Audiences', *The Star*, 18 February 1930: 'Nurse White has been called back to duty.'
[74]Passenger List, RMS *Aquitania*, arriving Southampton 25 March 1927. 1st Class alien passengers: Horace Liveright, publisher, age forty-three.
[75]David J. Skal, *Something in the Blood: The Untold Story of Bram Stoker, the Man who Wrote Dracula* (New York/London: The Liveright Publishing Company, 2016), 518.
[76]'Dracula to Open Wednesday at Fulton', *The Brooklyn Citizen*, 2 October 1927, 20. Balderston deemed Florence Stoker's requirement that only dialogue already in the book be used in the play, a caveat Hamilton Deane had to follow, as 'one of the most curious play situations that ever existed': see John Balderston, 'Incomplete sketch

Peggy Webling and the Story behind Frankenstein

in America, the Deane script remained as the version performed in England, where Deane continued to run Dracula in the provinces after the London run.

Frankenstein: Productions and Revisions

Deane was making good money with *Dracula*, so it is not exactly surprising that *Frankenstein* would appeal to him. His collaboration with Peggy was a happy melding of mutual interests. Coming on the heels of the impending New York production of *Dracula*, Deane must have seen *Frankenstein* as a serendipitous windfall with the possibility of another lucrative success. And things moved amazingly fast. After Peggy and Deane signed a contract on 14 October 1927, with Deane having an option on the play for six months,[77] preparations for an opening in December went into high gear. Deane chose to play not the role of Henry Frankenstein, the creator, but his creation, whom Peggy named 'Frankenstein' because, 'while the Monster is never given a name by Mary Shelley, it was necessary in a play for him to be known by the same name as the student who was his creator.'[78] And the reason that Peggy changed the name of 'Victor Frankenstein' in Shelley to 'Henry' was partly because she disliked the name Victor,[79] but more importantly to honour the friend of her youth, Henry Page, for whom she named a character 'Henry' in every novel she wrote.[80]

Peggy went to Preston, Lancashire, for the premiere on Wednesday, December 7th, at the Empire Theatre ('a very big house', she said).[81] She wrote to Josephine from the Red Lion Hotel on Church Street in the afternoon before the performance, sharing her thoughts about Deane as Frankenstein ('[he] will make a very intense "F."'), her worries about improving the last act, and Deane's determination to 'turn every stone to make "F." a success, "pulling and tugging it together when once he has seen how it goes before an audience."' She ended the letter by saying 'I can't realize the day has come, I have thought of "F." so much & put so much emotion into it.'

Her letter two days later began with a jubilant '*SUCCESS!*' For Peggy, hearing the calls for 'Author' on an opening night were 'the greatest professional thrills in a writer's life.'[82] This is how she described hearing *her* call:

> If you could have heard the call – enthusiastic, determined – for Author; if you could have seen me hurrying all the way from the middle of the circle . . . to the side

---

(autobiography)', John L. Balderston Papers, 1915–1950, *T-Mss 1954-002, Box 1, folder 7, pp. 4–5, Billy Rose Theatre Division, New York Public Library for the Performing Arts.

[77] Peggy to Josephine, 16 October 1927; Webling, *Story of a Pen* (MS page 113), 305.
[78] Webling, *Story of a Pen* (MS page 112), 304.
[79] Webling, *Story of a Pen* (MS page 114), 305; the name 'Victor' was transferred to her character Victor Moritz (originally Shelley's Henry Clerval).
[80] Ibid., MS page 94. (See also Chapter 1, pp. 20, 50.)
[81] All quotations in this paragraph from Peggy's letter to Josephine, 7 December 1927.
[82] Webling, *Story of a Pen* (MS page 114), 305.

of the stage. And Mr Deane led me on & then presented me . . . with a wonderful bouquet, so big – a great sheaf – that it almost reached my shoulder! Ethel said I looked little on that great stage. Mr Deane thinks, & so do I, we can work this play up into a really great thing – I don't mean by that that it needs extensive alterations, but one can never see some things until a play is actually before an audience.[83]

Because of her previous training, Peggy saw the play as both playwright and performer; she was struck by Deane's ability to play 'F.' 'with quite extraordinary pathos'.[84] (The idea that Frankenstein should be written and played to induce pity was something she wanted to make clear from the outset.) She could see that the Prologue 'worked' – 'The Prologue *grips* the people. . . . You can hear a sort of murmured "Oh!" go through the house when F. first moves; he is made up white – almost gray in colouring . . . & his eyes – just for the time when he comes to life – look as if they glittered.' But she also realized that the last act needed work – 'I am going . . . to write in a scene in the last act. I ought to have thought of it, but I didn't until I saw it (the whole act) rehearsed.'[85]

All in all, the performance was a great success, enthusiastically received by a packed house.[86] Peggy had been nervous, when she compared her play with *Dracula*, that the quiet moments in her play would be lost on those who were used to more spectacular thrills. 'At the same time, if it got hold of such a crowd at all, I thought it might work them up to a high state of excitement.'[87] She and Deane both knew that the play had to be done with 'sincerity and unwavering gravity' for the audience to 'take it seriously'.[88] It could not be played as a mere tongue-in-cheek thriller. That the audience accepted Frankenstein not just as an irredeemable monster, but as someone to be pitied (many reviews of the play mention this) shows that they accomplished their goal. Viewers also saw the 'innocent Katrine', Henry Frankenstein's lame sister, who treats Frankenstein with kindness, as a 'symbol of compassion'.[89] Her accidental death by drowning at the hands of Frankenstein 'was always received in the provinces, and afterwards in London, with silent attention.'[90] Even if some in the audience only went to see *Frankenstein* for the thrills, others were touched by its underlying pathos.[91]

The audience reaction on that first night in Preston was not a fluke. Deane had done hardly any publicity before the performance, possibly hoping to avoid the kind of press reception *Dracula* had had in London, but more likely to obtain a true read from the

---

[83] Peggy to Josephine, 9 December 1927.
[84] Ibid.
[85] Ibid.
[86] Webling, *Story of a Pen* (MS page 114), 305.
[87] Ibid.
[88] Webling, *Story of a Pen* (MS page 114), 305.
[89] Ibid.
[90] Ibid.
[91] Ibid., (MS pages 115–16), 305–6, conveyed in slightly different wording.

audience without advance prejudice.[92] Afterwards, a notice in London's *Daily Telegraph* mentioned its success:

> Last week there was produced at Preston a new play by Peggy Webling, the popular novelist, named 'Frankenstein', founded on the old novel bearing that title. It was presented by Hamilton Deane, and so decisive was its success that, as soon as he can find a home for it in town, he will remove it here.[93]

With such an embrace of *Frankenstein*, Deane immediately put it into the repertoire with *Dracula* and his other plays, performing it in the provinces over the next two years. Despite the note in the *Telegraph*, Frankenstein would not come to London until 1930.

The main reason for this was the revisions that inevitably come in writing and producing a play. Peggy was already aware that 'the last act isn't strong enough' and planned to add 'a violent scene between Henry and F.'[94] By 15 January 1928, she had rewritten the last act, adding 'the demand of F. (as in the book,) for a mate, and Henry's refusal to make one', followed by the new violent scene with Henry in which he is overpowered but unhurt.[95] Frankenstein still leapt to his death from the crag as she had previously written it. She also strengthened the meeting between Emilie (Henry's betrothed) and Frankenstein in Act II.[96] These alterations, though, were not enough. 'That fatal third act!' – Peggy and Deane 'both admitted that future success depended on a drastic change'.[97]

'Another revolution in F!'[98]

On 29 February 1928, Peggy and Lucy went to the matinée at the Borough Theatre, Stratford, where Deane was running *Dracula* for the week. Afterwards Deane brought up the persistent weakness of the third act, and told Peggy that 'he had had an idea that he was very diffident of suggesting to me, but when he *did* I instantly saw the possibilities'.[99] She ruefully noted in her literary memoir that 'it ought to have occurred to *me* – and I suddenly saw what to do. It meant a third act entirely different from the original one, much better and stronger.'[100] As she explained in an illuminating 2 March 1928 letter, it meant she would have to 'entirely re-write the last act – except for the little scene . . .

---

[92] *The Era* had a small notice on 7 December, 1927, 8: 'Tonight he [Hamilton Deane] is giving another new play, "Frankenstein," dramatised by Peggy Webling.'
[93] 'Theatrical Notes', the *Daily Telegraph*, 15 December 1927, 17. The only other London notice of the Preston production was in 'Chit Chat', *The Stage*, 15 December 1927, 14–15 (also mentioning an eventual London production).
[94] Peggy to Josephine, 7 December 1927.
[95] Peggy to Josephine, 15 January 1928.
[96] Ibid.
[97] Webling, *Story of a Pen* (MS page 116), 306.
[98] Peggy to Josephine, 2 March 1928.
[99] Ibid.
[100] Webling, *Story of a Pen* (MS page 117), 306.

between Waldman and F. in which the latter tries to understand that it is God alone who can help and pity him, as Deane says that always "gets over" and *he* considers it the most touching thing in the whole play.'[101] This would be the seventh re-write for *Frankenstein*, but it would make 'an end as thrilling as the prologue'.[102]

Since her January letter mentioned that she had already added Frankenstein's demand for and Henry's refusal of a mate, Deane's idea on that leap-year day must have been to have Henry die as well as Frankenstein, making clear to Peggy that Henry's refusal to make a mate would compel Frankenstein to kill him (Henry had not died in the 1927 version). So along with Henry's refusal to make a mate, she needed to incorporate Henry's death into the act as well.[103] At some point after her conversation with Deane, she put Frankenstein's demand for a mate, with Henry's reluctant consent to do it, as the closing scene of the second act.[104] This prepared the way for the third act finale, where Henry destroys his instruction scroll and the elixir of life (and thus the ability to animate the mate) because of the possibility, she said, to people 'the world with monsters – there's a situation for you!'[105] And then 'F. will kill Henry and die himself by a flash of lightning, thereby carrying out the thought that he comes to life in a storm and ends in a storm – Henry dies by his own wicked act, indirectly, and F. dies by the forces of nature.'[106]

This key letter establishes that by March of 1928, acting on Deane's crucial comment, Peggy had worked out the new third act and the scenes that would be used in the final version of the play. Peggy's September 1928 version of the end of Act II and Act III in the Library of Congress reflects the earlier changes, and is substantially the same as the 1930 production, except for the two last lines of the play.[107] Henry's death, along with Frankenstein's, becomes the counterpoint to Frankenstein's coming to life in the Prologue, with equal dramatic impact. The new version of the play (probably including the new end of Act II) was ready for the production in Nottingham the week of 10 June 1928 (programme in Webling Archive), and would be performed for the whole week. Underscoring how important the changes were to her, Peggy actually went to Nottingham's Theatre Royal for the performance on the 11th, and was introduced by Deane. The review in the *Nottingham Evening Post* said that 'it carries a thrill right from the appearance of the gruesome being called to life by a crazy scientist, and works up to a grim closing scene', and that 'Peggy Webling, the well-known novelist-dramatist, prepared a stage version that does her much credit.'[108]

---

[101] Peggy to Josephine, 2 March 1928.
[102] Ibid.
[103] That this interpretation is close to what Peggy decided to do by early March is borne out by Hamilton Deane's comment around 19 February 1930 to R. C. of *The Era*, 'The Technique of Terror' (see n. 64), that 'The whole of "Frankenstein" works up cumulatively to the end of the last act when Henry is killed. That is the climax of the play ...'.
[104] This probably occurred before June 1928, when the newly revised play was presented in Nottingham; the version copyrighted with the Library of Congress in September contains all these changes.
[105] Peggy to Josephine, 2 March 1928.
[106] Ibid.
[107] For discussion of this, see Chapter 3, p. 92.
[108] 'Review of This Week's Shows', *The Nottingham Evening Post*, 12 June 1928, 4.

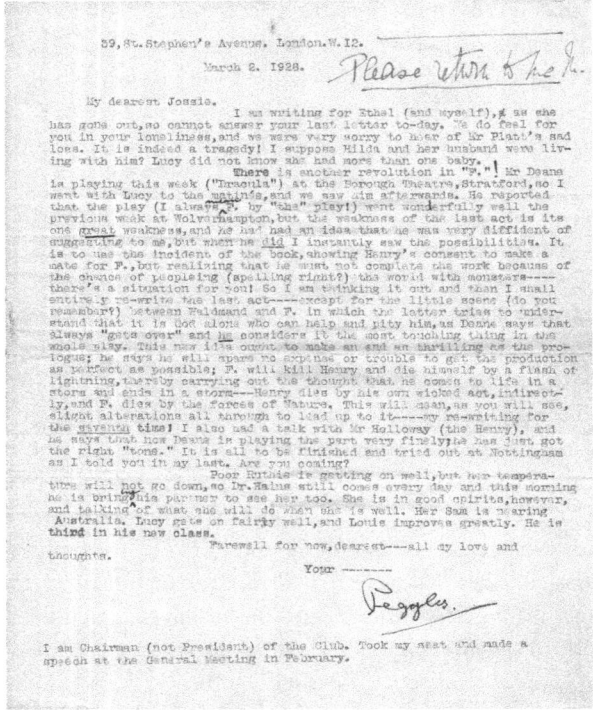

Figure 2.6 Peggy's letter of 2 March 1928: 'another revolution in "F."!' (Webling Archive)

Though these were significant changes to the play, they would not be the last. Peggy kept revising. More alterations were made to the second act in the autumn, chiefly a transposition of the scenes between Frankenstein and Katrine, and Frankenstein and Emilie, 'so that all the excitement now comes right at the end'.[109] These were incorporated into the performances at the Winter Gardens Theatre, New Brighton (near Liverpool). As she had in Nottingham, Peggy went to New Brighton to see her play in December.[110] Someone else also saw it there – John L. Balderston.

'[T]hat Frankenstein of my existence – John Balderston'[111]

When we last heard of Balderston, he was rewriting Hamilton Deane's version of *Dracula* for the American version produced on Broadway by Horace Liveright in 1927. John Lloyd Balderston (1889–1954) was born in Philadelphia, although for a significant part

---

[109] Peggy to Josephine, 13 December 1928.
[110] Ibid.: 'On Monday I am off to New Brighton for a week of "F."'
[111] Peggy to Josephine, 8 January 1930.

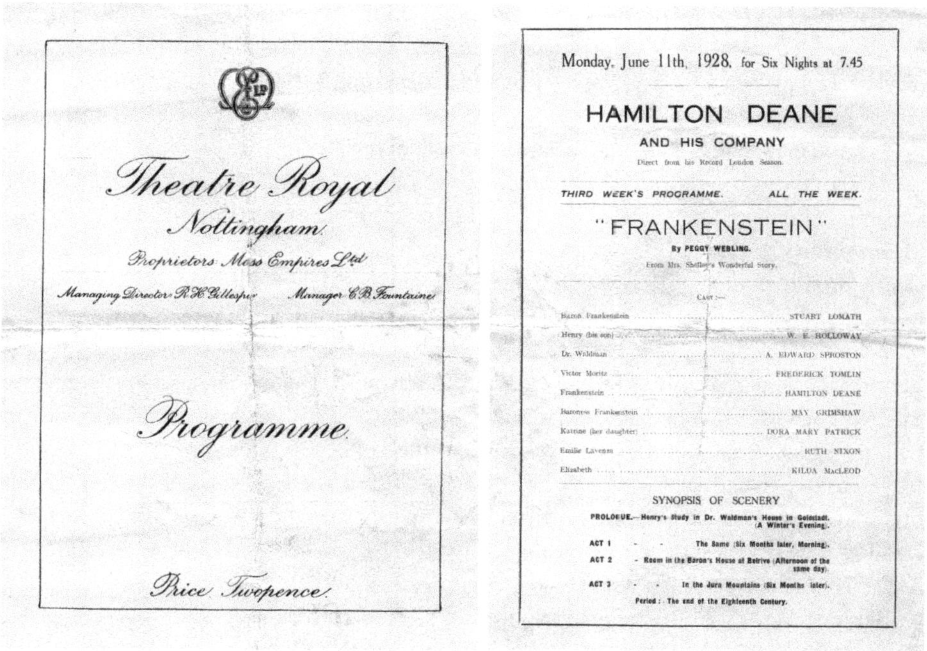
Theatre Royal
Nottingham.
Proprietors Moss Empires Ltd
Managing Director R. H. Gillespie Manager C. B. Fountaine
Programme.
Price Twopence.

Monday, June 11th, 1928, for Six Nights at 7.45

HAMILTON DEANE
AND HIS COMPANY
Direct from his Record London Season.

THIRD WEEK'S PROGRAMME. ALL THE WEEK.

"FRANKENSTEIN"
By PEGGY WEBLING.
From Mrs. Shelley's Wonderful Story.

CAST :—

Baron Frankenstein	STUART LOMATH
Henry (his son)	W. E. HOLLOWAY
Dr. Waldman	A. EDWARD SPROSTON
Victor Moritz	FREDERICK TOMLIN
Frankenstein	HAMILTON DEANE
Baroness Frankenstein	MAY GRIMSHAW
Katrine (her daughter)	DORA MARY PATRICK
Emilie Lavenza	RUTH NIXON
Elizabeth	KILDA MacLEOD

SYNOPSIS OF SCENERY

PROLOGUE.—Henry's Study in Dr. Waldman's House in Golstadt. (A Winter's Evening).
ACT 1 - - The Same (Six Months later, Morning).
ACT 2 - Room in the Baron's House at Belrive (Afternoon of the same day).
ACT 3 - - In the Jura Mountains (Six Months later).
Period : The end of the Eighteenth Century.

Figure 2.7 Frankenstein at the Theatre Royal, Nottingham, 11 June 1928 (Webling Archive).

of his working life he was based in England as a newspaper correspondent, editor and dramatist. He attended the Journalism School at Columbia University between 1912 and 1914, though he was never a matriculated student.[112] From 1914 to 1917 he worked as a war correspondent for the McClure Newspaper Syndicate, as a director of information for Great Britain and Ireland with the US Embassy in London[113] and as an international reporter based in London from 1918 on. From 1920 to 1924 he was editor of *The Outlook*, a weekly news and culture magazine; at the same time he was also chief correspondent and European manager for Joseph Pulitzer's *New York World*, a job he held until 1931 when the *World* folded.[114] In November and December 1925, writing for the *New York World* and the North American Newspaper Alliance, he reported from Luxor and Cairo, Egypt, on the treasures found in Tutankhamen's tomb.[115]

[112]Columbia University Catalogue, 1912/1913, 337: a list of 'Non-Matriculated Students' included 'Balderston, John Lloyd'; Columbia University Catalogue 1913/1914, 338, 'Non-Matriculated Students, Balderston, John Floyd [*sic*]'.

[113]John Balderston, 'Incomplete sketch (auobiography)', John L. Balderston Papers, 1915–1950, *T-Mss 1954-002, Box 1, folder 7, p. 2, Billy Rose Theatre Division, New York Public Library for the Performing Arts.

[114]Balderston, 'Incomplete sketch', pp. 3–4.

[115]E.g. 'King Tut's Body Taken from Coffin', *Great Falls Tribune* (Montana), 12 November 1925, 1; 'Writer Learns of New Tut Finds as Soldiers Shadow Him', *The Buffalo News* (New York), 14 November 1925, 2; 'Tomb of Tutankhamen Holds the World's Great Treasures of Art: Gems, Vases, Translucent Lamps of Exquisite,

Peggy Webling and the Story behind Frankenstein

Since the *World* allowed him time to do other things as long as he put on his reporting hat as needed, and *The Outlook* was humming along, Balderston also began writing plays.[116] His first success was *Berkeley Square*, co-written with J. C. Squire, and based on Henry James' posthumous unfinished novel, *The Sense of the Past*. It premiered in London on 6 October 1926 at St Martin's Theatre, to excellent reviews.[117] Earlier we saw Balderston's relationship with Liveright and Deane regarding *Dracula*. Deane had not forgotten it. He had apparently been writing to Balderston (and Liveright) well before Peggy wrote the changes to *Frankenstein*, asking him to revise it.[118] This behind-the-scenes correspondence was clearly unknown to Peggy, who wrote the revision in good faith. She had also copyrighted her latest version of *Frankenstein* with the US Library of Congress on 7 September 1928 (which contained all of the changes up to that point),[119] and the play was doing well in the provinces. Now, writing in November to Balderston, Deane disingenuously claimed to have 'revised it myself', and was doing good business 'with the new version ... every whit as big as we did with Dracula previous to the London production.'[120] The gist of the letter was to persuade Balderston to hop on the *Frankenstein* bandwagon. And Balderston, finally sold, sent Deane's November letter to his agent, Harold Freedman, adding that 'two London theatres have been offered for the play, but Deane is holding it up until he sees me.'[121] This scheme was, fortunately for Peggy, destined to fail.

Balderston duly came to New Brighton to see the play in December of 1928. Deane must finally have told Peggy about Balderston after this visit. She told Josephine later that he 'was so impressed that he kept Deane up till three in the morning discussing it.'[122] And in the middle of January, she hinted at 'news that will surprise you', having to do both with the artistic and financial sides of the play.[123] 'It has all been very exciting & not a little agitating, but I do believe it will turn out well. I will only say, that a *very big* possibility – for me – is now hanging in the balance, & yet it is not *all* delightful.'[124] And there matters stood – when a sudden tragedy intervened.

Incomparable Beauty', *The Anaconda Standard* (Montana), 20 December 1925, 40; The 'Incomplete sketch', p. 4, also mentions 'King Tut'.

[116]Balderston, 'Incomplete sketch', p. 4; mentioned also in the John L. Balderston Papers, 1915–1950 (*T-Mss 1954-002, Box 1) are his plays *The Brook Kerith* (1916), *Tongo* (1924) and *The Clown of Stratford* (c. 1925–1927). In 1922 his *A Morality Play for the Leisure Class* (one-act) was produced in New York.

[117]E.g., 'Two Authors – and Another, Enthralling Play at the St. Martin's', *Daily Herald*, 7 October 1926, 5.

[118]Skal, *Monster Show*, 97: 'Hamilton Deane ... had been pestering Liveright, as well as Balderston, for almost two years about a stage adaptation of Frankenstein by a certain Miss Peggy Webling. ... In November 1928, Deane wrote to Balderston ...' Skal suggests that Deane had been writing to Balderston before November 1928, but note that Deane only learned of Peggy's play in September of 1927, fourteen months – not almost two years – before he wrote the November letter.

[119]US Library of Congress, *Catalogue of Copyright Entries*, no. 9, 1928, 4458: 'Frankenstein; a play in a prologue and 3 acts, based upon Mrs. Shelley's well known book, by P. Webling. © 1 c. Sept. 7, 1928; D 86282.' The copyright for this is now held by Dorian Gieseler Greenbaum.

[120]Skal, *Monster Show*, 97, quoting Deane's letter of November 1928 to Balderston.

[121]Ibid., quoting Balderston's note to Freedman accompanying Deane's November letter.

[122]Peggy to Josephine, 24 March 1929.

[123]Peggy to Josephine, 17 January 1929.

[124]Ibid.

On 20 February 1929, after only a few weeks of illness, her beloved sister Ethel died from pneumonia.[125] Peggy was 'sorely stricken'[126] and could not even go into the house where she had lived with Ethel without breaking down. Everything was put on hold. Ethel had been the mainstay of the household, the guiding centre who kept family and house together, as well as doing her own work painting miniatures up to the end. Her nephew Louis McRaye called her 'a saint'.[127] Peggy sent a notice of her death to the London correspondent for the *Derby Daily Telegraph*, who wrote a lovely tribute, saying that neither Ethel nor Peggy were 'spoilt by the success which came to them and fitted them like a becoming mantle.' The column mentioned *Frankenstein*, 'a work which owed much . . . to the kindly inspiration of Ethel, and its production will constitute a memorial to a very charming and very great lady.'[128]

It was not until the middle of March 1929 that Peggy was able to think about Frankenstein again. An important letter written on the 24th of that month explained the enigmatic statements in her 17 January letter:

> Dearest, I *may* come to the U.S.A. & Canada as soon as I can afford it. All depends upon Frankenstein. In the greater matter of my unspeakable loss I have forgotten to tell you that it is *practically* settled that a Mr John Balderston – an American who wrote that brilliant play, 'Berkeley Square,' now running in London – is to collaborate with me in a version of 'F.' for the American stage. There has been any amount of talk & correspondence between him, Mr Deane & myself.[129]

'[T]here must be vital changes to suit America', Balderston said.[130] And having done the same with Deane's script for *Dracula*, he would be the one to do them for *Frankenstein*. Harold Freedman, Balderston's agent, came over from New York to make the contract. Peggy 'agreed to let him come in with me', but not before she showed 'the contract . . . to the Author's Society, & which Farquharson had altered on all the points with which I could not agree.' Peggy sent him the current copy of the play, and he guaranteed to finish the adaptation in six months or forfeit 'the small money he has paid me'; if he couldn't do this, 'he pays me a hundred pounds for a nine months option.' 'But', she said, 'I believe he *will* do it.' Her confidence would be misplaced.

Peggy was more complimentary about Balderston's previous work than he was to hers – he called *Frankenstein* 'inconceivably crude' and 'illiterate'.[131] She said of him, 'He is a very clever, peculiar man, with an extraordinary sense of the dramatic – a great

---

[125] Death Certificate, General Record Office (UK), Deaths 1929 January–March quarter, Kensington, 1a 409, no. 380: cause of death 'lobar pneumonia following influenza'.
[126] Peggy to Josephine, 24 March 1929.
[127] Personal conversation with this writer.
[128] 'Ethel Webling', *Derby Daily Telegraph*, 23 February 1929, 5.
[129] Peggy to Josephine, 24 March 1929.
[130] All information and quotations in this paragraph from letter of 24 March 1929.
[131] Skal, *Monster Show*, 97, 98.

sense of the theatre – combined with practical skill & artistic feeling. . . . This play of his, "Berkeley Square," is exceedingly fine.' The contract (for which Balderston paid Peggy £20)[132] stipulated that in England, any adaptation would be cited as by Peggy Webling and John Balderston. In the United States it would be 'by John Balderston and Hamilton Deane, adapted from the play by Peggy Webling'. She added, 'It is rather absurd to have Deane's name, but I *had* to give way on that point.'[133] The two would share equally in the profits, whether 'play, film rights, "talkies" – everything'. She was reassured that Deane had 'tremendous faith in him, & also says he is absolutely straight in business.'[134]

So why did Peggy call him 'that Frankenstein of *my* existence'? Principally because, though he had 'great ideas' for 'increasing its horror and dramatic possibilities', he only produced 'wearisome correspondence' and 'a hopeless manuscript of which not a line could be used'.[135] And on top of that he did not finish the adaptation within six months, so she consented to extend the contract for another nine months – this time being paid the required £100.[136] While waiting for Balderston to get on with it, however, something rather more exciting happened – Hamilton Deane, at last, decided to bring the play to London. He, too, had had enough of Balderston's promises without delivery.

'I've got a play running in London!'[137]

It came about when Peggy went to Chester for a night to talk to Deane, and he asked her to make an alteration in the second act.[138] She finished it by the 19th of October 1929, and Deane pronounced it 'most excellent'.[139] *Frankenstein* had been seeing increased business and enthusiastic reviews throughout the late summer and autumn.[140] Some notices had even advertised it 'prior to its London production',[141] but Peggy wasn't putting her eggs in that basket just yet. She wanted certainty and, finally, she got it. At the end of November she wrote: 'Now for the thrilling news – Frankenstein is to be produced next year, on Monday, February 10, at the Little Theatre', the same theatre where *Dracula* had opened in 1927. And even better, 'It will be *my* version, as Mr Balderston has not

---

[132]Ibid., 98. This was 'the small money he has paid me' that she mentioned in the 24 March 1929 letter.
[133]It was done because of Balderston's and Deane's previous success with *Dracula* (letter of 24 March 1929).
[134]Webling quotations in this paragraph from letter of 24 March 1929.
[135]Webling, *Story of a Pen* (MS page 118), 307.
[136]Peggy to Josephine, 3 October 1929 for the contract extension; the amount of £100 was mentioned in the 24 March letter.
[137]Peggy to Josephine, 13 February 1930.
[138]Peggy to Josephine, 3 October 1929.
[139]Peggy to Josephine, 19 October 1929.
[140] *Birmingham Gazette*, 27 August 1929, 9: 'One can also prophesy for it a vogue surpassing that of "Dracula" . . . and unlike "Dracula," it has sanity and a well-told, convincing story'; *Midland Daily Telegraph*, 10 September 1929, 5: 'has "Dracula" and other notable thrillers beaten to a frazzle'; *Liverpool Echo*, 24 October 1929, 4: 'Remarkable scenes of enthusiasm . . . attended the final curtain of "Frankenstein"'.
[141]E.g. *Runcorn Weekly News* (Cheshire), 11 October 1929, 10.

written his & neither Mr Deane nor I cared for his ideas.'[142] As December and the two-year anniversary of *Frankenstein* came and went, with no word from Balderston that his version was finished, it was just as well, for 'It is now decided to my great satisfaction ... that he has nothing whatever to do with the play in this country.'[143] And, she wrote indignantly, 'He wanted Deane to postpone till his version was ready! Thank Heaven Deane said "No!" & so it is settled.'[144]

In preparation for the London debut, Deane ordered new furniture, scenery and costumes for the women, and engaged a publicity man named Stanley Hale.[145] A book of clippings from the Hamilton Deane Papers at the Westminster Archives[146] holds hundreds of notices, interviews and reviews – Hale did his work well. Deane hired a new Henry, a new Emilie (the fifth) and a new Baroness.[147] Henry would now be played by Henry Hallatt, an up-and-coming actor who bore a striking physical resemblance to Deane.[148] The *doppelgänger* theme, which was part of Peggy's conception from the beginning, would be well served. The play also acquired a description above the title: instead of the succinct 'Frankenstein' used in the provinces over more than two years, 'Frankenstein' was now preceded by 'An Adventure in the Macabre:' in the London production's programme. This was probably Deane's or publicist Stanley Hale's idea, since none of Peggy's versions ever used such a phrase.[149]

As the time for the opening approached, Peggy went to see her agent, John Farquharson, to deal once more with the Frankenstein of *her* existence. Balderston was supposed to be working on an American version and production of *Frankenstein*, but, true to form, was now requesting yet another extension of six months (which would bring it to the end of 1930) to write and get someone to produce *Frankenstein* in the United States. Peggy agreed and got another advance.[150] But his delays and lack of results were infuriating all the same.

Meanwhile, the Little Theatre was redecorated in 'pale cream with small blue medallions' and the seats upholstered in a rich red,[151] and the lobby contained a display of Peake's earlier version, *Presumption; or, The Fate of Frankenstein.*[152] Peggy was given

---

[142]Quotations in this and the previous sentence from Peggy's letter to Josephine, 25 November 1929.
[143]Peggy to Josephine, 31 December 1929.
[144]Ibid.
[145]Peggy to Josephine, 5 January 1930.
[146]Catalogue no. 2992/HD/32.
[147]Peggy to Josephine, 5 January 1930. The letter was accompanied by four clippings from *The Times, Morning Post, Daily Telegraph* and *Daily News*.
[148]Peggy to Josephine, 5 January and 28 January 1930.
[149]See the discussion about this in Chapter 3, p. 75 n.35.
[150]Peggy to Josephine, 8 January 1930.
[151]Peggy to Josephine, 13 February 1930.
[152]Peggy to Josephine, 27 April 1930: 'Yes, there have been many versions of "F." in dramatic form, but not for some time. We had a play-bill on view at the Little Theatre (at least, Mr Deane had), of the very first, when the monster was played by the well known actor Cooke, and Mrs Shelley professed herself delighted with his performance. The latest was by Stephen Phillips, but it was (I believe) in one act, and Henry Ainley played the big part; one of the papers said it was not a patch on mine.' (This last probably refers to a Frankenstein clipping

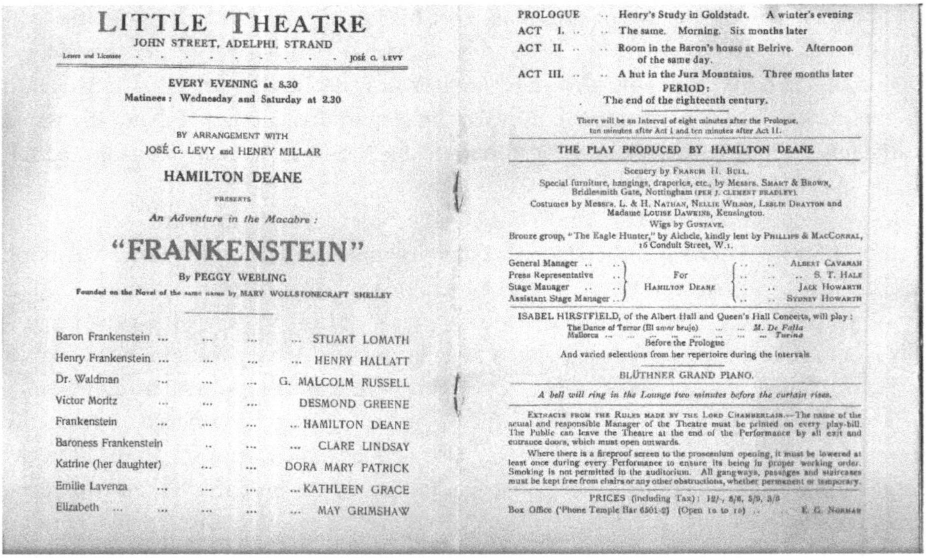

LITTLE THEATRE
JOHN STREET, ADELPHI, STRAND
Lessee and Licensee . . . . JOSÉ G. LEVY

EVERY EVENING at 8.30
Matinees: Wednesday and Saturday at 2.30

BY ARRANGEMENT WITH
JOSÉ G. LEVY and HENRY MILLAR

HAMILTON DEANE
PRESENTS
An Adventure in the Macabre:

"FRANKENSTEIN"

By PEGGY WEBLING
Founded on the Novel of the same name by MARY WOLLSTONECRAFT SHELLEY

Baron Frankenstein	STUART LOMATH
Henry Frankenstein	HENRY HALLATT
Dr. Waldman	G. MALCOLM RUSSELL
Victor Moritz	DESMOND GREENE
Frankenstein	HAMILTON DEANE
Baroness Frankenstein	CLARE LINDSAY
Katrine (her daughter)	DORA MARY PATRICK
Emilie Lavenza	KATHLEEN GRACE
Elizabeth	MAY GRIMSHAW

PROLOGUE .. .. Henry's Study in Goldstadt. A winter's evening
ACT I. .. .. The same. Morning. Six months later
ACT II. .. .. Room in the Baron's house at Belrive. Afternoon of the same day.
ACT III. .. .. A hut in the Jura Mountains. Three months later

PERIOD:
The end of the eighteenth century.

There will be an Interval of eight minutes after the Prologue, ten minutes after Act I and ten minutes after Act II.

THE PLAY PRODUCED BY HAMILTON DEANE

Scenery by FRANCIS H. BULL.
Special furniture, hangings, draperies, etc., by Messrs. SMART & BROWN, Bridlesmith Gate, Nottingham (PER J. CLEMENT BRADLEY).
Costumes by Messrs. L. & H. NATHAN, NELLIE WILSON, LESLIE DRAYTON and Madame LOUISE DAWKINS, Kensington.
Wigs by GUSTAVE.
Bronze group, "The Eagle Hunter," by Aichele, kindly lent by PHILLIPS & MACCONNAL, 16 Conduit Street, W.1.

General Manager .. .. For HAMILTON DEANE .. .. ALBERT CAVANAH
Press Representative .. .. S. T. HALE
Stage Manager .. .. JACK HOWARTH
Assistant Stage Manager .. .. .. SYDNEY HOWARTH

ISABEL HIRSTFIELD, of the Albert Hall and Queen's Hall Concerts, will play:
The Dance of Terror (El amor brujo) ... ... *M. De Falla*
Mallorca ... ... *Turina*
Before the Prologue
And varied selections from her repertoire during the intervals.

BLÜTHNER GRAND PIANO.

A bell will ring in the Lounge two minutes before the curtain rises.

EXTRACTS FROM THE RULES MADE BY THE LORD CHAMBERLAIN.—The name of the actual and responsible Manager of the Theatre must be printed on every play-bill. The Public can leave the Theatre at the end of the Performance by all exit and entrance doors, which must open outwards.

Where there is a fireproof screen to the proscenium opening, it must be lowered at least once during every Performance to ensure its being in proper working order. Smoking is not permitted in the auditorium. All gangways, passages and staircases must be kept free from chairs or any other obstructions, whether permanent or temporary.

PRICES (including Tax): 12/-, 8/6, 5/9, 3/6
Box Office ('Phone Temple Bar 6501-2) (Open 10 to 10) .. E. G. NORMAN

Figure 2.8 Playbill of *Frankenstein*, Little Theatre, London, 1930 (Webling Archive).

fifteen tickets for opening night.[153] She bought a ring velvet dress, black and flecked with a moony blue colour, with a black velvet cloak to match.[154] On 7 February *The Bookman* paid for her to be photographed by Edward Hoppé, *the* photographer at the time. Josephine sent a telegram: 'Darling, best wishes, love, success for the night of nights – With you in thought always, am writing – J.'[155] On the morning of February 10th, like a woman about to go into labour, Peggy did the laundry! – all the while thinking of 'THE PLAY' and those she loved, especially Ethel. She was ready well before it was time to go, so she 'sat quietly by the gas fire in my room, trying to be quite still and send good thoughts to everybody concerned in the production.'[156] When they got to the theatre Peggy, her family and friends sat in the last two rows of the stalls, the only place they could have ten seats together (five in one row, five in another). Her nephew Louis remembered sitting next to G. K. Chesterton.[157] The stalls filled quickly, nearly all with men (mostly critics). The rest is here in Peggy's own words:

In the 2 January *Morning Post*, that Peggy cut out and sent to Josephine on 5 January 1930, referring to the play as 'not an achievement which his best admirers would wish to remember'.)

[153]Peggy to Josephine, 6 February 1930. Five went to her agent, her publicist and others. The other ten were for family and friends.

[154]Peggy to Josephine, 21 January 1930.

[155]Text of the telegram written on the back of the letter of 21 January 1930 (Webling Archive).

[156]Letter of 13 February 1930.

[157]Personal conversation with the writer.

we had *all* the best, dramatic critics in London there, a very difficult, sophisticated audience. But the play went well from the start, not the hint of a laugh in the wrong place, and really *prolonged* applause at Deane's first exit in the first act, and again when he went out with Katrina. . . . After the second act I went behind . . . straight to Deane's room. . . . I said: 'Well, Mr Deane, what do you think?' 'I think we're *all right*,' he answered: 'We've turned the corner.' At that minute along came the boy – 'Third act!' 'Come with me,' said Deane. 'I want you to stand on the prompt side and leave it to me whether you take a call or not. Will you?' 'Certainly,' said I. . . . The stage hands do the thunder and final flash of lightning most wonderfully . . . – you never heard such a crash and flash and rush of excitement. Then the curtain began to go up and down, the first twice on H.D. and Mr Hallatt, then Deane alone five times, then (as there were mingled shouts of 'Speech!' and 'Author!') he made a capital, witty little speech to this effect: 'Ladies and gentlemen. I thank you most sincerely for the very kind way you have received this – this – weird little play. That is the case for the defence. The case for the prosecution you will hear tomorrow' – there was a great laugh from the men in the house – 'But the verdict, after all, is in your hands.' . . . Then . . . he came to the back and nodded to me and took my hand and led me forward. They said I looked so small, as he is so huge. He stepped behind me. I bowed, they shouted 'Speech!' so I just thanked them, turned to Deane, and we smiled and down came the curtain finally. *I'VE GOT A PLAY RUNNING IN LONDON, I HAVE!*[158]

The critics were kind to Deane, less kind to Peggy, but 'I suffer (as a playwright) by this perpetual comparison with Dracula, which is . . . a fifth rate play, considered as a literary work.'[159] Even so, 'all the critics have had to acknowledge that it is a striking and exciting play.'[160] Some said it was better than Dracula.[161] Most importantly, it was 'a box office Press'[162] and they even got a clever cartoon from Punch: 'I burst out laughing when I saw it at a railway station.'[163] And 'The best papers – The Times, the Daily News and Punch – have praised my work.'[164] E. A. Baughan of the *Daily News* wrote that 'she has done her

---

[158] Letter of 13 February 1930.
[159] Ibid.
[160] Peggy to Josephine, 23 February 1930.
[161] E.g. 'On its merits it deserves a bigger success than "Dracula"', 'Monster Incredible but Real', *Evening News*, 11 February 1930, 6; '"Frankenstein" is a much better play than "Dracula"', 'Those Thrillers', *Daily Express*, 12 February 1930, 6; Vaughan Dryden, 'This is a far far better play than Dracula', 'Provincial Actors in London', *Sporting Times*, 15 February 1930, 7; 'As an eerie thriller, Frankenstein is ten times as good as "Dracula"', 'A Real Thriller', *Reynolds's News*, 16 February 1930, 6; 'Whether it will run as long as "Dracula" is a moot point. It is an infinitely better play', 'Potted Plays', *Sunday Graphic*, 16 February 1930, 19.
[162] Letter of 13 February 1930.
[163] Peggy to Josephine, 23 February 1930. She saved the cartoon, too.
[164] Ibid.

Peggy Webling and the Story behind Frankenstein

Figure 2.9 Cartoon of *Frankenstein* in *Punch*, 19 February 1930, 219 (Webling Archive).

work well', *Punch* called it 'an interesting and intelligent adaptation' and *The Times* said 'Miss Webling . . . has unquestionably succeeded in bringing the monster to life'.[165]

Balderston and Liveright redux

The opening in London, and the resultant publicity, finally got the attention first of Balderston and then, through him, of Horace Liveright. Balderston couldn't believe his eyes when he looked at the theatre reviews after *Frankenstein* opened. How could the play he had called 'inconceivably crude' be a success?[166] How could 'highbrow' publications like *Punch* and *The Nation and Athenaeum* have even paid attention to it?[167] In fact, from the first time they made contact, Balderston had belittled and underestimated Peggy. So Deane's London production caught him by surprise. Instead of realizing that in spite

---

[165]E. A. Baughan, *Daily News*, 11 February 1930, 12; *Punch*, 19 February 1930, 219; *The Times*, 11 February 1930, 12, though its reviewer added 'but the play in which she exhibits this wild beast is as flimsy as a bird cage'.
[166]Skal, *Monster Show*, 97, citing Balderston's note to Harold Freedman (see above, n. 121).
[167]Ibid., 105, citing Balderston to Liveright, 24 February 1930.

of his views about her there may have been something worthy in her play, he doubled down, remarking, when he saw 'all raves' in the evening papers, 'It does take the biscuit, for you never saw such a text or such actors.'[168]

Even as he began to negotiate with Peggy about a New York production, he described her as 'totally ignorant and inexperienced' – apparently in the ways of theatrical contracts – and '[t]hat's why we have to shake some cash under her nose and sew her up quickly.'"[169] Of course the misogynistic, not to mention ageist, Balderston was just as eager as Peggy – if not more – to make a deal for the money it would bring *him*. But evidently this was not becoming in a female playwright. He sneeringly said: 'She thinks she's written a hell of a play and [that] I would probably spoil it.'[170] That, of course, is exactly what she thought. So she went into a new round of negotiation with her eyes wide open.

Peggy and Balderston came to an agreement on 24 February 1930 (see Appendix 3), in which Balderston agreed to write an adaptation of her play within a year of the date of the agreement, paying her $500 as an advance on royalties. If Balderston failed to produce, he would pay her an additional $250 for six months or $500 for one year. All 'monies and royalties' from grants, sale of rights and licences would be split, 50-50, between them. Balderston's adaptation would be known in America as 'by the authors of Dracula or by John Balderston and Hamilton Deane', followed by 'adapted from the play by Peggy Webling', and the 'new play shall be registered by the Adaptor [Balderston] at the Library of Congress, Washington, under the joint names of John Balderston and Peggy Webling.'[171] These were rather shrewd moves by someone supposedly so 'ignorant and inexperienced'.[172] In the end, Balderston's adaptation *was* registered with the Library of Congress as 'by John Balderston and Peggy Webling'.[173]

Now, however, she would be dealing not only with Balderston, who was at least a known quantity, but Liveright as well. She would discover that he was flamboyant, opinionated, prone to exaggeration and fabrication, and possessed a high, but unmerited, opinion of his own abilities as a writer.

The first indication of his loose relationship with the truth was when Liveright announced to the New York press as early as 26 January 1930, sixteen days *before* the London opening, that he had 'bought' *Frankenstein* for America.[174] Of course this was not true, though it was typical of Liveright's bombastic and rash style. As Peggy remarked to Josephine, 'Your hustling New York pressmen have anticipated my news! Mr Liveright

---

[168]Ibid., 104, citing Balderston to Liveright, 11 February 1930.
[169]Ibid. The quotation comes from Balderston's letter to Liveright, 11 February 1930 (personal communication with David J. Skal, 16 January 2023).
[170]Skal, *Monster Show*, 104, citing (411) letter from Balderston to Liveright, 11 February 1930.
[171]'Memorandum of Agreement' between Peggy Webling and John Balderston, dated 24 February 1930 (in the Webling Archive, initialed by John L. Balderston).
[172]Skal, *Monster Show*, 104.
[173]Library of Congress, *Catalogue of Copyright Entries 1931*, no. 3, 1614.
[174]'News and Gossip of the Times Square Sector', *New York Times*, 26 January 1930, page X (Section 8).

has *not bought* "F.," for I should not dream of selling it.'[175] She was, though, in negotiations for a New York production with him and Balderston, and a contract dated 26 February 1930 was signed by the three parties (see Appendix 3).[176] Liveright's agent had seen the play twice, and apparently the deal was proposed on the strength of his assessment. She happily reported that 'we are getting wonderfully good terms from Liveright, and it is understood that Mr Balderston shall do his version (of course founded on mine) in time for the production within a year, Liveright paying a sum down for the option. . . . I now look for Balderston to pull off the big money deal.'[177]

From Peggy's perspective, things were moving along and, after all, Liveright had paid them a $1000 advance.[178] She could not know that Liveright was actually nervous at making a deal without having seen the play himself. In his and Balderston's back and forth about the play, Balderston had to reassure him (while at the same time expressing amazement at its popularity).[179] Liveright did eventually show up in London on the 20th of March, and saw *Frankenstein* on the 21st.[180] She also did not know that Liveright was in increasing financial difficulties.

Cracks appeared at the beginning of April: 'I have had some absurd clippings from American papers, for Liveright appears to be an impulsive gentleman who talks to everybody.'[181] *Frankenstein* closed in London on April 12th, and Deane went on tour with it soon after.[182] Balderston was supposed to be writing the adaptation that would play in New York, but Peggy heard nothing from him for weeks. Having been down this road before, she added, 'I hope he is getting on with it.' In the meantime *she* finished two acts of the new play she was writing for Deane, *Reprieve*.[183] Balderston apparently was not as industrious.

Things were about to get even dicier, on a number of fronts. First, Deane was seriously considering going to America to star in the New York production, but after listening to Liveright talking 'like a Napoleon of the theatre', pontificating on his own views about how to write the new play and full of 'fool ideas', Deane saw him as the humbug he was.[184] Liveright's antics convinced Deane that the last thing he wanted was to be in a play produced by Horace Liveright: Balderston wrote that Deane 'so cordially dislikes him that he would not sign up even though offered what amounts to a thousand dollars

---

[175] Peggy to Josephine, 23 February 1930.
[176] See letter of 23 February 1930. This contract is in the Webling Archive. Peggy mentions in a letter of 16 March 1930 that she signed 'a lengthy document with Mr Liveright'; she received the contract from John Farquharson on 15 March 1930 (the envelope from Farquharson is dated 14 March 1930 as sent, 15 March 1930 as received and labelled in Peggy's handwriting '"F" U S A Contract').
[177] Quotations and information from Peggy's letter of 23 February 1930.
[178] Peggy to Josephine, 27 April 1930.
[179] Skal, *Monster Show*, 105–6.
[180] 'Horace Liveright, Book Publisher', arrived on the *Bremen* from New York on 20 March 1930. Balderston had also told Peggy (related in her letter to Josephine of 16 March), that Liveright would be in London by the end of the week.
[181] Peggy to Josephine, 4 April 1930.
[182] 'Frankenstein's Future', *Daily Telegraph*, 27 March 1930, 17.
[183] Quotations for this and the previous two sentences from letter of 27 April 1930.
[184] Skal, *Monster Show*, 106, citing Balderston to agent Harold Freedman, 24 March 1930.

a week'.[185] Worse, Liveright's attempts to take over impinged on Balderston's relationship with Deane, which had been good up to that point.[186]

Peggy was mercifully detached from these shenanigans: 'I hear there are alarums and excursions but I have nothing to do with *that*'.[187] In midsummer Balderston sent Liveright a draft of the first two acts. Liveright, predictably, did not approve.[188] The news travelled: on August 1st Peggy reported that 'Liveright does not like Balderston's chief alterations – at which I do *not* grieve! But they're going to "boom it big", and I hope we make some money.'[189] Balderston, already perturbed with Liveright falling behind on *Dracula* royalties and other payments, consented to work with Louis Cline, another collaborator proposed by Liveright.[190] But it was clear the end was coming. Liveright needed to produce the play before he could exercise his 50 per cent option on a film, but he was out of funds.[191] It was time for Balderston to consider other options.

Those options led to the west coast. Balderston found out in December 1930 that Universal might be interested in buying another horror film (they were filming 'Dracula' at the time).[192] As Peggy put it later, Balderston's 'army of advisers and friends, agents and managers, turned their attention to Hollywood.'[193] The rights to produce *Frankenstein* in New York reverted to the playwrights on 1 February 1931.[194] The film of 'Dracula' opened on Thursday, 12 February 1931 (Tod Browning, the director, refused to open it on Friday the 13th).[195] In early March, Peggy wrote to Josephine with some good news: 'Mr Balderston has again taken up a six month's option on "Frankenstein," and I'm sure he wouldn't part with his good money a second time unless he felt very confident of getting it back out of the play.'[196]

On 11 March 1931, Balderston copyrighted his version of *Frankenstein* with the Library of Congress, under the authors' names of John Balderston and Peggy Webling.[197] When Balderston and his agent, Harold Freedman, approached Universal, Carl Laemmle, Jr, the young production head at Universal, did not drop the ball. Dracula's film rights had been sold for $40,000. But Universal's finances in early 1931 were parlous. So, as Skal reports, Harold Freedman brokered an elegant compromise: the two playwrights would receive

---

[185]Ibid., citing Balderston to Freedman, 9 April 1930.
[186]Ibid., 107.
[187]Peggy to Josephine, 4 April 1930.
[188]Skal, *Monster Show*, 108.
[189]Peggy to Josephine, 1 August 1930.
[190]Skal, *Monster Show*, 108–9.
[191]Skal, *Screams of Reason*, 117.
[192]His wife had sent him a cable with news of Liveright: 'HORACE ASES EXTENSION OPTION BELIEVING UNIVERSAL WILL BACK PRODUCTION...'; see Skal, *Monster Show*, 109 (story repeated in Skal, *Something in the Blood*, 537–8).
[193]Webling, *Story of a Pen* (MS page 120), 308.
[194]Skal, *Monster Show*, 109.
[195]Skal, *Hollywood Gothic*, 140–2; see also *Los Angeles Evening Express*, 16 February 1931, 17.
[196]Peggy to Josephine, 5 March 1931.
[197]US. Library of Congress, *Catalogue of Copyright Entries*, no. 3, 1931, 1614: 'Frankenstein: a play in 3 acts, by John Balderston and Peggy Webling. © 1 c. Mar. 11, 1931: D unpub. 9603.'

Peggy Webling and the Story behind Frankenstein

half that amount, $20,000, but to compensate for the smaller sum would also receive 1 per cent of the gross sales.[198] On 8 April 1931, John Balderston and Peggy Webling signed a contract with Universal Pictures to produce *Frankenstein* as a film, receiving $20,000 plus 1 per cent of the worldwide gross.[199] From Peggy's perspective, 'We were made an exceedingly good offer and immediately accepted it'. Of the 1 per cent, she added:

> It was a small royalty, but when one considers that the film was the biggest success the company had had for two years and ran in all parts of the world for two years and a half . . . it will be seen that this pen of mine at last had made a little fortune.[200]

This contract would later come to play an important role for Webling's estate and its heirs. 'Frankenstein' premiered in the United States on 21 November 1931. Peggy saw it, at the Orpheum Theatre in Seattle, in early December. She had come in September to visit her sister Rosalind in Vancouver, and they travelled across the border to see the film.[201] It was part of her nine-month trip to Canada and America, using some of the money she earned from Frankenstein.[202] She also bought annuities for herself and her sister Lucy.[203] Her long ago feeling of someday writing a play that would be a hit had become reality. How long lasting it would be she could never have guessed.

A brief afterword

Peggy's story does not end here, of course, and there is much more to explore in the next chapter concerning her literary legacy. We shall close this chapter with one unforeseen,

---

[198] Skal, *Monster Show*, 128.
[199] Ibid. See also Forry, *Hideous Progenies*, 92; on 105, n. 26, he quotes from the contract:

> '(1) The dramatic composition entitled "Frankenstein" based upon the novel by Mary Wollstonecraft (Mrs. Percy B. Shelley) which said dramatic composition was registered for copyright in the United States of America by and in the name of PEGGY WEBLING, September 7th, 1928 under entry NO. D86282.
>
> (b) The dramatic composition as adapted by . . . JOHN L. BALDERSTON based upon the aforesaid dramatic composition, written by PEGGY WEBLING, which said composition was copyrighted as follows: by and in the name of JOHN LLOYD BALDERSTON and PEGGY WEBLING under the date of March 11th, 1931 under Entry NO. D89603. . . .'

[200] This and the previous quotation from Webling, *Story of a Pen* (MS page 120), 308.
[201] U. S, Border Crossings from Canada to U. S., 1895–1960, database online at ancestry.com. National Archives, Washington, DC, Manifests of Alien Arrivals at Blaine, Washington, 1924–56; Record Group Title: Records of the Immigration and Naturalization Service, 1787–2004; Record Group Number: 85; Series Number 2675039; Roll Number: 023. Webling, Margaret (Peggy) Arrived Dec. 3, 1931, for 2 day visit. 'Destination: Seattle. To Orpheum, to see Frankenstein (she is author of it).'
[202] Outbound voyage: Margaret Webling, Novelist, on *Athenia* to Montreal, leaving 12 September 1931. Inbound voyage: Margaret Webling, Novelist, leaving New York on *Laconia*, arriving Liverpool 21 June 1932.
[203] She had written about this wish to Josephine back on 27 April 1930: 'As you know, I want to buy myself an annuity, then I shall be safe for the future, and I dream of also buying one for Lucy.'

but happy, consequence of Webling's *Frankenstein*. It goes back to the 1931 contract that gave her and Balderston 1 per cent of the gross worldwide receipts from the film. Though Peggy had continued living her life more or less as she had before *Frankenstein*, John Balderston had made a significant change to his. He left his life in London to go to Hollywood as a screenwriter, moving to Beverly Hills and living a more lavish lifestyle. By the early 1950s he was suffering financially and in ill health.[204] It had not been lost on him that Universal had produced seven additional films about Frankenstein based on the 1931 original, films that would not have existed without it. Balderston believed the studio owed him royalties on all of them. So in 1952, John Balderston and the estate of Peggy Webling sued Universal Pictures Company, Inc. for their 1 per cent of the gross on the subsequent spinoffs from the original Frankenstein film.[205] After 'protracted and involved litigation', the suit was settled in May 1953 for an undisclosed sum, believed to be more than $100,000 (over $1,116,000 today).[206] As for the proceeds, Louis McRaye, Peggy's nephew and the executor of her estate, explained where some of it went. He had been ordained at St John Lateran in Rome in 1962, and in later years was fond of telling the story, with a twinkle in his eye, that he was the only person ever to have his seminary education paid for by the money earned from Frankenstein.[207]

---

[204] Skal, *Screams of Reason*, 180.
[205] Donald F. Glut, *The Frankenstein Legend: A Tribute to Mary Shelley* (Metuchen, NJ: The Scarecrow Press, 1973), 45; Gregory W. Mank, *It's Alive: The Classic Cinema Saga of Frankenstein* (San Diego and New York: A. S. Barnes and Company, Inc., 1981), 13.
[206] 'Hollywood Report', *NY Times*, 24 May 1953, p. X5; see also Glut, *Frankenstein Legend*, 45; Mank, *It's Alive*, 13 and n.; Skal, *Screams of Reason*, 180.
[207] Personal communication with this writer.

CHAPTER 3
FROM PEAKE TO WHALE, AND WEBLING'S MISSING LINK
Bruce Graver

Peggy Webling's *Frankenstein* marked a significant new direction in the history of stage adaptations of Mary Shelley's novel. Unlike earlier Frankenstein plays, Webling went to extraordinary ends to make the creature sympathetic by altering 'the hideous and revolting appearance' of the creature,[1] by minimizing the horrific violence that has been the bread and butter of most *Frankenstein* adaptations, and by presenting him as a slave-like victim of intolerable abuse. As the first woman to write a dramatic version of Shelley's story, Webling was also sensitive to the social implications for women of an artificial means of creating new life, and she thus anticipated by some fifty or sixty years the feminist reinterpretations of the novel that began in the 1970s.[2] By setting the opening acts of the play indoors, in the studies or sitting rooms of her major characters, Webling is also able to demonstrate visually the disruption to the domestic world that Frankenstein's researches have caused, and she does so in ways that the earlier adaptations, which were set largely out of doors, could not.[3] Most interesting of all, Webling portrayed Frankenstein and his creature as *doppelgängers*, an idea she might have borrowed from the 1910 Edison film, directed by J. Searle Dawley, but it is also likely that the insight was her own[4] – in any case, in no earlier dramatic production were the two central characters presented as doubles of each other.[5] Earlier historians of the reception of *Frankenstein*

---

[1]Webling, *The Story of a Pen*, MS page 111, 304 in this volume.
[2]See, for instance, Sandra M. Gilbert and Susan Gubar, *The Madwoman in the Attic: The Woman Writer and the Nineteenth-Century Literary Imagination* (New Haven: Yale University Press, 1979), 213–47; Mary Poovey, *The Proper Lady and the Woman Writer* (Chicago: University of Chicago Press, 1984), 114–42; and Margaret Homans, *Bearing the Word: Language and Female Experience in Nineteenth-Century Women's Writing* (Chicago: University of Chicago Press, 1986), 100–19. Homans, 302, has a note that summarizes earlier feminist readings of *Frankenstein*.
[3]In the two earliest surviving scripts, the final act is set outdoors in the Jura mountains. In the later scripts of 1928 and 1930, Act III is also set indoors, in a hut in the Jura mountains.
[4]Webling had used doubling as a plot device before, in her novel *Boundary House* (London: Hutchinson & Co., 1916). There the elderly toymaker Fob marries a young woman, Richenda Gay, who strongly resembles his deceased wife.
[5]That Victor Frankenstein and his creature are *doppelgängers* has been a commonplace in *Frankenstein* criticism since at least Muriel Sparks's *Child of Light: A Reassessment of Mary Wollstonecraft Shelley* (Hadleigh Essex: Tower Bridge, 1951), 134–7. For earlier overviews of this matter, see David Ketterer, *Frankenstein's Creation: The Book, The Monster, and Human Reality* (Victoria: English Literary Studies Monograph Series, 1979), 56–65; and Anca Vlasopolos, 'Frankenstein's Hidden Skeleton: The Psycho-Politics of Oppression', *Science Fiction Studies* 10, no. 2, *Science Fiction in the Nineteenth Century* (July, 1983): 125–36.

have, with few exceptions, dismissed Webling's effort.[6] My aim in this chapter is to demonstrate that they were wrong to do so. But to understand her achievement, it is necessary first to examine the principal nineteenth-century Frankenstein plays and how they shaped the popular understanding of Shelley's story. I will then look at two early versions of Webling's play, one from 1923 and never performed, and the other the script used in the play's performance debut on 7 December 1927. A 1928 revised script, as well as the prompt script for the 1930 London production, will be considered afterwards.

Early *Frankenstein* adaptations

Stage adaptations of *Frankenstein* are almost as old as the novel itself. Richard Brinsley Peake's was the first, and his 1823 *Presumption; or, the Fate of Frankenstein* was not only successful in its initial run – it was regularly revived for the next 30 years, spawned numerous parodies and burlesques, and provided a signature role for actor T. P. Cooke, who performed as the creature some 365 times, both in Peake's play and in a French adaptation, *Frankenstein, ou le Monstre et le magicien*, by Merle and Béraud.[7] Merle and Béraud's play was itself performed on the London stage in 1826, 'freely translated' by John Kerr,[8] and Henry Milner, who had already staged *Frankenstein, or the Demon of Switzerland*, in the same year produced *Frankenstein, or The Man and the Monster*

---

[6]Brian Taves, *Robert Florey: The French Expressionist* (Duncan, OK: BearManor Media, 2014), 158, writes that 'the Webling piece was hardly original, but was based on many previous stage adaptations', a statement that is patently wrong. Steven Earl Forry, *Hideous Progenies: Dramatizations of 'Frankenstein' from Mary Shelley to the Present* (Philadelphia: University of Pennsylvania Press, 1990), 92–3, notes correctly that 'the play's tone and content differ from any previous treatment of the novel', but concludes that it 'is a pretty dreary treatment' of Shelley's work. David Skal, *The Monster Show: A Cultural History of Horror* (New York: Farrar, Straus, and Giroux, 1993), 97–8, calls Webling's work 'a stilted, preachy, fussy piece of theatre' and quotes John Balderston's assertion that her play was 'illiterate'. Susan Tyler Hitchcock is less openly dismissive than others, considering Webling's drama 'a morality play about the limits of human knowledge', but her summation of the play, with its allusion to Robert Browning, demonstrates obvious condescension: 'Webling's *Frankenstein* concluded with all again right with the world.' Hitchcock, *Frankenstein: A Cultural History* (New York: W. W. Norton & Company, 2007), 139–42. Lester D. Friedman and Allison B. Kavey, *Monstrous Progeny: A History of the Frankenstein Narratives* (New Brunswick: Rutgers University Press, 2016), 85–7, devote barely a page to Webling's play, repeating information from Forry and Skal, and quoting some lines of the play that were not part of the London production, as if they were. Michael Chemers, *The Monster in Theatre History* (London: Routledge, 2018), 65, calls Webling's play 'a lackluster affair', even though he refers only to Forry's account of it. Audrey Fisch, *Frankenstein: Icon of Modern Culture* (East Sussex: Helm Information, 2009), 161–71, is one of the few historians of the Frankenstein story to appreciate the importance of Webling's achievement: 'her treatment of the novel', writes Fisch, 'is . . . central . . . to the reshaping of the Frankenstein tradition' (Fisch, 162).

[7]Forry, *Hideous Progenies*, 3, 5–11. The original title page gives only Antony Béraud's first name as author; the Bibliothèque nationale de France catalogue lists his full name, Antony Béraud.

[8]Kerr's chief alterations include changing the central character's name from 'Zametti, célèbre alchimiste vénitien du 16e. siècle' to Frankenstein, and adding several songs. His text otherwise follows the French original fairly closely. For the French original, see *Le Monstre et le magicien, mélodrame-féerie en trois actes par mm. Merle et Antony*, seconde édition (Paris: Bezou Libraire, 1826). https://gallica.bnf.fr/ark:/12148/bpt6k311832c .texteImage# (accessed 31 December 2022). The original title page gives only Antony Béraud's given name.

(1826). Milner's adaptation proved to be nearly as popular as Peake's, and was also the first to stage the scene in which the monster is created, a scene that was central to the novel and became, with significant variations, a standard part of later adaptations.[9] Both Milner's and Peake's plays were subsequently retitled *Frankenstein, or the Monster*, blurring the distinction between the creature and his creator that persists to this day.[10] And as William St Clair has shown, until copyright on the novel expired in the 1880s, the plays, both in performance and in print, were far more widely available than Shelley's book. Through most of the nineteenth century, then, the stage adaptations had far more influence on the popular understanding of the Frankenstein story than the novel itself.[11]

At the same time, the stage adaptations radically simplified Shelley's vision. As its title suggests, *Presumption* presents the Frankenstein story as one of a man who has, through his scientific investigations, transgressed the divinely prescribed boundaries of human knowledge: he calls his work 'impious labour', he immediately regrets it, and he calls his creature a demon and a fiend (as do the stage directions), implying that Frankenstein, like Dr Faustus, has summoned up a devil.[12] *The Monster and Magician* has a more overtly Faustian focus. Set in sixteenth-century Italy, Frankenstein uses the books of 'Albert and Faust', as well as a set of 'cabalistical instruments', to call up a fiery genie, who gives him a vase containing 'the reward of my labours', that is, the elixir of life which he uses to animate the creature.[13] He later calls his work a 'crime', and asks the creature 'to engulph me in that hell from which I have dragged thee'.[14] This creature is more overtly a demon, conjured literally from hell. Milner's play has Frankenstein proclaim that his creation will be 'that best of victories, a victory o'er the grave',[15] echoing Paul's peroration about Messianic redemption in 1 Cor. 15:55, and inviting the charges of blasphemy that the Frankenstein plays in fact received. Milner's Frankenstein also immediately regrets his work, calls the creature a demon and exclaims (in an open reference to Peake): 'Mine is a guilt a thousand times more black, more horrible. I am the father of a thousand murders. Oh! presumption, and is this thy punishment?'[16] When 'zealous friends of morality' and societies 'for the prevention of vice' protested the plays and attacked them for blasphemy and impiety, the theatrical producers defended themselves by asserting that 'the striking moral exhibited in this story, is the fatal consequence of that presumption which

---

[9]Forry, *Hideous Progenies*, 11–12.
[10]William St Clair, *The Reading Nation in the Romantic Period* (Cambridge: Cambridge University Press, 2007), 53.
[11]Ibid., 365–8.
[12]My text for Peake is from *Seven Gothic Dramas 1789-1825*, ed. Jeffrey Cox (Athens, OH: Ohio University Press, 1992), 385–415. Frankenstein calls his work 'impious labour' in Act II, Scene i, 400. And in Act I, Scene i, Frankenstein's servant, Fritz, remarks: 'Now, my shrewd guess, sir, is that, like Doctor Faustus, my master is raising the devil', 389.
[13]My text is from Forry, *Hideous Progenies*; quotations are from Act I, Scene 1, 208, 210.
[14]Act II, Scene 1, ibid., 217.
[15]The text for Milner's play is from Forry, *Hideous Progenies*; the quotation is from Act I, Scene 2, 193.
[16]Act I, Scene 8, ibid., 198.

attempts to penetrate, beyond prescribed depths, into the mysteries of nature',[17] or, as the *Theatrical Observer* put it:

> The moral here is striking. It points out that man cannot pursue objects beyond his obviously prescribed powers, without incurring the penalty of shame and regret at his audacious folly.[18]

The plays, insofar as they considered themselves serious representations of Shelley's novel (this would not include the many burlesques and farces on the Frankenstein theme), presented her story as a simple moral lesson: human knowledge must have its limits, and those who pursue knowledge so that they may acquire the creative powers of God are doomed.

But, as Anne Mellor has argued in her classic study of the novel, Shelley was not just interested in telling the story of a man using scientific research to play God. '*Frankenstein*,' writes Mellor, 'is a book about what happens when a man tries to have a baby without a woman.'[19] Victor Frankenstein believes that the knowledge he has gained through his research will enable him to create a more perfect human being, and this belief rests on a far more sinister one: that natural reproduction involving women is fundamentally flawed. His solitary quest to create new life is a misogynistic attempt to bypass and perhaps eliminate the role of women in the creation of new life. Frankenstein himself is so obsessed with this quest that he does not seem to realize the deep misogyny of it. But when he later rips the naked female creature limb from limb on his laboratory table, his fear of sex and his repressed hatred of women could not be more vividly demonstrated. 'What Victor Frankenstein truly fears is female sexuality', writes Mellor. 'Horrified by this image of uninhibited female sexuality, [he] violently reasserts a male control over the female body, penetrating and mutilating the female creature at his feet in an image which suggests a violent rape.'[20] It is thus ironically fitting that the creature attacks and kills Elizabeth Lavenza on her marriage bed, a victim of both murder and possible rape.

Not surprisingly, none of the nineteenth-century dramatic adaptations of *Frankenstein* approach Shelley's story from quite this perspective. None of them include the making of the female creature, so questions about rape, the female body and the propagation of monsters never arise, as they do in the novel. Like the novel, the plays show the irony of Frankenstein labouring to make new life while neglecting a woman whom he supposedly loves, but they do so in strikingly different ways, and always without Shelley's horrific violence on the marriage bed. In *Presumption*, for instance, Elizabeth is cast as Frankenstein's sister, and Frankenstein himself is engaged to Agatha de Lacey: Peake is alone among the playwrights to include a version of the de Lacey episode from the

---

[17] Forry, *Hideous Progenies*, 5–9.
[18] Quoted in Cox, ed., *Gothic Dramas*, 386.
[19] Anne Mellor, *Mary Shelley: Her Life, Her Fiction, Her Monsters* (New York and London: Routledge, 1989), 40.
[20] Mellor, *Mary Shelley*, 119–20.

novel. Agatha, like her whole family, has been separated from Frankenstein by political exile: due to their resistance to the powers governing France, the de Laceys have been forced to flee their home and country. So Peake's Frankenstein cannot be easily charged with preferring experiments in his laboratory to normal human relations: the separation from Agatha was not his fault. When Frankenstein hears of Agatha's return, he cries: 'Agatha! dearest Agatha! her name recalls my sinking spirits. . . . Oh, would that I had never been robbed of her! 'Twas her loss that drove me to deep and fatal experiments!'[21] Here Frankenstein's obsessive attempt to create new life is presented as a substitute for the domestic life French political intrigue has denied him. This substitute, however, ironically leads to the destruction of his domestic happiness, as the monster strangles Agatha and later dies with Frankenstein in an avalanche. But, as Jeffrey Cox has argued, in the end domestic happiness wins out: the surviving characters are all paired off, sadder but wiser for Frankenstein's errors,[22] and the English audience can, with some justification, blame his fate on Napoleonic France.

In *The Monster and Magician*, Frankenstein has been married and has a son, Antonio, but his wife has died, and although the play does not reveal her cause of death, it seems likely that she may have died in childbirth. When the play begins, he is engaged to be married to Cecilia, who, like Agatha of *Presumption*, seems to be a fount of virtue who 'will . . . protect [him] from the wrath of heaven' that his necromantic conjuring may unleash.[23] Cecilia's brother tries in vain to persuade him to give up his magic, but Frankenstein will not, telling him that if he succeeds in his purpose, it will bring 'to Cecilia ages of glory and felicity'.[24] Apparently, he is doing it all for her. The monster later kills both Antonio and Cecilia, the latter with a bullet from Frankenstein's gun intended for Frankenstein himself: so much for glory and felicity. In the final scene, Frankenstein dies with the creature in a boating accident on the Mediterranean: their boat is struck by lightning, nature itself punishing those who have transgressed its boundaries.[25] So Frankenstein's quest for glory for himself and his family fails. But this is not a Frankenstein engaged in serious scientific research: instead, he is a conjuror of demons, of the sort that traditionally earn divine retribution. The chance that Frankenstein's first wife died in childbirth leaves open the possibility that his motive to gain the illicit elixir may have been in some sense humanitarian. In any case, making him a widower is an innovation in the Frankenstein story that no other stage or film adaptation repeats.

Milner's play also presents Frankenstein as a married man and a father: his wife is Emmeline Ritzberg and they are parents to a 'Child'.[26] Frankenstein, however, has deserted

---

[21] Act II, Scene 1, Cox, ed., *Gothic Dramas*, 401.
[22] Cox, ed., *Gothic Dramas*, 68.
[23] Act I, Scene 1, Forry, *Hideous Progenies*, 209.
[24] Act I, Scene 1, ibid., 209.
[25] Act III, Scene 4, where the stage direction reads: 'a thunderbolt descends and severs the bark, the waves vomit forth a mass of fire and the Magician and his unhallowed abortion are with the boat engulphed in the waves.' Ibid., 226.
[26] Oddly enough, the child is never named, and is apparently not even listed in the Dramatis Personae: see Forry, *Hideous Progenies*, 189.

his family in order to pursue his scientific researches in Italy, where he is employed as a natural philosopher by the Prince de Piombino, whose estate is in Sicily, 'near the foot of Mount Etna.'[27] When Emmeline first appears, she has just crossed the Alps and the length of Italy on foot, searching in vain for her husband, and when she subsequently collapses from weariness, the monster saves her. But his horrific appearance so appalls her that she fails to recognize his instinctive kindness for what it is, 'utters a piercing shriek', and her father shoots the creature in the shoulder and drives him away.[28] In the next scene, we are told in a stage direction that 'The Monster expresses that his kindly feelings towards the human race have been met by scorn, abhorrence, and violence',[29] so he murders Prince Piombino's son Julio, and later attempts, unsuccessfully, to murder Emmeline and her son. He finally dies by leaping into Mount Etna, having first fatally stabbed Frankenstein, who dies in Emmeline's arms. For Milner, then, Frankenstein's quest for knowledge has led to irresponsible neglect, and there is little question that he deserves his punishment. But Emmeline's presence in the final scene reminds us of the social implications for women of what he has done, with a clarity that the adaptations by Peake and Merle and Béraud lack.

Closely related to Frankenstein's quest to create new life is his failure to care for the creature he has made. In the novel, Frankenstein was so disgusted by his creature's appearance that he abandoned him, and the creature became a kind of oversized feral child, modelled after the contemporary case of Victor of Aveyron (1788–1828).[30] In the creature's narrative, Shelley carefully charts the process by which his perceptions develop, and later, in his hideout in the de Lacey's woodshed, we watch him acquire language, learn to read, educate himself with the works of Milton, Volney and Plutarch, and attempt to interact with the de Lacey family. But his appearance is so offensive that even the human beings whom he cares for reject him, and that provokes his violent responses. The plays simplify this process. In none of the plays, for instance, does the creature become the well-read, articulate being of Shelley's novel: in fact, the reason T. P. Cooke could perform the role in both English and French adaptations is that the creature never speaks in either play. He is similarly silent in Milner's play – as the stage directions indicate, the creature expresses his feelings through pantomimed gestures rather than in language. In *Presumption*, in lines lifted almost word for word from the novel, Frankenstein describes his disgust at the moment of creation:

> I saw the dull yellow eye of the creature open, it breathed hard, and a convulsive motion agitated its limbs. What a wretch have I formed, [his legs are in proportion and] I had selected his features as beautiful – 'beautiful'! Ah, horror! his cadaverous

---

[27]Ibid., 190.
[28]This occurs in Act I, Scenes 5 and 6, ibid., 196.
[29]Act I, Scene 6, ibid., 196.
[30]For a recent discussion of this matter, see Noah Heringman, 'Science and Human Animality in Mary Shelley's *Frankenstein*', *The Wordsworth Circle* 50, no. 1 (Winter, 2019): 136–7.

skin scarcely covers the work of muscles and arteries beneath, his hair lustrous, black, and flowing – his teeth of pearly whiteness – but these luxuriances only form more horrible contrasts with the deformities of the Demon.[31]

Later in the scene, when 'The Demon . . . approaches [Frankenstein] with gestures of conciliation', Frankenstein attacks him with a sword, which 'the Demon' promptly 'snatches . . . [and] snaps in two', 'throws [Frankenstein] violently on the floor' and escapes through a window.[32] A similar sequence happens in the scenes with the de Laceys. There Peake dramatizes the creature's gradual acquisition of limited forms of knowledge: he burns himself on a fire, learning its properties by experience, he watches how the de Laceys need various things and then secretly supplies them himself, in acts of goodwill. He even saves Agatha from drowning in a rivulet after she screams and faints upon seeing him. But the thanks for his benevolence is a gunshot wound, and that injury provokes his vengeance: he sets fire to their cottage, and later murders Agatha. Frankenstein's failure to care for his creation thus leads directly to the play's tragic outcome. *The Monster and Magician* does not give the creature much opportunity to show potential benevolence. As in *Presumption*, when the creature first appears, rather than care for him, Frankenstein tries to kill him with a sword, and the creature quickly disarms him, again snapping the sword in two. But there is no mention of the creature's initial conciliating gestures: this creature is a fiend from hell, on whom human nurture and care would have little effect. Later the creature sees Cecilia 'and regards her with rapture' (there is a similar scene in *Presumption* between the creature and Agatha), and the conflict between the creature and Frankenstein is presented as a struggle between rival lovers, both of whom act with undisguised brutality. When their boat is sunk by a lightning bolt, it is difficult to feel much sympathy for either Frankenstein or the creature, and there is no one left to mourn them. *The Man and the Monster* is closer to *Presumption*, in that the creature initially shows benevolence to Emmeline and 'the Child', and turns violent only when he has been rebuffed and injured. Ironically, in saving Frankenstein's family, the creature proves himself to be more of a traditional father/protector than Frankenstein himself, who has neglected to care for both his laboratory creation and his wife and child. But that, of course, is before human beings try to injure him, and their attacks turn the creature's benevolence into malevolence and despair, leading to the murder–suicide that ends the play.

Enter Peggy Webling

Later Victorian Frankenstein dramatizations, such as *Frankenstein; or, the Model Man* (1849) and *Frankenstein, or, The Vampire's Victim* (1887), are what Audrey Fisch has

---

[31] Act I, Scene 3, Cox, ed. *Gothic Dramas*, 398.
[32] Ibid., 399.

called 'burlesques and extravaganzas',[33] so when Peggy Webling was inspired one day in 1920 to write a *Frankenstein* play, it was one of the few serious stage adaptations of the novel to be undertaken in almost a century. Could she have seen one of the burlesques in her youth? Perhaps: her early experiences in the theatre surely put her in a position to do so. But there is no evidence, in her surviving letters and manuscripts in the Webling Archive, that she did.[34] Her play, entitled *Frankenstein: A Play in a Prologue and Three Acts (Based upon Mrs. Shelley's well known book)* in every surviving script,[35] marks a radical departure from earlier serious treatments of Shelley's novel. It survives in four complete versions: a 1923 script prepared at the request of an unnamed actor and never performed;[36] a 1927 script, which opened at the Empire Theatre in Preston, Lancashire, in December of that year;[37] a 1928 script, deposited for copyright in the Library of Congress, Washington, DC, on 7 September 1928;[38] and a prompt script used in the 1930 London production in the West End at the Little Theatre.[39] In the play, Webling changed several of the characters' names: Victor Frankenstein has become Henry Frankenstein, and Henry Clerval has become Victor Moritz,[40] name changes that are preserved in the Universal films *Frankenstein* (1931) and *Bride of Frankenstein* (1935), directed by James Whale. She has also changed Elizabeth Lavenza's first name to Emilie, and rather than a younger brother, William, Henry Frankenstein has a younger sister, Katrine (occasionally spelled Katrina, in some of the scripts). Katrine seems to be modelled on Charles Dickens's Tiny Tim: she is disabled and walks with a crutch, and

---

[33] Fisch, *Frankenstein*, 131. Forry, *Hideous Progenies*, 227–50, includes a text of *Frankenstein; or, the Model Man*.
[34] In *The Story of a Pen*, MS page 110, 303, Webling mentions having read a cheap edition of the novel as a child, and makes no mention of, for instance, *The Vampire's Victim*, the burlesque she most likely could have seen. There is some evidence that she knew of Stephen Phillips's one-act Frankenstein adaptation, *Aylmer's Secret*, which ran at the Adelphi Theatre in London from 4 to 15 July 1905. For further discussion of this matter, see pp. 78–9 below.
[35] The phrase 'An Adventure in the Macabre', by which Forry and others refer to the play, was not Webling's: it is first used by Deane in promotional interviews for the play (*Official Theatre Guide*, 27 January 1930, signed 'E. B.'). It then appears in the London playbills either above or below Webling's title, always in a different typeface from *Frankenstein*. It should be considered as a kind of advertising slogan, probably developed by Stanley Hale, Hamilton Deane's publicity agent. It appears in the London playbills and in a Blackpool playbill, dated 12 May 1930, just after the closing of the London run; it does not appear in the 1929 Nottingham playbills (see Figure 2.7 above), nor does it appear in the playbill for the Lyceum Theatre, Sheffield (27 October 1930) (See Figure 3.1).
[36] This script was registered 16 January 1923 at the Incorporated Society of Authors, Playwrights and Composers. This script is now in the Webling Archive. In it, Henry Frankenstein and the creature are double-cast.
[37] This script, now in the British Library, was licensed by the Lord Chamberlain's Office on 25 November 1927. It opened in Preston on 7 December 1927.
[38] Webling copyrighted this script and deposited it in the Library of Congress in expectation of her play being performed in New York. See Chapter 2, 56 n. 119.
[39] This script can be found in the Hamilton Deane Papers at the Westminster City Archives, where it is catalogued as 2992/HD/164.
[40] According to her unpublished memoir, *The Story of a Pen* (MS pages 94), 114, 305, Webling put 'a Henry in all my stories', and particularly disliked the 'name of Victor'. Why she changed Clerval to Moritz, the family name of the unjustly accused servant Justine, remains a mystery, but she does invent a Pastor Clerval, a minor character who never appears but serves as the pastor to the Frankenstein family.

Figure 3.1 Playbill of Frankenstein, The Lyceum Theatre, Sheffield, 27 October 1930 (Private Collection).

is the incarnation of loving benevolence in the play. Dr Waldman, Henry and Victor's university professor, has become a central character in the play, although he was a minor figure in the novel and does not appear at all in the earlier stage adaptations. And there is no de Lacey family, no polar explorers and no townspeople, as Webling has been careful to limit the size of her cast and the necessity for scene changes: until the last act, hers is strictly a drawing-room drama. More striking are Webling's changes to the creature himself. Rather than an angry monster wreaking vengeance on Frankenstein and his family, the creature is presented sympathetically, as the slave-like victim of his creator's abuses. He is not oversized,[41] as in the novel, nor is his appearance described as particularly frightening.[42] In the 1923 and 1927 scripts, there are no on-stage murders, and the deaths that do occur are the result of the creature's ignorance, not his malevolence or attempts at revenge. Nor is the creature inarticulate, as he is in the other stage adaptations: Henry has taught him a few words, and the play depicts the process by which the creature acquires increasingly complex words and ideas, as he comes to understand human experience and the world around him. Most interestingly, Webling presents Frankenstein and his creature as *doppelgängers*. The stage directions indicate that they are to be dressed alike, and they share the name Frankenstein – in fact, Henry himself is responsible for the naming, understanding that the creature is in some sense

---

[41]Such was her original conception, but Webling recounts in her memoir: 'I wish Mary Shelley could have seen him – six feet three in height; uncouth; lithe as an animal.' *The Story of a Pen* (MS page 116), 306. Skal, *The Monster Show*, 101, records that Deane wore elevator shoes, increasing the height difference between the creature and Henry Frankenstein.

[42]Hamilton Deane, however, in performance seems to have taken liberties with his makeup in order to make the creature seem more outlandish than the script describes. According to David Skal, who interviewed an actor from the touring production of Webling's *Frankenstein* after the London run, Deane painted his face 'blue, green, and red, with thick red lips', apparently in imitation of T. P. Cooke's makeup when playing the creature in *Presumption*. Skal, *The Monster Show*, 101. This suggests that Deane not only knew Peake's play, but was familiar with the acting tradition associated with it. Although a playbill from *Presumption* was displayed at the London performances, there is no clear evidence that Webling knew Peake's play.

an extension of himself. As he explains to Dr Waldman in Act I of all versions of her play: 'I call him by my own name. He *is* Frankenstein.'[43] Finally, Webling engages herself with a question that was at the heart of the scientific debate that inspired the novel, but was ignored by all the previous stage adaptations: she attempts to trace the process by which the creature develops or awakens a soul, a process that is closely connected to his ability to express himself in language.

The doubling of Frankenstein and his creature, and the question of whether the creature can possess a soul suggest that Webling may have been familiar with the two silent film versions of Frankenstein, the 1910 Edison film, *Frankenstein*, directed by J. Searle Dawley, and *Life Without Soul* (1915), directed by Joseph Smiley.[44] Unfortunately, Smiley's film is now lost and is known only by a few stills and a review in *The Moving Picture World*, in which the reviewer praises the actor playing 'Brute Man' (so the creature is named) for 'actually awaken[ing] sympathy for the monster's condition'.[45] But since it premiered in New York, and is not known to have been shown in London, there seems to be little chance that Webling saw it. The Edison film, however, was a London production that she may have seen, or seen written up in *The Edison Kinetogram*. Once only known from its synopsis, Dawley's *Frankenstein* was rediscovered in the late 1970s, and is now readily available at the US Library of Congress website, as well as on YouTube in several restored versions.[46] Like Webling's play, it excludes any violence: 'the Edison Company' explains a publicity blurb in *The Edison Kinetogram*, 'carefully tried to eliminate all the actually repulsive situations and to concentrate its endeavours upon the mystic and psychological problems that are to be found in this weird tale.'[47] The psychological emphasis can be seen in one of the film's early title cards: 'Instead of a perfect being', which had been Frankenstein's aim, 'the evil in Frankenstein's mind creates a monster.'[48] That is, the creature is to be understood as a psychological projection of Frankenstein that, through a gradual magico-chemical process in a large smoking cauldron, has taken physical form. Or, as the synopsis of the film explains, 'the creation of the monster was only possible because Frankenstein had allowed his normal mind to be overcome by evil and unnatural thoughts'.[49] Towards the end of the film, after Frankenstein and Elizabeth have been joined in marriage, another title card appears, stating: 'The creation of an evil mind is overcome by love and disappears.'[50] Or, as the synopsis puts it: 'With the strength of Frankenstein's love for his bride and the effect of this upon his own mind,

---

[43]See 130.
[44]These are discussed by Fisch, *Frankenstein*, 149–55.
[45]Quoted in Fisch, *Frankenstein*, 154.
[46]https://www.loc.gov/item/2017600664/ (accessed 14 June 2023). References below are to this version of the restored film.
[47]*The Edison Kinetogram,* London, Vol. I, no. 1 (15 April 1910): 1. Cited and quoted in Fisch, *Frankenstein*, 149; she cites a copy in the British Film Institute.
[48]The title card appears at 2:26.
[49]Quoted by Fisch, *Frankenstein*, 152.
[50]The title card appears at 11:18.

the monster cannot exist.'[51] So in the following scene, the creature stares at itself in a full-length mirror, 'holds out its arms entreatingly'[52] and disappears, leaving only his reflection behind. Frankenstein enters, sees the creature's image in the mirror, which almost instantly disappears 'under the effect of love and his better nature'[53] and is replaced by his own reflection. Then Elizabeth enters the room and the two embrace, free of the effects of Frankenstein's evil ambitions, and therefore free of the monster. We are meant to think they will live happily ever after.

There is no documentary evidence that Webling knew the Edison film, but her sympathetic treatment of the creature suggests that she may have had some familiarity with an earlier, and seldom noticed, Frankenstein play: *Aylmer's Secret,* by Stephen Phillips. *Aylmer's Secret* was a one-act play, produced in July, 1905, as a prelude piece for an Adelphi Theatre production of Shakespeare's *The Comedy of Errors*; it ran briefly in London from July 4 to 15 and was badly reviewed in both *The Sketch* and *The Morning Leader*. *Aylmer's Secret* is set in contemporary London. Aylmer, a chemist, has concealed himself in a laboratory in his Soho flat, where he has discovered, as he proclaims in over-wrought blank verse, the secret of life. His daughter, Miranda, confronts him in the first scene, complaining (in prose) that he prefers science to her, a charge that Aylmer tries unsuccessfully to defend himself against. At the end of the scene, he pours his elixir of life into the body he has made, and slowly it comes to life. Scene 2 occurs three months later. We learn that Aylmer, like Victor Frankenstein, abandoned his creation, who has been wandering the streets of London as one of the homeless, scorned and rejected by all. The creature has returned to Aylmer's flat, fully able to speak in elaborate blank verse, and there he reproaches Aylmer, and then meets Miranda, who sympathizes with him and calls him friend. The two seem to be falling in love, but Aylmer enters the room, sees them holding hands, is appalled, and orders his daughter to give up her affection and leave the room. Very reluctantly, she obeys. In the third scene, Aylmer threatens to kill his creature, but the creature, because he lacks anyone to love him, conveniently dies all on his own. At the end of the play, Miranda re-enters, asks her father who the creature was, and Aylmer replies 'my Child'. For all its absurd improbabilities, Phillips's play, like Webling's, presents the creature sympathetically, and his interactions with Miranda show what he could have become, had his maker taken care to nurture him. Henry Ainley, who played the creature, was strikingly handsome, which helps to explain why Miranda could fall in love with him so effortlessly, and photographs of the performance show that he used no ghastly makeup to hide his good looks.[54]

---

[51]Quoted by Fisch, *Frankenstein*, 150.
[52]Ibid., 152.
[53]Ibid.
[54]Photographs of the performance, published in the 19 July edition of *The Sketch*, show Ainley, both before and after animation. As the caption puts it: the creature is shunned 'for no apparent reason since it is most presentable'. 'Heard in the Green-Room', *The Sketch: A Journal of Art and Actuality* 51, no. 651 (19 July 1905): 27.

Could Webling have seen this play? Probably not, given its short run at the Adelphi. But on 11 February 1930, *The Morning Post* reviewer of Webling's *Frankenstein* wrote that her play 'was certainly a far better adaptation than that by the late Stephen Phillips', and this prompted her to write to her sister Josephine: 'The latest [dramatic adaptation of *Frankenstein*] was by Stephen Phillips, but it was (I believe) in one act, and Henry Ainley played the big part; one of the papers said it was not a patch on mine.'[55] Webling's remark does not necessarily imply familiarity with the play itself: she only *believes* it was in one act, and recalls that Ainley, who by 1930 had established himself as one of Britain's finest Shakespearean actors, had 'the big part'. Nor could she have read *Aylmer's Secret* before writing *Frankenstein*: the play remained unpublished until February, 1921, when it appeared in a New York edition of his *Collected Plays*.[56] No British edition ever appeared. By February 1921, Webling had already conceived of her version of the play, may have written the Prologue and was in discussions with Matheson Lang about producing it. Her remark to Josephine thus seems to be derived from accounts of Phillips's play related by Lang or the other actors and theatrical managers she corresponded with.[57]

In any case, Webling's conception of the creature, her handling of the *doppelgänger* theme and her version of the creation scene are very different from the Edison film, the Phillips play and all earlier Frankenstein adaptations. In the 1923 and 1927 scripts, she showed little interest in the science and the chemical process that produced the creature: all that takes place offstage, and how it takes place is left deliberately vague. The 1928 and 1930 scripts speak of an elixir of life that finally appears in the third Act,[58] but what it is and how it is made is unclear, nor is there anything like the pyrotechnically-striking creation scene, as in the Dawley film: in Webling's play, the creature just wakes up and comes to life. Nor did Webling have much interest in scenes of horror and violence. For Webling there is no oversized deformed monster roaming the stage laying waste innocent victims, only a character who is dressed like Henry himself, whom he calls by his family name, and who, in the 1923 double-cast version, is played by the same actor. There is a homicide: the creature inadvertently drowns Henry's younger sister, Katrine. But that happens offstage, and it is not described as an act of violence: the creature simply didn't know what he was doing. On stage the only thing he kills is a pet dove that he squeezes

---

[55] *The Morning Post*, 11 February 1930. Peggy Webling to Josephine, 27 April 1930, 301.
[56] Stephen Phillips, *Collected Plays* (New York: The Macmillan Company, 1921). The copyright page states that the volume was 'Published February, 1921'. It was copyrighted with the Library of Congress on 1 March 1921, and notices of it appeared in newspapers at the end of the first week of March.
[57] Matheson Lang is the most likely source. He had appeared with Ainley in *The Merchant of Venice* in 1901, and both were trained in Frank Benson's acting school. Benson was the director of both the 1901 *Merchant* and *Aylmer's Secret*. See Lucie Sutherland, *George Alexander and the Work of the Actor-Manager*, Palgrave Studies in Theatre and Performance History (Cham: Palgrave Macmillan, 2020), 144, 149 n.31. Webling met with Lang in February 1921, to discuss production of her *Frankenstein*, the month before Phillips's *Collected Plays* was available in New York. See p. 40, above.
[58] In all surviving scripts, Victor Moritz mentions that as a youth, Henry sought for an 'elixir of life', but only in the 1928 and 1930 scripts does he use an elixir to give life to his creature.

Peggy Webling and the Story behind Frankenstein

Figure 3.2 Scene from Act I of *Frankenstein*, Little Theatre, London, 1930, l. to r. Henry, Frankenstein, Dr Waldman, Victor Moritz. Courtesy of the Mander and Mitchenson Theatre Collection, University of Bristol.

too tightly, not understanding his own strength and what the effects would be: again, an act of ignorance, not malevolent violence.

If these two stock features of *Frankenstein* adaptations – weird science and horrific violence – are not Webling's concern, just where does her interest lie? To address this question, it is first necessary to give a brief plot summary, since other accounts of her play are not entirely accurate.[59] I will begin with the 1923 script, which survives in the Webling Archive. The play, as its title indicates, is divided into a Prologue and three Acts. In the 1923 Prologue, which takes place in Henry Frankenstein's study at Dr Waldman's house in Goldstadt,[60] Henry reveals to Waldman and Moritz the aim of his experiments. The two men are sceptical and properly appalled, but at its end the creature dramatically comes to life[61] – and awkwardly, since Henry and a body double (Webling calls him 'the Substitute') have to quickly change places, one of them slipping through a slit in the stage backdrop; when they are both on stage at once, one of them must stand with his back to the audience, or with his face hidden. Here, for instance, are the stage directions when the creature first appears:

---

[59]Most errors about the plot occur when scholars mix up details from different versions of the play, or are unaware of all of the surviving scripts. For instance, Penny Chalk discussed Webling's play in her 2018 PhD thesis, 'Adaptation as an Intertextual Mode of Practice' (University of Portsmouth), having consulted the 1927 version housed in the British Library, which she wrongly calls 'the last surviving copy of this play', 87. Therefore she was unaware of the revised third act, even though earlier scholars like Forry and Fisch had referred to it, as did the reviews of the London production. Forry mixes up the Webling and Balderston scripts, in one instance ascribing to her play this line, that only occurs in Balderston's version: 'The Elixir – the Elixir of life! I found some of the formula in those old black letter books—I worked out the rest for myself'. Forry, *Hideous Progenies*, 93.

[60]Webling's shortened version of Ingolstadt, which she has moved from Germany to Switzerland along the shores of Lake Geneva.

[61]Henry had initiated what he calls his 'discovery', about which he 'shall say no more'. Prologue, *Frankenstein* 1923, Webling Archive. The 1927 script is identical at this point, 119.

(**Waldman** lifts cloth and throws it over the back of the lounge so that it completely covers the Substitute, falling to the floor in front. This lounge must be constructed in such a way that the Substitute can, when he is so concealed, drop to the ground between the seat and the back, and crawl through the slit in scenery behind him. He does this, puts on a high stock like **Henry** and goes to door *L.* to wait, with a lamp in his hand, to take the place of **Henry** later on) (*Frankenstein* 1923, Webling Archive)

From stage directions like this, it is easy to see why Webling eventually thought the double-casting unworkable.[62]

Act I takes place in the same room, six months later. Rather than rejecting his creature, as in the novel, Henry has kept him imprisoned in a room without windows, torturing or violently whipping him into submission, as if he were a beast or a slave. Victor Moritz asks if the creature obeys him, and Henry replies: 'Does a frightened slave obey? Does a beaten hound obey?' (*Frankenstein* 1923, Webling Archive). Baron Frankenstein, his father, shows up to take Henry home to Belrive; the Baron is a comic figure, who says Henry is

Too fond of books and learning. Too serious – thinks too much. If you want to be happy, doctor, and live to a jolly, gay old age, don't *think*. It's dangerous. Men who think so much, doctor, are generally too long in the legs, lean and grizzly-bearded.[63] (*Frankenstein* 1923, Webling Archive)

According to the stage directions, Waldman then strokes his grizzled beard. There follows a curious scene in which Frankenstein (the creature) appears and sees the sun for the first time, and is taught, by Dr Waldman, about flowers, trees and beauty (in that order). Then Emilie Lavenza also arrives from Belrive, also looking for Henry, with whom she reluctantly shares a loving embrace, after complaining angrily about his neglect. At the end of the Act, Frankenstein bursts into the room as Henry and Emilie are speaking, he and Henry struggle, Frankenstein nearly strangles his 'master', and Emilie gets very confused (as do the 1923 stage directions – imagine staging this with a body double):

(Re-enter Actor as **Frankenstein**, gripping the Substitute – as **Henry** – by the throat and struggling, the latter's back being towards the audience. **Emilie** gives a scream. . . . **F.** throws **Henry**, who is not strangled. He falls face downwards,

---

[62]Or as Webling put it in *The Story of a Pen* (MS page 113), 304, 'I realized it [the double-casting] could not be done effectively.'
[63]The Universal film also presents the Baron as a comic buffoon; Taves, 131, wrongly attributes the characterization to James Whale. The Baron's buffoonery was in fact exaggerated by John Balderston in his revision of Webling's script, which Whale did work with, especially when the Baron offers the creature wine in Act II. In Webling's scripts, the creature spits the wine out in disgust; in Balderston's, he guzzles it. See Forry, *Hideous Progenies*, 274, for Balderston's version.

Figure 3.3 Scene from *Frankenstein*, Little Theatre, London, 1930: Henry Frankenstein and Emilie Lavenza. *Daily Chronicle*, 11 February 1930. Courtesy of the Westminster City Archives.

F. releases his hold, looking intensely surprised at what he has done.) (*Frankenstein* 1923, Webling Archive)

At the Act's end, Emilie flies back to Belrive, her horse at a full gallop, with Frankenstein in hot pursuit on foot, while Henry, Waldman, Victor and the Baron follow along in a carriage.

For Act II the scene switches to the Baron's drawing-room in Belrive, where Emilie recounts to the Baroness and Katrine what just happened. There is an odd scene in the 1923 script in which the Baron meets Frankenstein and, like Emilie, gets very confused, and that is followed by an even odder sequence in which Emilie speaks first with Henry and then with Frankenstein. Henry tries to explain to her his motive for making the creature:

> I think I was possessed by a devil to begin such a work. All that was dark and hidden and evil in my man's nature gave me power. I was driven on by the pride of Lucifer, and in the minute of my triumph I fell. As Frankenstein came to life, my heart died in my breast. I had turned my world into Hell. There was only one hope – one dream – one consolation left – *You*! Emilie, your love still shone in the blackness of my despair.[64]

This speech seems to echo the Edison *Frankenstein*, and is the strongest evidence that Webling may have known Dawley's film. Later in the Act, the creature speaks with

---

[64] Henry's speech is unchanged in the 1927 and 1928 versions of the play. In the 1930 prompt script, it has been revised to: 'My wicked pride conceived this inhuman monster – my devilish power brought it to life – . . . I have turned my world into Hell. Will you *desert* me? Will you drive me to *destruction*? Can't you understand my agony – my shame – my remorse? Emilie! Emilie! My only hope is in you. Love me! Try to forgive me! – pray for me!' See pp. 147, 202, and 260, below.

Emilie, and attracted by her beauty, attempts to embrace her. Emilie is not entirely unresponsive. 'You are so like your master', she remarks, which of course he is in the double-cast version. When he then 'swings her up into his arms', the stage directions state: 'She resists his embrace feebly.' (*Frankenstein* 1923, Webling Archive). Then Katrine appears, convinces Frankenstein to release Emilie, and treats him with kindness he has never before experienced. He is enchanted, and is eager to go boating with her. But then he drowns her in the river outside the castle, without realizing what he is doing. Act II ends with Waldman explaining to Frankenstein that he has killed Katrine, and what death is. With the creature himself beginning to understand love and death, grief and guilt, we see him beginning to develop a more complex understanding of human experience, as well as a more advanced vocabulary: this is how Webling dramatizes the development of his soul.

The final Act is very short: Frankenstein, in a fit of despair at having slain Katrine, has run off to the Jura mountains, just north of Lake Geneva. Henry, Emilie and Waldman follow him there, and Waldman convinces the creature that only in heaven can he and Katrine be reunited. Frankenstein seems to be fully convinced and flings himself from a towering cliff, the unnatural creature hoping to be joined for eternity with the kind but disabled young woman. And there it ends. And perhaps we are to assume that Henry and Emilie have a happy married life. Or perhaps not.[65]

As this summary suggests, Webling's adaptation is not simply the tragedy of a man who learns too much and transgresses divine laws. It focuses on the creature who only gradually comes to understand who he is and what he has done. Rather than a gothic monster out for vengeance, the creature is a pathetic sufferer who both is, and is not, fully human. For Henry, Frankenstein is 'a brute, a brute' that he must keep locked in a room in the dark where he cannot be seen, and who must be beaten and threatened like a beast – at one point in Act I, the creature even curls up on the floor, as the stage directions say, 'like a dog'. Henry controls his behaviour by inflicting pain, in a palpably sado-masochistic kind of way, and early in the play the only emotion Frankenstein knows is fear. When Frankenstein first appears, he is called a 'devil' in the shape of Henry, and a 'thing without a soul'.[66] So central to Webling's play is one of the key questions of Shelley's novel: can a life form created by a human being possess an immortal soul, and what would that consist of?[67]

---

[65] A word needs to be said about the possible borrowings from Dawley's film. In the play, it is Henry who thinks Frankenstein is necessarily a creation of the evil in his mind. Emilie, Victor, and to a lesser extent Waldman also see the creature as evil, Emilie partly because he assaulted her. But Katrine does not, and her scene with the creature shows what might have happened had the creature received proper nurture. In other words, what is presented as a truth in the film – that the creature is a projection of the evil in Frankenstein's mind – is only an opinion in Webling's play, and an opinion that subsequent events in the play dispute.
[66] Victor says this in the 1923 version; the lines are Henry's, slightly modified, in the 1927 script.
[67] For a discussion of the contemporary medical debates that form much of the background of Shelley's novel, see Richard Holmes, *Age of Wonder* (New York: Pantheon Books, 2008), 305–36.

She begins to address this question later in Act I, when the creature escapes confinement and sees the sun and the natural world for the first time. The great fire in the sky, he learns from Waldman, is good, and the sight of flowers and trees gives him pleasure – for the first time he experiences pleasure, and his affective response is delight, an elative emotion, as the Stoics might say, not a contractive one like fear. Delight is his appropriate response to beauty, a new word that Waldman teaches him – and thus Frankenstein begins to learn abstract concepts. 'You shall go into the garden when the sun sets', Waldman promises, to which Frankenstein responds, 'I want to go there now. Now! There is – there is – Tell me.'

Waldman   There is beauty in the garden

F.   Is that – the word? Beauty. Beauty.

Waldman   Yes, the fresh grass, the wind, the flowers.

F.   And the great – flowers – are they called beauty?

Waldman   You mean the trees. It is all beautiful.

F.   *(spreading his arms wide)* All – beautiful – all.

When Emilie Lavenza arrives shortly afterwards, his understanding of beauty grows more complicated. He feels delight because she is beautiful, but because she is human and female, he also begins to feel the more powerful emotion of desire, or, as Frankenstein himself later names it, love. And when Henry attempts to deny him what he desires, the creature feels anger for the first time, which precipitates the struggle that ends the first Act.

The second Act complicates Frankenstein's emotional development further. There is, as already mentioned, a very awkward scene between Henry and Emilie, in which Henry tries to explain to her what he has done, and Emilie, filled with horror, rejects his embrace and, like Greta Garbo, wants to be alone. That is immediately followed by an even more uncomfortable scene between Emilie and Frankenstein, who like his maker attempts to embrace her. Curiously, Emilie is both reluctant and yielding at one and the same time, which, due to the double-casting, makes some sense: soulless or not, Frankenstein at least shows an interest in her, and he does bear an exact resemblance to the man she supposedly loves. As Emilie explains to Henry in Act III, 'There was some call from his body to mine that I could not deny. It was as if one heart, torn asunder, throbbed in his breast and in my own. . . . He is part of you, and part of myself, and we are all one.' But in spite of this 'call', she rejects the creature, for reasons that also make sense. 'I . . . love . . . the woman', stammers Frankenstein. 'No! No!' Emilie responds, 'I hate you. I can't breathe the same air!' So Frankenstein expands his emotional repertoire yet again: 'Hate', he says, 'horrible! horrible!' (*Frankenstein* 1923, Webling Archive).

It is Katrine who intervenes, separating the creature from Emilie, allowing her to escape offstage. Katrine is the first human being to show Frankenstein any kindness or

Figure 3.4 Scene from Act II of *Frankenstein*, Little Theatre, London, 1930: Katrine and Frankenstein. Courtesy of the Mander and Mitchenson Theatre Collection, University of Bristol.

affection, and as Webling explained in her memoir, is 'a symbol of compassion'.[68] She touches him gently, and when she helps him stand up, he asks 'Why . . . did you . . . do that?' She responds with puzzled looks, so he explains: 'No one . . . has done that before. My master . . . will not touch me. The men . . . there . . . will not touch me.' Moved by his words, in a gesture of sympathy, she invites him to go outdoors with her to see the 'beautiful world'. Although she cannot walk without a crutch, she has a boat that she rows on the river outside the castle. So she invites the creature to join her for a boat ride. Fatal mistake. Frankenstein thinks the water is beautiful, and that the leaves and flowers that float and sink in the water are also beautiful. He drops Katrine in the water as well, thinking she would float beautifully on the water also, and she sinks and drowns. As he later explains, 'I wanted to see her float . . . on the water. "Oh! Oh!" she cried. Then I pressed her down . . . under the water. Beauty . . . beauty . . . her hair . . . her face . . . under the water.' And after Waldman explains what happened, Frankenstein learns new emotions: sorrow and grief. He runs off in despair to the Jura mountains, to the north of Belrive, with Waldman, Henry and Emilie in pursuit.

Webling eventually realized that the original final act of her play, in the 1923 and 1927 versions, was weak and rather too short. In both versions, Dr Waldman tracks Frankenstein down, explains to him that Katrine's soul is in heaven and that if Frankenstein wants to be with her, he could do so by dying. Frankenstein is convinced, and, thinking he will be one with Katrine, leaps to his death from a cliff. How Webling intended this scene to be played is hard to determine. One can take Waldman's pietisms as straightforward and well intended, as Forry seems to have done when he dismissed her play as filled with 'religious diatribe'.[69] Or one can see his arguments in a more cynical way as a self-serving, and hypocritical, means of manipulating an ignorant creature. The

---

[68] So Webling calls her in *The Story of a Pen* (MS page 115), 305.
[69] Forry, *Hideous Progenies*, 93.

latter reading is more interesting, it makes better sense of Waldman's encouragement to suicide (which is hardly an orthodox Christian way to heaven), and it is entirely consistent with Webling's portrayal of the creature as a sympathetic victim, abused by men. The creature's death leaves Waldman, Henry and Emilie standing together near a hut in the Jura mountains, and Webling gives Waldman the last word: 'Your guilty work is destroyed, but his soul has returned to its Creator.' Soulless no longer, Frankenstein has returned to his 'Creator', and we are to suppose that Henry will abandon his questionable scientific pursuits and marry Emilie, even as we wonder what Waldman, or Webling, meant by Frankenstein's 'Creator'.

Webling's drama makes the creature, Frankenstein, into a much more interesting character than was usual in stage adaptations of the novel, which was her manifest intention. As she wrote in her unpublished memoir, Deane, who played the creature, 'aroused compassion in his audiences, as I meant that he should.'[70] To arouse compassion, she has carefully traced Frankenstein's psychological development, which is measured in

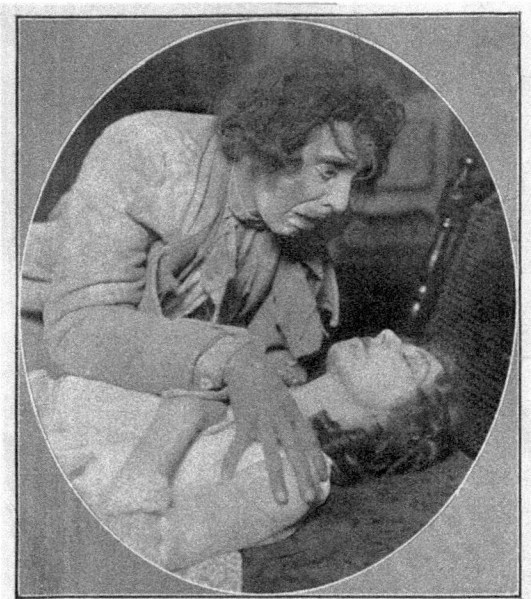

Figure 3.5 Scene from Act II of *Frankenstein*, Little Theatre, London, 1930. Frankenstein holds the drowned Katrine in his arms. *The Graphic*, 22 February 1930, 28. Courtesy of the Westminster City Archives.

---

[70]Webling, *Story of a Pen* (MS page 111), 304.

the play by his widening experience of human emotion, and by the end of the play, it is evident that, whatever else Henry has done, he has succeeded in creating a fully human being, who through suffering and sorrow has developed what the play calls a soul. At the same time, she shows how that being has been deformed by the physical and emotional abuse that Henry has inflicted upon him. Henry admits to having tortured Frankenstein and regards him as a slave-like possession – 'Is he not mine – mine!' he exclaims in Act I. He has steadfastly refused to regard his creature as a human being, and thus he has deprived him of the physical and emotional nurture that human beings deserve and require. Victor Moritz is almost as abusive, especially in the 1923 script. Among the male characters, only Waldman seems to regard him as anything but subhuman, and it is easy to see how Henry's violence and failure to educate led directly to Frankenstein's assault on Emilie and the accidental murder of Katrine. The principal women of the play, on the other hand, view Frankenstein differently. Katrine, in her simplicity and unaffected kindness, shows us what the creature might have been, if treated humanely and acculturated properly: the physically disabled girl understands, either intuitively or from her own experience with disability, the psychological damage that has been done to the creature, and attempts to heal him. Emilie is horrified by what Henry has done – why spend time in a laboratory and charnel houses when there is an easier and much more pleasurable way to create new life? – and that affects her view of the creature initially, and damages it irreparably when he attempts to sexually assault her. But at the same time, she has the most complex understanding of the relationship of Henry, Frankenstein and herself, however much the idea disturbs her. She feels genuine erotic attraction to the creature, as well as revulsion, and can articulate her mixed emotions quite clearly.

The double-casting of Henry Frankenstein and his creature was not Webling's original conception. It was undertaken, as she wrote in her memoir, at the request of

> a certain young actor, then on the crest of the wave, [who] persuaded me to alter the play so that the two parts, creature and creator, could be taken by the same man. . . . I realized it could not be done, so *Frankenstein* was once again hidden in a drawer.[71]

The script accepted by Hamilton Deane and performed in Preston, Lancashire, beginning 7 December, 1927, was thus a return to her original conception: the two characters would resemble each other and dress alike, but would be played by different actors.[72] The Preston production did not substantially depart from the thematic ideas of the 1923 script; it mainly involved assigning back to Henry Frankenstein speeches that, in the double-cast version, he could not have spoken when he and the creature were on stage together. Most of these occur in Acts I and II, where lines originally given to Henry have

---

[71] Webling, *Story of a Pen* (MS page 113), 304.
[72] According to Webling's letter of 16 October 1927, she had sent both versions to Deane, and he rejected the double-cast version. See 284–5.

Figure 3.6 Scene from Act I of *Frankenstein*, Little Theatre, London, 1930. Henry threatens Frankenstein. *Reynolds's News*, 16 February 1930, 6. Courtesy of the British Library.

been reassigned to Victor Moritz or, less frequently, Dr Waldman. For example, in Act I (1923), when the creature first appears, this exchange occurs:

Victor	*(whispering)* Look at him! He resembles Henry in every line of his body –
Waldman	But how different! (**Waldman** *sits, looking at* **F.** *with frowning severity.* **Victor** *moves to the opposite side of the table.* **F.** *makes an uncouth sound of fear, hiding his face)*
F.	Burn! Burn! Fire – *(he looks wildly around the room)* Where – is – my master? *(springs to* **Waldman** *and tries to cling to him.* **Waldman** *spurns him away.* **F.** *points to window)* Fire!
Waldman	Yes, but a good fire – a bright, grand fire. Go! *(threatens to strike him.* **F.** *moves to centre doors, frequently looking over his shoulder fearfully at* **Waldman**. *At first he bends forward, gazing up into the sky, then slowly stretches out his hands and rubs them in the hot rays, rears himself to his full height, arms lifted over his head, and stands amazed at the brilliance.* **Waldman** *rises)*

Waldman	*(as if the words were forced out of him)* Man – devil – what are you?
F.	*(with a long drawn breath)* Oh – great fire! *(ne takes a step forward and lays his hands on the glass doors, staring out into the garden, then pulls his shirt open so that the heat may fall on his breast)* Great – soft – fire. *(another pause, then he suddenly lies down and curls himself up like a dog)*
Waldman	*(sharply)* Frankenstein! *(F. does not move)* Frankenstein! *(F. stretches himself at full length to be more comfortable.* **Victor** *advances and stirs him with his foot)*
Victor	Frankenstein! *(F. pulls himself into a kneeling position and lays his face down on* **Victor's** *foot. Then looks up at him humbly.)*
F.	You are – like – my master – *(offers to take his hand.* **Victor** *quickly draws back)*

In contrast, here is the exchange in the 1927 script:

Victor	*(whispering)* Look at him, doctor! He moves like a half blind animal.
Waldman	Hush! *(***Henry*** sits, looking at* **F.** *with frowning severity.* **Waldman** *and* **Victor** *move to the opposite side of the table, farther away.* **F.** *makes an uncouth sound of fear, hiding his face)*
F.	Burn! Burn! Fire! *(springs to* **Henry** *and tries to cling to him.* **Henry** *spurns him away.* **F.** *points to window)* Fire!
Henry	Yes, but a good fire – a bright, grand fire. Go! *(Threatens to strike him.* **F.** *moves towards the centre doors, frequently looking over his shoulder fearfully at* **Henry.** *At first he bends forward, gazing up into the sky, then slowly stretches out his hands and rubs them in the hot rays, rears himself to his full height, arms lifted over his head, and stands amazed at the brilliance.)*
Waldman	*(as if the words were forced out of him)* Man – devil – what are you?
F.	*(with a long drawn breath)* Oh – great fire! *(he takes a step forward and lays his hands on the glass doors, staring out into the garden, then pulls his shirt open so that the heat falls on his breast)* Great – soft – fire! *(Another pause, then he suddenly lies down and curls himself up like a dog.)*
Henry	*(sharply)* Frankenstein! *(F. does not move)* Frankenstein! *(F. stretches himself at full length to be more comfortable.* **Henry** *advances and stirs him with his foot)* Frankenstein! *(F. pulls himself into a kneeling position and lays his face down on* **Henry's** *foot. Then he looks up at him humbly)*
F.	You are – my master!

Peggy Webling and the Story behind Frankenstein

As this passage shows, the 1927 script is not so much a revision of the 1923 script as it is a reversion to an earlier version that unfortunately does not seem to have survived.[73] Lines that originally belonged to Henry have been given back to him, clarifying that he and he alone is responsible for the abuse his creature has suffered. In both versions, the key phrase is Waldman's line 'Man – devil – what are you?' From Henry's point of view, the creature is a devil or a brute, to be physically intimidated so that he can maintain control. Waldman is not so sure, and later in the scene he encourages Frankenstein's pleasure in the natural world, and teaches him one of his first abstract ideas: beauty. This teaching begins the humanization of Frankenstein, allowing the audience to feel compassion for him, as Webling intended.

From Preston to London

Frankenstein opened at the Empire Theatre in Preston, Lancashire, on 7 December 1927, and it was well received. Webling and Deane, however, came to realize that the ending was weak. It certainly did not include the fireworks of a thunderbolt, or an erupting volcano, or the sudden violence of an avalanche, as the nineteenth-century stage plays did. Her initial impulse was to add what none of the earlier stage adaptations had included: the making of a female creature. In an entirely new third Act she apparently added the creature's request for a mate and Henry's attempt to comply. The new Act III, however, did not satisfy either her or Deane, and sometime in March, 1928, she had a breakthrough. As she recalled in her unpublished memoir:

> Frankenstein had been running for several weeks before I fully realised that the third act was *no good*. . . . All Hamilton Deane's skill could not save it. A night came when we both admitted that future success depended on a drastic change. . . . Indeed, I spent many nights and many days haunted by Frankenstein. . . . Then Hamilton Deane had an idea – it ought to have occurred to *me*.[74]

Hamilton Deane's suggestion was to follow the novel even more closely by having the creature kill his maker, and Webling, as she put it, 'suddenly saw what to do'.[75] She moved the creature's request to the end of Act II, turning it into the pivotal moment

---

[73] A notation on the 1923 script, dated 20 July 1927, mentions the existence of an earlier script. It reads: 'Not handed to Miss Webling as she found it was an earlier version she required' (Webling Archive). That is, in preparing the script for Deane, she needed an earlier script in which Henry and the creature were not double-cast, but apparently that version was not on file at the Society of Authors, Playwrights, & Composers, so she had to look elsewhere for it.

[74] Webling, *The Story of a Pen* (MS page 117), 306.

[75] Forry, *Hideous Progenies*, 99–100, and Friedman and Kavey, *Monstrous Progeny*, 88, both attribute the addition of the request for a female companion to Balderston. That was simply not the case, as the 1928 script, which predates Balderston's by 2 years, demonstrates.

of the play. As Frankenstein is learning from Waldman what it means to have killed Katrine and is experiencing intense grief for the first time, Henry bursts into the room, looking to avenge his sister's death. Waldman stops him. 'Henry, think! Think! He is not responsible. He doesn't understand', Waldman protests. 'You cannot kill him. He is bound to you more closely than a brother of the same flesh and blood. He is yours – you made him.' (210) The creature, on the other hand, can think only of Emilie and his desire for her. 'I love the woman. Give her to me', he demands, and when Henry refuses explaining that, 'No living woman will give herself to you. No woman in the world can love *you*', Frankenstein responds: 'You made Frankenstein – you can make a mate *for* Frankenstein.' (211) And if Henry does not, Frankenstein threatens to kill both him and Emilie Lavenza. So Henry accedes to his request, and Frankenstein asserts his power over him, reversing the dynamics of Act I.

F.   You will make me a mate – another Frankenstein –?

Henry   God forgive me! Yes!

F.   (*putting his out-spread hand over* **Henry's** *face as he forces him backwards*) I am your master now! You are my maker, but I am – your master. Your master! Your master! (*he throws* **Henry** *insensible to the ground, and stands triumphantly over him with both arms out-spread*) (212)

The key word here is master. Treated like an abused slave from the moment of his creation, tortured and beaten by his 'master', Frankenstein has asserted his strength and claimed mastery over his maker. He treats his creator as he has been treated.

Webling has moved Act III of the 1928 version six months later,[76] to give Henry time to finish making the female creature. Like the earlier versions, it is set in the Jura mountains, but rather than outdoors in 'a mountain pass', the action occurs in a hut where Henry has once again isolated himself. The 'female Frankenstein' is lying on a 'low couch' at the rear of the stage, visible throughout the Act. To instil her with life, Henry must administer an 'elixir of life', for which he has written a secret formula in 'cipher', on a single scroll of paper that he keeps locked in a cabinet. (The explicit use of an elixir of life is new to the 1928 play, and is first mentioned in the revised prologue, as Henry brings the creature to life.) When Act III opens, Waldman enters the hut and attempts to convince Henry not to fulfil his promise. As they talk, Frankenstein appears and reappears at the windows of the hut, anticipating the creation of his mate, surveilling and threatening Henry at one and the same time. There is much talk about souls. Waldman thinks Henry is endangering his soul by making a female creature; Henry says he will lose his life if he doesn't, and worries about 'the dark spirit of evil' he will awaken when he animates her. He then exits to his bedchamber to rest, and Frankenstein enters the hut. He and Waldman discuss his grief over the death of

---

[76]In the 1923 and 1927 versions, Act III takes place 'the following dawn'.

Katrine, and Waldman consoles him by saying 'In the depths of sorrow the soul awakes.' As in the earlier versions, Waldman assures the creature that in death God may forgive him, and he will be reunited with Katrine. But one wonders how sincere Waldman is being, given what he has just said to Henry. In any case, the invitation for the monster to commit suicide does not work this time: the desire to have his own mate outweighs his desire to be reunited with Katrine. When Henry returns, this exchange occurs:

Waldman   Henry! Henry! You will buy your freedom at too great a price. Listen to the truth before it is too late. Think of the awful possibilities – realize what it will mean to give a woman like himself to Frankenstein. *(they look at each other with a sudden flash of understanding)*

Henry   I *know*!

Waldman   *(his horror increasing every minute)* It will mean that she will be his – it will mean that she will bear him children –

Henry   I tell you, Dr. Waldman, I *know*.

Waldman   But you have not thought that the children of Frankenstein and the unnatural mate of Frankenstein, will be the children of *your* guilty mind, the work of *your* sinful hands! *(***Henry** *remains immovable, staring down into* **Waldman's** *face)* Do you remember the day at Belrive, after Katrina's death, when Frankenstein told you to choose?

This argument convinces Henry to destroy the written formula, and pour the remaining elixir on a brazier, where it burns spectacularly. Frankenstein witnesses the scene, and fulfils his threat: he seizes Henry by the throat and strangles him. In this version of the play, Waldman does not have the last word; Webling assigns it instead to the desperate creature.

> Shall each man have his wife – each beast his mate – and I be alone. I killed him – because he robbed me – of all *she* would have given me. All men hate me – and now – I hate myself. *(looks down at* **Henry***)* He is dead who brought me to life, and I – shall be dead soon – and find – God. Rest! Rest! Dead – very soon – soon – rest – rest – *(he groans and moves blindly towards the centre doors. There is a vivid flash of lightning that strikes him and he falls, instantly, shattered. A terrific roll of thunder.* **Waldman** *stands immovable, gazing at* **Henry's** *dead body)*.

This is certainly a more spectacular ending, with all its fireworks, and one wonders whether Deane, who seems to have known *Presumption* well, introduced the idea of the lightning bolt. In a later version of *Presumption* Peake changed the climactic death of the creature and his creator from an avalanche to a fatal lightning bolt, which he borrowed

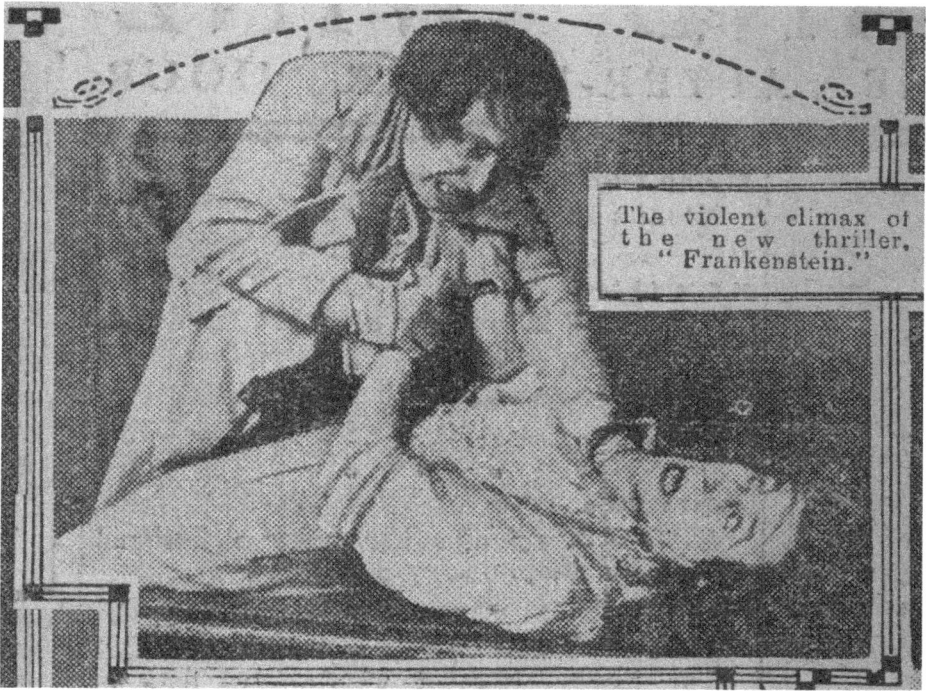

Figure 3.7 Scene from Act III of Frankenstein, Little Theatre, London, 1930. Frankenstein strangles Henry. *Sunday Pictorial*, 16 February 1930, 12. Courtesy of the British Library.

from the ending of *The Man and Magician*. Besides, it is much easier to flash a light and imitate thunder than to stage an avalanche.[77]

If the 1928 ending is more spectacular, it is also a vast improvement over the earlier ones. First of all, Webling has developed more sides to Frankenstein's character. In the earlier versions, he is an abused creature who, overcome with grief and guilt at Katrine's death, runs off to the mountains in despair. In Webling's revision, he has become the alienated being of Shelley's novel, conscious of how damaged and abused he has been, seeking the love and companionship that he believes would heal him but that human beings deny him, and using the only means to get it that he has been taught: anger, threats and violence. When his prospect for love is irrevocably cut off, he takes revenge on his maker, and afterwards his anger and hatred change to despair and self-loathing, and he wishes only for 'Rest'. Does he find God? Webling leaves that question unanswered.

---

[77]Forry, *Hideous Progenies*, 7–8, gives an account of a disastrous Birmingham production of *Presumption*, in which the theatre did not have enough white canvas for the avalanche, and substituted instead a stage elephant, apparently painted white. According to a reviewer, the stage elephant 'came down before the cue was given him, so that *Franky* and his *Demon* were obliged to seek death from some other source than excessive *snow-ball*.'

Peggy Webling and the Story behind Frankenstein

The failure to make the female creature gives Webling the chance to complicate Henry's character as well. She could not, of course, depict Henry ripping the naked female body to pieces, as Victor Frankenstein does in the novel.[78] But the on-stage presence of her body throughout Act III is a reminder of the intimate work he has been engaged in, alone in his mountain hut, and his disgust at what he has done lays bare the misogyny at the heart of his whole enterprise. 'I was upheld at Goldstadt', Henry tells Waldman,

> by the false dream of my own greatness. I thought I could control and master the being of my own creation. But in making – that – I have been overwhelmed by fear and abhorrence of the task. For hours – for days – I have wandered about the hills, unable to return to this accursed place. I have been afraid to come in – afraid to touch it – afraid of myself.

Rather than nurture and educate, Henry has sought to control, master and dominate, and he has failed: Frankenstein, he says, has 'conquered my manhood', just as earlier he ascribed the making of the creature to his 'man's nature'. He abhors the making of the female creature, convinced that he would be awakening a 'dark spirit of evil', if he brings her to life. Later in the Act, he agrees with Waldman that making the female will be 'monstrous' because 'she will bear him children'. Like the hero of Shelley's novel, then, Henry fears the sexuality of the beings he has created, because he has no prospect of controlling it. Henry's masculinity, his 'manhood', we see, consists in his ability to control others, not in his willingness to join with others in the nurturing of new life. It is thus appropriate that Webling wrote Emilie out of the final act: Henry's attempt to create life isolated him from human contact before, and it has done so again, this time with the irony of a well-draped female corpse visible on the stage. The revised ending also alters our view of Dr Waldman. In convincing Henry not to give life to the female body, Waldman argues that Henry is endangering his soul. His argument is essentially a reiteration of Frankenstein's demand at the end of Act II: choose, the creature tells Henry – create a female Frankenstein or die. Choose, implores Waldman, between making the female creature and death. And it is Waldman who articulates the fearful prospect that convinces his former student to sacrifice himself: 'But you have not thought that the children of Frankenstein and the unnatural mate of Frankenstein, will be the children of *your* guilty mind, the work of *your* sinful hands!'[79] Waldman's subsequent discussion with Frankenstein, in which he repeats the pietisms about God and Katrine and an afterlife from the earlier ending, rings even more hollow: he has just called the creature an irredeemable demon, so he can't believe that the creature will find God, forgiveness

---

[78] Webling's stage directions in fact state that the drapery covering the female creature 'must be arranged in such a way that it can be lifted without the audience actually seeing the figure'. 213.
[79] These are almost the same arguments that Victor Frankenstein makes in the novel, with one exception: Victor considers the possibility that the female creature might hate her male partner. That argument Waldman never makes.

and Katrine in a heavenly afterlife. He just wants Frankenstein to kill himself. In this version, Frankenstein may wish for death, and may even be intending to commit suicide. But a lightning bolt intervenes, and Waldman gets what he wished for.

The 1928 script was the version of Webling's play that Hamilton Deane produced in various British provincial theatres between 1928 and 1930; it was also the version sent to the American author, John Balderston, who had contracted with Webling and Deane to adapt her play for performances in New York City. Balderston himself later wrote that this version had been performed more than 700 times over a period of 9 years, and if these numbers are accurate, they are astonishing, and a testament to the quality of both Webling's writing and Deane's acting.[80] But it was not the 1928 version that most audiences saw: there is a later surviving script, recently discovered by Dorian Greenbaum in the Hamilton Deane Papers at the Westminster City Archives in London: the prompt script for the 1930 London production. This script is, for the most part, assembled from typescripts of both the 1927 and 1928 versions, into which someone has entered a number of handwritten revisions: we believe the hand, in most cases, to be that of Hamilton Deane. It is impossible to say with certainty whether these revisions were authored by Deane, or whether he was transcribing changes Webling herself composed. Their correspondence suggests that they are more likely to be Webling's, but it is also apparent that the two had become, to some extent, collaborators, as is often the case with performers and playwrights. Some of these revisions are minor changes of wording, the sort of thing that actors insist upon to make the delivery of lines seem more natural. Several are more extensive: there are revisions of the 1927 script towards 1928 (these appear at the end of Act II, for the most part), there are revisions in the 1928 script towards 1930, especially in Act III, and there are handwritten insertions throughout. Because the prompt script is the latest version of the play to survive, and is the basis of the London production, the one most playgoers and the London theatre critics would have seen, we have chosen to reproduce it fully in this book, in spite of its complexity.

There are important differences between the 1928 play and the 1930 prompt script. First of all, there is a significant omission in the play's prologue. In the 1928 script, Henry is more specific about how he brought Frankenstein to life than he had been in previous versions. In the versions of 1923 and 1927, he merely calls it 'my discovery', which must remain a 'secret'. 'An hour ago I used my discovery to animate the senseless body – I'll say no more of that, no more! The secret shall live and die with me', he says. (119) And in the early versions, we never find out what his secret was, since he does not have to use it again to make a female creature. But in the 1928 script, when he shows Waldman and Moritz Frankenstein's inanimate body, he claims: 'my elixir is at work.' Now the reference to the elixir here anticipates what will happen in the reworked final Act, where Henry shows the elixir to Dr Waldman and eventually destroys it. In preparing the text for the London stage, however, Webling decided to revert to the earlier version: the prompt script has

---

[80]The John L. Balderston Papers, 1915–1950, part of the Billy Rose Theatre Collection, New York Public Library, 'Analysis of Frankenstein by Peggy Webling', *T-Mss 1954-002, Box 1, folder 13, item 2, p. 1.

no mention of the elixir in the Prologue. Until Act III, we are left wondering just what Henry Frankenstein discovered. She apparently decided that this uncertainty was an effective device for creating suspense: as Hamilton Deane put it, the key to shocking an audience is 'through a process of suggestion .... [B]y using a few of the legitimate tricks of the theatre, of which the chief one is suspense, we manage, I think, to build up that atmosphere in which it is possible to create the maximum sensation.'[81]

An even more significant change occurs in Act III itself. Frankenstein's final speech, which had ended the 1928 script, has been changed, and rather than having it end the play, Webling has added a speech by Waldman, a reworked version of the 1927 conclusion, to serve as a kind of moral. Here again is the 1928 speech:

> Shall each man have his wife – each beast his mate – and I be alone. I killed him – because he robbed me – of all *she* would have given me. All men hate me – and now – I hate myself. *(looks down at* **Henry***)* He is dead who brought me to life, and I – shall be dead soon – and find – God. Rest! Rest! Dead – very soon – soon – rest – rest. (220)

And here is how Webling changed it for the London production:

> Killed – my master! Then his soul – his soul – with little Katrina – I am alone – alone *(he gives a deep, long moan)* I must find – my way – to God – alone – alone – where shall I find – Him! He will help me – I must go – into the night! How shall I find – the way – how shall I find the way –[82] (279)

The 1928 speech emphasizes the anger Frankenstein feels at the loss of his mate and the hatred he feels towards the man he has just murdered. Webling has rewritten it to emphasize instead the grief he feels for Katrine, and therefore she makes his death wish a yearning for a reunion with her, as it was in the earliest versions, rather than an escape from a life he can no longer bear. The result is a Frankenstein who is a more sympathetic figure than the apostle of vengeance of the 1928 script. As in early versions, though, we are left to wonder how to take Waldman's pious moral, which has here been expanded from the 1923 and 1927 endings. 'He is dead', says Waldman, referring to the creature.

> The guilty work is destroyed, but his soul has returned to its Creator. *(turns and looks tenderly and solemnly down at* **Henry***)* Man! Man! From God alone is the breath of life! (280)

---

[81]'The Technique of Terror. Mr. Hamilton Deane's Definition', *The Era*, 19 February 1930, 9.
[82]The London reviewer of *Frankenstein* for *The Illustrated Sporting and Dramatic Review*, 8 March 1930, 512, confirms that the prompt script was the version performed at The Little Theatre. Of the ending, he writes: 'Down goes the poor monster in a heap, to meet the God he was just setting forth to seek.'

Waldman's pietisms elide altogether the abuse Henry has heaped upon the manchild he created, and Waldman's assumption about the creature's soul is just as ambiguous as it was before. If his soul 'awakened . . . [i]n the depths of pain and sorrow', does that guarantee a divine origin? And if it has a divine origin, how does that justify Henry's abuse? Waldman's final, tendentious admonition to Henry's corpse is contradicted by the play itself: Henry gave the breath of life to his creature, and could have given it again to his mate. But he chose not to, persuaded by Waldman.

Frankenstein comes to Hollywood

It remains to talk about John Balderston's reconception of Webling's play and its transformation into James Whale's Universal film in 1931. As we have already shown, sometime in 1929 Balderston received a script, namely a copy of the 1928 version on deposit at the Library of Congress.[83] He had contracted with Deane and Webling to revise it for the American stage, just as he had successfully revised Deane's *Dracula* some years earlier. As Dorian Greenbaum has shown in our earlier chapters, Webling came to regard Balderston as a nemesis, Deane's feelings about him were not much better, and Balderston himself took his sweet time with his work, finishing it only when the finances of his sponsor, Horace Liveright, had been so weakened that his version of the play could not be produced in New York. Nor did Balderston have much regard for Webling and what she had written: he famously dismissed her work as 'illiterate', and his judgement has been echoed, we believe wrongly, by most of the historians of Frankenstein reception.[84] Luckily for both Balderston and Webling, Carl Laemmle, Jr, of Universal Pictures became interested in producing another horror feature, capitalizing on the success of *Dracula*, the 1931 Universal film based on the Balderston/Hamilton Deane theatrical version of Bram Stoker's novel. And the provincial and London success of Webling's *Frankenstein* – by 1931, it had been performed well over 200 times – led him to purchase the rights to the Balderston–Webling play.[85]

Balderston has taken considerable liberties with Webling's text. From the beginning he shows much more interest in the arcane science that produced the creature than Webling had: this Henry Frankenstein tells of his experiments with galvanic batteries on toads, cats, and dogs, brags of stealing body parts from dissecting labs, including a brain, proudly admits to desecrating a grave, and claims to have found part of the formula for 'the Elixir of Life . . . in those old black letter books, [and] worked the rest out for myself'. None of this is in Webling's play. Balderston also stages the creation

---

[83]That this was the version sent to Balderston is shown by the full title Balderston uses for his 'Analysis of Frankenstein by Peggy Webling' (see n. 80 above): 'Analysis of Frankenstein by Peggy Webling' as deposited in the copyright office, Washington, D86282, on September 7, 1928' (*T-Mss 1954-002, Box 1, folder 13, item 2, p. 1).
[84]See note 6 above.
[85]Forry, *Hideous Progenies*, 92, speculates that 'Universal purchased the rights to forestall any unnecessary competition; that is, so that two adaptations of *Frankenstein* would not play simultaneously in New York'.

scene more fully than Webling did: the body Henry has made is connected, by wires, to a machine run by a galvanic battery, we see him pour the elixir down its throat (how it swallows is not explained), and slowly the creature comes alive. 'I have made life out of matter that is dead', exults Henry. 'You make yourself equal with God – that was the sin of the fallen angel!' responds Waldman.[86] Waldman's response signals another of Balderston's changes: he makes the professor both a scientist and a priest, and much more emphatically the latter. From the beginning of the play he is the source of orthodox Christian commentary and admonition about Henry's doings. When Henry reminds Waldman of their discussion about 'the mystery of life', Waldman quickly interjects: 'We know that life comes from God, from God alone. . . . It is presumption . . . to push our enquiries so far. . . . We must remember that we can deal with matter, not with spirit, which is the breath of God.'[87] If Webling's play becomes preachy in places, Balderston's is tendentious throughout, especially when Waldman is on stage, and he never, like Webling, undercuts Waldman's authority. Instead, he consistently juxtaposes Henry's scientific ambitions with Waldman's pietisms. The final scene is painful to read: Waldman pulls out a crucifix[88] just as Frankenstein is about to kill him (a leftover prop from *Dracula*?), and gives a very short sermon on Jesus, the soul, and how God loves everyone, even Frankenstein. So Frankenstein prays, with outstretched arms, 'God help me.'[89] And we are to believe God does: for at that moment Frankenstein is struck by lightning and dies. One wonders what Mary Shelley, daughter and wife of avowed atheists, would have thought.

Balderston's other innovations in the Frankenstein plot include arranging a marriage between Henry and Amelia Lavenza (so he renamed Webling's Emilie) in the second Act, which, rather than occurring on the next day, takes place 'Several weeks later'.[90] The wedding does not occur: the creature's inadvertent murder of Katrina prevents it. But preparations for the wedding provide a backdrop for another Balderstonian innovation: a love quadrangle he creates between Henry, Amelia, Victor Moritz and Katrina (Balderston consistently calls her Katrina, rather than Katrine). Balderston introduces the quadrangle at the beginning of Act II. Amelia opens the Act by saying to Victor

---

[86] My text for Balderston's *Frankenstein* is that in Forry, *Hideous Progenies*, 251–86. The quotation occurs in Act I, Scene 1 (a revision of Webling's Prologue), 258. This line is recast in perhaps the most famous line (often censored) from Whale's film: 'Now I know what it feels like to be God.'

[87] Act I, Scene 1, Forry, *Hideous Progenies*, 254. Waldman's speech is a revision of a similar speech in the Prologue of all versions of Webling's script: 'I warn you, solemnly, against the sin of vain presumption. From God alone is the breath of life. Be warned!' Balderston, however, has Waldman repeat the word presumption in two consecutive speeches, and the word comes back multiple times in his script. The phrase 'sin of vain presumption' can be traced to *Pneumatologia: A Treatise on the Soul of Man*, in *The Whole Works of the Reverend Mr. John Flavel*, vol. 1 (Glasgow: John Orr, Bookseller, 1754), 374. John Flavel (1630–1691) was a Puritan divine: see Brian H. Cosby, *John Flavel: Puritan Life and Thought in Stuart England* (Lanham, MD: Lexington Books, 2014), ix, 14–20.

[88] Never mind that the play takes place near Geneva, in a famously Protestant Swiss canton.

[89] Act III, Forry, *Hideous Progenies*, 286.

[90] Act II, Scene 1, ibid., 268.

Moritz 'She loves you', meaning Katrina, to which Victor responds, 'she's too good for just ordinary life, she's different from other people, it's impossible to think about things like marriage, and children.' And a few lines later, as Victor continues to disavow feelings for Katrina, the real issue emerges: 'I'm not going to bring up MY love, my feelings for you,'[91] he says. So Katrina loves Victor, Victor loves Amelia, and Amelia and Henry love each other, even though he has neglected her for months at a time while making his creature. The plot changes certainly create tensions in the story, but mainly they are used to set up the revamped concluding Act. Amelia is present in the Balderston version of Act III, and convinces Henry not to make the female creature: 'If it's me he wants, I'd rather – I'd rather he had his way . . . than you should do it again – make again – commit that sin over again. . . . You can't – you can't – people the world with monsters', she protests.[92] So the horror about making monsters is displaced from Waldman and Henry, to a woman who is ready to be raped by Frankenstein, and who apparently believes that won't produce children. And when Henry and the creature are dead, Amelia is given the play's last word: 'Victor. Take me away. Take me away. Victor, don't ever leave me, don't ever leave me.'[93] Like *Casablanca*, is this the beginning of a wonderful friendship?

The most important change that Balderston made was to make the creature far less sympathetic than in any of Webling's different versions. Not only is he described as a demon, fiend or monster by almost every other human in the play – Katrina being the lone exception – but the scenes in which Webling depicted him sympathetically are severely altered. For instance, in Act I when Waldman (in Webling's play) teaches Frankenstein about beauty, Balderston has Henry do most of the teaching while carrying a whip, and although the creature does learn about beauty (the line 'All beautiful . . . All' has been cut), he is also learning about hatred at the same time. 'I know I oughtn't to hate him, Dr. Waldman', exclaims Henry, 'but he's part of me and I hate myself. He oughtn't to exist.'[94] So on the heels of teaching him about the beauty of nature, Henry immediately jumps his creature from behind and tries to strangle him. The scene with Katrina in the second Act is also altered to make Frankenstein appear the worse. The moving lines about no one ever touching him are cut, Katrina, even while being kind, is trying to get him to 'go away a little while, until just after the wedding', and a reference to Amelia leads Frankenstein to respond, 'savagely', 'No! Frankenstein master now. Frankenstein mate. Frankenstein woman'.[95] There are also reports of random murders Frankenstein has already committed, and the time elapsed between Acts I and II has allowed Frankenstein to visit the de Laceys (who are mentioned but not named), where he learns about reading. Afterwards he steals Henry's secret formula and arranges to have one of his future victims read it to him. When he demands a mate at the end of Act

---

[91] Act II, Scene 1, ibid.
[92] Act III, ibid., 284.
[93] Act II, ibid., 286.
[94] Act II, ibid., 264.
[95] Ibid., 275–7.

Peggy Webling and the Story behind Frankenstein

II, then, it is not just a logical deduction – you made me, you can make a female like me. Instead, he makes his demand with knowledge of exactly how Henry did it in the first place.

Webling and Deane were right to be frustrated with Balderston, both for the delays in producing a revised script, and for his failure either to see and appreciate what Webling was doing, or his conscious decision to ignore it. Webling's abused creature has become, certainly by the end of the play, the demon that most other characters describe him as. And most of the complexities and ambiguities of character that Webling was justly proud of have been erased. Instead, there is a constant hammering of religious truisms: Henry has sinned, Henry delights in his sin like Satan, Henry repents and is punished for his sin, and the creature, in the end, gets what he deserves. Could he, with proper parenting and nurture have turned out well, as both Shelley and Webling clearly imply? Balderston's play never really takes that possibility seriously. Even in his nearly redeemable moments, Balderston's Frankenstein cannot control outbursts of hatred and violence: either he has become what his maker perceives him as, or he is, as Waldman repeatedly asserts, an embodiment of Henry's sin that is incapable of good. Webling was right: it was 'a hopeless manuscript of which not a line could be used.'[96]

The opening credits of the Universal *Frankenstein* state that the film was 'based upon the composition by John L. Balderston' and 'adapted from the play by Peggy Webling'. Almost every historian of the Frankenstein phenomenon notes that James Whale preserves Webling's name changes, with one minor exception: he retains from the novel the name Elizabeth Lavenza, where Webling called her Emilie. And Whale also preserves Webling's name of the town as Goldstadt, where the whole of the movie is set. But these same historians also note that there is surprisingly little of the Balderston/Webling script and plotting in the movie; those lines that are preserved, as Webling predicted, are hers, not Balderston's. Some have speculated that Universal bought the rights to the play to keep it off the New York stage, where it would serve as a competitor to their film.[97] Perhaps that was the case. But it is not our purpose to trace the complicated history of the filming of the Universal *Frankenstein*, with its multiple screenwriters, changes of directors and censorship difficulties. We simply maintain the uncontroversial position that, without the popularity of Peggy Webling's play in London and provincial British theatres, the film would not have been made. It is important, therefore, to articulate more exactly than other accounts have done, just what in the film had its origins in Peggy Webling's imagination, and how James Whale adapted those things to fit his own conception of the Frankenstein story.

The most important thing to consider is Whale's presentation of the creature. Both Whale and Karloff are on record as wanting to present the creature sympathetically,[98]

---

[96]Webling, *Story of a Pen* (MS page 118), 307.
[97]So speculates Forry, *Hideous Progenies*, 92.
[98]Robert Horton, *Frankenstein* (London and New York: Wallflower Press, 2014), 21, notes that both Whale and Karloff 'viewed [the monster] as a blameless, childlike creature'. David Skal, *Screams of Reason: Mad Science*

and their ways of doing so are clearly derived from the Webling play. In the film, as in her play, the creature suffers abuse from virtually all of the men around him. We don't see Henry talk about beating him, as we do in the play, nor does he call him a slave, but Fritz, his assistant, both taunts and beats him, and becomes the creature's first victim, killed in an act of self-defence. Henry Frankenstein is clearly complicit in this abuse: he fights with the creature in an attempt to subdue him, has apparently done little to discipline Fritz for his taunting, has chained the creature in a windowless room in the depths of his tower (we are clearly to think of it as a dungeon), and has given no attention whatsoever to anything beyond creating him. What to do with the creature later seems not to have crossed Henry's mind – he offers him no education, no nurture, no love, and his instinctive reactions to things the creature does are usually violent. Waldman is even more grotesquely complicit: he makes the bizarre decision to anaesthetize the creature and dissect him while still alive. When the creature wakes up at the last second and kills the doctor as he reaches for his scalpels, it is another act of self-defence, although everyone else in the film calls it murder, refusing to grant the creature anything like human dignity or human rights. The famous scene in which Fritz steals the 'abnormal' brain (Abby Normal, said Marty Feldman in *Young Frankenstein*) is supposed to mitigate audience sympathy, but in context it seems just a bit of comic business that does not wholly square with the later events of the plot. This scene, writes Skal, was added late in the screenwriting process, and 'amounted to a major subversion of Shelley's moral'.[99] Not to mention Balderston–Webling's.

There are two scenes in the film that originate from Webling's play, both of which are designed to elicit sympathy for the creature. The first is in Henry Frankenstein's Gothic tower, where he has been keeping the creature in utter darkness, locked away and perhaps in the dungeon. But Henry has let him out, and for the first time the creature sees and feels sunlight. Karloff's pantomime expresses his unutterable joy at the new and pleasurable sensations, and it is evident that these are not the reactions of an abnormal brain. The scene is adapted from the similar one in Act I of Webling's play, in which the creature has been released from the dark room where he has been confined and takes delight in his first contact with the 'soft fire' of the sun. (186) Waldman goes on to teach him the words for sun, garden, flowers, trees and finally beauty. But Whale's creature, like the monsters of Peake and Milner, cannot speak, so the process of language acquisition, which Webling uses to show the increasing sophistication of the creature's perceptions, is lost. And in the film Fritz breaks the scene up, taunting the creature with a flaming torch, and turning his delight into fear and anger. The scene ends with the men wrestling the creature to the floor. As a result of these changes our sympathy for the creature is

---

and Modern Culture (New York: W.W. Norton & Company, 1998), 128, credits Francis Edwards Faragoh with 'going back to the Balderston–Webling play and Shelley novel to reinstate the crucial element of pity for the monster.' At 129, Skal also quotes Karloff that he conceived of the monster 'as a pathetic creature who, like us all, had neither wish nor say in his creation and certainly did not wish upon itself the hideous image which automatically terrified humans whom it tried to befriend.'
[99] Skal, *Screams of Reason*, 128.

mitigated by his alternately pitiable and beastly actions. That is the general tendency of Whale's film: we can pity the creature, but not too much.

The most famous borrowing from Webling is the scene between the creature and the child Maria at the lake shore, which is Whale's adaptation of the encounter between Katrine and the creature in Act II of Webling's play. In the film, the creature is wandering aimlessly outdoors, as he does in the novel, and when he meets Maria, she calls him 'friend,' as Katrine does in Webling's play, and the two of them cast daisies on to the surface of the lake. The creature feels intense pleasure at the beautiful sight. Then, when they run out of flowers, and apparently thinking Maria will float just as beautifully, he throws her into the lake, where she drowns. The scene is meant to reflect the childish innocence that Whale and Karloff believed should characterize the creature at his best, but the two of them disagreed about how to end the scene. Karloff thought he should gently lay Maria upon the water, whereas Whale, invoking an idea of the story as ritual, thought she must be thrown.[100] In other words, from Whale's point of view, this death not only should happen, it must happen with an act of thoughtless violence, in order to be in accord with his conception of the Frankenstein myth. Webling, on the other hand, puts the drowning of Katrine offstage, and although Whale does give us a brief sense of the creature's confusion and chagrin at what he has done to Maria, we have nothing like the moment when Frankenstein carries Katrine's corpse back from the river, confused and grief-stricken, beginning to learn things that his maker had wholly neglected to teach him. Instead, Maria's father carries her body from the lake to the town, arousing the townspeople, in their Dirndls and Lederhosen, to vengeance. Whale's conception of the story would not allow for the level of sympathy that Webling's scene evokes. By so doing, he avoids the overstated sentimentality with which Webling presents Katrine: in her play, she is little Katrine, who has a little room, and a little boat, and everyone, except herself, feels sorry for her. But at the same time, Whale all but erases the 'symbol of compassion' that Webling used to show both the full humanity of the creature and to reveal by contrast the extent of Henry Frankenstein's abuses.

Other borrowings from Webling include the elevation of Henry's father to the rank of Baron Frankenstein, and her characterization of him as a comic figure, full of himself and ignorant, primarily interested in the quality of his wine. The expanded role of Dr Waldman is also a Webling innovation that Whale preserves. More important is her characterization of Henry Frankenstein as frenzied and half-mad. Colin Clive, whom Whale cast in the role, brilliantly projects these qualities, while maintaining a tight control over his performance that consistently pushes things to the edge, without quite going over. One wonders, in fact, if Clive had seen Henry Hallatt perform as Henry Frankenstein on the London stage. Webling's remark in her memoir, that Clive 'went from London to the States on purpose to play' the role, suggests he may well have attended the Little Theatre performance of her play. (308)

---

[100]Gregory William Mank, *It's Alive: The Classic Cinema Saga of Frankenstein* (San Diego: A. S. Barnes & Company, 1981), 31–2.

We also owe to Webling the sequel to Whale's *Frankenstein*, *The Bride of Frankenstein* with its creation of the female creature. As Balderston wrote in his 'Analysis of "Frankenstein" by Peggy Webling', 'Balderston was hired by Universal three years later (in 1934) to turn the dramatic material in the play version into a screen play which should involve the creation of a mate'.[101] In a companion document, called 'Analysis Mary Shelley's Novel – "Frankenstein"', Balderston wrote this about the creation of a female mate: 'It will be seen at once that the elements of this were used in our play, that they were all discarded in the first film and you will recognize my successful attempt to get a sequel made to get some of these things back, treated in our way of course, not Mary Shelley's.'[102] Our way, however, means Balderston's way, who is credited with the screenplay for 'Bride of Frankenstein', and his way only vaguely reflects anything in Webling's original. There is one borrowing, however, that is well worth mentioning. The scene with the blind fiddler is adapted from Webling's scene between Katrine and the creature, as well as the scene when Waldman teaches the creature to speak. As in the play, the kindness of the blind man suggests what the creature could have become, given proper human nurture and education, and the episode is designed to evoke precisely the kind of sympathy that both Webling and Karloff thought necessary to the Frankenstein story.

There are, then, in the Universal *Frankenstein* films episodes and moments both touching and horrifying that have their origins in Peggy Webling's vision of Mary Shelley's book. As the first woman to adapt the novel for the stage, she placed her indelible mark on the Frankenstein story, perpetuated in James Whale's classic films, and in our cultural perceptions of this enduring myth of the limits of modern science.

---

[101] The John L. Balderston Papers, 1915–1950, *T-Mss 1954-002, Box 1, folder 13 item 2, p. 6. It seems to be related to the lawsuit filed by Balderston and the Webling estate against Universal pictures in the early 1950s.
[102] This document is also part of the John L. Balderston Papers in the Billy Rose Theatre Collection, New York Public Library, *T-Mss 1954-002, Box 1, folder 13 item 1, p. 16 (3rd page of 3).

PART II
TEXTS OF WEBLING'S *FRANKENSTEIN*

EDITORIAL PROCEDURES

Our edition of Peggy Webling's *Frankenstein* consists of full transcriptions of three versions of the play: the 1927 script, first performed in Preston on 7 December 1927; the 1928 script, copyrighted and deposited at the Library of Congress on 8 September 1928; and the 1930 prompt script, used for the London production at the Little Theatre in 1930. Our rationale for choosing these three versions, out of the four that survive, is this: we wish to show the version of the play that was first performed, the one closest to Webling's original vision, we wish to show the version (1928) that was sent to John Balderston and formed the basis of his revised text of the play, and we wish to show the final version that most theatre-goers would have experienced both in London and in later tours in provincial theatres.

In transcribing the typescripts, we have striven to represent Webling's spelling and punctuation as faithfully as possible. Obvious misspellings have been silently corrected, as have obvious punctuation errors. For instance, Webling or her typist often seems to have hit the comma key at the end of sentences instead of the period key, and almost always has failed to correct the error.

We have also interpreted her underlinings as indicating italic type. In most versions of the play, the stage directions are underlined, and thus they have been represented in italic type. Some words and phrases in the dialogue are also underlined to indicate emphasis, and these are also represented in italics.

The prompt script presents special problems, since it has several revisions of different kinds. Some are entered by hand in ink or pencil. We believe most of these are in the hand of Hamilton Deane, who may have been responsible for the revisions, but more likely is entering revisions that he and Webling have mutually agreed upon. In a handful of cases, the editor has had to decipher the handwriting and determine its place in the text. In addition to the handwritten revisions, there are several sheets and half-sheets of typed revisions, marked with indications that they are to replace specific sections of the script. These are almost certainly Webling's own revisions. Halfway through the prompt script the habit of underlining stage directions has been dropped by the typist. We have continued to represent them in italics, for consistency. Finally, the revised third Act does not contain the opening stage directions; apparently they were considered irrelevant for the prompter. We have inserted the opening stage directions from the 1928 script, for the sake of coherence. Also, the prompt script sometimes uses the spelling Katrine and sometimes uses Katrina. We have retained this inconsistency.

Frankenstein (1927)

First Performed at Preston, Lancashire
7 December 1927

FRANKENSTEIN
A Play in a Prologue and Three Acts
(Based upon Mrs. Shelley's well known book)
By
Peggy Webling

FRANKENSTEIN

Characters:

Baron Frankenstein
Henry (his son)
Dr. Waldman (of the University of Goldstadt, Switzerland)
Victor Moritz
            and
Frankenstein

Baroness Frankenstein
Katrine (her daughter)
Emilie Lavenza
Elizabeth

Prologue:

Henry's study in **Dr. Waldman's** house in Goldstadt. A winter evening. Six months are supposed to elapse.

Act I: The same as the Prologue. Morning.

Act II: Room in the **Baron's** house at Belrive. Afternoon of the same day.

Act III: A pass in the Jura Mountains. The following dawn.

Period:
The end of the Eighteenth Century.

FRANKENSTEIN

Prologue

Henry's *study in* **Dr. Waldman's** *house at Goldstadt. A winter evening. A small room lighted by an oil lamp. Centre doors, hidden by long, dark curtains which are slightly open. There is a lounge standing across the corner of the room, with a small table nearby. Big arm chairs by the fire; writing desk, shelves of books. The walls are hung with anatomical drawings. Doors R. and L., both opening away from the audience. It is almost dark when the curtain rises. A flash of lightning through the slit in the curtains over centre doors, followed by a long roll of thunder. The sound of a storm is heard. which gradually dies away as the Prologue proceeds, but there is occasional thunder and lightning to the end. The stage is empty. A loud knocking at the door L., and* **Victor Moritz's** *voice is heard outside.*

Victor	Henry! Henry Frankenstein! Henry! Where are you? *(Enter* **Victor**, *wearing a heavy cloak and hat pulled down over his brows. He glances round the room, removes his hat and shakes the water off. As he crosses towards opposite door it is unlocked and* **Henry** *enters, speaking as he does so.)*
Henry	Who is it? Ah, Victor! *(He closes door behind him and advances quickly with out-stretched hand.)* Did you knock before? I am glad you have come before Dr. Waldman.
Victor	Did you expect me on such a night?
Henry	Of all men in the college you are most welcome. *(As they shake hands a gust of wind blows open the centre doors behind the curtains.* **Henry** *goes to them.)* Good God! What a night! *(Closes and bolts doors, arranging curtains and turns up lamp a little.)* Take off your wet cloak, Victor. I'll hang it by the stove in my other room. This fire is too small to dry a rag. *(Offers to take his friend's cloak and hat)*
Victor	Let me take them into your room. *(Goes towards door R.)*
Henry	*(Quickly)* No, Victor, no. You can't go into my room. Give it to me — and your hat— *(Exit* **Henry** *with cloak and hat. For the few seconds he is absent* **Victor** *stands by the fire, warming his hands and feet. Re-enter* **Henry**. *He has the key of the door in his hand and locks it, putting the key in his pocket)*
Victor	*(carelessly)* Why do you lock your inner door and leave the other open?
Henry	No reason. I expect Dr. Waldman. *(he throws a log on the fire)* Pull up a chair. How the wind howls! I think it's found its way from the lonely Jura

Mountains to Goldstadt. Listen! Doesn't it take you back to old Belrive? *(They sit down.* **Victor** *lights his pipe. He leans back comfortably in his chair, stretching his feet to the fire.* **Henry** *is restless and nervous, frequently changing his position and fidgeting. He often stoops forward, clasping his hands on either side of his head.)*

Victor   I'm glad that it can't take us back to old Belrive — literally.

Henry   Why are you glad?

Victor   If we suddenly found ourselves in your father's house, or in mine — no smoking all night, or free talk, or late supper, but long evening prayers, after yawning over a good, dull book, or listening to the damned soliloquy that elderly gentlemen call conversation. No disrespect to the Baron, Henry, or my own worthy father.

Henry   *(Gloomily)* I don't agree with you. If the wild wind could blow me back to Belrive at this minute, I'd rush out into the night — what's that? Hush! Didn't you hear — ? *(He rises and goes to door R., stooping to listen and signing to the other to be quiet)*

Victor   What on earth is the matter?

Henry   Hush! Listen! *(a pause)* It's all right. It was nothing — my imagination. Nothing! *(he paces up and down the room)*

Victor   What is wrong with you, Henry? —You look as nervous and unstrung as a sick girl. Are you ill? Had any bad news? You're over-worked, that's it! *(Goes on smoking complacently)* Classes, lectures, reading, writing, and all the rest of the old grind has been too much for your nerves. I know you're the most promising man of your time and we're all proud of you. Old Professor Kempe calls you the new light of natural science. Dr. Waldman is always dinning your achievements in chemistry into our long-suffering ears. The Principal of the University declares —

Henry   *(impatiently)* Don't talk such nonsense, Victor.

Victor   It's the truth. We all admit it. *(then in a serious tone)* My dear Henry, what is the good of your labours if you half kill yourself? Why do you spend all your days and nights in study? What is your end and aim? Why have you cut yourself adrift from your companions and oldest friends?

Henry   *(Stopping a minute to lay his hand on the other's shoulder)* No, no, not that, Victor.

Victor   Yes, yes, Henry. I never see you. Look here! Has a man in the college crossed your threshold for the past three months?

Frankenstein (1927)

Henry   Yes, Dr. Waldman dined with me recently.

Victor   Dr. Waldman! A book-worm like yourself. A grave, learned man, old enough to be your father. *He's* no companion for Henry Frankenstein.

Henry   He understands me. He's the greatest and kindest man I've ever met.

Victor   (*lightly*) Then why do you welcome such a fellow as me? I'm no pedant — no scientist ——

Henry   (*sitting on the arm of his friend's chair*) Because we've known each other all our lives, Victor. I love you like a brother. I wish — I wish you'd come to see me more often.

Victor   To speak the truth, when I do come you're so absent minded, or so absorbed in your own thoughts, that I only feel in the way. Don't apologize. It was just the same when we were boys at Belrive. You wanted to be an alchemist in those days, studying how to turn base metals into gold, or discover the elixir of life. What fools we are when we're young!

Henry   No, youth is the age of true wisdom.

Victor   Was it true wisdom of you to believe in alchemy, or hunt for the philosopher's stone? No, the wisest step you ever took, my friend, was on the day you gave it up and engaged yourself to our pretty neighbour, Emilie Lavenza.

Henry   (*staring in front of him, sadly*) Yes, that was wise.

Victor   (*inquisitively*) How is the charming Emilie?

Henry   Well — at home.

Victor   Have you seen her lately?

Henry   (*with constraint*) Not for — some months.

Victor   You astonish me. Goldstadt is only a ride from Belrive, and you both love riding.

Henry   I have been absorbed in study. All my time, my thoughts, my energies have been devoted to a certain work. But it is done at last. Victor! I am glad you have come to-night. I am thankful that I sent for you, although I am afraid ——

Victor   (*in surprise*) My dear Henry, why *afraid*?

Henry   Because — because this will be the greatest and the most wonderful night in the whole course of my life — or the most terrible and bitter. To-night

	I shall conquer the world of science, or fall into black despair. To-night I shall triumph, or fail, in the most daring and marvellous experiment ever attempted by mortal man.
Victor	Henry!
Henry	Oh, don't think I'm a madman. Don't be frightened. You know me of old. I've got the courage of the devil.
Victor	A devilish courage when your blood is up.
Henry	Yes, but to-night I must be calm and cool as the Jura hills. I must control myself. I must! I must! *(he paces the room again in agitation)*
Victor	What have you done? What do you mean by all this wild talk?
Henry	Stop with me, Victor, and you shall learn. Don't leave me till I tell you to go. You belong to my old life. *(very affectionately)* You come from my home. Swear you'll stand by me whatever happens.
Victor	Of course I'll stand by you. *(a roll of thunder)* My dear boy, where's this courage of the devil you brag about? You're shaking from head to foot, and your pulse — (**Henry** *drags his hand away*)
Henry	*(wildly)* If *you* had waited, and waited, and longed for to-night as I have done — if *you* knew what was hanging in the balance ——
Victor	Why don't you tell me? *(a knock at the door L.* **Henry** *starts violently, then speaks in a loud voice)*
Henry	Who's there? Who is it?
Waldman	*(outside)* Dr. Waldman.
Henry	*(earnestly, as he hurries to open the door)* Don't leave me, Victor. Come in, Dr. Waldman! *(enter* **Waldman***)* I was afraid you had forgotten your promise.
Waldman	Oh, no, but I was reading in my room upstairs and the hour slipped past. I didn't mean to miss our appointment, Henry. Victor Moritz, is it not?
Victor	Yes, sir. *(they shake hands)*
Henry	Will you sit in the arm chair, doctor? Victor, please lock the door. (**Victor** *does so while* **Henry** *pulls chair forward for* **Waldman***)*
Waldman	What a night of storm! The wind and rain have been fighting for mastery and the wind is beaten. Can we not have a little more light, Henry? Does this mysterious experiment of yours require a dark room and crashes of thunder? *(thunder far away)*

Frankenstein (1927)

Henry	If you like, sir. *(He turns up the lamp making the stage light.* **Waldman** *and* **Victor** *sit by fire,* **Henry** *at table, facing audience)*
Waldman	*(lighting his pipe)* That is more cheerful. *(a pause)* Well, Henry? Your class is seated and admirably attentive.
Henry	Do you remember, sir, supping with me in this room about six months ago? We were all alone.
Waldman	Very well. I'm afraid we talked nearly the whole of the night.
Henry	The sun was rising before I got to sleep. Do you remember all that we said, Dr. Waldman?
Waldman	*(smiling)* No, indeed.
Henry	Not the gist of the talk — the subject?
Waldman	We discussed the origin of life.
Henry	Yes, and the possibility of science, in the far future, being able to discover the secret of creation.
Waldman	*(smiling again)* I recollect leaving that supposition to my junior, Henry. You must forgive the inexperience and modesty of age. *(turns deliberately to* **Victor***)* Have you read Ludenburg's latest treatise, Moritz?
Victor	Not yet, but I have heard ——
Henry	Stay, Victor! *(entreatingly)* Dr. Waldman, I beg you not to attempt to turn me from my purpose. If you disapprove of our former discussion, believe me you will alter your opinion to-night.
Waldman	Our former discussion, my young friend, was futile and fruitless. Wild exaggeration and unsupported tales of marvels have nothing whatever to do with science. Forgive my bluntness. We were both rather foolish on that occasion. Let us forget it. So I wish you'd tell me, Moritz, whether you have heard that Herr Ludenburg's most original treatise is ——
Henry	*(striking the table excitedly)* No, doctor! No! By Heaven, you *shall* hear me.
Waldman	*(resignedly)* Well, well, well! Don't get excited, dear boy.
Henry	*(rapidly)* You know — you both know — how deeply I have devoted myself to natural philosophy, and particularly chemistry, in the most comprehensive sense of the term. But you do *not* know the years that I have spent in deep and occult study of the secrets of life, before and since

	I came to Goldstadt. One question haunted me day and night — one problem I would have given the best years of my life to solve — the secret of the principle of life. I have studied physiology and anatomy, birth and death. I understand the natural growth and decay of the human body. I have long lost all sense of restraint and moderation. I have sought my subjects in the hospital and the grave.
Waldman	*(smiling slightly)* Well, well, well!
Victor	*(to* **Waldman***)* What does he mean by that?
Waldman	*(looking at* **Henry** *as if doubting his reason)* God knows.
Henry	I tell you I have handled the newly dead. I have spent nights and days in vaults and charnel-houses. I have learned the processes of corruption, the secrets of the flesh, but always before my mind — a light in the darkness — I hoped to discover the cause of generation. At last — at last — *(he rises)* when my strength was nearly gone, when I was haggard and worn with labour — when I had tasted the bitter cup of despair — I saw the flaming of the torch! I had found the secret of giving life. The desire and dream of humanity had burst upon me. It was too much for my heart and brain. It was mine! It was mine! *(drops again into his chair and covers his face with his hands, visibly trembling with excitement)*
Victor	My dear Henry! *(wonderingly)*
Waldman	*(sternly)* Tell us your meaning in plain words. Master yourself.
Henry	*(lifting his head slowly)* I — I'm sorry, doctor. I — I — I'm over-worked and unnerved. What a fool I am! Forgive me. Victor, will you get that little bottle and glass from the shelf yonder — thank you. *(***Victor** *brings them.* **Henry** *vainly tries to pour a dose)* This is too absurd! My hand shakes. Victor, pour it out for me — there — *(he indicates the dose,* **Victor** *pours it and* **Henry** *drinks)*
Waldman	*(looking at bottle)* Be careful how you use this drug.
Henry	That is better. I beg your pardon, doctor, for all my wild talk.
Waldman	Let's hear no more of it.
Victor	But Henry was telling us of his discovery, doctor.
Henry	*(eagerly)* Do you believe in me, Victor?
Victor	I — I hardly know what to say.
Henry	Wait till the end. *Wait*, doctor.

Frankenstein (1927)

Waldman	We must follow you step by step. Describe your work in detail.
Henry	That is impossible. I have told you the truth as surely as the sun shines in heaven. I can bestow animation upon lifeless matter.
Waldman	No, no, Henry Frankenstein. You ask too much of our faith in you, my poor friend. No, no, no.
Henry	Hear me out, Dr. Waldman. My ambition, after this great discovery, was to prove its practical truth. I hesitated for a long time. Then I determined to prepare an object — a form — a body — for the vital experiment.
Waldman	*(astounded)* Do you mean a human body?
Henry	Yes. I began to dream of the creation of a being like ourselves, the physical man complete.
Waldman	*(protestingly)* My friend! My friend!
Henry	I set to work. I — *(covers his face for a second)* I can't tell you everything I did. You would think I was a cunning madman. Look! *(holding out his hand)* I'm shaking from head to foot, my mouth is parched, and my head swims at the mere recollection of the awful task. *(in a hoarse whisper)* In a dark cellar beneath the ground I made the Thing I had dreamed of. It was horrible — horrible — but I could not stop. I collected all the gruesome parts from secret haunts of death. I crept, like a murderer, night after night to my frightful labour — *(again overcome, he covers his face with his hands)*
Waldman	*(calmly and emphatically)* And at the end you *failed*.
Henry	No, I succeeded! The Thing is finished. To-night I shall perfect my work and give it life.
Victor	Impossible!
Waldman	Oh, Science! What falsehood is spoken in thy name!
Henry	An hour ago I used my discovery to animate the senseless body — I'll say no more of that, no more! The secret shall live and die with me. *It* is there, locked in my room. *(points to inner door)* Victor, old schoolfellow, will you come with me? We will bring It here. Will you come?
Victor	Yes. What do you want me to do?
Henry	Help me. Doctor, wait for us — *(Exit* **Henry**. **Victor** *is about to follow when he turns and speaks quickly)*
Victor	What do you think, Dr. Waldman? Has Frankenstein gone out of his mind?

Waldman	*(slowly)* God knows what he has done. Go with him. *(Exit* **Victor**. **Waldman** *rises and stands over the fire, looking frowningly towards the door. A flash of lightning, followed by thunder.* **Waldman** *shudders. Re-enter* **Henry** *and* **Victor**, *carrying the in-animate body of* **Frankenstein** *in, with a big, black cloth thrown over it)*
Henry	There — down upon the lounge — steadily, Victor — *(They place him on the lounge, and* **Victor** *straightens his back with an outward breath).*
Victor	A dead weight. Who is this hidden man? *(makes gesture to pull away drapery)*
Henry	Not yet! *(stopping him)*
Victor	How still! I think he must be insensible. What do you say, doctor? *(looking over his shoulder at* **Waldman***)* I do not want to touch him — how cold it seems to be all of a sudden! *(moves away from the lounge)*
Henry	Dr. Waldman may touch him. Doctor, you have heard Victor's question. Tell him the condition of this man — feel his pulse — *(***Henry** *draws the cloth sufficiently on one side to show a shoulder and arm. A pause.* **Waldman** *lifts the limp hand to feel his pulse, puts it down again and stoops for a second over him, listening for breathing. Another pause)*
Waldman	There is no life in this man.
Henry	*(looking from one to the other impressively)* There is no life in this man.
Victor	*(indignantly)* Henry, you have gone too far. It's ghastly. This is a corse. It's horrible.
Henry	No, he is not dead, for he has never lived. You shall look upon the creature I have made with these hands. Draw the cloth from the face, one of you. *(They hesitate)* Victor?
Victor	No — no — I ——
Henry	Then Dr. Waldman! *(A slight pause, then* **Waldman** *pulls aside the cloth enough to show the head and shoulders of* **Frankenstein**. *He is dressed like* **Henry** *in dark, plain clothes, but* **Henry** *wears a high, black stock, and* **F.'s** *shirt is open, showing his throat and a piece of chest. The men's faces express fear mingled with amazement)*
Waldman	*(gaspingly)* My God!
Victor	It is the death mask of a strange, inhuman being. Look, doctor! Look at the great lips and brow! *(gazes confusedly at his friend, then again at* **F.***)*

Frankenstein (1927)

Waldman	*(running his hand down the figure)* This is the physical body of a young, strong man.
Henry	Now you see my accomplished labour.
Waldman	There is no vital force in it.
Henry	*Not yet!* But my secret is at work. The hour of waiting is nearly over. Shall I triumph or shall I fail?
Waldman	I warn you, solemnly, against the sin of vain presumption. From God alone is the breath of life. Be warned!
Henry	You are too late. He lives!
Waldman	No — no —— *(he again takes* **F.**'s *wrist.* **Victor** *and* **Henry** *strain forward. The storm is heard very faintly. The doctor lays down the hand and turns to* **Henry**) You have failed!
Henry	*No!* I have succeeded. Look! (**Henry** *slowly draws drapery off* **F.** *After a slight pause,* **F.** *very slowly clenches and unclenches his hand hanging down at side of lounge. Then stretches his arms over his head and raises himself on one elbow.* **Henry** *utters a wordless exclamation, or groan, but the other men remain speechlessly gazing.* **F.** *stands up, thrusts both hands in front of him, as if groping in the dark, his head sunk on his chest. After a few seconds he lifts his head, in the full light of the lamp, his mouth a little open, eyelids quivering. At last he opens his eyes and stares blankly in front of him.*)

End of Prologue.

FRANKENSTEIN

Act I

The same scene as Prologue. Six months later. A bright summer morning. The curtains drawn away from the centre doors to show a garden flooded with sunshine, arranged to give an impression of distance. The doors closed. Enter **Dr. Waldman** *and* **Baron Frankenstein**, *talking as they come.*

Baron I am glad. to have met you, doctor. Very fortunate. Very fortunate.

Waldman The pleasure is mutual, my dear Baron. (**Waldman** *closes the door L.* **Baron** *holds his hat in his hand. He glances round the room eagerly as he comes in*)

Baron Henry is not here, I see. Perhaps he is in the other room. *(He turns towards the door R.)*

Waldman *(stopping him)* No, your son isn't at home. He is — er — at a lecture, or at one of the professors' classes. It's no use looking for him elsewhere in the house, Baron. *(he speaks hurriedly and with some confusion)*

Baron No matter. No matter. I'll wait for him. Don't let me detain you, doctor.

Waldman You're not detaining me. I've nothing to do.

Baron *(surprised)* Fortunate man! Nothing to do towards the end of term. In my young days it was the students who had nothing to do and the masters who worked. Times have evidently changed for the better. Why doesn't Henry leave his doors open? *(he goes to centre doors and pulls the handles)* What the devil — *(shakes the doors)*

Waldman *(mildly)* No, the bolt — allow me — *(he draws back the bolts top and bottom and throws the doors wide)*

Baron Thanks. That's better. Ugh! It's hot! *(he stands between doors looking out.* **Waldman** *moves away, watching him with a thoughtful expression, perplexed and anxious)* Charming little garden! I drove around the edge of that wood in the distance — *(pointing)* beautiful bit of road, smooth and shady. The prettiest bit of road between Goldstadt and Belrive. *(turns back into the room)* Won't you sit down, Dr. Waldman? *(they sit)* When d' you think my too studious son will return? He doesn't expect me, or I'm sure I should have found him at home.

Waldman Oh, at any minute. Why do you call Henry your "too studious" son? It's a rare fault in a young man, but I'm afraid he's guilty of it.

Baron	No? Well, it's not an inheritance from his father. A good boy, doctor, but weak here — weak — *(tapping his forehead)*
Waldman	Henry? I don't agree with you. *(smiling)*
Baron	Too fond of books and learning. Too serious. Thinks too much. If you want to be happy, doctor, and live to a jolly, gay old age, don't *think*. It's dangerous. Men who think so much, doctor, are generally too long in the legs, lean and grizzly-bearded.
Waldman	*(stroking his own beard)* True, my dear Baron.
Baron	Look at me! *I'm* not a thinking man. *I'm* not profound.
Waldman	No one would ever suspect you of it.
Baron	*(failing to see any sarcasm in the reply)* I hope not, thank God. Now, look at Henry. You know what a fine, amiable looking boy he is ——
Waldman	Ah! *(he leans his head on his hand, tapping his foot softly on the ground)*
Baron	An only son, doctor, with a father who never thwarted him, a mother who adores him, a dear little sister, a beautiful home, and one of the sweetest and best girls in the world waiting to marry him. Is he happy and content? No! He throws it all on one side for the sake of his studies. He's mad on his studies. It's only ten miles to our house — ten miles from door to door — but he hasn't spent a single day with his parents and his sweetheart for six months. Six months! It's a shame, doctor, it's a confounded shame! *(he begins to walk about the room in agitation)*
Waldman	Don't let it trouble you too much, my friend. No doubt, when Henry leaves college —
Baron	Hang college! I wish I'd never let him come to college. There's our neighbour's son, Victor Moritz — *he* hasn't forgotten his family.
Waldman	Victor Moritz has neither the genius nor application of your son.
Baron	I wish my son had the genius for making other people happy and the application to devote himself to his father and mother. Our little Katrine longs for him. There never was a brother half so kind as Henry used to be. She's not like other girls, our little Katrine. She can't run about and play, or dance, or ride, or dream of a sweetheart. She's lame, doctor. *(he speaks very gently and tenderly)* She has always walked with a crutch, a tiny thing, barely to my shoulder.
Waldman	Lame, is she? That's a great affliction for you to bear.

Baron	True, true. But somehow Katrine makes you forget it. She's so happy and content. I'm not a poetical, sentimental man, doctor, but sometimes I think when I look at the child, that she can't belong to us — me and my good wife — although we have watched her grow from a baby to nearly a woman.
Waldman	How do you mean?
Baron	*(very earnestly)* I mean she is a bright and heavenly spirit, innocent, but wise. It seems as if the crutch alone held her to this earth and made her human. Free from that, she would be perfect. Do you smile at a father's fancy?
Waldman	No, no, it is a beautiful thought, Baron.
Baron	Her mother says she couldn't be happy in Heaven itself without Katrine. In this life we both listen for the tap of the little crutch, in the life to come we shall hear the flying footsteps of our child, running to meet us . . . God knows . . . *(he jumps up in a very different mood)* But all this talk has nothing to do with Henry. When did you say his confounded lecture would be over?
Waldman	I am not at all certain. Perhaps it would be better not to wait —
Baron	Not to wait? I haven't driven from Belrive to run back again without him. I've come to take him home, Dr. Waldman.
Waldman	To-day? Now? Impossible!
Baron	Why should it be impossible? Henry is not a prisoner at Goldstadt. *(he laughs a little)* You look positively frightened.
Waldman	*(hurriedly, forcing a smile)* Not at all, but you forget that it is term time and he is hard at work —
Baron	What of that? Have you never heard of a young man playing truant?
Waldman	You will not be able to persuade him to go.
Baron	I don't persuade, doctor. I command.
Waldman	I'm afraid he'll disobey your commands — hush! I think I hear your son's step. *(hastily)* Baron, you must be prepared for a change in Henry. Don't be alarmed, but I expect you'll find — hush! Here he is! *(Enter **Henry L**. He starts violently and stares at his father. There is a marked alteration in his appearance. He is haggard and pale, his dress neglected, his manner anxious and nervous)*

Frankenstein (1927)

Henry	Father!
Baron	My — dear — boy! Why, Henry! My son! *(shocked and surprised)*
Henry	*(glancing from one to the other)* Dr. Waldman! Father!
Baron	Are you pleased to see me, Henry?
Henry	Of course I'm very pleased. I — I was only a little surprised. *(they shake hands cordially. The* **Baron** *lays both hands on his son's shoulders)*
Baron	Why, what's the matter with you, Henry? Have you been ill? You should have told us. My poor boy!
Waldman	*(cheerily)* Oh, he's very well, my dear Baron. Only a little tired — he's quite himself — *(he steps behind* **Henry** *and shakes his head at the* **Baron**, *frowning and touching his lips)*
Baron	*(bewildered)* But he's not quite himself. He looks as if he'd seen a spectre. (**Waldman** *frowns and shakes his head again)* Eh? What? Why the devil are you scowling and wagging your head about at me, Dr. Waldman? What have I said?
Waldman	Nothing. I wasn't scowling at you.
Baron	But you were.
Waldman	Oh, no, you're mistaken. I always frown. It's a bad habit of mine.
Baron	*(softly)* Damned bad habit. What is wrong with you, Henry?·
Henry	*(irritably)* I'm well enough, Father. If I had been ill, of course I should have told you in my letters.
Baron	Your mother will break her heart —
Henry	My dear mother! Sit down, sir. Don't leave us, Dr. Waldman. What a pleasure to see you, Father! What a pleasure to hear your voice and feel your hand. *(he presses his own over it for a minute)* How is my mother? And Katrine? And our good old Elizabeth, and Gustave, and John, and all the others at home? *(They sit.* **Waldman** *strolls to the centre doors and stand there, looking out)*
Baron	Your mother is well, but Katrine misses you sadly. We believe she cries about it, although she never lets us see her tears.
Henry	Poor little Katrine!
Baron	She keeps all your letters and reads them over and over again. She has not been out in her little boat since you left home. I would gladly take her, but

	it's — "No, Father, I'll wait for Henry." She talks to her tame doves about her brother Henry. It's Henry, Henry all the time.
Henry	Go on, Father! I love to hear your voice. It is like a strain of familiar music. *(he sighs and leans back in his chair)*
Baron	*(drily)* Well, the music has been waiting for you patiently, although our good friend yonder wanted me to go away before you came home from your lecture. ·
Henry	I haven't been to any lecture this morning. ·
Baron	No?
Henry	No, I was — I was — in my bedroom overhead, reading.
Baron	Dr. Waldman assured me you were not in the house. Doctor! If you had let me go to Henry's other room above stairs I should have found him at once.
Waldman	I'm sorry, but I thought — it would disturb —
Henry	*(returning* **Waldman's** *expressive glance)* He was right, Father. You would have wakened me from a most refreshing sleep.
Baron	Sleep? Why, you said just now you had been reading.
Henry	*(embarrassed)* Did I? At all events, *(turning to* **Dr. W.***) you* know I mustn't be disturbed when I am reading, — *reading*, doctor.
Baron	Why, the boy's caught the bad habit of frowning and wagging his head. You both of you look so solemn and mysterious. No wonder, reading and sleeping all day! What is the latest study, Henry?
Henry	Hang the latest study! Tell me the news of Belrive. Talk to me of my mother and little Katrine.
Baron	And somebody else, Henry? You haven't asked a single question about Emilie Lavenza.
Henry	*(rising hastily)* Father, don't speak to me of her.
Baron	*(also rising)* What is the trouble, Henry? Can't you tell me the truth? Have you ceased to care for Emilie? Do you still love her?
Henry	*(passionately)* Do I love her? Emilie! Emilie!
Baron	You do? Then you have a strange way of showing your love. Mark my words, the most unselfish and constant of women will not take a man's love on trust if he never shows it. If she were your wife —

Frankenstein (1927)

Henry	*(interrupting in the same passionate manner)* I would to God she were my wife. She could save me. *(turning fiercely on the* **Baron***)* Why do you come here to torture me? Why do you talk of home and all the peace and happiness I have thrown away? Why do you tell me that I'm unworthy of Emilie Lavenza? Who knows the truth better than I? Father, I'm on the rack! Spare me —
Waldman	*(stepping between them and speaking sternly)* Henry! Henry! Control yourself. Be calm. *(then consolingly)* My dear Baron, you mustn't be alarmed. My young friend is over-wrought — words, words, words!
Henry	*(miserably)* Oh, doctor, this useless, eternal balm of yours on an open wound.
Waldman	*(ignoring him and continuing to the* **Baron***)* Now, if you'll only take my advice and leave me alone with Henry — my dear sir — pray hear me out. I know that I can do him good. Be persuaded. Be reasonable.
Baron	*(hotly)* I'm reasonable enough —
Waldman	Yes, yes, yes, but if you'll only leave me alone with Henry for ten minutes — five minutes — where are your carriage and horses?
Baron	In the stable of old Pastor Clerval, ready for Henry and me to drive back to Belrive.
Henry	I cannot come —
Baron	*(angrily)* You must!
Henry	Father, it is absolutely impossible! *(Played very quickly from this speech to the* **Baron's** *exit)*
Baron	You refuse, in spite of my command?
Henry	I refuse.
Waldman	Henry, let me speak to you alone.
Henry	Doctor, it's no use!
Baron	You have no respect for my wishes. You are deaf to your mother's prayers. But don't be mistaken, Henry — *(stepping close to him)* — I *will* know the reason before I go. Dr. Waldman, talk to the headstrong young fool. Teach him his duty if you can.
Waldman	*(almost pushing* **Baron** *out of the door)* Yes, I will, my dear Baron, but in the meantime —

Baron	In the meantime I'll wait for you at the Pastor's house, Henry. Come to me soon, or by Heaven I'll return here and drag you home. Good-bye, Dr. Waldman.
Waldman	Let me have the pleasure of showing you the way, Baron.
Baron	Pleasure! Pleasure! You seem to want the pleasure of kicking me out — (*Exit, talking,* **Waldman** *mildly and the* **Baron** *angrily.* **Henry** *sinks into a chair and buries his face in his hands. After a few seconds re-enter* **Waldman**. *He lays his hand on* **Henry's** *shoulder.* **Henry** *starts and raises his head.*)
Waldman	Come! Come! Why did you betray yourself to your father?
Henry	(*miserably and vaguely*) Why, what did I say?
Waldman	You were nervous, angry, unnatural. You must be more careful —
Henry	(*quickly*) Ah! What's that? There's a hand on the door. Who is it? (*a tap at door L.*)
Waldman	Quiet! Who is there?
Victor	(*outside*) May I come in? Victor Moritz.
Henry	It's Victor. Come in, Victor! (*Enter* **Victor**)
Victor	(*taking off his hat to* **Waldman**) Good morning, Dr. Waldman. How are you, Henry? (*They shake hands*)
Henry	Alive, Victor. (**Henry** *stares in front of him unhappily. The others exchange a troubled glance. A pause.* **Waldman** *draws a chair close to* **Henry**. **Victor** *leans against the table*)
Waldman	(*softly*) Where is — he? (**Henry** *points to door R.*) Alone? (**Henry** *nods*)
Victor	I saw, as I approached the house, that the shutters are closed. Is — he in semi-darkness?
Henry	Yes.
Waldman	You kept him all the winter months in the laboratory underground. But since you brought him to your rooms, a week ago, surely he has seen the sunlight?
Henry	Only through the cracks of the shutters. I forbade him to touch them.
Victor	Does he obey you?
Henry	(*contemptuously*) Does a frightened slave obey? Does a beaten hound obey?

Frankenstein (1927)

Victor   But he is as strong as yourself.

Waldman   How have you mastered him?

Henry   Don't ask me, doctor. It is better not to know.

Victor   But he is your equal in height and —

Henry   (*rising, angrily*) Victor, Victor! What is strength of muscle and sinew compared to the cunning of the brain? What is the courage of a wild beast compared to the cruelty of man?

Victor   (*recoiling a little*) Have you tortured him?

Henry   (*opening and then clenching his out-stretched hand*) Is he not *mine — mine*?

Waldman   Can he speak?

Henry   Yes. I have taught him, day after day, night after night. He is never out of my thoughts. When I fall asleep, from sheer exhaustion, I meet him in dreams of horror. (*he sits down again in his old attitude of despair*)

Waldman   Can he learn from your teaching? Does he understand?

Henry   As a child understands, but now and again there is a flash of deeper thought across his narrow mind. He is elemental, unconscious of his own strength, a brute — a brute! You have both seen him and he remembers you.

Victor   I can't bear to look at him. He is strangely like yourself in gesture and movement — in his great hands, his face, his body, but a sullen devil looks at me out of his eyes.

Henry   (*with a groan*) Spare me, Victor!

Victor   (*with greater earnestness*) No one can see him. Your father, above all, must never see him. You must follow the Baron to Pastor Clerval's house and induce him to go back to Belrive at once.

Henry   How can I do that? You know how obstinate he is. He will not leave without me, and how can I promise to go home?

Waldman   But he *must not* come here again — (*Loud knock or blow, on door R.*) What is that?

Henry   Ah! It is Frankenstein.

Waldman   (*in surprise*) Frankenstein?

Peggy Webling and the Story behind Frankenstein

Henry I call him by my own name. He *is* Frankenstein. *(Knock repeated)*

Victor What does he want?

Henry He wants to come in here. He has never seen the sun shine as it does today.

Waldman Let him come in.

Henry Are you not afraid?

Waldman No, no.

Victor We are two strong men.

Henry *(warningly as he goes towards door R.)* Remember, we must keep him beneath our feet. *(he unlocks the door R.* **Waldman** *and* **Victor** *retire to back of stage watching)* Frankenstein! *(A pause)* **(Henry** *speaks again in harsh, commanding tones)* Frankenstein! Come here, I say! Frankenstein! *(Enter* **Frankenstein** *slowly. He is in dark, loose clothes, with his shirt open at the neck. He is bending forward, slightly stumbling, instinctively shielding his eyes from the light with his hands. As he comes into the full light of sunlight he suddenly crouches on the floor, frightened.)*

Victor *(whispering)* Look at him, doctor! He moves like a half blind animal.

Waldman Hush! **(Henry** *sits, looking at* **F.** *with frowning severity.* **Waldman** *and* **Victor** *move to the other side of the table, farther away.* **F.** *makes an uncouth sound of fear, hiding his face)*

F. Burn! Burn! Fire! *(springs to* **Henry** *and tries to cling to him.* **Henry** *spurns him away.* **F.** *points to window)* Fire!

Henry Yes, but a good fire — a bright, grand fire. Go! *(Threatens to strike him.* **F.** *moves towards the centre doors, frequently looking over his shoulder fearfully at* **Henry**. *At first he bends forward, gazing up into the sky, then slowly stretches out his hands and rubs them in the hot rays, rears himself to his full height, arms lifted over his head, and stands amazed at the brilliance.)*

Waldman *(as if the words were forced out of him)* Man — devil — what are you?

F. *(with a long drawn breath)* Oh — great fire! *(he takes a step forward and lays his hands on the glass doors, staring out into the garden, then pulls his shirt open so that the heat falls on his breast)* Great — soft — fire! *(Another pause, then he suddenly lies down and curls himself up like a dog.)*

Henry *(sharply)* Frankenstein! **(F.** *does not move)* Frankenstein! **(F.** *stretches himself at full length to be more comfortable.* **Henry** *advances and stirs him*

	with his foot) Frankenstein! *(F. pulls himself into a kneeling position and lays his face down on **Henry's** foot. Then he looks up at him humbly)*
F.	You are — my master!
Henry	Frankenstein, look out of the windows. That is my garden. Say it after me. Garden.
F.	*(in an expressionless tone)* Garden.
Waldman	Those are trees, and flowers and a blue heaven over all.
F.	Heaven — over — all.
Henry	That is the sky, and the great fire is called the sun.
F.	*(quite bewildered)* The sky — the sun — the sun — *(He looks out for a while, then lies down again muttering)* The great fire — the sun — the sun — *(begins to fall asleep)*
Henry	Wake up! Come here and kneel beside me — farther off — your touch is repulsive — *(**F.** kneels at a little distance)* Frankenstein, what is this? *(puts out his hand)*
F.	*(very slowly)* Your hand.
Henry	*(points to **F.**'s hand)* And this?
F.	My — hand.
Henry	What is your name?
F.	Frankenstein.
Henry	Do you remember my name? *(**F.** stares at him dumbly)* What *am* I?
F.	Man. *(mutters the word to himself several times)* Man — man. Master — man. Frankenstein — man. *(Gives it up and points to centre doors)* I want — the sun.
Henry	No, you mustn't go into the sun now. You must stop here beside me. Now, listen. Look at me. Look me in the eyes! *(at first **F.** shrinks almost to the ground and then obeys him)* Tell me your thoughts.
F.	My — thoughts.
Henry	What do you think of me — of us — of this other man? *(**Victor** comes a little nearer)*
F.	*(Looking at them fixedly in turn)* You are — big — big — you are — you are — like each other, but I — *(stops helplessly)*

Peggy Webling and the Story behind Frankenstein

Henry Well, go on. What else do you want to say?

F. Are there men like — like — Frankenstein? *(indicating himself)*

Henry No. *(Spoken together)*

Victor Oh, no.

F. *(repeating in the same tone)* No. Oh, no! Then — then — *(he clenches both hands beneath his chin, trying to think)*

Henry What now? (**Victor** *makes an impatient movement*)

Waldman Silence, Victor!

Henry What now, Frankenstein?

F. Why — why — why are there no men — like me?

Henry I can't tell you. You wouldn't understand.

F. *(To* **Victor***)* Are you — like my master? Do you — do you *(he clenches his hand and lifts it and frowns darkly)*

Victor Does your master hate you?

F. Yes. Hate — hate — what does that mean?

Henry How can I answer? *(Rising and speaking to* **Waldman***)*

Waldman It is impossible for him to understand. What can you say?

Henry I don't know, doctor. I don't know! *(He sits on the lounge in an attitude of dejection.* **Waldman** *stands pondering.* **Victor** *watches* **F.***, who slowly creeps towards* **Henry** *and points to his eyes)*

F. What is that? Your eyes are wet. (**Henry** *rises with an angry sound and goes to centre doors with* **Victor***.* **F.** *touches his own eyes and looks at his hand. Sits on lounge in* **Henry's** *favourite position, bending forward with his hands clasped between his knees.)* All men — hate me. Hate Frankenstein — hurt Frankenstein —*(Suddenly yawns, stretches himself and lies down on the lounge to sleep, muttering incoherently.* **Henry** *returns and stands over him. He slowly stoops and holds his hands over* **F.'s** *throat)*

Waldman *(quickly and softly)* Henry, what are you doing?

Henry *(In an equally low tone)* It would be no sin — no sin — but have I the strength? *(Clasps* **F.'s** *throat, as if to strangle him.* **Waldman** *and* **Victor** *start forward.)*

Frankenstein (1927)

Waldman Henry — (**F.** *opens his eyes at the touch and stares at him.* **Henry** *tightens the clutch.* **F.** *gives a guttural gasp, instinctively catches* **Henry's** *wrists, and there is a second's struggle. Then* **F.** *throws* **Henry** *off. The latter reels back a few steps.* **F.** *stares at him wonderingly*)

Henry Keep off! His hands are like steel, Dr. Waldman. I think that he would kill —

F. (*interrupting quickly*) Kill? Kill! (*then in his usual slow way*) What does that mean? (*he repeats his gesture of throwing* **Henry** *off*)

Henry (*angrily*) Frankenstein, why did you throw me off? Dog! How dare you touch me!

F. (*stretching out his arms, clenching and unclenching his fists*) I — threw you off! (*passes his hands with great swiftness down* **Henry's** *arms from his shoulders*) A man — tall — strong — (*he suddenly realizes his own size*) Frankenstein is tall — strong — (*he stands quite erect*)

Henry (*fiercely*) Down! Crouch upon the ground — or I will make you — (**F.** *crouches, but unwillingly, and covers his mouth with his hands*)

F. No! No!

Henry Then lay your face upon my foot — don't touch my hand — (**F.** *obeys him, but not so cringingly as he did before*)

F. (*pointing to the garden*) Let me go — out there. (**Henry** *turns away*)

Waldman Not now, Frankenstein. You shall go into the garden when the Sun sets.

F. The sun sets.

Waldman When the great fire in the sky is burnt out. To-night.

F. To-night?

Waldman Yes, before we go to sleep.

F. I want to go there — now. *Now!* There is — there is — (*pleadingly*) Tell me.

Waldman There is beauty in the garden.

F. Is that — the word? Beauty. Beauty.

Waldman Yes, the fresh grass, the wind, the flowers.

F. (*spreading his arms wide*) All — beautiful. All —

Henry	Hush! What's that? *(a knock at the door L.)* Stand back! (**Henry** *lays a hand on* **F.**'s *arm and signals to* **Victor** *to open door*)
Henry	See who it is, Victor. (**Victor** *opens the door a little*)
Victor	Good heavens! It is — *(he goes out, nearly closing door behind him)*
Henry	Be silent, Frankenstein! Stand still.
F.	What — is — it? *(Re-enter* **Victor***, closes door and looks in an agitated way at* **Henry** *and* **Waldman***, still grasping the handle)*
Victor	*(softly)* Henry! Doctor! It's Emilie Lavenza! She has ridden over from Belrive to see Henry. The door was open and she came into the house. What shall we do? (**Henry** *is astounded*)
Waldman	We must send her to find the Baron — no, stay! Let me think — let me think — *(a second's pause)*
Henry	I know! Yes! Frankenstein, go you into the other room and stop there. Do you understand? At once — on the instant! Go!
F.	*(cowering and pointing to door L.)* Who is — there?
Henry	*(stamping)* Go, I say! (**Waldman** *opens door R.* **F.** *exits quickly, scowling darkly over his shoulder at the men.* **Waldman** *closes door and locks it.*)
Waldman	Now, Henry — Victor! (**Victor** *opens the other door. Enter* **Emilie Lavenza***. She stops short, staring at* **Henry***. She is a handsome, bright, high-spirited girl of about twenty-three, wearing a riding costume and hat. Her manners are frank and unaffected)*
Victor	*(hastily)* This is one of our professors, Emilie. Allow me to present Dr. Waldman — Miss Lavenza.
Waldman	I have heard so much of Miss Lavenza that I seem to know her already.
Emilie	*(offering her hand in an abstracted way)* I am pleased to meet you, Dr. Waldman. I have come to see Henry.
Henry	Yes, I am here.
Emilie	I knew the Baron was driving into Goldstadt to-day. Was it very bold of me to follow him on horseback, doctor? We are all distressed over Henry's long absence from home, especially his mother and little sister Katrine.
Waldman	It was kind and good of you, Miss Lavenza, but at the same time — *(she does not heed him)*

Frankenstein (1927)

Emilie	*(almost inaudibly)* Is this really Henry!
Waldman	Moritz and I will leave you together. *(then very seriously, in a fatherly way to* **Emilie***)* Miss Lavenza, let me entreat you, as an old and true friend of Henry's, to forgive him for his seeming neglect. There is a reason for it that even you would not be able to understand. Trust him and believe him. Henry! *(in a lower voice)* Do not forget the man in your other room. Be careful!
Victor	*(expressively to* **Henry***)* If you want us we shall be near at hand. Good-bye! *(he bows to* **Emilie***)*
Waldman	Come, Moritz! *(Exit* **Waldman** *and* **Victor**. **Henry** *closes the door after them. He then turns and faces* **Emilie**. *They look at each other eagerly and curiously, as people do after separation.)*
Emilie	Oh, how changed! *(in a pained voice)*
Henry	Oh, how unchanged! *(he goes towards her with out-stretched hands)*
Emilie	Are you glad to see me?
Henry	Glad? Glad? *(He seizes her hands and presses them passionately to his lips and then tries to clasp her in his arms. She steps back quickly)*
Emilie	No, no, Henry —
Henry	*(still trying to embrace her)* Oh, why not? My darling! My love! My darling!
Emilie	*(as she goes into his arms)* Oh, if you must — you must —
Henry	*(incoherently as he kisses her)* I have you again — you, you! I've waited for this for months — sweetest — dearest —
Emilie	*(gently pressing his face away and looking pityingly into it)* My poor Henry! How pale and worn and old you look. An old man! I was not prepared for this. What *can* have happened to you? Now, let me go. Dear, let me go! *(he releases her. She sits down and he kneels beside her holding her hand)* Why have you deserted us all for so long? If I were not the most forgiving and faithful creature in the world I should never speak to you again. I thought you loved me.
Henry	*(again kissing her hand)* I do! I do!
Emilie	Then why haven't you been to see me, or written to me?
Henry	I have written.

Emilie	*(firmly withdrawing her hands)* Twice in six months, empty, formal notes. Who cares for a letter invented with obvious effort and constraint? Take them back! It would be better if you had not written at all. *(takes two letters out of her pocket and tosses them on the table.)*
Henry	If you only knew!
Emilie	If I only knew — what? You have mystified your father and mother. Although you ignore all their affection and authority, perhaps *I* shall not plead in vain. *(with winning tenderness, lightly twining her arm round his neck)* Dearest, what is your secret? Why are you so changed and unhappy? Won't you tell me? Can't you trust me?
Henry	Trust you, Emilie? Against the world!
Emilie	Then tell me, or come back to Belrive with your father and me.
Henry	My father is now on his way home, I hope.
Emilie	Let us ride after him together, you and I.
Henry	*(with an effort)* It is impossible for me to leave Goldstadt to-day.
Emilie	*(coaxingly)* To-morrow then? Promise me to come back to us to-morrow.
Henry	*(drearily)* No, no, no.
Emilie	*(with great tenderness)* Yes, yes, yes! Promise me!
Henry	*(rising and moving away)* I am a phantom-haunted man. *(desperately)* Do you think I would refuse you if I dared to promise? But I'm afraid — *(looking about him wildly)*
Emilie	*(also rising)* Phantom-haunted? Afraid? Of what are you afraid? The very air of this room is full of mystery. You look distraught. You are different from the man I loved. I feel as if I couldn't breathe here — *(faintly)* Open the doors wide, Henry. Give me a little air! (**Emilie** *stands against the door-post. He watches her wretchedly)* Ah, how sweet and refreshing! It gives me new life to feel the wind. *(she takes off her hat and pushes her hair back from her forehead. Looks at him again, smiling a little)* Oh, Henry, I'm afraid we've been much too serious with each other. Don't let us talk of phantoms and misery and cruel letters. I'll forget them. *(points to letters on table)*
Henry	Emilie, if you knew —
Emilie	Well? You said that before. "Emilie, if you knew!" But you refuse to tell me anything. Never mind! *(fondly)* You shall tell me all about this mystery of yours when we are at Belrive. Then my love will teach you to forget it.

Frankenstein (1927)

Henry	I can never forget it.
Emilie	*(taking his hand for a minute)* Henry, what is it? Let me try to guess. Where shall I find the clue? In this room? *(drops his hand looking curiously round)* Do you study here — work here?
Henry	Not very often.
Emilie	Where then?
Henry	In my laboratory.
Emilie	*(pointing to door R.)* Is that your laboratory?
Henry	*(very emphatically, stepping forward so as to prevent her going to the door)* No, not there.
Emilie	*(gaily)* Another mystery! Who is the man Dr. Waldman whispered was in that room?
Henry	Did you hear that?
Emilie	Yes, and why did he say "Be careful"? *(sudden, loud knock on door R. They both start)* What's that?
Henry	Nothing — nothing.
Emilie	Nothing? *(knock repeated)* There is it again. *(with sudden suspicion)* Who is the man concealed in that room? Henry, who is it?
Henry	Don't be frightened. I will speak to him. I'll make him be quiet. Stand away from the door — farther! *(he gently pushes her towards the other side of the room)*
Emilie	Why, your hand shakes! You are so pale! *(fearfully)* Let me see the hidden man.
Henry	No, no! I'll speak to him. (**Henry** *goes to door R., opens it and speaks in a harsh voice)* Be silent! Stand back! Stand back, I say! *(then in agitation)* No, you can't come here. Stop where you are — hands off, Frankenstein! (**Henry** *disappears for a minute into inner room)*
Emilie	Frankenstein! *(all to be played very quickly, with increasing excitement. Re-enter* **Henry**, *struggling with* **F.***)* Henry! Henry! What are you doing? Oh, Heaven! — (**F.** *throws off* **Henry's** *hands with violence and sees* **Emilie** *for the first time. She stares at him, gives a shriek, and rushes away through the centre doors.)*
F.	Who was — that? Went out — ran — I will follow —

Henry	*(wildly)* No! No! Waldman! Victor! *(as he shouts these words,* **Henry** *goes to centre doors, closes, bolts and stands with his back against them)* Victor! *(enter* **Waldman** *and* **Victor** *quickly)*
F.	I will follow — let me go! *(pleadingly)*
Henry	Stop him for God's sake!
F.	*(pointing out)* Who — was that?
Victor	Emilie Lavenza — a woman?
F.	Was that — a woman? I will follow — *(approaches* **Henry** *menacingly)*
Henry	Stand back, you brute! You thing without a soul! You shall not follow her — stand back!
F.	Let me go —
Henry	Curse you to Hell — no! **(Henry** *strikes at* F., *but* F. *catches his hand and holds it.* **Waldman** *and* **Victor** *spring forward, but* F. *breaks away from them all)*
F.	I *will go — the woman —* (*he thrusts* **Henry** *on one side, rears himself to his full height, looking brutal and fierce, then stoops forward, smashes open the doors with one blow and exits. The others look after him in fear and horror.)*

End of Act I.

FRANKENSTEIN

Act II

*Later in the same day. A room on the first floor of the **Baron's** house at Belrive. A homely, comfortable room, with porcelain stove (not lighted), book-cases, flowers, easy chairs, tables, etc. A big casement window R, through which the afternoon sun is warmly glowing, showing a clear, blue sky. A small slit of a door R. Another L. A wicker cage, on a stool, near window. This must contain two real and one artificial doves, the last named concealed from view. Whenever **Katrine** passes the cage she stoops to look at the birds, or softly coo to them. The **Baroness**, a plainly dressed, serene type of middle-aged woman, is discovered, sewing. **Katrine** sits near to the window, also sewing. She stops working, leans one elbow on the sill and looks out dreamily. She is lame. Her crutch is leaning against the wall beside her. **Katrine** is very slight and short, about fifteen years old, pale, with flaxen hair. She is appealing and sweet in expression, her whole appearance being spiritual and unconsciously pathetic.*

Baroness   Katrine, lean out the window. Do you see any sign of your father coming?

Katrine   *(Pulls herself up and looks out)* No, dear Mother. No. There is not a single carriage in sight on the road by the river.

Baroness   I do hope our Henry will return with him.

Katrine   *(clasping her hands ecstatically and speaking as if her brother stood before her)* Dear Henry, do come home to us! Your books are here and a quiet room. Your boat is asleep on the water, with her sails furled like a bird's wings. The garden waits for you. The house is empty without you. Henry do come home!

Baroness   *(smiling at her)* To whom are you talking, sweetheart? Your brother can't hear you.

Katrine   *(whimsically)* Not with his ears, Mother, but with his spirit.

Baroness   He is very unkind to keep away from his good little sister for so long.

Katrine   *(leaving the window to press her face lovingly against the **Baroness's** cheek)* It's harder for you than for me, harder for Father, and much, much harder for Emilie. Think, Mother! Henry hasn't seen my two birds! *(stoops to cage)* Coo, coo, you pretty doves! Coo, coo! *(leans on sill again)* Mother! I think I see — is that? — *(pause)* Yes! It's Emilie Lavenza, galloping along the river road.

Baroness   Is it Emilie — alone?

Katrine	Yes. She sees me and waves her hand. Emilie! Emilie! *(signals out of the window)* She is coming nearer. Emilie! Our John has run out and is taking her horse.
Baroness	Why should Emilie be galloping along the river road?
Katrine	Perhaps she has been to Goldstadt to see Henry. She knew that Father was going there to-day — ah! here she is! *(Enter **Emilie Lavenza** L. She looks pale and agitated. The **Baroness** rises and advances quickly)*
Baroness	My dear Emilie!
Emilie	Baroness! I am so over-joyed to see you! I'm so thankful to be here. *(She and the **Baroness** kiss affectionately)*
Katrine	Why — Emilie — dear! *(looking at her anxiously)*
Emilie	Little Katrine! *(kisses **Katrine**)*
Katrine	How ill you look! What has happened to you? Are you frightened? What have you seen?
Emilie	Frightened? What have I *seen*? Nothing, nothing.
Baroness	Have you been to Goldstadt, my dear?
Emilie	Yes. How did you know that?
Baroness	Katrine suspected it. Where is the Baron?
Emilie	I don't know. I haven't seen him.
Katrine	*(drawing her by one hand towards a chair)* Sit down, Emilie dear.
Emilie	*(as she drops into the chair)* Thank you. *(takes off her hat)*
Baroness	Where is Henry?
Emilie	Henry? I — I — I'm afraid Henry is — *(she stops in confusion)*
Katrine	Not ill, dear? Is he ill?
Emilie	No, no. He was well and I spoke to him, but he is greatly changed. He refused to come home with me. I — I hardly know how to tell you what happened. *(**Katrine** draws a stool beside **Emilie's** chair and takes her hand. The **Baroness** bends eagerly forward)* We were talking together, in his room, when suddenly there was a loud blow on the door leading to his inner room. A man was hidden there. He was locked in, for I saw Henry turn the key. Dr. Waldman had warned him to be careful with this man. I heard the words myself.

Frankenstein (1927)

Baroness   Who was it?

Emilie   I can't tell you. Henry opened the door and called out to him, "Stand back! Hands off, Frankenstein!" He spoke to the strange man as Frankenstein.

Baroness   His own name!

Emilie   Yes, and there was a scuffle and they came into the room together. I looked at the strange man and I was frightened — intensely frightened. He looked at me — stared at me — and I was filled with horror.

Baroness   Emilie!

Emilie   I felt as if I were looking on a creature without a soul — a brute-beast in the body of a man. I rushed away. My instinct was to fly — anywhere, anyhow — so I mounted my horse and put him at a gallop. I think I galloped all the way from Goldstadt to Belrive. I should have gone home, but your house was nearer than ours — Baroness! Katrine! *(appealingly)* Let me stop here for a little while. I can't go out alone. I'm afraid — I'm afraid — *(She hides her face, almost crying.)*

Baroness   Of course you shall stop as long as you please, my dear child.

Katrine   *(pressing her cheek to one of* **Emilie's** *hands)* Stop with *me*. Dear one! Dear one!

Emilie   Yes, I am sure that with you — *(As she says this there is a sound of voices below the window and clatter of horses' hoofs)* Ah! That must be your father. *(she goes to window)* Yes, it is the Baron and several other men. Why, there is Henry!

Katrine   *(joyously)* Henry! *(she hurries to window)* Father! Henry at last!

Baron   *(outside)* John! Max! hillo there!

Emilie   I can't meet Henry just yet — *I can't!* Let me go upstairs to your little sitting room, Katrine. Pray let me go. Come with me!

Baroness   *(drawing* **Emilie's** *hand through her arm)* You're still trembling. *(To* **Katrine***, as they go towards door)* Meet your father, sweetheart. Send Henry to us by-and-bye — soon. Come, Emilie! *(Exit* **Baroness** *and* **Emilie** *R.* **Katrine** *picks up her crutch and goes as quickly as she can towards door L. It opens as she draws near. Enter* **Baron***, talking fussily as he comes, with* **Henry***,* **Waldman***, and* **Victor***)*

Baron   Where are you, Baroness? Ah, little Katrine! *(kisses her)* Where's your mother? Did you hear me shouting for John and Max? No promptitude! No preparation! No civility!

Peggy Webling and the Story behind Frankenstein

Katrine Henry!

Henry Little Katrine! *(eagerly)* Has Emilie returned to Belrive?

Katrine Yes.

Henry Thank God! Dear Katrine! *(they embrace affectionately)* Dr. Waldman, this is my sister Katrine. (**Waldman** *takes her hand and kisses it*)

Katrine *(smilingly)* Dr. Waldman! I'm glad to see you, Victor.

Victor And I to see you, Katrine.

Katrine So you came home with Father after all, Henry? Poor, tired Henry! *(she reaches up her hand to smooth his cheek)*

Henry Have you missed me so much, little Katrine?

Baron *(throwing down his hat and gloves)* Where is your mother? Sit down, Dr. Waldman.

Henry Where is Emilie?

Katrine She is in my little sitting-room, with Mother. She wants to see you by-and-bye.

Henry Is she well? Is she quite safe, Katrine?

Katrine Of course she is quite safe, dear Henry.

Henry I'm glad. I'm thankful. (**Henry** *goes to the window and stands still, looking anxiously out. The* **Baron** *and* **Katrine** *exchange a troubled glance*)

Baron What's the matter with you, my son. Come and sit down. You're at home. You've escaped from your prison at Goldstadt.

Henry Prison indeed!

Baron We'll have a glass of wine after our drive. Katrine, open the door, my little heart, and call to Elizabeth to bring us a bottle here and some glasses, for our visitors, and your brother and me.

Victor I'll tell her, Katrine.

Katrine Thank you, Victor. (**Victor** *starts for door*)

Baron *(stopping him)* No, it is not your place. Come, Henry, fetch the wine, or call to Elizabeth. Pull up a chair. Don't stare out of that window.

Henry *(ignoring his father)* Can I go up to your little room, Katrine? Shall I find Emilie there?

Katrine	Yes, with Mother.
Henry	I must speak with Emilie alone. I'll greet my dear mother and ask her to leave us.
Baron	Oh, these moony, abstracted lovers! Won't you have a glass of wine before you go, Henry? *(Enter* **Elizabeth***, carrying a tray)* Why, Elizabeth, you must be a good fairy to appear just when we wanted you. Set it down. Set it down. Now, Henry ——
Henry	No, Father. Excuse me, Dr. Waldman. Katrine, take me to Emilie.
Katrine	*(as they go towards door R.)* You wish to be alone with her.
Henry	After a little while. I want her to see me first hand in hand with you. *(he puts out his hand, she takes it. Exit* **Henry** *and* **Katrine** *R.)*
Baron	Well, well, all the more wine for us. Doctor, let me fill your glass.
Waldman	*(as he does so)* Thank you, Baron. Enough — enough —
Baron	*(to* **Victor***)* Now, my boy, and don't you say, "Enough — enough — !" You needn't wait, Elizabeth.
Elizabeth	There is a man at the door who is asking for you, Baron.
Baron	*(putting down his glass after drinking)* Who is it?
Elizabeth	*(in a puzzled tone, glancing over her shoulder)* I don't know. All he said was "Master — Master!"
Waldman	*(with a quick look at* **Victor***)* What is he like?
Elizabeth	*(again glancing over her shoulder)* I don't know. His hair is blown over his face. He is very tall, and big, and — strange.
Waldman	I know who it is.
Baron	*(in surprise)* Do you?
Waldman	Yes, Victor Moritz and I know this man.
Elizabeth	*(in an agitated manner)* Oh, I hear him on the stairs. He has followed me.
Waldman	*(quickly to* **Baron***)* This man is a friend of Henry's. He is rough and uncouth, but — here he is! *(***F.** *appears at door L. He is bare-headed, his hair straggling over his face, his clothes and boots flecked with dust. He stands on the threshold staring at the other men. After a second he takes a step forward, thus enabling* **Elizabeth** *to pass behind him and exit.)*

Peggy Webling and the Story behind Frankenstein

Baron   Good Heavens!

F.   Are you — angry with me?

Waldman   Be silent. Do as I tell you. Come farther into the room.

F.   *(gazing round)* Strange — place. *(revolves slowly then points to* **Baron***)* What is that? Is it — a man?

Baron   *(half angrily)* Do you think I'm a horse?

F.   I — don't know. Are you — a horse?

Baron   Upon my word.

F.   Why are you — you — *(indicates his hair)* all white, and all — all red — *(indicates his face)* and all — round — big — *(indicates his size)*

Baron   You're not very civil, my young friend.

F.   Civil? *(ponders)* I — don't know what you mean. Let me — look at you — turn — turn — *(suddenly lays his hands on* **Baron's** *shoulders and twists him round)*

Baron   *(indignantly)* How dare you!

F.   You are — you are — fat — round — he — *(points to* **Waldman***)* is long — long — long — so — so — *(he mimics, first the* **Baron**, *then* **Waldman**.*)*

Waldman   Be silent! Pardon him, my dear Baron.

F.   Where — is — the woman?

Waldman   Hush!

Victor   You will never see her again.

F.   *(more vaguely than usual)* Never — never — what does that mean?

Baron   You haven't told me this young man's name, Dr. Waldman.

Waldman   His name? It is — *(he is embarrassed, glancing at* **Victor***)* It is —

Baron   Yes? What is your name, sir? *(To* **F.***)*

F.   My name? Frankenstein.

Baron   What? Our name? Frankenstein? Does he claim to be one of the same family?

Waldman   No, no.

Frankenstein (1927)

Baron *(To* **F.***)* Where were you born?

F. I do — not know.

Baron You don't know? Who were your father and mother?

F. I do — not know.

Baron: How old are you? (**F.** *looks blank.* **Baron** *speaks with laboured distinctness*) How long is it since you first saw the light?

F. The light? *(points to window)* Yesterday.

Baron *(to* **Waldman***)* Poor idiot! Well, young Frankenstein, will you drink a glass of wine? Sit down.

Waldman Sit down beside me, Frankenstein. *(He obeys, staring at* **Baron.** *They all drink.* **F.** *tastes his and instantly withdraws glass from his lips with an exclamation of dislike)*

Baron *(incredulously)* You don't care for this?

F. No! *(coolly hurls glass out of window)*

Baron *(rising indignantly)* What the devil —

Waldman *(fiercely)* Frankenstein!

Victor You brute!

F. I want — to drink — to drink — *(notices a bowl of flowers on the table, snatches out the flowers, gives them a twist and throws them on the ground. Drinks the water noisily.)*

Waldman My dear Baron, forgive him, he doesn't understand —

Victor Give me that bowl! *(takes bowl just as* **F.** *is about to throw it out of the window)*

Baron You should beg my pardon, young man. (**F.** *stares at him, then goes to window. His manner is changed. He is no longer afraid of the men)*

F. The great fire is — burning — low. The sun! The sun! The sun! *(points down)* There is water — shining water — look! Shining water.

Baron Have you never seen a river before?

F. River? Water.

Baron Well, the water down there is called a river.

F.	Water — sun — shining —
Baron	*(half to himself)* Look at him now! He's a strange creature. I can't understand him — *(he folds his arms and steps closer, watching* **F.** *with growing distrust)*
Victor	*(softly to* **Waldman***)* What are we to do, doctor? Shall I go for Henry?
Waldman	Yes — no! We must distract the Baron's attention. I'll get him away. *(goes to* **Baron***)* Have you forgotten your promise as we drove from Goldstadt, Baron?
Baron	*(absently, staring at* **F.***)* What promise was that?
Waldman	To show me your garden and stables. What of the new mare? I'm longing to see her. Come, Baron! *(puts his hand through the* **Baron's** *arm)* Is she really such a little jewel?
Baron	*(with interest)* A jewel, doctor, a little beauty!
Waldman	I'll go with the Baron, Moritz. You stop here with Frankenstein.
Baron	No, no, Victor. I don't want to lose sight of Frankenstein. Come with us! *(to* **F.***)*
Waldman	*(reassuringly to* **Victor***)* Well — very well.
F.	*(eagerly)* Out there — to the water — and the sun?
Victor	Wherever we choose to take you.
F.	*(excitedly)* The sun — the shining water — this way — this way — *(he coolly thrusts* **Baron** *on one side and exits L.)*
Baron	Of all the vulgar young louts —
Waldman	Follow him, Moritz! *(exit* **Victor** *quickly)* He is ignorant and ill bred, Baron. He means no harm. It's only — only — his boyish, sportive way —
Baron	*(as they go out)* Boyish! Sportive! Those are not my words for damned impertinence. I beg your pardon, doctor, but upon my life I never met —
Waldman	Neither did I, Baron —— *(Exit* **Waldman** *and* **Baron.** *As they disappear enter* **Emilie** *R., closely followed by* **Henry***)*
Henry	Believe me, dearest, it's the truth.
Emilie	*(in an agitated, incredulous voice)* How can I believe you, Henry? Impossible!

Frankenstein (1927)

Henry Emilie! My darling! Before God I have done this thing I tell you. I have created this being. I call him "Frankenstein" like myself. Don't you understand my agony? Can't you realize my remorse? *(She looks at him steadily, her fear gradually changing to pity)* I think I was possessed by a devil to begin such a work. All that was dark and hidden and evil in my man's nature gave me power. I was driven on and on by the pride of Lucifer, and in the minute of my triumph I fell! As Frankenstein came to life, my heart died in my breast. I had turned my world into Hell. There was only one hope — one dream — one consolation left. You! Emilie, your love still shone in the blackness of my despair. My punishment was more than I could bear, but I believed that you would understand, you would pity, you would save me.

Emilie *(despondently)* What can I do? What can I do?

Henry Love me. Try to forgive me. Pray for me.

Emilie *(laying her hand timidly on his shoulder)* Let me go away, Henry. Leave me to myself. Let me go back to your sister's little room. I want to be alone — to think — to realize — *(presses her hand to her forehead)* I am bewildered and unnerved — can't you see? —

Henry Would you rather go home?

Emilie I can't go home. I feel too weak and wretched. Your mother will let me stop here to-night.

Henry Oh, yes —

Emilie I will sleep in little Katrine's room. Even to be near Katrine and touch her hand will give me peace and rest.

Henry Shall I send one of the servants with a message to your home?

Emilie Not one of the servants, Henry. My poor mother will be so anxious. She knew that I was riding into Goldstadt this morning. She has been greatly troubled by your long absence. Will you go yourself? *(he makes a slight gesture of dissent)* To please me, Henry. Talk to her. Tell her that your love for me is unchanged. Assure her that I'm well and happy. I will be home to-morrow.

Henry Are you indeed happy?

Emilie Not now — but I shall be in the future. We shall both be happy again — some day, my poor Henry.

Henry Very well. I will go. *(a pause)* Before I go — *(opening his arms)*

Emilie	*(drawing back)* No — no — not yet. Give me time. Don't let us see each other again to-day. I'll stop in Katrine's little room. I will pray for you. Farewell! *(she puts out one hand)*
Henry	Farewell! God bless you, dear! *(he gently kisses her hand, looks at her most tenderly for a second, and exits L.* **Emilie** *gazes sadly after him, then slowly turns to the window and leans wearily against the frame with eyes closed. She moves, after a few seconds, glances at the doves' cage and bends down, abstractedly looking at the birds. Her back is to door L. Enter* **Frankenstein**. *He is panting. She turns at the sound and stands erect, looking amazed.)*
Emilie	You again! *(gaspingly)*
F.	The — woman! The same — woman — *(She steps back as he advances a little, with an expression of fear)* I saw — you — there — *(points vaguely before him)* in the place — where my master lives. I — threw down my master — my master — *(he imitates the action of breaking open the glass doors)*
Emilie	*(quickly)* Who are you? What is your name?
F.	Frankenstein. I — saw you — I — followed you —
Emilie	You followed me? Why?
F.	I saw you — quick, quick, quick! *(with a movement of his hands)*
Emilie	Did you see me ride away from Goldstadt?
F.	I — ran — I saw — saw you — far — far — *(holds his hands over his eyes as if watching her disappear in sunshine)* You — you —
Emilie	I was gone. I galloped away.
F.	I — saw my master — men — horses — that man — white — with a whip.
Emilie	Do you mean the old man, the Baron? You saw his carriage, with Henry in it.
F.	There was — noise — noise — on the road. Quick! Quick! *(imitates plying a whip)*
Emilie	Where were you?
F.	*(not understanding her, touches his breast)* I? Frankenstein?
Emilie	Yes.
F.	I? I ran — so — *(He bends down as if running and illustrates all the following sentences with appropriate gestures)* I ran, white all over me — white.

Frankenstein (1927)

Emilie   You mean the dust of the road?

F.   I ran — there — they could not see me.

Emilie   You ran at the side of the road, under the trees and through the woods?

F.   I ran — so — *(stooping low down)* they could not see me. Quick! Down — up — trees all round me — leaves. Grass — under my feet. I fell — so! Cut — my hands. I — saw my master and the old man — quick. I — I sprang up — up — down — branches struck me — I tore them off — so! so! Water — I drank — so! *(imitates drinking)* Quick! The great fire burns — burns — pain! Pain! *(he clutches at his heart, imitating exhaustion)* I ran — I ran — I wanted — you! You! You!

Emilie   *(shrinking from him more and more)* Did you see your master come here?

F.   I saw — my master — quick! There — *(points vaguely to door L.)*

Emilie   Your master drove up to this house with his father, and you followed them in? Where is the Baron now?

F.   *(pointing again to door L.)* Down there — I crept away — I want you! *(throwing out his arms)*

Emilie   *(in breathless alarm)* Don't come near me. I will shriek ——

F.   *(trying to understand)* Shriek? You will — cry out?

Emilie   Yes.

F.   When I cry out — *(in a hoarse whisper)* my master — stops my mouth — pain! — pain! *(covers his mouth with his hands)* I — will so stop — yours! *(slowly approaches her)* Come — close to me! Come! Come!

Emilie   *(faintly)* No.

F.   I — I — woman! What have you — done to me? I — I —

Emilie   *(as if the words were torn from her against her will)* Do you love me? No — no — *(trying to keep away from him)*

F.   Love! Love! What is love? Pain — joy — beauty — come to me ——

Emilie   *(almost falling towards him)* Frankenstein — no —

F.   Love — love — love! *(at the last word he swings her up into his arms, but does not kiss her. She resists his embrace feebly. At that second the door R. opens and* **Katrine** *enters. As she starts and stops on seeing them,* **Emilie** *pushes* **F.** *away and leans back against his arms clenched round her)*

Emilie	*(faintly and desperately)* Let me go ——!
F.	You — you — I love — you! Mine!
Katrine	Emilie! Frankenstein! *(advances quickly as she can)* Let her go! *(She boldly lays her hand on his chest. He looks at her in utter amazement. His grasp of **Emilie** loosens. She moves away from him still trembling. His arms drop to his sides.* **Katrine** *still retains her position and speaks calmly and slowly)* I don't know why she looks so frightened. I don't quite understand, but you must not hold her like that again. It is not right. Emilie, come back to my room. *(puts out her hand to **Emilie**, but does not turn her eyes from **F.**'s face)* You stop here till I return.
Emilie	Katrine, let us go! *(they turn towards door R.)*
F.	I — love — the woman — *(blankly staring at **Katrine**)*
Emilie	Katrine, don't leave me! *(to **F.**)* No, no! I hate you. I can't breathe in the same air — horrible! Horrible!
Katrine	*(to **F.**)* Wait here for me. *(exit **Katrine** and **Emilie** R.)*
F.	Hate — horrible! horrible! I — want — the woman! *(He walks backwards and forwards in an agitated state for a few seconds, then stops at the window, looking out. Suddenly turns his face upwards, lifting his hands to point at a bird. Then he glances at the doves, takes up the cage and looks closer, puts it down again in such a position that the audience cannot see inside, opens door, thrusts in his hand and pulls out the artificial bird from where it has been concealed, shuts cage door roughly and takes bird to window. His attention is attracted by something below, so he leans out, crushing the bird on the sill beneath his two hands. When he looks at it again he does not understand that it is dead, but is puzzled by its quietude and throws it out, saying—*
F.	Fly! *(As it falls, he looks down, pointing to it wonderingly. Re-enter **Katrine**, unheard. She gazes at him from the door, crosses room, and, after a slight hesitation, touches him on the arm. He turns quickly and stares at her. She does not withdraw her hand. He looks down at it and then again into her face.)*
Katrine	Did you come here with Henry?
F.	Yes.
Katrine	Then you are very welcome. I am pleased to see you. What is your name?
F.	Frankenstein.
Katrine	So you told me. Is it truly Frankenstein? You must be my cousin, or my — oh! *(she catches sight of the cage, goes to it and kneels down, distressed)* Oh,

Frankenstein (1927)

	my doves! My pretty, pretty doves! One of them has gone. Sweetest dove, where is your gentle mate? *(with her face close to cage)*
F.	It has gone — out there.
Katrine	*(rising and going to window beside him)* Did it fly into the blue?
F.	No. It fell down — down — to the water — going on and on — still — on the water.
Katrine	Then it must be dead. I was so fond of both my doves. *(She leans beside F. on the sill. He looks at her shoulder resting against his, then touches her face very carefully)*
F.	What — are you doing? There are drops of water coming out — of your eyes. I have seen water — in my master's eyes like that.
Katrine	They are tears.
F.	Tears?
Katrine	*(very simply)* Yes. I am sorry — unhappy, and I am crying. Have you never cried?
F.	No. *(puzzled for a second, then points down to the river again)* I like — to see them — float.
Katrine	The leaves?
F.	And — the bird! *(**Katrine** sits down near the cage, resting her crutch on the side of her chair, looking at him thoughtfully. After a few seconds he turns to her, picks up her crutch and examines it curiously)*
Katrine	Please give me back my crutch. *(he takes no notice)* Give me back my crutch. I can't walk without it.
F.	Can you — fly — like the bird?
Katrine	*(smiling a little)* No, indeed.
F.	Could you — float along the water?
Katrine	*(shakes her head)* Do give me back my crutch. (**F.** *holds it out to her humbly. She puts her hands forward for him to help her to rise. After a pause, he does so)*
F.	Why — did you do that? I? — *(stops helplessly)*
Katrine	I don't know what you mean.

F.	You gave me — your hands. May I feel them — again? *(stretches out his own, palm upwards.* **Katrine** *lays her hands on them for a second)* No one — has done that — before. *(she gently withdraws her hands)* My master — will not touch me. The men — there — *(points vaguely)* will not touch me. That woman — hates me. Do you hate me?
Katrine	No, no, my poor friend.
F.	Friend? What is that?
Katrine	I am your friend. Why do you look so sad? So strange!
F.	Sad? I do — not know.
Katrine	This is such a beautiful world, with so many kind and good people in it. Look at the flowing river and the drifting clouds. Let us go out of doors.
F.	Out there?
Katrine	Yes, I am always running out of doors.
F.	Can you — run?
Katrine	*(half sadly)* No, I am lame, and I get tired so easily. But I love to feel the soft air and lean over the side of my little boat, touching the water with my fingers. It whispers "Little Katrine! Little Katrine!"
F.	*(slowly repeating the words in her voice)* Little Katrine! Little Katrine!
Katrine	Will you come with me?
F.	Yes. I — will come.
Katrine	*(laying her finger on her lips as she opens the door R.)* Look! This opens on a narrow staircase, above it is my own little room, below is a door leading to the river bank where my boat is lying. Come!
F.	You do not — hate me?
Katrine	Why should I hate you? Come!
F.	To the water — where the leaves float — and the bird —
Katrine	Yes, I will show you the way — it's such a narrow stair — take my hand.
F.	*(as he does so)* You are — little Katrine —
Katrine	This way — — *(Exit* **Katrine** *first, her hand stretched behind her, lightly holding his. Exit* **Frankenstein**. *A slight pause, then the voices of men heard outside. Enter* **Baron**, **Waldman**, *and* **Victor**)

Frankenstein (1927)

Baron (*as he comes in*) Of course I'm glad you and Henry came, doctor, though I admit it was very surprising. The boy refused to leave Goldstadt this morning and you encouraged him. Do sit down. I want to talk to you. (*They sit, all at a distance from the window*)

Waldman (*To* **Victor**) Where is Frankenstein?

Victor He eluded me when we were left alone in the orchard.

Baron Let well alone. Perhaps he has run away or followed Henry to the Lavenzas' home. This Frankenstein, as you call him, is the man I want to talk about, Dr. Waldman. Do you know him well?

Waldman I — I know him well, Baron. You mustn't take his roughness ill. He's only ignorant and ——

Baron Only ignorant! My hound has better manners. He took a glass of wine and threw it out of the window. You saw him do it. I've never met a man before, however ignorant, who hasn't learned where to toss wine. (*indicates his mouth*) But here's the point. There's something strange about him. (*draws his chair close to* **Waldman**) I wouldn't say so to Henry, for he'd only laugh at me, but my blood runs cold in my body when I look at young Frankenstein.

Waldman (*forcing a smile*) Really, my dear Baron!

Baron Truth, sir, truth. He seems to me like an evil thing — no man at all as we know men.

Waldman Well, Henry must get him away from Belrive.

Baron I shall tell Henry to have nothing more to do with him. My son is not his keeper.

Waldman Take my advice, Baron, leave the matter in your son's hands entirely.

Baron Henry must give me a promise to renounce him.

Waldman It will be far wiser to trust to his discretion.

Victor I'll do my best with Henry to take Frankenstein away.

Baron (*looking with surprise from one to the other*) What! Both of you? (*with sudden suspicion*) What are you hiding from me?

Waldman Nothing, my good sir, nothing.

Victor (*boldly*) There is nothing to hide, Baron.

Baron	That's a lie — it's a lie, Victor Moritz. You know it is. *(rises)* Who is this man calling himself by my name? Where does he come from? How long has my son been in his power?
Waldman	Henry is not in his power.
Baron	False again! I see it in your face. Henry and Victor are afraid of him and you know the reason, Dr. Waldman.
Waldman	I assure you very solemnly, Baron ——
Baron	*(getting very angry)* I'm not a fool. I'm not in dotage. Why did my son stop away from home for six months and rush here to-day in pursuit of this Frankenstein? Why did you both come with him? What have you done with the man? *(to* **Waldman***)* Where is he now?
Waldman	I wish to God I knew.
Baron	*(turning appealingly to* **Victor***)* Victor, you're a good, kind fellow. Tell me what you know of Frankenstein. I entreat you to tell me.
Victor	*(embarrassed)* Baron, I — I know so little of Frankenstein.
Baron	Do you know his people, his home, his character?
Victor	No.
Baron	Where did you first meet him? *(a pause)* Well?
Victor	In Goldstadt. In — in Henry's rooms.
Baron	Then he is Henry's friend, not yours, or Dr. Waldman's?
Victor	*(more and more troubled)* Yes, he — Henry knew him first.
Baron	What did Henry tell you about him?
Victor	*(desperately)* Baron, I can't answer this volley of questions. Ask your son yourself. *(enter* **Henry***)* Here he is. I am not responsible for Frankenstein.
Baron	Then, Henry, *you* are responsible.
Henry	*(after an irresolute pause)* Yes.
Baron	Tell me the truth about him.
Henry	How can I tell you, Father? You wouldn't understand ——
Baron	*(in a towering rage)* There's one thing I do understand. You are all determined to deceive me. Where has Frankenstein gone? I'll find him!

Frankenstein (1927)

	Frankenstein! Frankenstein! *(he takes a quick step towards the door L., it opens and* **Elizabeth** *enters, very white and agitated)* Elizabeth! *(All look at her in surprise. To be played rapidly)*
Elizabeth	Oh, Baron! Baron! Where is my mistress? Something terrible has happened — oh, gentlemen! it's too dreadful — she's gone! She's gone! Our little angel! Let me go to her poor mother — *(she hurries towards door R.)*
Henry	Elizabeth! *(spoken together)*
Waldman	What do you mean?
Elizabeth	*(looking over her shoulder)* He's bringing her in. I met him at the door — oh, Lord have mercy! — *(a pause.* **Waldman** *instinctively lays his hand on the* **Baron's** *shoulder. They stare at open door L. Enter* **Frankenstein***, carrying* **Katrine** *in his arms. She is drowned. Her dress clings to her figure and water drips from her hair. His eyes are wide with wonder as he looks from one to another. For a second they are too shocked to speak)*
F.	*(blankly)* Little Katrine!
Baron	Oh, God! My child! Henry — —
Waldman	*(calmly and authoritatively)* Quick, Moritz, pull out the lounge — put her down here — *(***Waldman** *and* **Victor** *pull lounge forward.* **F.** *lays* **Katrine** *down upon it, profile to the audience. The men bend over her.* **F.** *stands aside, still staring blankly)*
Baron	My little girl! *(turning to* **Elizabeth***, while* **Waldman** *feels* **Katrine's** *pulse, etc.)* Go to my wife — don't let her come here. Tell Emilie — go to my poor wife — *(Exit* **Elizabeth***, crying)*
Henry	Doctor— —
Waldman	Silence. Control yourselves. *(he lays his hand on the* **Baron's** *arm)* My poor friend, your child is —
Victor	Dead?
Waldman	She has been drowned.
Henry	Can nothing be done?
Waldman	Nothing.
Henry	*(brokenly, bending over back of lounge)* Our little Katrine! My own loving little girl! Shall we never hear you speak again? Will you never look at us again? *(hides his face on back of lounge)*

Baron	I must go to my wife — my poor wife — the mother of my child — where is my wife — *(Exit* **Baron**, *blindly)*
Waldman	*(to* **F.***)* Where did you find her? What do you know of this?
F.	*(bewildered)* She took me — there — *(points to door R.)* down to the boat. I — I — pushed it away — from land — on the water. The leaves floated — on the water — like the white bird — shining water —
Waldman	Go on! Go on! What then?
F.	*(with expressive gestures for all words)* I took — her hands. I — lifted her and laid her — down on the water — *(looks at them vaguely)*
Waldman	Go on, Frankenstein.
F.	She held my hands — but I shook her off. I wanted — to see her like the bird — on the water. "Oh! Oh!" she cried. Then I pressed her down — under the water. Beauty — beauty — her hair — her face — under the water — *(he bends forward towards the girl on the lounge)*
Waldman	You held her under the water — ah! —
F.	Down — down. I held her. Long time. Down! Then — then — I took her out. She was still — still — like that — *(pointing to her)*
Henry	Oh, you have killed my sister — murderer! *(He makes a movement towards* **F.** **Waldman** *and* **Victor** *check him)*
Victor	Henry —
Waldman	Remember, he doesn't understand.
Henry	*(sinking into a chair)* He has killed Katrine — little Katrine — *(buries his face in his hands and remains immovable)*
F.	*(staring at the other men)* I — killed little Katrine —
Waldman	Yes, she will never speak to us again.
F.	*(very slowly beginning to realize the truth)* Never — speak again. Never take my hand! She — did not hate me. She — touched me — *(he creeps towards the lounge, bends down, then raises his head and whispers)* Is she — asleep?
Waldman	She is dead.
F.	She looks — the same —
Waldman	No, she is utterly changed. You have killed her.

Frankenstein (1927)

F.   Changed? Changed? I have — killed her? *(he is silent a few seconds, then raises his voice, close to her)* Katrine! Little Katrine! Look at me. Never — never — *(wildly appealing to* **Waldman***)* What — does it mean? I am hurt — I am hurt — *(gasping and laying his hand on his heart)* Pain — pain — but not with my master's blows. Help me! Help me! Help me, men! Is there — no one — in the world — to help me? *(Looking up to Heaven)* Katrine! Katrine! I know — what I have done. I know! Sorrow — sorrow — pain — I — I understand — *(He breaks into a storm of uncontrollable grief and throws himself down on the ground in front of the lounge. The other men watch him in an awe-stricken way. Silence, except for the sound of* **Frankenstein** *weeping)*

End of Act II.

FRANKENSTEIN

Act III

The following dawn. A pass in the Jura Mountains. Beautiful, desolate scenery, with a group of crags at the back of the stage. It is nearly dark when the curtain rises. There is a long bar of light across the sky, which gradually intensifies and deepens in colour as the act proceeds, until the stage glows with soft light. Silence for a few seconds, broken by the sound of **Frankenstein** *breathing heavily as he approaches. He enters, dragging a long, torn branch, which he drops. He is bare-headed, his clothes are torn and dusty, and he limps painfully. He stands still, staring about him and into the sky. He is haggard and exhausted, and sits down upon the bole of an old tree, muttering to himself.*

F. Men — men — kill — kill — Frankenstein — *(a pause, then in a louder voice)* Little Katrine! *(listens)* Where is the great fire? Oh! Oh! Pain! *(he groans and covers his face with his hands)* Sleep — sleep — sleep — love — kill — sleep *(He rises and limps towards the rocks, stretching himself beside one of them. A pause. Men's voices in the distance. Enter* **Victor***)*

Victor This way, Henry! This is where we saw the shape disappear. I'm on level ground here. This way! *(a slight pause, then enter* **Henry***, also wearing a cloak and hat over the same clothes)*

Henry It was yonder that we saw him, Victor — there — *(points)* creeping through the undergrowth.

Victor I can see nothing in the distance, Henry.

Henry You are right. It has gone. I'm like a bewitched man. Wherever I turn I seem to look upon Frankenstein, but he always eludes me and escapes.

Victor Where is your father with the other men?

Henry We out-stripped them long ago.

Victor I hope the Baron has gone home. This man hunt is too hard for him.

Henry It is no man hunt. It is a hunt for a wild beast, a murderer, a devil in human shape.

Victor What will you do when we find him? Will you shoot at sight?

Henry No. Oh, Victor, you forget the strange, terrible link there is between us. He is *mine* — nearer to me than a brother *(begins to pace the stage)*

Victor I never forget, but he is no longer *your* creation. That is over. He has become —

Frankenstein **(1927)**

Henry	*(On a level with the rock and catching sight of* F.*)* Look! Look there!
Victor	It is he.
Henry	At last! At last!
Victor	What shall we do?
Henry	Hush! Don't wake him. Let me think! *(glances L. and moves away from* F.*)* I can hear footsteps and voices — softly, Victor — who is it yonder?
Victor	Two of your father's men?
Henry	No. Look again. I think it's Dr. Waldman. *(a pause)* It *is* Waldman — with a woman.
Victor	A woman?
Henry	A woman, Victor. Oh, it's Emilie Lavenza. *(in great surprise)*
Victor	Is it possible?
Henry	Oh, yes, I could never be mistaken in *her*! *(Enter* **Waldman** *and* **Emilie**, *the latter closely muffled in a thin mantle and wearing a plain hat)* Dr. Waldman! Emilie!
Emilie	*(hurrying to him)* Forgive me, Henry! *(turns to* **Waldman***)* Tell him why I came with you.
Waldman	I went home with the Baron, when I parted from you, a couple of hours ago. This poor girl has been watching and waiting all night.
Emilie	I couldn't sleep after I heard about Katrine. I was haunted by the fear of your meeting *him*.
Henry	Frankenstein?
Emilie	Yes, the murderer of Katrine — *(hides her face on* **Henry's** *shoulder)*
Henry	We hoped to meet him. We have been hunting all night — doctor! Victor and I have succeeded.
Waldman	You have found Frankenstein?
Henry	We have found him. *(together)*
Victor	Yes, doctor.
Waldman	Where is he?
Henry	He is here! *(points to* F.*)*

Peggy Webling and the Story behind Frankenstein

Waldman *(as he goes to look at him)* Is he asleep?

Henry Yes, he is sleeping heavily.

Waldman What are you going to do?

Henry We must go for help.

Victor Why? We are three men against one.

Henry But he is so cunning and quick. Remember how he swept you both on one side when you tried to keep him in my room at Goldstadt. Remember how he eluded Victor in the orchard and found his way into our house at Belrive.

Emilie How did he escape you after the death of poor little Katrine?

Henry Easily. He sprang away from us all like a wild beast. We gathered a party of friends and our servants together and we have followed his tracks from sunset. Now the dawn is breaking. *(turns quickly to **Victor**)* Victor, will you go down to Belrive and see my father? Tell him we have found Frankenstein.

Victor Of course I'll go. But what will you do if he awakes before our return?

Henry Advise me, doctor.

Waldman You and I must stop here and do our best to govern him.

Victor That may be impossible.

Henry I know he will be furious over the sight of me. My power over him is gone.

Waldman I am not afraid to be alone with him. He may not wake. He must be worn out — poor wretch!

Henry *(looking at **F**.)* Devil! Devil!

Victor I'll start at once. But what of Emilie?

Emilie *(earnestly)* Let me stop with you, Henry. I'm not frightened when I'm with *you*. Victor doesn't pass my home on his way to your father's house. I can't go with him, and I daren't go alone.

Henry *(after pondering a second)* Well — go, Victor! Leave everything else to us. Go to Belrive.

Victor Goodbye! *(Exit **Victor** quickly)*

Frankenstein (1927)

Henry	Goodbye!
Waldman	I will watch beside him. (**Waldman** *goes to back of stage and sits on bole of tree near* **F.**, *turned away from the audience*)
Emilie	You are not angry with me for coming, Henry?
Henry	(*passionately*) My darling! Let me hold you in my arms. Close! Close! Kiss me once more. Love me as you loved me in the happy, happy days before he lived to curse us. (*After a second she gently disengages herself from his embrace*)
Emilie	I believe your strange and terrible story. But tell me why is this man — this Frankenstein — so like and yet unlike yourself?
Henry	Do you find him so?
Emilie	When I was alone with him yesterday, I felt — I felt —
Henry	You could never love him, Emilie? You could never let him take *my* place in your heart?
Emilie	(*vehemently*) Never! Never! But when we were alone together — I don't understand myself — I was drawn towards him by a wild, resistless power. I was helpless — a bird before a serpent, a spar on a rushing river, paper thrown into a fire!
Henry	(*seizing her hands*) But you love *me*! You love *me*! You will marry *me*.
Emilie	(*earnestly*) My mind and my judgment were untouched, watching him, hating him, afraid of him. But my senses were all bewildered. There was some call from his body to mine that I could not deny. It was as if one heart, torn asunder, throbbed in his breast and in my own. Our blood ran in the same swift current. He is part of you and part of myself, and we are all one — oh, my poor love! My poor darling! Do I hurt you so much? (*She suddenly draws his head down on her shoulder in the tenderest pity. After a second he looks up, still clasping her in his arms*)
Henry	Part of me . . . of you . . . we are all one . . . (*a pause*)
Waldman	(*coming forward*) Henry! Henry! Frankenstein is waking.
Henry	Waking?
Waldman	Yes. Be quiet. Don't startle him.
Emilie	I'll go away. He must not see me.
Waldman	Wait for Henry in the shadow of that rock — (*points L.*)

Peggy Webling and the Story behind Frankenstein

Emilie	He will attack Henry — he is angry with him. Come with me! *(to* **Henry***)*
Henry	I mustn't desert Dr. Waldman.
Waldman	Quick — He moves. I am best alone. Stop within call, Henry!
Henry	Go, darling! I'll come — *(exit* **Emilie** *hurriedly L.)* Are you not afraid, Dr. Waldman?
Waldman	*(with a quiet smile)* I am not afraid — look! He is drawing himself together like an animal. Go, Henry.
Henry	*(Looking towards rock at back)* The hunted beast! The slayer of my sister . . . I shall be near at hand, doctor! *(Exit* **Henry** *L.* **Waldman** *walks slowly back and stands still, as if studying* **F.** *closely)*
F.	Master! Where — is Frankenstein? *(He rises, steps quickly forward, then gives a cry of pain, and stares blankly at* **Waldman***)*
Waldman	Be still, Frankenstein.
F.	Where — is my master? I have run — hidden — all night — *(he shudders)* The wet fell on me. I dropped — there — *(points L.)* My hands are — hurt — my foot — pain — pain — *(drawing a little closer)* Where is — little Katrine?
Waldman	Don't speak of her.
F.	She floated, like the leaf — and the bird — on the water. You say I — I killed her. She was kind to me. Will you — be kind to me?
Waldman	Stand away from me.
F.	Where — is the — woman? I — I — love the woman.
Waldman	What does it mean, to love?
F.	*(drearily)* I — do not know. Nothing, nothing! *(again trying to approach)* Take me — to that place — down there — where I saw little Katrine.
Waldman	No!
F.	*(still pleading)* Take me!
Waldman	You can never go to that house again. There is blood upon your hands.
F.	On my — hands? Blood? My hands —
Waldman	How can I make you understand? Sit down there — not close to me — I will talk to you. **(Waldman** *sits on bole of tree)*

Frankenstein (1927)

F.	*(looking up into sky)* The great — fire is alight.
Waldman	Sit on the ground, Frankenstein. (**F.** *obeys him*) Now, do you understand why your master and the woman hate you?
F.	*(brooding)* No. Why do they — hate me? I want — the woman. I can kill — my master.
Waldman	No, no, not that.
F.	*(innocently)* I love the woman. I can — kill him — so! *(he stretches out his hands, clenches and opens them again)*
Waldman	Listen! If you kill your master the woman will only hate you more and more. She would die and go to him.
F.	*(simply bewildered)* She would die — *and go to him?*
Waldman	Yes, try to understand. You know that Katrine is dead?
F.	The little thing — Katrine.
Waldman	She is dead.
F.	I know. I know. I wept — so — for her — it hurt me — hurt me — *(hides his face in his hands)*
Waldman	Yes, but the pain awakened your soul. In the depths of pain and sorrow the soul awakes.
F.	*(looking up with a gleam of intelligence)* Soul? My soul? What do you mean?
Waldman	*(very distinctly)* Katrine is dead. She can't speak to us. Her body will never move again, but her soul is not dead.
F.	Then — then — where is her — soul? What do you mean?
Waldman	Her soul is with God.
F.	*(repeats the word slowly, with eyes half closed and hands out-stretched, as if groping in the dark)* God. Where — is God?
Waldman	I cannot tell you.
F.	Would God hate me?
Waldman	No, no. He alone could forgive you and help you.
F.	He would — take my hand — like the little thing. Katrine! *(a pause, then he rises and goes close to* **Waldman**, *who also rises)* Show me — the way to Him.

Peggy Webling and the Story behind Frankenstein

Waldman   You must wait. You must be patient.

F.   Wait? But the great fire is coming again. The men will — hurt me — pain! *(he paces backwards and forwards.* **Waldman** *watches him, half curiously, half in terror of what he is going to do)* Did the bird's soul fly to God — when it fell — down — down — was the bird dead?

Waldman   Yes.

F.   Katrine — is dead. Did her — soul fly to God?

Waldman   Yes, yes.

F.   *(a second's silence, then* **F.**'s *face changes as an inspiration comes to him)* Then — if *I* were dead — (**Waldman**, *fascinated by his expression, goes out of his way, then suddenly calls aloud),*

Waldman   Henry! Henry! *(Enter* **Henry**, *who stands immovable, at a signal from* **Waldman***)* Hush! Hush! *(***F.*** looks around, as if in search of something. Then he suddenly becomes exultant and springs up the high rock at back of stage. He stands still on the top, profile to audience, gazing upward, then below)*

F.   The great fire — down — down! Water — trees — shining water — My soul will find — God! Little Katrine! Rest — rest — down — down — down — *(he turns to audience for a second, an expression on his face of wild excitement and hope, then leaps off the rock out of sight.* **Henry** *climbs a little way after him, and leans far forward, gazing where* **F.** *fell. As this takes place enter* **Emilie**, *who looks at him in amazement)*

Emilie   Where is Frankenstein? The men are coming.

Waldman   Too soon and too late. He sprang from the rock.

Henry   His body is shattered. He is dead. My guilty work is destroyed! *(turns to* **Emilie** *with an appealing gesture)* Forgive me!

Waldman   Your guilty work is destroyed, but his soul has returned to its Creator. *(***Emilie*** stretches out her arms, and* **Henry** *takes a step downwards, and so they remain looking at each other. Silence. The light of day very intense as the curtain slowly falls.)*

End of Play

Frankenstein (1928)

Registered and Copyrighted with the United States Library of Congress
7 September 1928

FRANKENSTEIN
A Play in a Prologue and Three Acts
(Based upon Mrs. Shelley's well known book)
By
Peggy Webling

FRANKENSTEIN

Characters:

Baron Frankenstein
Henry, his son
Dr. Waldman (of the University of Goldstadt, Switzerland)
Victor Moritz
              and
Frankenstein

Baroness Frankenstein
Katrina, her daughter
Emilie Lavenza
Elizabeth

Prologue:

Henry's study in **Dr. Waldman's** house in Goldstadt. A Winter evening. Six months are supposed to elapse.

Act I.   The Same as the Prologue. Morning.

Act II.   Room in the **Baron's** house at Belrive. Afternoon of the same·day.

Act III. Hut in the Jura Mountains. Six months later.

Period.
    The end of the Eighteenth Century.

FRANKENSTEIN

Prologue

Henry's *study in* **Dr. Waldman's** *house at Goldstadt. A Winter evening. A small room lighted by an oil lamp. A fire glowing in the grate. Centre doors, hidden by long dark curtains which are slightly open. A table and arm chairs by the fire. The walls are hung with anatomical drawings. A skeleton in a case at the back of the stage. Doors R. and L. It is almost dark when the curtain rises. A flash of lightning through the slit in the curtains, followed by a long roll of thunder. The sound of a storm is heard, which continues intermittently throughout the act. The stage is empty. A loud knocking at the door R., and* **Victor Moritz's** *voice is heard outside.*

Victor	Henry! Henry Frankenstein! Henry! Where are you? (*Enter* **Victor**, *wearing a heavy cloak and hat pulled down over his brows, and carrying a lantern. As he crosses towards opposite door it is unlocked and* **Henry** *enters, speaking as he does so.*)
Henry	Who is it? Ah, Victor! (*he closes door behind him and advances quickly with out-stretched hand.*) Did you knock before? I am glad you have come before Dr. Waldman.
Victor	Did you expect me on such a night?
Henry	Of all men in the college you are most welcome. (*as they shake hands a gust of wind blows open the centre doors behind the curtains.* **Henry** *goes to them.*) The doors have blown open. Good God! What a night! (*closes & bolts doors, and turns up lamp a little.*) Take off your wet cloak, Victor. I'll hang it by the stove in my other room. This fire is too small to dry a rag. (*offers to take his friend's cloak and hat.*)
Victor	Let me take them into your room. (*goes towards door L.*)
Henry	(*quickly*) No, Victor, no. You can't go into my room. Give it to me — and your hat — (*Exit* **Henry** *with cloak and hat. For the few seconds he is absent* **Victor** *puts down his lantern in the corner of the fire-place and warms his hands. Re-enter* **Henry**. *He has the key of the door in his hand and locks it, putting the key into his pocket*)
Victor	(*carelessly*) Why do you lock your inner door and leave the other open?
Henry	No reason. I expect Dr. Waldman. Pull up a chair. How the wind howls! I think it's found its way from the lonely Jura Mountains to Goldstadt. Listen! Doesn't it take you back to old Belrive? (**Victor** *sits down and lights his pipe.* **Henry** *is restless and nervous, pacing up and down the room*)

Peggy Webling and the Story behind Frankenstein

Victor I'm glad that it can't take us back to old Belrive — literally.

Henry Why are you glad?

Victor If we suddenly found ourselves in your father's house, or in mine — no smoking all night, no free talk, or late supper, but long evening prayers, after yawning over a good, dull book, or listening to the damned soliloquy that elderly gentlemen call conversation — No disrespect to the Baron, dear Henry, or my own worthy father.

Henry *(gloomily)* I don't agree with you. If the wild wind could blow me back to Belrive at this minute, I'd rush out into the night — what's that? Hush! Didn't you hear — ? *(he goes to door L., stooping to listen and signing to the other to be quiet)*

Victor What on earth is the matter?

Henry Hush! Listen! *(a pause)* It's all right. It was nothing — my imagination — nothing. *(he paces the floor again)*

Victor What is wrong with you, Henry? You can't sit still for five minutes. You look as nervous and unstrung as a sick girl. Are you ill? Had any bad news? You're over-worked, that's it — yes, you're over-worked. Classes, lectures, reading, writing, and all the rest of the old grind has been too much for your nerves. I know you're the most promising man of your time and we're all proud of you. Old Professor Kempe calls you the new light of natural science. Dr. Waldman is always dinning your achievements in chemistry into our long-suffering ears. The Principal of the University declares ———

Henry *(impatiently)* Don't talk such nonsense, Victor.

Victor It's the truth. We all admit it. *(then in a serious tone)* My dear Henry, what is the good of your labours if you half kill yourself? Why do you spend all your days and nights in study? What is your end and aim? Why have you cut yourself adrift from your companions and oldest friends?

Henry *(stopping a minute to lay his hand on the other's shoulder)* No, no, not that, Victor.

Victor Yes, yes, Henry. I never see you. Look here! Has a man in the college crossed your threshold for the past three months?

Henry Yes, Dr. Waldman dined with me recently.

Victor Dr. Waldman! A book-worm like yourself. A grave, learned man, old enough to be your father. *He's* no companion for Henry Frankenstein.

Frankenstein (1928)

Henry He understands me. He's the greatest and kindest man I've ever met.

Victor *(lightly)* Then why do you welcome such a fellow as me? I'm no pedant — no scientist —

Henry Because we've known each other all our lives, Victor. I love you like a brother. I wish — I wish you'd come to see me more often.

Victor To speak the truth, when I do come you're so absent minded, or so absorbed in your own thoughts, that I only feel in the way. Oh, don't apologize. It was just the same when we were boys at Belrive. You wanted to be an alchemist in those days, or discover the elixir of life. **(Henry** *starts)* What fools we are when we're young!

Henry *(looking towards the inner room)* No, youth is the age of true wisdom.

Victor Was it true wisdom of you to believe in alchemy, or hunt for the philosopher's stone? No, the wisest step you ever took, my friend, was on the day you gave it up and engaged yourself to our pretty neighbour, Emilie Lavenza.

Henry *(staring in front of him, sadly)* Yes: that was wise.

Victor *(inquisitively)* How is the charming Emilie?

Henry Well — at home.

Victor Have you seen her lately?

Henry *(with constraint)* Not for — some months.

Victor You astonish me. Goldstadt is only a ride from Belrive, and you both love riding.

Henry I have been absorbed in study. All my time, my thoughts, my energies have been devoted to a certain work. But it is done at last. Victor! I am glad you have come tonight. I am thankful that I sent for you, although I am afraid — *(he stops)*

Victor *(in surprise)* My dear Henry, why afraid?

Henry Because this will be the greatest and the most wonderful night in the whole course of my life — or the most terrible and bitter. Tonight I shall conquer the world of science, or fall into black despair. Tonight I shall triumph — or fail — in the most daring and marvellous experiment ever attempted by mortal man.

Victor Henry!

Henry	Oh, don't think I'm a madman. Don't be frightened. You know me of old. I've got the courage of the devil.
Victor	A devilish courage when your blood is up.
Henry	Yes, but tonight I must be calm and cool as the Jura hills. I must control myself. I must! I must! *(he becomes more agitated).*
Victor	What have you done? What do you mean by all this wild talk?
Henry	Stop with me, Victor, and you shall learn — don't leave me till I tell you to go. Swear you'll stand by me whatever happens.
Victor	Of course I'll stand by you. *(a roll of thunder)* My dear boy, where's this courage of the devil you brag about? You're shaking from head to foot, and your pulse — (**Henry** *drags his hand away*)
Henry	*(wildly)* If *you* had waited, and waited, and longed for tonight as I have done — if *you* knew what was hanging in the balance ——
Victor	Why don't you tell me? *(a knock at the door R.* **Henry** *starts violently, then speaks in a loud voice)*
Henry	Who's there? Who is it?
Waldman	*(outside)* Dr. Waldman.
Henry	*(earnestly, as he hurries to open the door)* Don't leave me, Victor. Come in, Dr. Waldman! *(Enter* **Waldman***)* I was afraid you had forgotten your promise.
Waldman	Oh, no, but I was reading in my room and the hour slipped past. I didn't mean to miss our appointment, Henry. Victor Moritz, is it not?
Victor	Yes, sir. *(they shake hands)*
Henry	Will you sit in the arm chair, doctor? Victor, please lock the door. (**Victor** *does so while* **Henry** *and* **Waldman** *sit on opposite sides of the table by fire)*
Waldman	What a night of storm! The wind and rain have been fighting for mastery and the wind is beaten. Can we not have a little more light, Henry? Does this mysterious experiment of yours require a dark room and crashes of thunder? *(thunder far away)*
Henry	If you like, sir. *(He turns up the lamp, making the stage light)*
Waldman	That is more cheerful. *(a pause)* Well, Henry? Your class is seated and admirably attentive.

Henry	Do you remember, sir, supping with me in this room about six months ago? We were all alone.
Waldman	Very well. I'm afraid we talked nearly the whole of the night.
Henry	The sun was rising before I got to sleep. Do you remember all that we said, Dr. Waldman?
Waldman	*(smiling)* No, indeed.
Henry	Not the gist of the talk — the subject?
Waldman	We discussed the origin of life.
Henry	Yes, and the possibility of science, in the far future, being able to discover the secret of creation.
Waldman	*(smiling again)* I recollect leaving that supposition to my junior, Henry. It is beyond me. You must forgive the inexperience and modesty of age. *(turns deliberately to* **Victor***)* Have you read Ludenburg's latest treatise, Moritz?
Victor	Not yet, but I have heard ——
Henry	Stay, Victor! *(entreatingly)* Dr. Waldman, I beg you not to attempt to turn me from my purpose. If you disapprove of our former discussion, believe me you will alter your opinion tonight.
Waldman	Our former discussion, my young friend, was futile and fruitless. Wild exaggeration and unsupported tales of marvels have nothing whatever to do with science. Forgive my bluntness. We were both rather foolish on that occasion. Let us forget it. So I wish you'd tell me, Moritz, whether you have heard that Herr Ludenburg's most original treatise is ——
Henry	*(striking the table excitedly)* No, doctor! No! By Heaven, you shall hear me.
Waldman	*(resignedly)* Well, well, well! Don't be excited, dear boy.
Henry	You know — you both know — how deeply I have devoted myself to natural philosophy, and particularly chemistry, in the most comprehensive sense of the term. But you do *not* know that I have spent years in deep and occult study of the secrets of life, before and since I came to Goldstadt. One question haunted me night and day — one problem I would have given the best years of my youth to solve — the secret of the principle of life. I have studied physiology and anatomy, birth and death. I understand the natural growth and decay of the human body. I have long lost all sense of restraint and moderation. I have sought my subjects in the hospital and the grave.

Peggy Webling and the Story behind Frankenstein

Waldman Well, well, well!

Victor *(to **Waldman**)* What does he mean by that?

Waldman *(looking at **Henry** as if doubting his reason)* God knows.

Henry I tell you I have handled the newly dead. I have spent nights and days in vaults and charnel-houses. I have learned the processes of corruption, the secrets of the flesh, but always before my mind — a light in the darkness — I hoped to discover the cause of generation. At last — at last — when my strength was nearly gone, when I was haggard and worn with labour, when I had tasted the bitter cup of despair — I saw the flaming of the torch! I had found the secret of giving life. It was too much for my heart and brain. The desire and dream of humanity had burst upon me. It was mine! It was mine! *(drops into his chair and covers his face with his hands, visibly trembling with excitement)*

Victor *(wonderingly)* My dear Henry!

Waldman *(sternly)* Tell us your meaning in plain words. Master yourself.

Henry *(lifting his head slowly)* I — I'm sorry, doctor. I — I — I'm over-worked, unnerved. What a fool I am! Forgive me. Victor, will you get that little bottle and glass from the desk yonder — thank you. (**Victor** *brings them.* **Henry** *tries to pour a dose)* This is too ridiculous. My hand shakes. Victor, pour it for me — there — *(he indicates the dose. Victor pours it.)*

Waldman *(smelling the glass)* Be careful how you use this drug. (**Henry** *drinks eagerly, gasping as he finishes)*

Henry That is better. I beg your pardon, doctor, for all my wild talk.

Waldman Let us hear no more of it.

Victor But Henry was telling us of his discovery, doctor.

Henry *(eagerly)* Do you believe in me, Victor?

Victor I — I hardly know what to say.

Henry Wait till the end. *Wait*, doctor.

Waldman We must follow you step by step. Describe your work in detail.

Henry That is impossible. I have told you the truth as surely as the sun shines in heaven. I can bestow animation upon lifeless matter.

Waldman No, no, Henry Frankenstein. You ask too much of our faith in you, my poor friend. No, no, no!

Frankenstein (1928)

Henry	Hear me out, Dr. Waldman. My ambition, after this great discovery, was to prove its practical truth. I hesitated for a long time. Then I determined to prepare an object — a form — a body — for the vital experiment.
Waldman	*(astounded)* Do you mean a human body?
Henry	Yes. I began to dream of the creation of a being like ourselves — the physical man complete.
Waldman	*(protesting)* My friend! My friend!
Henry	I set to work. I — *(covers his face for a second)* I can't tell you everything I did. You would think I was a cunning madman. Look! *(holding out his hand)* I'm shaking from head to foot, my mouth is parched, and my head swims at the mere recollection of the awful task. *(in a hoarse whisper)* In a dark cellar beneath the ground I made *the Thing* I had dreamed of. It was horrible — horrible — but I could not stop. I collected all the gruesome parts from secret haunts of death. I crept, like a murderer, night after night to my frightful labour. I — I — *(again overcome, he covers his eyes with his hands)*
Waldman	*(calmly and emphatically)* And at the end you failed.
Henry	No, I succeeded! The Thing is finished. To-night I shall perfect my work and give it life.
Victor	Impossible!
Waldman	Oh, Science, what falsehood is spoken in thy name!
Henry	An hour ago I used my discovery to animate the senseless body — I'll say no more of that, no more! The secret shall live and die with me. *It* is there, locked in my room. *(points to inner door)* Victor, old schoolfellow, will you come with me? We will bring it here. Will you come?
Victor	Yes. What do you want me to do?
Henry	Help me. Doctor, wait for us! *(Exit* **Henry** *L.* **Victor** *is about to follow when he turns and speaks quickly)*
Victor	What do you think, Dr. Waldman? Has Henry Frankenstein gone out of his mind?
Waldman	*(slowly)* God knows what he has done. I must see this to an end. Go with him! *(Exit* **Victor**. *A flash of lightning, followed by thunder.* **Waldman** *shudders. Re-enter* **Henry** *and* **Victor**, *carrying the inanimate body of* **Frankenstein** *on a low couch, with a big black cloth thrown over it)*

Peggy Webling and the Story behind Frankenstein

Henry Steady, Victor!

Victor A dead weight! Who is this hidden man? *(makes gesture to pull away drapery)*

Henry Not yet!

Victor How still! I think he must be insensible. What do you say, doctor? I do not want to touch him. How cold it seems all of a sudden! *(he moves away from the couch)*

Henry Dr. Waldman may touch him. Doctor, you have heard Victor's question. Tell him the condition of this man — feel his pulse — *(***Waldman** *draws the cloth sufficiently to show the shoulder and arm of* **Frankenstein**. *A pause. He lifts the hand and feels the pulse, puts it down and stoops for a second over him. The hand drops to side of couch. Another pause)*

Waldman There is no life in this man.

Henry *(looking from one to the other impressively)* There is no life in this man.

Victor *(indignantly)* Henry, you have gone too far. It's ghastly. This is a corse. It's horrible.

Henry No, he is not dead, for he has never lived. You shall look upon the creature I have made with these hands. Draw the cloth from the face, one of you! *(they hesitate)* Victor!

Victor No — no — I ——

Henry Then Dr. Waldman! *(a slight pause, then* **Waldman** *pulls aside the cloth enough to show the head and shoulders of* **Frankenstein**. *The men's faces express fear mingled with amazement)*

Waldman *(breathlessly)* My God !

Victor It is the death mask of a strange, inhuman being. Look, doctor! Look at the great lips and the brow! *(gazes confusedly at his friend, then again at* F.*)*

Waldman *(runs his hand down the figure)* This is the physical body of a young, strong man.

Henry Now you see my accomplished labour.

Waldman There is no vital force in it.

Henry *Not yet.* But my elixir is at work. The hour of waiting is nearly over. Shall I triumph or shall I fail?

Frankenstein (1928)

Waldman	I warn you, solemnly, against the sin of vain presumption. From God alone is the breath of life. Be warned!
Henry	You are too late. He lives!
Waldman	No — no — *(he takes* **Frankenstein's** *wrist.* **Victor** *and* **Henry** *strain forward. The storm is heard faintly. The doctor drops the hand and turns to* **Henry***)* You have failed!
Henry	No, I have succeeded. Look! *(After a slight pause* **F.** *slowly clenches and unclenches his hand, and raises it over his head. He draws a breath with a groan, lifts his head, opens his eyes and glares at* **Henry***, then sinks back with another groan, while the men watch him in speechless dismay).*

End of Prologue.

————————————————————

FRANKENSTEIN

Act I

The same scene as Prologue. Six months later. The curtains drawn away from centre doors to show a garden flooded with sunshine, arranged to give an impression of distance. The doors closed. Cabinet containing skeleton also closed. Enter **Waldman** *and* **Baron Frankenstein**, *talking as they come.*

Baron I am glad to have met you, doctor. Very fortunate. Very fortunate.

Waldman The pleasure is mutual, my dear Baron. (**Waldman** *closes the door R.* **Baron** *holds his hat in his hand. He looks round the room eagerly as he comes in)*

Baron Henry is not here, I see. Perhaps he is in the other room. *(goes towards door L.)*

Waldman *(stopping him)* No, no, your son isn't at home. He is — er — at a lecture, or at one of the Professors' classes. It's no use looking for him elsewhere in the house, Baron. *(He speaks hurriedly and with some confusion)*

Baron No matter. No matter. I'll wait for him. Don't let me detain you, doctor.

Waldman You're not detaining me. I've nothing to do. *(lays down his hat and stick)*

Baron *(surprised)* Fortunate man! In my young days it was the students who had nothing to do and the masters who worked. Times have evidently changed for the better. Why doesn't Henry leave his doors open? *(he goes to centre doors and pulls the handles)* What the devil——

Waldman *(mildly)* No, the bolt — allow me — *(he draws back the bolts top and bottom and throws the doors wide)*

Baron Thanks. That's better. Ugh! It's hot! *(he stands between doors* **Waldman** *watching him with an anxious and perplexed expression)* Charming little garden! I drove around the edge of that wood in the distance, the prettiest bit of road between Belrive and Goldstadt. *(turns back into room)* Won't you sit down, Dr. Waldman? *(they sit)* When do you think my too studious son will return?

Waldman Oh, at any minute. Why do you call Henry your "too studious" son? It's a rare fault in a young man, but I'm afraid he's guilty of it.

Baron Well, it's not an inheritance from his father. A good fellow, doctor, but weak here — weak! *(tapping his forehead)*

Frankenstein (1928)

Waldman Henry? I don't agree with you.

Baron Too fond of books and learning. Thinks too much. If you want to be happy and live to a gay old age, *don't think*. It's dangerous. Look at me. *I'm* not profound.

Waldman *(drily)* No one would ever suspect you of it.

Baron *(failing to see any sarcasm in the reply)* I hope not. Now, you know what a fine, spirited fellow Henry is —

Waldman *(very sadly)* Ah!

Baron An only son, doctor, with a father who has never thwarted him, a mother who adores him, a dear little sister, and one of the sweetest girls in the world waiting to marry him. Is he happy and content? No! He throws it all on one side for the sake of his studies. It's only ten miles ride to our house, but he hasn't spent a single day with his parents and his sweetheart for six months. It's a shame, doctor, it's a confounded shame! *(he begins to pace the room in agitation)*

Waldman Don't let it trouble you too much, my friend, no doubt, when Henry leaves college —

Baron Hang college! There's our neighbour's son, young Victor Moritz — *he* hasn't forgotten his family.

Waldman Victor Moritz has neither the genius nor application of your son.

Baron You don't know how our little Katrina longs for Henry. There never was a kinder brother than he used to be. She's not like other girls, our little Katrina. She can't run about, or dance, or ride, or dream of a sweetheart. *(very gently and tenderly)* She's lame, doctor. She has always walked with a crutch.

Waldman That's a great affliction for her to bear.

Baron True, true, but Katrina's so happy and cheerful. Sometimes I think she can't belong to us — me and my good wife —

Waldman How do you mean?

Baron I mean she is a bright and heavenly spirit. It seems as if the crutch alone held her to this earth and made her human. In this life we both listen for the tap of that little crutch; in the life to come we shall hear the flying footsteps of our child, running to meet us . . . Heaven knows . . . *(then in a different mood)* But all this talk has nothing to do with Henry. When did you say his confounded lecture would be over?

Waldman	I am not at all certain. Perhaps it would be better not to wait ——
Baron	Not to wait? I've come to take him home, Dr. Waldman.
Waldman	Today? Now? Impossible!
Baron	Why should it be impossible? Henry is not a prisoner at Goldstadt. *(he smiles)* You look positively frightened.
Waldman	*(forcing a smile)* Not at all, but he is so hard at work.
Baron	What of that? Have you never heard of a young student playing truant?
Waldman	You will not be able to persuade him to go.
Baron	I don't persuade, doctor. I command.
Waldman	I'm afraid he'll disobey your commands — hush! I think I hear your son's step. *(hastily)* Baron, you must be prepared for a change in Henry. Don't be alarmed, but I expect you'll find — hush! Here he is! *(Enter **Henry** L. He starts violently & stares at his father. There is a marked alteration in his appearance. He is haggard & pale, his dress neglected, his manner anxious & nervous)*
Henry	Father!
Baron	My — dear — Henry! Why, Henry! My son! *(shocked and surprised)*
Henry	*(glancing from one to the other)* Dr. Waldman! Father!
Baron	Are you pleased to see me, Henry?
Henry	Of course I'm very pleased. I — I was only a little — a little surprised. *(they shake hands. The **Baron** lays his hands on his son's shoulders)*
Baron	Why, what's the matter with you, Henry? Have you been ill? You should have told us. My poor boy!
Waldman	*(cheerily)* Oh, he's very well, my dear Baron. Only a little tired — he's quite himself — *(he steps behind **Henry** & shakes his head at the **Baron**, frowning & touching his lips)*
Baron	*(bewildered)* But he's not quite himself. He looks as if he'd seen a spectre. (**Waldman** *frowns & shakes his head again)* Eh? What? Why the devil are you scowling and wagging your head about at me, Dr. Waldman? What have I said?
Waldman	Nothing. I wasn't scowling at you ——
Baron	But you were.

Waldman	Oh, no, you're mistaken. I always frown. It's a bad habit of mine.
Baron	*(softly)* Damned bad habit. What is wrong with you, Henry?
Henry	I'm well enough, Father. If I had been ill, of course I should have told you in my letters.
Baron	Your Mother will break her heart.
Henry	My dear Mother! Sit down, sir. Don't leave us, Dr. Waldman. What a pleasure to see you, Father! What a pleasure to hear your voice, and feel your hand. *(He presses his own on it for a minute)* How is my Mother? And Katrina? And our good old Elizabeth, and Gustave, and John, and all the others at home? *(they sit.* **Waldman** *strolls to the centre doors and stands there, looking out)*
Baron	Your mother is well, but Katrina misses you sadly. We believe she cries about it, although she never lets us see her tears.
Henry	Poor little Katrina!
Baron	She keeps all your letters and reads them over and over. She has not been out in her little boat since you left home. I would gladly take her, but it's — "No, Father, I'll wait for Henry." She talks to her tame doves about her brother Henry. It's Henry, Henry all the time.
Henry	Go on, Father! I love to hear your voice. It is like a strain of familiar music.
Baron	*(drily)* Well, the music has been waiting for you patiently, although our good friend yonder wanted me to go away before you came home from your lecture.
Henry	I haven't been to any lecture this morning.
Baron	No?
Henry	No, I was — I was — in my bedroom overhead, reading.
Baron	Dr. Waldman assured me you were not in the house. Doctor! If you had let me go to Henry's other room I should have found him at once.
Waldman	I'm sorry, but I thought — it would disturb him —
Henry	*(returning* **Waldman's** *expressive glance)* He was right, Father. You would have awakened me from a most refreshing sleep.
Baron	Sleep? Why, you said just now you were reading.

Henry	Did I? *(embarrassed)* At all events, *you* know *(turns to* **Waldman***)* I mustn't be disturbed when I am reading, — *reading*, doctor.
Baron	Why, you have caught the bad habit of frowning and wagging your head now! You both of you look so solemn & mysterious. No wonder, reading and sleeping all day. What is the latest study, Henry?
Henry	Hang the latest study! Tell me the news of my mother and little Katrina.
Baron	And somebody else, Henry? You haven't asked a single question about Emilie Lavenza.
Henry	*(rising hastily)* Father, don't talk to me of her.
Baron	*(also rising)* What is the trouble, Henry? Can't you tell me the truth? Have you ceased to care for Emilie? Do you still love her?
Henry	*(passionately)* Do I love her? Emilie! Emilie!
Baron	You do? Then you have a strange way of showing your love. Mark my words, the most unselfish and constant of women will not take a man's love on trust for ever. If she were your wife ——
Henry	*(interrupting in the same passionate manner)* I would to God she were my wife! She could save me. Why do you come here to torture me? Why do you talk of home and all the peace and happiness I have thrown away? Why need you tell me that I'm unworthy of Emilie Lavenza? Who knows the truth better than I? Father, I'm on the rack! Spare me —
Waldman	*(stepping between them)* Henry, Henry, control yourself. Be calm. *(then consolingly)* My dear Baron, you mustn't be alarmed. My young friend is overwrought — words, words, words!
Henry	*(miserably)* Oh, doctor, this useless, eternal balm of yours on an open wound.
Waldman	*(ignoring him and continuing to the* **Baron***)* Now, if you'll only take my advice and leave me alone with Henry — my dear sir, pray hear me out! — I know that I can do him good. Be persuaded! Be reasonable.
Baron	*(hotly) I'm* reasonable enough —
Waldman	Yes, yes, yes, but if you'll only leave me alone with Henry for ten minutes — five minutes — where are your carriage and horses?
Baron	In the stable of old Pastor Clerval, ready for Henry and me to drive back to Belrive.
Henry	I cannot come —

Frankenstein (1928)

Baron	*(angrily)* You must!
Henry	Father, it is absolutely impossible! *(played very quickly from this speech to* **Baron's** *exit)*
Baron	You refuse, in spite of my command?
Henry	I refuse.
Waldman	Henry, let me speak to you alone.
Henry	Doctor, it's no use.
Baron	You have no respect for my wishes. You are deaf to your Mother's prayers. But don't be mistaken, Henry, I *will* know the reason before I go. Dr. Waldman, talk to this headstrong young fool. Teach him his duty if you can.
Waldman	Yes, I will, my dear Baron, but in the meantime — —
Baron	In the meantime, I'll wait for you at the Pastor's house, Henry. Come to me soon, or, by heaven, I'll return here and drag you home. Good-bye, Dr. Waldman.
Waldman	Let me have the pleasure of showing you the way, Baron.
Baron	Pleasure! Pleasure! You seem to want the pleasure of kicking me out — — *(exit, talking,* **Waldman** *mildly and the* **Baron** *angrily.* **Henry** *sinks into a chair and buries his face in his hands. After a few seconds re-enter* **Waldman**. *He lays his hand on* **Henry's** *shoulder.* **Henry** *starts and raises his head.)*
Waldman	Come, come! Why did you betray yourself to your Father?
Henry	*(miserably and vaguely)* Why, what did I say?
Waldman	You were nervous, angry, unnatural. You must be more careful —
Henry	Ah! What's that? There's a hand on the door. Who is it? *(knock at door R.)*
Waldman	Quiet! Who is there?
Victor	*(outside)* May I come in? Victor Moritz.
Henry	It's Victor. Come in, Victor! *(enter* **Victor***)*
Victor	Good morning, Dr. Waldman. My dear Henry, how are you? *(goes to* **Henry***, bends over table, and takes his hand)*
Henry	Alive, Victor. *(He stares in front of him unhappily. The others exchange a troubled glance.)*

Waldman	*(very softly)* Where is — *he*? Alone? *(***Henry** *nods)*
Victor	I saw, as I approached the house, that the shutters are closed. Is — he — in semi-darkness?
Henry	Yes.
Waldman	You kept him all the winter months in the laboratory underground. But since you brought him to your own rooms, a week ago, surely he has seen the sunlight?
Henry	Only through the cracks of the shutters. I forbade him to touch them.
Victor	Does he obey you?
Henry	*(contemptuously)* Does a frightened slave obey? Does a beaten hound obey?
Victor	But he is as strong as yourself.
Waldman	How have you mastered him?
Henry	Don't ask me, doctor. It is better not to know.
Victor	But he is your superior in height and — —
Henry	Victor, Victor! What is strength of muscle and sinew compared to the cunning of the brain? What is the courage of a wild beast compared to the cruelty of man?
Victor	*(recoiling a little)* Have you tortured him?
Henry	*(opening and then clenching his out-spread hand)* Is he not mine — mine? Is he not my terrible creation?
Waldman	Can he speak?
Henry	Yes. I have taught him, day after day, night after night. He is never out of my thoughts. When I fall asleep, from sheer exhaustion, I meet him in dreams of horror. But there is something worse, even worse, than his hated face and cowering body — his voice, his strange, unearthly laugh — —
Waldman	*(in surprise)* His laugh?
Henry	No! That is the wrong word. There is no laughter, no mirth, nothing human in that appalling cry. It is harsh and wild — *(he is, for a few seconds, frantic with fear)* it deafens my ears and beats in my brain until I feel I shall go mad — shall go mad —

Waldman	*(appealingly)* Henry! Henry!
Henry	*(hardly giving* **Waldman** *time to speak)* I can never hear it without terror. I tell you it will drive me mad. All my false ambition — my wicked pride — my filthy work among the dead — all my shame and misery is echoed in that voice. I cannot bear it! I cannot bear it! *(he sinks down in a chair, but quickly masters his emotion and lifts his head, speaking to* **Waldman** *vaguely and wretchedly)* What were you saying? What did you ask me?
Waldman	Can he learn from your teaching? Does he understand?
Henry	As a child understands, but now and again there is a flash of deeper thought across his narrow brain. He is elemental, unconscious of his own strength — a brute, a brute!
Victor	Is he so very strong?
Henry	Yes, strong and quick and agile. I have seen him leap like an animal on its prey, but he has never realized his powers. You have both seen him, and he remembers you, Dr. Waldman.
Victor	I cannot bear to look at him. He is so strangely like yourself in gesture and movement — his hands, his face, his colour, but a sullen devil looks at me out of those eyes.
Henry	*(with a groan)* Spare me, Victor!
Waldman	*(earnestly)* No one can see him. Your father, above all, must never see him. Henry you must follow the Baron and induce him to go back to Belrive.
Henry	How can I do that? You know how obstinate my Father is. He will not leave without me. I cannot promise to go home and leave him there! *(points to door L.)*
Waldman	But the Baron must not come here again — *(Loud cry from the inner room. They all start)* What is that?
Henry	Ah! It is Frankenstein.
Waldman	*(in surprise)* Frankenstein?
Henry	I call him by my own name. He *is* Frankenstein. *(Noise repeated)*
Victor	What does he want?
Henry	He wants to come in here. He has never seen the sun shine as it does today.

Peggy Webling and the Story behind Frankenstein

Waldman Let him come in.

Henry Are you not afraid?

Waldman No, no.

Victor We are three strong men.

Henry *(warningly as he goes to door L.)* Remember, we must keep him beneath our feet. *(He unlocks the door L.,* **Waldman** *watching him anxiously,* **Victor** *retreating a little up stage)* Frankenstein! *(a pause.* **Henry** *speaks again in harsh, commanding tone)* Frankenstein! Come here, I say! Frankenstein! *(Enter* **F.** *slowly. He bends forward, instinctively shielding his eyes with his hands. As he comes into the full stream of sunlight he suddenly crouches down, frightened.)*

Victor *(whispering)* Look at him, doctor! He moves like a half blind animal.

Waldman Hush! *(***F.*** makes an uncouth sound of fear)*

F. Burn! Burn! Burn! Fire — *(he looks wildly around the room)* My master! *(runs to* **Henry** *& tries to cling to him.* **Henry** *spurns him away.* **F.** *points to window)* Fire!

Henry Yes, but a good fire — a bright, soft fire. Go! *(threatens to strike him.* **F.** *moves to centre doors, frequently looking over his shoulder fearfully at* **Henry**, *and slowly warms them in the sunshine)*

Waldman *(drawing near, as if the words were forced out of him)* Man — devil — what are you?

F. *(with a long drawn breath)* Oh — great fire! *(another pause)* Great — soft — fire! *(he slowly lies down and curls himself up like a dog)*

Henry Frankenstein! *(kicks him)* Frankenstein! *(***F.*** rises)* Frankenstein, look out of the window. That is my garden. Say it after me. Garden.

F. *(in an expressionless tone)* Garden.

Henry Those are trees, and flowers, and the blue heaven over all.

F. Heaven — over — all.

Henry That is the sky, and the great fire is called the sun.

F. *(quite bewildered)* The sky — the sun — the sun — *(he looks out for a second and prepares to lie down again)* The great — fire — the sun — *(begins to fall asleep)*

Frankenstein (1928)

Henry	Wake up! Come here and kneel beside me — farther off — (**F.** *kneels at a little distance.* **Henry** *puts out his hand*) Frankenstein, what is this?
F.	*(very slowly)* Your — hand.
Henry	*(points to* **F.**'s *hand)* And this?
F.	My — hand.
Henry	What is your name?
F.	Frankenstein.
Henry	Do you remember my name? (**F.** *stares at him dumbly*) What am I?
F.	Man. *(mutters the word to himself)* Man — man. Master — man. Frankenstein — man. *(gives it up and points to centre doors)* I want — the sun.
Henry	No. You mustn't go into the sun now. You must stop here. Now, listen! Look at me! Look me in the eyes. *(at first* **F.** *shrinks almost to the ground, and then obeys him)* Tell me your thoughts.
F.	My — thoughts.
Henry	What do you think of us — of me — of these other men?
F.	*(looking at them fixedly in turns)* You are — big — big — you are — you are — like each other, but I — *(gives it up helplessly)*
Henry	Well, go on. What else do you want to say?
F.	Are there — men — like — like — Frankenstein? *(indicating himself)*
Henry	No.
Victor	*(quickly on* **Henry's** *denial)* Oh, no!
F.	*(repeating in the same tone)* No! Oh, no! Then — then — *(he clenches both hands beneath his chin, trying to think)*
Henry	What now? (**Victor** *makes an impatient movement*)
Waldman	Silence, Victor!
F.	Why — why — why are there no men — like me?
Henry	I can't tell you. You wouldn't understand.
F.	*(turns to* **Victor**) Are you — like my master? Do you *(he imitates a blow and a kick)*

Peggy Webling and the Story behind Frankenstein

Victor Does your master hate you?

F. Yes. Hate — hate — what does that mean?

Henry How can I answer?

Waldman It is impossible for him to understand. What can you say?

Henry I don't know, doctor. I don't know! (**F.** *slowly comes to* **Henry** *and touches his cheek.* **Henry** *draws back*)

F. What is that? Your — eyes are wet. (**F.** *shakes his head, touches his own eyes, then sinks into chair by table*) All men — hate me. Hate Frankenstein — hurt Frankenstein — (*droops forward, hands clasped between his knees.* **Henry** *comes up behind him*)

Waldman Henry! (*spoken together*)

Victor What do you —

Henry Now! (*clasps* **F.**'s *throat, as if to strangle him*) It would be no sin — no sin — (**F.** *gives a guttural gasp and instinctively catches* **Henry**'s *wrists. There is a brief struggle, then* **F.** *throws* **Henry** *off. The latter reels back a few paces.* **F.** *stares at him wonderingly, still seated.* **Waldman** *steps between them*) Keep off, Dr. Waldman! His hands are like steel. I think that he could kill —

F. (*loudly and fiercely, springing to his feet*) Kill! Kill! Kill? What does that mean? (*vaguely again*)

Henry (*angrily*) Frankenstein, why did you throw me off? How dare you touch me!

F. (*pleadingly*) Let me go — out there — (*points to garden*)

Waldman Not now, Frankenstein. You shall go into the garden when the sun sets.

F. The sun sets.

Waldman When the great fire in the sky is burnt out. Tonight.

F. Tonight?

Waldman Yes, before we go to sleep.

F. I want to go there now. Now! There is — there is — (*unhappily pleading for help*) Tell me! There is — there is —

Waldman There is beauty in the garden.

F.	Is that — the word? Beauty. Beauty.
Waldman	Yes, the fresh grass, the wind, the flowers.
F.	Are the great — flowers called beauty?
Waldman	You mean the trees. It is all beautiful.
F.	*(spreading his arms wide)* All — beautiful. All — *(a knock at the door R.)*
Henry	Hush! What's that? *(Henry thrusts F. out of the way: signals to Victor)* See who it is, Victor! *(Victor opens door a little)*
Victor	Good heavens! *(he goes out quickly, nearly closing door behind him)*
Henry	Stand still, Frankenstein. *(sternly)*
F.	*(his curiosity awakened)* What — is — it? *(Re-enter Victor. Closes door and looks in an agitated way from Henry to Waldman, still grasping the handle behind him)*
Victor	Henry — doctor — it's Emilie Lavenza! She has ridden over from Belrive. The door was open and she came into the house. What shall we do?
Henry	*(astounded)* Emilie? Here!
Waldman	*(speaking at the same second)* We must send her to find the Baron — no, stay! Let me think —
Henry	I know what to do. Yes! Frankenstein, go you into the other room and stop there. Do you understand? At once! On the instant — go!
F.	*(pointing to door R.)* Who — is there?
Henry	*(fiercely)* Go, I say!
F.	*(cowering, but still pointing to door)* I — will see —
Henry	*(threatening him with his hand)* Go! *(he is frightened and retreats as Henry advances. F. makes an ugly sound — half menace half in fear — and exits quickly L. Waldman closes and locks the door after him, leaving the key in it)*
Waldman	Now, Victor! *(Victor opens the other door. Enter Emilie Lavenza. She is a handsome, self-possessed girl of about twenty-three. She wears a riding costume and hat. She stops short on the threshold, staring at Henry)*
Victor	*(hastily)* This is one of our Professors, Emilie. Allow me to present Dr. Waldman — Miss Emilie Lavenza.

Peggy Webling and the Story behind Frankenstein

Waldman	I have heard so much of Miss Lavenza that I seem to know her already.
Emilie	*(with a curtsey)* I am pleased to meet you, Dr. Waldman. I have come to see Henry.
Henry	Yes, I am here.
Emilie	*(advancing into room & gazing at him wonderingly)* Is this really — you?
Waldman	Moritz and I will leave you together. *(then very seriously & kindly to* **Emilie***)* Miss Lavenza, let me, as an old and true friend of Henry's, entreat you to forgive him for his seeming neglect. There is a reason for it that even you would not be able to understand. Trust him & believe in him. *(in a lower voice as* **Emilie** *turns to* **Victor***)* Do not forget the man in your other room. Be careful.
Victor	*(expressively to* **Henry***)* If you want us we shall be near at hand. Good-bye! *(he bows to* **Emilie***)*
Waldman	Come, Moritz! *(Exit* **Waldman** *and* **Victor**. **Emilie** *&* **Henry** *look at each other eagerly & curiously)*
Emilie	Oh, how changed!
Henry	Oh, how unchanged! *(he goes towards her with out-stretched hands)*
Emilie	*(as if to gain time)* Are you glad to see me?
Henry	Glad? Glad? *(he seizes her hands & presses them passionately to his lips and then tries to clasp her in his arms. She yields after a momentary refusal)* Oh, my dear! My dear! I've waited for this for months — *(kissing her)*
Emilie	My poor Henry! How pale and worn you look. An old man! I was not prepared for this. Now, let me go. Dear, let me go! *(he releases her. She sits and he kneels beside her, holding her hand)* Henry, why have you deserted us all for so long? If I were not the most faithful woman in the world I should never speak to you again. I thought you loved me.
Henry	*(again kissing her hands)* I do! I do!
Emilie	Then why haven't you been to see me, or written to me?
Henry	I have written.
Emilie	*(firmly withdrawing her hands)* Twice in six months! Empty, formal notes! Who cares for a letter written with obvious constraint? Take them back — better if you had not written at all. *(throws two letters on the table)*

Frankenstein (1928)

Henry	If you only knew!
Emilie	If I only knew — what? You have mystified your Father and Mother, and saddened the life of your poor little sister Katrina. Although you ignore all their affection & entreaties, perhaps I shall not plead in vain. *(very tenderly)* Dearest, what is your secret? Why do you look so unhappy? Can't you trust me?
Henry	Trust you, Emilie? Against the world!
Emilie	Then tell me, or come back to Belrive with your Father. Let us ride after him together.
Henry	*(with an effort)* It is impossible for me to leave Goldstadt today.
Emilie	*(coaxingly)* Tomorrow then? Promise me to come back to us tomorrow.
Henry	No, no, no.
Emilie	Promise me! I implore you, Henry. Think of Katrina — remember our happy old life at Belrive. Why do you refuse? Tell me — I will be answered. Tell me, Henry.
Henry	*(rising and moving away, speaking desperately)* It would be better for Katrina never to see me again — better for you to forget our love — better for you all if I had never lived. Do you think I would refuse you if I dared to promise? I am a phantom-haunted man.
Emilie	*(catching eagerly at the words)* Phantom-haunted? Now you are telling me the truth.
Henry	Yes, the awful truth.
Emilie	A phantom-haunted man? What do you mean by that? You look distraught. You frighten me. Henry, come away! *(putting her hands round his neck)* Come to Belrive. My love will teach you to forget.
Henry	I can never forget.
Emilie	Let me help you. Nothing can change my love. What is your strange and terrible secret? Where shall I find the clue? The very air of this room is full of mystery. What have you done? Do you study here — work here?
Henry	*(embarrassed and troubled)* Not — not very often.
Emilie	Where then?
Henry	In my laboratory.

Emilie	*(moving towards inner room)* Is that your laboratory?
Henry	*(very emphatically, as he stops her)* No, not there. You must not go there.
Emilie	*(suddenly suspicious)* Why not? Oh, I remember — who is the man Dr. Waldman whispered was in that room?
Henry	Did you hear that?
Emilie	Yes, and why did he say "Be careful"?
F.	*(in a loud, imperative voice from the inner room)* Master! *(they both start)*
Emilie	Who is the man concealed in that room? Henry, who is it?
Henry	Stand back — I will make him be quiet — farther away — *(he pushes her across the room, then unlocks and opens door L.)* Frankenstein!
Emilie	*(in amazement)* Frankenstein! (**Frankenstein** *bursts into the room with* **Henry**. *They stand facing the girl in exactly the same attitude. She screams)* Henry, who is this? You are both alike! I am afraid — let me go — let me go — *(she rushes out.* **Henry** *follows her to the door)*
F.	Who — was that? Went out — ran away — I will follow —
Henry	You follow a woman — no!
F.	Was that — a woman? I will follow —
Henry	No! Back, Frankenstein! You shall not go. I am your master. Down at my feet! *(he lifts his hand to strike* **F.**, *but* **F.** *catches his wrist and they stand for a second, both drawn to their full height staring into each other's eyes. Then* **F.** *throws* **Henry** *off, wrenching his arm so that he gives a cry of pain.)*
Henry	*(shouting)* Victor! Victor! Waldman! Help! Help! *(Enter* **Waldman** *and* **Victor**. *They seize* **F.** *He slowly pushes* **Victor** *to his knees and then throws him down, jerks his arm from* **Waldman** *and turns to* **Henry**)
F.	I — will — go! *(Exit* **F.**, *the others staring after him)*

End of Act I.

FRANKENSTEIN

Act II

*Later in the same day. A room on the first floor of the **Baron's** house at Belrive. A homely, comfortable room, book-cases, flowers, easy chairs, a table, etc. A bowl of roses in the middle of this table. A balcony at the back of the stage L. showing a clear, blue sky beyond. A small slit of a door R. Another L. A wicker cage, on a stool near window. This must contain two real and one artificial doves, the last named concealed from view. Whenever **Katrina** passes the cage she stoops to look at the birds, or softly coo to them.*

*The **Baroness**, a plainly dressed, serene type of woman, is discovered sewing. **Katrina** sits beside her, singing. She rises & goes to the doves' cage. She is lame. Her crutch is resting beside her. **Katrina** is very slight and short, about fifteen years of age, pale, with flaxen hair. She is appealing and sweet in expression, her whole appearance being spiritual and unconsciously pathetic.*

Baroness Katrina, lean out the window. Do you see any sign of your Father coming?

Katrina No, dear Mother. No. There is not a single carriage in sight on the road along the river.

Baroness I do hope our Henry will return with him.

Katrina *(clasping her hands ecstatically together and speaking as if her brother stood before her)* Dear Henry, do come home to us! Your books are here and a quiet room. Your boat is asleep on the water, with her sails furled like a bird's wings. The garden waits for you. The house is empty without you. Henry, do come home!

Baroness *(smiling at her)* To whom are you talking, sweetheart? Your brother can't hear you.

Katrina *(whimsically)* Not with his ears, Mother, but with his spirit.

Baroness He is very unkind to keep away from his good little sister for so long.

Katrina *(pressing her cheek lovingly against the **Baroness's** hair)* It is harder for you than for me, harder for Father, and much, much harder for Emilie. Think, Mother! Henry hasn't seen my two birds! *(stoops to cage)* Coo, coo, you pretty doves! Coo, coo! *(gives a little start and goes to balcony)* Mother! *(sound of approaching horse)* I think I see — is that? — *(pause)* Yes! It's Emilie Lavenza galloping along the river road.

Baroness Is it Emilie — alone?

Katrina	Yes. She sees me and waves her hand. Emilie! Emilie! *(the sound of the horse stopping)* She is coming nearer. Our John has run out and is taking her horse.
Baroness	Why should Emilie be galloping along the river road?
Katrina	Perhaps she has been to Goldstadt to see Henry. She knew that Father was going there today — ah! here she is! *(enter **Emilie Lavenza**. She looks pale and agitated. The **Baroness** & **Katrina** advance quickly)*
Baroness	My dear Emilie!
Emilie	Oh, Baroness! I am overjoyed to see you! *(they kiss)* I'm so thankful to be here.
Katrina	What is the matter, Emilie dear?
Emilie	Little Katrina! *(kisses **Katrina**)*
Katrina	How ill you look! What has happened? Why were you galloping along the road at such a furious pace?
Baroness	Have you been to Goldstadt, my dear?
Emilie	How did you know that?
Baroness	Katrina thought of it. Where is the Baron?
Emilie	I don't know. I haven't seen him.
Katrina	Sit down and rest, Emilie dear.
Emilie	*(as she drops into a chair)* Thank you.
Baroness	Have you seen Henry? Where is he?
Emilie	Oh, yes, I have seen him. I went to his rooms. But I'm afraid he is — *(she stops confusedly)*
Katrina	Not ill, Emilie? Is he ill?
Emilie	No, no. He said he was quite well, but he seems to be greatly changed. He refused to come home with me. I saw — dear Baroness, I hardly know how to tell you what happened. We were together, standing in his room, when suddenly there was a strange sound from the inner room. A man was locked in, for I saw Henry turn the key. Dr. Waldman had warned him to be careful with this man.
Baroness	Who was it?

Emilie	I can't tell you. Henry called him "Frankenstein."
Baroness	Did he speak to the strange man by his own name?
Emilie	Yes, this other Frankenstein looked at me — stared at me — and I was filled with terror.
Baroness	Emilie!
Emilie	He looked to me like a thing without a soul — a brute beast in the body of a man. Then I rushed away. My instinct was to escape — anywhere — anyhow — I think I galloped all the way from Goldstadt to Belrive. I should have gone home, but your house was nearer than ours — *(appealingly)* Dear Baroness, let me stop here for a little while. I am afraid —
Baroness	Of course you shall stop as long as you please, my child.
Katrina	*(pressing her cheek to **Emilie's** hand)* Stop with me. Dear one! Dear one!
Emilie	Yes, I am sure that with you, Katrina — *(as she says this there is the clatter of horses' hoofs quickly approaching)* Ah! That must be your Father! *(goes to balcony)* Yes, it is the Baron and two other men. Why, there is Victor Moritz and Dr. Waldman.
Katrina	*(also hurrying to balcony)* Is Henry there?
Emilie	I do not see him.
Baron	*(outside)* John! Max! Hillo there!
Katrina	*(turning back sadly into room)* No Henry.
Emilie	*(quickly)* I do not want to meet Victor and the doctor. They will question me about your brother. Let me go to your little sitting room, Katrina. Pray let me go! Come with me.
Baroness	No, I'll come with you, my dear. There! *(draws **Emilie's** hand through her arm)* You're still trembling. *(to **Katrina**, as they go towards door R.)* Ask your Father about Henry, sweetheart. Come to us with the news as soon as you can. Now, Emilie! *(Exit **Baroness** and **Emilie**. **Katrina** goes as quickly as she can towards door L. It opens as she draws near. Enter **Baron**, talking fussily as he comes, followed by **Waldman** and **Victor** in an anxious, hurried manner)*
Baron	Come in! Come in! Where are you, Baroness? Ah, little Katrina! *(kisses her)*
Victor	*(almost interrupting him)* Is Emilie Lavenza here?

Katrina	Yes, she is here.
Victor	*(softly, half to himself)* Thank God!
Baron	Dr. Waldman, this is my daughter Katrina. (**Waldman** *kisses her hand*)
Katrina	*(smiling)* Dr. Waldman. I'm very glad to see you, Victor.
Victor	And I to see you, Katrina. *(also kisses her hand)*
Katrina	*(to **Victor**)* Why did you ask so anxiously for Emilie? *(then to **Baron**)* I wish Henry had come with you.
Baron	Oh, your brother's mad!
Katrina	*(protestingly)* Father dear!
Baron	*(throwing down his hat and gloves)* He refused to drive with us, but mounted his own horse and galloped off to the Lavenzas' house. He was riding like the devil. Sit down, Dr. Waldman.
Waldman	Thank you, Baron. *(quickly to **Victor**)* Go on to the balcony, Moritz, and look out for Henry. Give him the signal we arranged at Goldstadt that all is well — she is safe —
Victor	*(equally quickly)* I will, doctor. (**Victor** *goes on to balcony and shows, by the way he leans & watches, that he is very eager to see* **Henry**)
Baron	Where is your Mother?
Katrina	She is in my little room with Emilie. Shall I call her?
Baron	No matter. Did you hear me shouting for John and Max? No civility! No promptitude! I must show you my garden and stables, doctor. I've got a new little mare — a jewel! She is —
Victor	*(turning towards the room)* Henry is coming, Dr. Waldman! *(sound of* **Henry** *approaching on horseback.* **Victor** *waves his handkerchief up and down several times)*
Waldman	*(as **Victor** does this)* Is he alone?
Victor	Yes.
Waldman	*(to **Baron**)* That is our signal to your son that all is well. (**Henry** *is heard getting nearer & nearer)*
Baron:	He knows that all is well. What do you mean?
Victor	*(bending forward over balcony)* She is here. She came here. Emilie is here!

Frankenstein (1928)

Katrina Henry at last! *(horse's hoofs stop)*

Baron I said he started riding like the devil. He must have ridden like twenty devils! *(Enter **Henry** quickly, hat and whip in hand, speaking as he enters)*

Henry Is she safe, doctor?

Waldman Yes —

Katrina Henry!

Henry Dear Katrina! *(they embrace affectionately, and she puts a rose from the bowl on the table in his coat)*

Katrina So you have come home after all, poor, tired Henry! *(she reaches up her hand to smooth his cheek)*

Henry Have you missed me so much, little Katrina? Where is Emilie now?

Katrina She is with Mother —

Henry *(interrupting)* Is she well? What did she say to you? She is quite safe, Katrina?

Katrina Of course she is quite safe, dear Henry.

Henry Oh, I'm thankful! I'm thankful! Oh, the agony of dread — I'm thankful! *(he turns towards balcony as if unable to control himself. **Waldman** & **Victor** whisper to each other unheard as the **Baron** speaks)*

Baron What is the matter with you, my son? You're at home. You've escaped from your prison at Goldstadt.

Henry A prison indeed!

Baron We'll have a glass of wine after our drive.

Waldman *(nervously)* Thank you, Baron, but perhaps Moritz and I had better go with Henry in search of — of — *(he stops uncertainly)*

Victor Henry's friend — *(with similar hesitation and nervousness)* the man from Goldstadt — the stranger —

Baron We want no strangers here. Katrina, go to the stairs, my little heart. Call to Elizabeth to bring us a bottle of wine and some glasses.

Victor I'll tell her, Katrina.

Katrina Thank you, Victor.

Baron	*(stopping him)* No, no, it is not your place. Come, Henry, fetch the wine, or call to Elizabeth. Don't stare out of that window.
Henry	*(ignoring his Father)* Can I go up to your little room, Katrina? I'll greet my dear Mother and ask her to leave us. I must see Emilie by herself.
Baron	Oh, these moony, abstracted lovers! Won't you have a glass of wine before you go, Henry?
Henry	No, Father. Excuse me, Dr. Waldman. Katrina, take me to Emilie.
Katrina	*(as they go towards door R.)* But you wish to be alone with her.
Henry	Yes, after a little while. I want her to see me first hand in hand with *you*. *(they take hands. Exit* **Henry** *and* **Katrina** *R.)*
Baron	Well, well, all the more wine for us! *(Enter* **Elizabeth**, *carrying a tray with wine and glasses)* Why, Elizabeth, you must be a good fairy to appear just when we wanted you. Set it down, set it down. Now, doctor — *(he pours wine)*
Elizabeth	If you please, there is a man at the door asking for you, Baron.
Baron	*(passing wine to* **Waldman***)* Who is it, Elizabeth?
Elizabeth	*(in a puzzled voice, glancing nervously over her shoulder)* I don't know. All he said was, "Master — Master!"
Waldman	*(putting down his glass and starting to his feet.* **Victor** *also springs up)* Ah! I know who it is!
Baron	*(in amazement at his manner)* Do you?
Waldman	Yes, he must not come in here. Moritz!
Victor	What shall I do?
Elizabeth	*(with a little cry)* I hear him on the stairs!
Waldman	*(softly to Moritz)* Too late! *(***Frankenstein** *bursts into the room. He is panting loudly, his hair is blown over his face, and his clothes & boots are flecked with dust.* **Elizabeth** *passes behind him & exits, keeping her eyes fixed on him till she disappears)*
Baron	*(rising, astonished)* Good Heavens!
F.	*(gazing about him blankly)* Strange — place!
Waldman	Silence! *(sternly)* Do as I tell you. Come farther into the room.

Frankenstein (1928)

F.	Where is — my master? Who is — that? *(points to* **Baron***)*
Baron	Who d'ye think I am? The master of the house.
F.	You are not — my master. *(points to* **Baron's** *hair & face)* Why are you — all white — all lined — are you — an old man?
Waldman	Be silent! Pray pardon him, my dear Baron, pray pardon him.
F.	*(to* **Victor***)* Where is — the woman?
Waldman	Hush!
Victor	You will never see her again.
F.	Never — never — what does that mean?
Baron	*(looking at* **F.** *very curiously)* You haven't told me this surprising young man's name, doctor.
Waldman	*(taken aback)* His name? It is — it is —
Baron	Yes? *(to* **F.***)* What is your name, sir?
F.	My name? Frankenstein.
Baron	What? Our name? Does he claim to be one of the same family?
Waldman	No, no.
Baron	Where were you born?
F.	I do — not know.
Baron	You don't know? Who were your father and mother?
F.	I do — not know.
Baron	Why did you come here?
F.	*(turning to* **Waldman** *&* **Victor***)* I saw you — there — where my master lives — *(with contempt)* My master! — I saw — the — woman —
Baron	What woman does he mean?
F.	I ran — I ran — far — far *(holds his hands over his eyes as if watching* **Emilie** *disappear in sunshine)*
Waldman	Did you see us — in the carriage — drive away?
F.	Noise — noise — on the road — *(looks at* **Baron** *and imitates plying a whip)* I followed —

Peggy Webling and the Story behind Frankenstein

Victor   Where were you?

F.   You did — not see me. I ran, white all over me — white.

Baron   Do you mean the dust of the road?

Waldman   Did you run at the side of the road?

F.   There — quick! quick! Down — up — tree all round me — grass — under my feet. I fell — so — branches struck me — I tore them off — so! so! Water — I drank — so! *(imitates drinking from his hands)* Quick! The great fire burns — burns! Pain! Pain! *(clutches at his heart, imitating exhaustion)* I ran — I ran — the woman was gone — I saw — my master —

Baron   Who *is* your master?

Waldman   *(quickly & emphatically interposing)* Do not listen to him, my dear Baron. He has no master — he doesn't know what he is saying — *(turns to F.)* Silence, silence, Frankenstein!

F.   *(unheeding him and pulling at his throat)* I want to drink — I want to drink — *(looks about him)*

Baron   I understand him now. Well, young Frankenstein, will you drink a glass of wine? Sit down.

Waldman   Sit down beside me, Frankenstein — speak no more. Moritz, sit on his other hand. *(they all drink. F. tastes his and instantly withdraws glass from his lips with an exclamation of disgust)*

Baron   *(incredulously)* You don't care for this?

F.   *(with a snarl)* No! *(coolly hurls glass out of window)*

Baron   *(rising indignantly)* What the devil —

Waldman   *(fiercely)* Frankenstein!

Victor   You brute!

F.   I want — to drink — to drink — *(notices the bowl of roses on the table, snatches out the flowers, throws them down and drinks the water noisily)*

Waldman   Give me that bowl! My dear Baron, he doesn't understand —

Baron   You should beg my pardon, young man! *(F. stares at him, makes a low sound of disgust and goes to balcony. He is no longer afraid of the men)*

F.   The great fire is — burning — low. The sun! The sun! The sun! *(points down)* There is — water! Look! Shining water!

Frankenstein (1928)

Baron	Have you never seen a river before?
F.	River? Water.
Baron	Well, the water down there is called a river. *(to the others)* He's a strange creature! I can't understand him — *(stares at F.)*
Victor	*(softly to Waldman)* What are we to do, doctor? Shall I go for Henry?
Waldman	Yes — no! We must distract the Baron's attention. I'll get him away. *(goes to Baron)* Have you forgotten your promise as we drove from Goldstadt, Baron?
Baron	*(still staring at F.)* What promise was that?
Waldman	Why, to show me your garden & stables. What of the new mare? Come, Baron, is she really such a little jewel?
Baron	A jewel, doctor, a little beauty!
Waldman	I'll go with the Baron, Moritz. You stop here with Frankenstein.
Baron	No, no, Victor. I don't want to lose sight of Frankenstein. *(to F.)* Come with us.
Waldman	Well — very well.
F.	*(eagerly)* Out there — to the water — and the sun?
Victor	Wherever we choose to take you.
F.	*(excitedly)* The sun — the shining water — this way — this way — *(he thrusts Baron on one side and exits L.)*
Baron	*(angrily)* Of all the vulgar young louts —
Waldman	Follow him, Moritz! *(exit Moritz running)* He is ignorant and ill bred, Baron. He means no harm. It's only — only — his boyish, sportive way — —
Baron	*(as they go out)* Boyish! Sportive! Those are not my words for damned impertinence. I beg your pardon, doctor, but upon my life I never met —
Waldman	Neither did I, Baron — *(Exit Waldman and Baron. As they disappear enter Emilie R., closely followed by Henry)*
Henry	Believe me, dearest, it's the truth —
Emilie	How *can* I believe you, Henry? Impossible!
Henry	Emilie! My dear love! Before God I have done this thing I tell you. I have created this being. I call him Frankenstein like myself. Don't you

	understand my agony? Can't you realize my remorse? *(she looks at him steadily, her fear changing to pity)* I think I was possessed by a devil to begin such a work. All that was dark and hidden and evil in my man's nature gave me power. As Frankenstein came to life, my heart died in my breast. I had turned my world into Hell. There was only one hope — one dream — one consolation left. *You!* Emilie, your love still shone in the blackness of my despair. I believed that *you* would understand, *you* would pity, *you* would save me.
Emilie	*(despondently)* What can I do? What *can* I do?
Henry	Love me. Try to forgive me. Pray for me.
Emilie	*(laying her hand timidly on his shoulder)* Let me go away, Henry. Leave me to myself. Let me go back to your sister's room. I want to be alone to think — to try to believe — *(presses her hand to her forehead)* I am bewildered and unnerved — can't you see — ?
Henry	Would you rather go home?
Emilie	I can't go home. I feel too weak and wretched. Your Mother will let me stop here tonight.
Henry	Oh, yes.
Emilie	I will sleep in little Katrina's room. To be near Katrina will give me peace and courage.
Henry	Shall I send one of the servants with a message to your home?
Emilie	Not one of the servants, Henry. My poor Mother will be so anxious. She knew that I was riding into Goldstadt this morning. Will you go yourself? *(he makes a slight gesture of dissent)* To please me! Tell her that your love for me is unchanged. Assure her that I'm well and happy. I will be home tomorrow.
Henry	Are you indeed happy?
Emilie	Not now — but I shall be in the future. We shall both be happy again some day — my poor Henry!
Henry	Very well. I will go. Goodbye!
Emilie	I *will* pray for you. Farewell! *(he kisses her hand)*
Henry	God keep you! *(Exit* **Henry.** **Emilie** *gazes sadly after him for a second. She then walks slowly to the doves' cage & looks abstractedly at them. Sighs and makes her way wearily towards the door R. Enter* **Frankenstein,**

Frankenstein (1928)

	quickly, *as if he had just eluded* **Henry**. **Emilie** *turns and sees him. She gives a slight cry)*
Emilie	Oh — you again!
F.	*(staring at her)* The woman! The — same — woman!
Emilie	*(gasping)* You frighten me. Who are you? Who are you?
F.	Frankenstein. I want — you! *(he takes a quick step, almost a leap towards her)*
Emilie	No — no! I will shriek —
F.	You will — cry out? When I cry out, my master stops my mouth — so! *(spreads his open hand over face)* Woman! Woman! What have you done to me? I — I — come to me! I — I —
Emilie	*(as if the words came against her will)* Do you — love me?
F.	Love! Love! What is that? Come close to me! Love — Pain — beauty — Come to me! *(he seizes her in his arms, crushing her to his breast, but not kissing her)* Mine! Mine! Mine! **(Katrina** *enters at door L. Her face expresses utter amazement. She advances quickly)*
Katrina	Emilie! Let her go! **(F.**'s *arms drop to his sides.* **Emilie** *falls back against the table, almost fainting.* F. *stares at* **Katrina**.*)* I don't know why she looks so frightened. I don't quite understand, but you must not hold her like that again. It is not right. Emilie, come back to my room. You stop here till I return. *(to* F.*)*
F.	I — love — the woman —
Emilie	No, no! I hate you. I can't breathe in the same air — horrible! horrible!
Katrina	*(to* F.*)* Wait here for me. *(Exit* **Emilie** *and* **Katrina***)*
F.	Hate! Horrible! Horrible! *(he walks backwards & forwards in an agitated state for a few seconds, wrings his hands, and then stops at the balcony. Suddenly turns his face upwards, as if watching the flight of a bird. Catches sight of the doves. Goes to them, takes one out (the artificial bird) and throws it in the air. Then looks down, as if watching it fall. Enter* **Katrina**, *unheard. She advances. He turns and stares at her as before)*
Katrina	Did you come here with Henry?
F.	I — do not know.
Katrina	Well, you are very welcome. What is your name?

Peggy Webling and the Story behind Frankenstein

F. Frankenstein.

Katrina Is it truly Frankenstein? Then you must be my cousin, or my — *(she catches sight of the cage and goes to it, distressed)* Oh, my doves! My pretty, pretty doves! One of them has gone. Sweetest dove, where is your gentle mate?

F. It has gone — out there.

Katrina Did it fly into the blue?

F. No. It fell down — down — on the water— still, on the water. Still! Still!

Katrina Did it float along the river?

F. Yes, like those leaves — on the water —

Katrina Then it must be dead. I was so fond of all my doves. *(F. touches her face very carefully)*

F. What — are you doing? I have seen — water — in my master's eyes — like that.

Katrina They are tears.

F. Tears?

Katrina *(very simply)* I am sorry — unhappy — and I am crying. Have you never cried?

F. No. *(points down to river again)* I like — to see them — float.

Katrina The leaves?

F. And — the bird! (**Katrina** *sits near the cage, looking at him thoughtfully. He picks up her crutch and examines it. She tries to rise)*

Katrina Please give me back my crutch. *(he takes no notice)* Give me back my crutch. I can't walk without it. *(he suddenly comprehends her meaning and gives it back. She puts out her hands for him to help her to rise. After a pause he does so)*

F. Why — did you do that?

Katrina I don't know what you mean.

F. You — gave me your hands. May I feel them again? (**Katrina** *lays her hands on his for a second)* No one — has done that before. My master — will not touch me. Those men — will not touch me. The woman — hates me. Do you — hate me?

Frankenstein (1928)

Katrina	No, no, my poor friend.
F.	Friend? What is that?
Katrina	I am your friend. Why do you look so sad?
F.	Sad? I do — not know.
Katrina	This is such a beautiful world, with so many kind and good people in it. Look at the flowing river and the drifting clouds. Let us go out of doors.
F.	Out there?
Katrina	Yes, I am always running out of doors.
F.	Can you — run?
Katrina	No, I am lame, and I get tired so easily. But I love to feel the soft air and lean over the side of my little boat, touching the water with my fingers. It whispers "Little Katrina! Little Katrina!"
F.	*(slowly repeating the words)* Little Katrina! Little Katrina!
Katrina	Will you come with me?
F.	Yes. I will come.
Katrina	*(as she goes towards the door R.)* Look! This opens on a narrow staircase; above is my own sitting room, below is a little door leading to the river bank where my boat is lying.
F.	*(as he goes to her)* You do not — hate me?
Katrina	Why should I hate you? Come!
F.	To the water, where the leaves float — and the bird —
Katrina	Yes, I'll show you the way. It's such a narrow stair — take my hand.
F.	*(as he does so)* You are — little Katrina —
Katrina	This way — *(Exit* **Katrina** *first, her hand stretched behind her holding his. Exit* **F.** *A slight pause. The sound of men's voices heard outside. Enter* **Baron**, **Waldman**, *and* **Victor**).
Baron	*(As he comes in)* Of course I'm glad Henry came, doctor, although I admit it was very surprising. He refused to leave Goldstadt this morning, and you encouraged him. Do sit down. I want to talk to you. (**Baron** *&* **Waldman** *sit at table*)
Waldman	*(anxiously to* **Victor***)* Where is Frankenstein?

Peggy Webling and the Story behind Frankenstein

Victor He eluded me when we were alone in the orchard.

Waldman *(nervous and annoyed)* Why did you let him do that?

Victor He is so swift — so cunning —

Waldman *(interrupting in a distressed, alarmed manner)* But where has he gone? Oh, Moritz! What is he doing now? (**Victor** *shakes his head with a troubled expression. He &* **Waldman** *are restless all through the scene*).

Baron This Frankenstein, as you call him, is the man I want to talk about, Dr. Waldman. Do you know him well?

Waldman I — I — yes, I know him well, Baron. You mustn't take his roughness ill. He's only ignorant and —

Baron Only ignorant! My dog has better manners. He took a goblet of wine and threw it out of the window. You saw him do it. I've never met a man before, however ignorant, who hasn't learned where to toss wine! *(indicates his mouth)* There's something strange about him. I wouldn't say so to Henry, for he'd only laugh at me, but my blood runs cold in my body when I look at young Frankenstein.

Waldman *(forcing a smile)* Really, my dear Baron!

Baron Truth, sir, truth. He seems to me like an evil thing — no man at all, as we know men.

Waldman Well, Henry must get him away from Belrive.

Baron I shall tell Henry to have nothing more to do with him. My son is not his keeper.

Waldman Take my advice, Baron, and leave the matter in your son's hands entirely.

Victor I'll do *my* best with Henry to take Frankenstein away.

Baron *(looking with surprise from one to the other)* What, both of you? *(with sudden suspicion)* What are you hiding from me?

Waldman Nothing, nothing, my good sir.

Victor *(boldly)* There is nothing to hide, Baron.

Baron That's a lie — it's a lie, Victor Moritz. You know it is. *(rises)* Who is this man calling himself by my name? Where does he come from? How long has my son been in his power?

Waldman Henry is not in his power.

Frankenstein (1928)

Baron False again! I see it in your face. Henry and Victor are afraid of him and you know the reason, Dr. Waldman.

Waldman I assure you solemnly, Baron ——

Baron *(getting very angry)* I'm not a fool. I'm not in my dotage. Why did my son stop away from home for six months, and rush here today in pursuit of this Frankenstein? Why did you both come with him? What have you done with the man? Where is he now? *(to **Waldman**)*

Waldman I wish to Heaven I knew.

Baron *(turning appealingly to **Victor**)* Victor, you're a good, kind fellow. Tell me what you know of Frankenstein. I entreat you to tell me.

Victor *(embarrassed, glancing for guidance to **Waldman**)* Baron, I — I know so little of Frankenstein.

Baron Do you know his people, his home, his character?

Victor No.

Baron Where did you first meet him? *(a pause)* Well?

Victor In Goldstadt. In — in Henry's rooms.

Baron Then he was Henry's friend, not yours, or Dr. Waldman's?

Victor *(more and more troubled)* Yes, he — he — Henry knew him first.

Baron What did Henry tell you about him?

Victor *(desperately)* Baron, I can't answer such a volley of questions. Ask your son himself. God knows *I* am not responsible for this Frankenstein.

Baron Then Henry is responsible?

Victor *(after a very slight, irresolute pause)* Yes, but you wouldn't understand —

Baron *(in a towering rage)* There's one thing I *do* understand. You are all deceiving me. Where has Frankenstein gone? Where is he hidden? I'll find him! Frankenstein! Frankenstein! *(as he moves quickly to door L., it opens and **Elizabeth** enters, very white and agitated)* Elizabeth! *(all look at her in surprise — to be played rapidly)*

Elizabeth Oh, Baron, Baron! Where is my mistress? Something terrible has happened. Oh, gentlemen, it's too dreadful! She's gone — she's gone — our little angel! Let me go to her poor mother — *(hurries towards door R.)*

Baron Elizabeth! *(spoken together)*

Waldman	What is the matter?
Elizabeth	*(looking over her shoulder)* He's bringing her in. I met him at the door — oh, Lord! have mercy —
Waldman	Quick, Moritz, pull out the lounge! *(***Victor** *obeys him. Enter* **F.**, *carrying* **Katrina** *in his arms. She is drowned. Her dress clings to her figure and water drips from her hair. His eyes are wide with wonder as he looks from one to another. For a second they are too shocked to speak)*
F.	*(blankly)* Little Katrina!
Waldman	Put her down here!
Baron	*(as he takes* **Katrina** *from* **F.** *and puts her down on lounge.* **F.** *only stares)* Oh, God, my child! Doctor, look! My little girl! Little Katrina! *(turns to* **Elizabeth**, *while* **Waldman** *feels* **Katrina's** *pulse, looks under her eyelid, etc.)* Go to my wife. Don't let her come here. Go to my poor wife. *(Exit* **Elizabeth**, *crying bitterly)*
Victor	Dr. Waldman, shall I —
Waldman	Silence! Control yourselves. *(lays his hand on* **Baron's** *shoulder)* My poor friend, your child is — *(stops)*
Victor	Dead?
Waldman	She has been drowned.
Baron	Oh, doctor! Can nothing be done?
Waldman	Nothing.
Baron	*(brokenly, bending over lounge)* Our little Katrina! My own loving little girl! *(more brokenly)* I must go to my wife — my poor wife — the mother of my child — I want my wife — *(Exit* **Baron** *R., blindly)*
Waldman	*(to* **F.***)* Where did you find her? What do you know of this?
F.	*(bewildered)* She took me *(points to door R.)* down to the boat. I — I — pushed it away from land. On the water. The leaves floated — like the bird — on the water —
Waldman	Go on! Go on! What then?
F.	*(with expressive gestures)* I took — her hands. I — lifted her and laid her down — on the water — *(looks at them vaguely)*
Waldman	Go on, Frankenstein.

Frankenstein (1928)

F.	She held my hands — but I — shook her off. I — wanted to see her — like the bird — on the water. "Oh! Oh!" she cried. Then — I pressed her down — under the water. Beauty — beauty — her hair — her face — under the water.
Waldman	You held her under the water — ah! —
F.	Down — down — I held her a long time. A long time. Then — then — I took her out. She was still — still — like that! *(points to her)*
Victor	You have killed Katrina. *(then in a deep, horrified way)* Murderer!
Waldman	Moritz, remember! He doesn't understand.
Victor	He has killed little Katrina.
F.	*(staring at them in turn)* I — killed little Katrina —
Waldman	Yes, she will never speak to us again.
F.	*(very slowly beginning to realise the truth)* Never — speak again. Never take my hand. She — was not afraid of me. She — touched — me. *(he creeps to lounge)* Is she — asleep?
Waldman	She is dead.
F.	She looks — the same —
Waldman	No, she is utterly changed. You have killed her.
F.	Changed? I have — killed her? *(raises his voice)* Katrina! Little Katrina! Look at me. Never — never — *(wildly appealing to* **Waldman***)* What — does it all mean? I am hurt — I am hurt — *(laying his hand on his heart)* pain — pain — but not with my master's blows. Help me! Help me! Help me, men! *(looking up to heaven)* Is there — no one — in the whole world — to help me? Katrina! Katrina! I know — now — what I have done. I know! Sorrow — sorrow — pain — I — I understand — *(he breaks into a storm of uncontrollable grief and drops down over* **Katrina***. Silence for a few seconds, the other men watching him in an awe-stricken way. Then* **Waldman** *beckons* **Victor** *with a slight gesture of his hand to come close to him)*
Waldman	My dear Moritz, we must take her away. Henry must not find her here — with him. Can you carry her up to her room?
Victor	Yes, doctor. Will you speak to him, or shall I? *(they both look doubtfully at* **F.***, then* **Waldman** *lays his hand on* **Victor's** *chest to keep him back)*
Waldman	Leave it to me. Do not say a word, I entreat you. This grief will pass and then — who knows? Keep still! *(gives* **Victor** *a warning, almost a stern,*

	look and advances to **F.***)* Frankenstein! *(speaks calmly, but draws back his hand as he is about to touch him)* Now, Frankenstein! Come! Rise to your feet. Rise! (**F.** *slowly lifts his head and slowly stands up*) She must be taken away. Do not look at her again. Listen to me, (**F.** *stares at him blankly*)
F.	What — am I — to do?
Waldman	Listen to me. When your master comes home —
F.	*(in a changed voice)* My master! Why did my master — not tell me — the shining water would kill? (**Waldman** *&* **Victor** *exchange an expressive glance, realising the sense of this question)*
Waldman	He will tell you what to do. Now, Moritz, carry her to her room — gently — gently — (**Victor** *lifts* **Katrina** *and slowly carries her out at door R.*)
Victor	*(as he exits)* Oh, Katrina! Poor, poor little girl!
F.	*(gazing after them in a dazed way)* Where — has she gone? Let me go with her.
Waldman	Not now, not now! (**F.** *turns miserably towards the balcony, takes a few steps and hides his face on the rail. Enter* **Henry** *L.*) Henry! Henry — Katrina —
Henry	*(in a deep, unhappy voice)* I know. I know. They told me at the door. *(with sudden fierceness)* Where is Frankenstein?
Waldman	He is there —
Henry	My sister's murderer! His accursed life shall pay for hers —
Waldman	*(with great earnestness)* Henry, think! Think! He is not responsible. He doesn't understand — my dear Henry, for God's sake, control yourself —
Henry	*(with stern determination)* He killed my sister. Let me go, Dr. Waldman!
Waldman	*(wildly, clinging to him)* No! No! You cannot kill him. He is bound to you more closely than a brother of the same flesh and blood. He is yours — you made him —
F.	*(with sudden passion)* You — made me! I am yours!
Henry	Yes. We grow — we are born — we are made by God. But I, a man, made *you*!
F.	Then you can help me. I — I love the woman. Give her to me.
Waldman	*(quickly)* No, no, he can never do that.

Frankenstein (1928)

Henry (*to* **F.**) Fool! She is mine — my wife to be — my own, my mate.

F. *Your* wife! *Your* mate! Not mine?

Henry Never — never yours. Listen to the truth, Frankenstein! (*goes close to him*) No living woman will give herself to you. No woman in the world can love *you*! (*they stand in the same position, staring into each other's eyes.* **Waldman** *drops behind, watching them tensely*)

F. Listen to me, my master! No woman will — ever love me? Must I be alone? No mate — for me? *You* can — make me one!

Henry (*recoiling*) I — can make you one?

F. Yes, my master! You made Frankenstein — you can make a mate *for* Frankenstein.

Waldman (*in horror*) What does he mean?

Henry (*never faltering in his gaze at* **F.**) I know what he means.

Waldman Oh — horror —

F. You *can*, my master.

Henry (*distractedly*) Never! Never!

F. You *must*, my master. Then I will go away — far away — for ever. You will — not see me again. I will take — my mate — far away — for ever....

Henry (*desperately*) If I refuse — Frankenstein — if I refuse —

F. (*slowly*) I will — kill you — I will — kill — your mate —

Henry No — No —

F. I will kill — your mate — then you —

Henry (*wildly and quickly to* **Waldman**) Oh, my friend! What am I to do?

F. Make me — a woman — and I will go away — for ever! Choose, my master! (*towering over* **Henry**)

Henry Help me, Waldman!

Waldman It is for you to choose —

F. If you do not — promise me — I will follow you — I will never leave you — I will destroy you! (*he takes* **Henry** *by the throat*)

Henry Frankenstein! I will do your bidding —

F.	You will make me a mate — another Frankenstein —?
Henry	God forgive me! Yes!
F.	*(putting his out-spread hand over **Henry**'s face as he forces him backwards)* I am your master now! You are my maker, but I am — your master. Your master! Your master! *(he throws **Henry** insensible to the ground, and stands triumphantly over him with both arms out-spread)*

End of Act II.

FRANKENSTEIN

Act III

Six months later. A lonely hut in the Jura Mountains. Night. The hut is bare and rough in appearance. A small door up stage R., leading to an inner room, and a second, wide door centre back, leading out of doors. Two narrow, uncurtained windows right and left of this door, through which is seen a view of desolate, mountainous country in bright moonlight. There is no carpet on the floor of the hut; a table on which a lamp stands; several wooden stools; a closed cabinet, a heavy wooden chest; a shelf of books; a brazier in which is a glowing fire; a number of surgeon's tools, measures and charts. Towards the back of the stage, placed crosswise, is a low couch, or bier, on which is lying the form of the female Frankenstein, covered in a long, dark drapery. This drapery must be arranged in such a way that it can be lifted without the audience actually seeing the figure.

When the curtain rises the lamp is turned low, the moonlight falling in a long, silver beam across the head and chest of the figure under its covering. **Henry** *is discovered, sitting on a stool by the brazier, his elbows on his knees, staring thoughtfully into the fire. After a pause* **Waldman** *is seen slowly approaching the centre doors. He knocks and* **Henry** *starts to his feet. Another pause.* **Henry** *goes to doors and throws them open.* **Waldman** *stands silently waiting, he is closely muffled in a cloak and leans on a stick.* **Henry** *reels back, astounded.*

Henry Great Heaven! Dr. Waldman!

Waldman My dear, dear Henry Frankenstein! *(stretches out both hands)*

Henry Is it possible? I am afraid to touch you, old friend. You come like a dream of the past — too dear, too wonderful to be real *(they clasp hands)*

Waldman Have I found you at last, Henry? It seemed to be years, not months, since you left us all at Belrive. May I come in?

Henry Come in! Come in! (**Waldman** *enters hut.* **Henry** *closes the door and turns up the lamp.* **Waldman** *takes off his hat, throws back his cloak and looks about him*) Let me take your hand again — the kindest, truest friend man ever had. *(they again clasp hands)* Why have you sought me out, Dr. Waldman? Have you come alone to this desolate place?

Waldman Victor Moritz brought me to the little village — a mere group of huts — five miles away.

Henry Good, dear Victor!

Waldman I would not let him come any farther. I have kept my word to you, Henry. Not a soul, except myself, knows that you are here. Your friends all think —

Henry	Stop, Dr. Waldman! Don't speak to me of my friends, or my home. Spare me that. *(almost angrily)* Sit down by the fire. The midnight hour is very cold. (**Waldman** *sits &* **Henry** *kneels by the brazier*) You have a great, courageous heart to come to me at my — my — awful work! *(he lays his hand on* **Waldman's** *knee)*
Waldman	How long have you been here, my poor Henry?
Henry	Two months. When I rushed away from Belrive — you remember? — I tried to hide myself from — from —
Waldman	Frankenstein? (**Henry** *nods*)
Henry	It was useless. He followed me like a beast of prey upon the scent. His face haunted me day and night. His voice was always in my ears. On the seashore — in mountain passes — in the depths of the forest — he found me out. *You know* my promise. You know what he wanted.
Waldman	*(quickly)* You must never do that.
Henry	*(in a low voice, drooping his head)* It is done.
Waldman	*(rising & drawing back from him)* Impossible! Impossible! *(as he says this* **Frankenstein's** *face is seen at window R., the moonlight full upon it, glaring in with a terrible expression of malignity).*
Henry	Look there! *(they both turn.* **F.** *passes on and stares in at the other window.* **Waldman** *draws near to* **Henry**, *and clutches his arm)*
Waldman	*(in a nervous whisper)* Is it Frankenstein? *(the moonlight from this point onward begins to be less bright)*
Henry	*(with the calmness of despair)* Yes, it is Frankenstein. He is here again! *(after an irresolute pause* **Henry** *rushes to the door, throws it open and looks in all directions)* He is gone, lost in the shadows of the rocks. Come here, doctor! (**Waldman** *goes to door*) There is nothing to be seen, but I know that *he* is lingering near. Day or night he never leaves me.
Waldman	Black clouds are drifting across the moon. It rains. *(sound of gusty rain)* There is a storm brewing over the distant hills — *(a slight flash of lightning followed by a faint peal of thunder far away).*
Henry	Come in, doctor, come in! *(he closes door again)* Sit down again by the fire.
Waldman	*(looking round)* This is a miserable hut. *(points to door R.)* What door is that?

Frankenstein (1928)

Henry It leads to my other room where I sleep, when I do sleep.

Waldman *(looking from one door to the other)* Do you not lock or bolt your doors?

Henry What need? I did so when first I came, but Frankenstein broke in one night when I was lying in the heavy sleep of utter exhaustion. I awoke to find him bending over me — oh, it was terrible! His eyes glared into mine, his hands were moving about my throat, his breath was icey cold upon my face. I couldn't move, or cry out, I was helpless. Then he dragged me up from my bed and made me come in here — to work!

Waldman *(stupefied)* To work — ?

Henry Yes, on that — on that! *(he points to recumbent figure. Another flash of lightning and distant thunder.* **Henry** *leans against the centre doors)* It was a night of storm at Goldstadt, like this, when I poured my elixir into the cold blood of Frankenstein and he came to life. Then I was swept with wild emotion — pride, ambition, triumph! Now I am in despair. *(very earnestly)* Do you dare to look upon the work that is nearly done? It is lying yonder. It but awaits the quickening touch. Do you *dare*?

Waldman Tell me what I shall see.

Henry A being like Frankenstein, but a woman — his mate. I was upheld at Goldstadt by the false dream of my own greatness. I thought I could control and master the being of my own creation. But in making — that — I have been overwhelmed by fear and abhorrence of the task. For hours — for days — I have wandered about the hills, unable to return to this accursed place. I have been afraid to come in — afraid to touch it — afraid of myself, but Frankenstein has always driven me back. His damnable threats against my life — against my love — have conquered my manhood and my soul. Waldman! Waldman! I shall be free tonight. When I give *her* to him *(point to figure)* a warm, living, breathing creature — I shall be free! *(***F.*** *looks in at window R., a flash of lightning showing his face)*

Waldman *(in a hoarse voice, pointing to window)* There — again!

Henry He is waiting — he understands — he knows the only thing there is to be done now. Come! Look upon her! *(***Henry*** *goes to figure and stands behind lounge, his hands upon the cloth as if to raise it)*

Waldman No! No! Do not raise that cloth. I cannot bear it. I will not look. No, no, Henry!

Henry What is there to fear in the un-living? What is flesh and blood — even such flesh and blood! — without life? What is the gross body compared to

	the dark spirit of evil that I shall awaken in it? *(He goes to* **Waldman**, *who has turned away, covering his face)* Oh, forgive me! Forgive me, doctor!
Waldman	My poor friend, what have I to forgive? *(they clasp hands)* I would to God that I could help you. *(he suddenly puts both hands on* **Henry's** *shoulder with great solemnity)* You must never do this thing.
Henry	I must.
Waldman	Then you will be lost eternally.
Henry	I must.
Waldman:	It is too late to undo the past — too late to save Katrina or the happiness of your home, but it is *not* too late to save your soul.
Henry	Do you think for a minute, friend, that if I deny Frankenstein his mate he will spare me? Do your realize the strength of his hate? Listen! *(lowers his voice, after glancing at the windows)* I have destroyed the principal tools with which I work, and the diary in which I described my progress every day. Only one sheet of cipher and one glass phial remain — in that locked cabinet. Here is the key hanging round my neck.
Waldman	One sheet of cipher and one glass phial in there? Well?
Henry	I will show you, but go to the window first and tell me if you can see — Frankenstein. (**Henry** *unlocks cabinet, or chest)*
Waldman	*(at window)* No. The lightning is playing over the distant sky. The storm is coming nearer and nearer.
Henry	Look, Dr. Waldman! *(he holds out a scroll and* **Waldman** *stands close to him, both speaking in lowered voices)* This is the secret formula that no man has ever read except myself. It tells me what to do before I use this — stand back — you must not touch it! *(he takes a glass phial out of the cabinet, covered with vivid red and yellow pieces of silk, and holds it up to the light. It is half filled with a colourless fluid)* The elixir that gives life — see! It looks like pure and sparkling water — *(a flash of lightning)* See! It flashes into the night and draws down the very fire from heaven — quick! quick! *(he wraps up the phial and thrusts it into the cabinet)* Back — back to your secret hiding place! *(he closes and locks cabinet, then staggers forward, his hand to his brow)* My head swims. I am as weak as a dying man. I must go and lie down upon my bed — I must rest — I must rest — before I end my work. *(points to figure)*
Waldman	*(with momentary fear)* Will you leave me alone?

Frankenstein (1928)

Henry You need not fear — (gives **Waldman** a dagger) He has no grudge against you. Sleep! If I could only sleep! (he groans and exits at door R. The storm goes on, still rumbling in the distance. **Waldman** looks fearfully round, then, after holding his hands as if in prayer, goes towards the fire. A pause. **F.'s** face appears at the window. **Waldman** does not see him. **F.** opens door slowly and enters. He is haggard and wild and limps badly. His clothes hang about him in rags and are stained with earth and rain. **Waldman** turns quickly. They stare at each other for a second.)

Waldman (in a breathless whisper) Frankenstein!

F. (looking round) Where has — he gone — the man?

Waldman Your master — be quiet — he is asleep.

F. (points to figure) She will — be mine — tonight — (he slowly goes to figure and passes his hands over the head, while **Waldman** watches nervously) He — will make her live — tonight. She is still — still — (he draws nearer to **Waldman** who shrinks away) Are you — afraid of me?

Waldman (dropping the dagger) No! I am not afraid, but I — I —

F. You hate me. All men hate — Frankenstein. You come from — from — tell me.

Waldman I come from Belrive.

F. That place — there — (points vaguely towards the door) where I saw — where — is little Katrina?

Waldman Don't speak of her.

F. You say I — I killed her. She was kind to me. Take me — to that place.

Waldman (fearfully) Stand away from me.

F. Take me — down there — where I saw little Katrina.

Waldman No! You can never go to that house again. There is blood upon your hands.

F. On my — hands? Blood. My hands — (utterly puzzled)

Waldman How can I make you understand? Sit down. I will talk to you. (**F.** sits on stool by fire, warming his hand) Do you understand why men should hate you? Do you know why your master hates you?

F. (brooding) No. I want — my woman. My master — will give me — the woman, or I will — kill him — kill him — so! (he clenches & unclenches his hands)

Peggy Webling and the Story behind Frankenstein

Waldman   No, no, not that!

F.   *(innocently)* I — *can* kill him —

Waldman   Listen to me. You know that Katrina is dead?

F.   The little thing — Katrina.

Waldman   She is dead.

F.   I know. I know. I wept so — for her — it hurt me — hurt me —

Waldman   Yes, but that pain awakened your soul. In the depths of sorrow the soul awakes.

F.   Soul? *(with a gleam of intelligence)* My soul? What do you mean?

Waldman   *(very distinctly)* Katrina is dead. Her body will never move again, but her soul is not dead.

F.   Then — then — where is her soul? What — do you mean?

Waldman   Her soul is with God.

F.   *(repeats the word slowly, with hands out-stretched, as if groping in the dark)* God! Where is — God?

Waldman   I cannot tell you.

F.   Would God — hate me?

Waldman   No. He alone could pity and help you.

F.   He would — take my hand — like the little thing, Katrina. *(he rises and takes a step towards* **Waldman***)* Show me the way — to Him.

Waldman   You must find a way for yourself.

F.   *(looking round helplessly)* I do not know — the way. Did the bird's soul fly to God — when it fell — down — on the water? Was the bird dead?

Waldman   Yes.

F.   Katrina is dead. Did her — soul fly to God?

Waldman   Yes, yes!

F.   I must — find the way....

Waldman   *(quickly)* Begone! Begone! I hear your master's step —

Frankenstein (1928)

F.   *(his expression instantly changing to ferocity as he gives a low snarl)* Tell — my master — I am there! *(points to the outer door)* I am here — I am there — I am everything! Tell my master — *(he points to the figure)* The hour has come — tell my master — *(exit quickly, passes before the window R., and disappears.* **Waldman** *closes the doors. Enter* **Henry**)

Henry   *(apprehensively, stopping short)* Frankenstein — ? *(the action of the scene to be gradually intensified from this point to end of act)*.

Waldman   Yes, he was here. He is waiting.

Henry   The hour has come.

Waldman   Those were the very words he used. *(goes to* **Henry**, *who is staring towards the window)* Could you not go to sleep? *(***Henry** *shakes his head without moving)* What are you going to do now? *(a slight pause)*

Henry   *(slowly)* End my work. Gain my freedom. *(as* **Henry** *crosses the stage towards the cabinet* **Waldman** *clutches his shoulders)*

Waldman   Henry! Henry! You will buy your freedom at too great a price. Listen to the truth before it is too late. Think of the awful possibilities — realize what it will mean to give a woman like himself to Frankenstein. *(they look at each other with a sudden flash of understanding)*

Henry   I *know*!

Waldman   *(his horror increasing every minute)* It will mean that she will be his — it will mean that she will bear him children —

Henry   I tell you, Dr. Waldman, I *know*.

Waldman   But you have not thought that the children of Frankenstein, and the unnatural mate of Frankenstein, will be the children of *your* guilty mind, the work of *your* sinful hands! *(***Henry** *remains immovable, staring down into* **Waldman***'s face)* Do you remember the day at Belrive, after Katrina's death, when Frankenstein told you to choose?

Henry   *(passionately)* Shall I ever forget?

Waldman   I bid you to choose now. Will you do this monstrous thing, with all its appalling consequences, or will you refuse before it is too late — too late?

Henry   *(triumphantly)* You shall see what I will do! *(he swiftly unlocks and throws open the doors of the cabinet. At that minute* **F.**'*s face appears at the window, but the others do not see him.* **Henry** *takes out the cloth-covered glass phial and the scroll. Places the former on the table and holds the latter towards* **Waldman**) Look, Waldman! Without this scroll my work could never have been accomplished. *(throws it on table & lifts up the phial)* Without the secret elixir I can never give life to that senseless body. My friend, I have chosen! *(the centre doors open and* **Frankenstein** *stands on the threshold, staring at them, still unperceived)* Look! Look! *(he tears the scroll into pieces. Comprehension of what he is doing dawns in* **F.**'s *face as he stoops forward watching.)* Now — (**Henry** *tears off the coverings of the phial)* Life to the emblem of life! Mystic flame to real flame! Fire to fire! *(he pours the liquid into the brazier, as the drops fall in, flames of a bright and beautiful colour leap up, while lightning plays across the windows.* **Henry** *speaks as this happens —)* My secret gone for ever! Burn! Burn! Gone for ever! *(***F.*** springs into the room with a howl of frenzy.* **Henry** *turns to meet him,* **Waldman** *reeling back, unheeded. The two face each other in silence for one breathing space)*

F.   Now — you cannot give me — her — *(points wildly to the figure)*

Henry   No! *(almost as the words are spoken* **F.** *leaps at* **Henry**'s *throat, like an animal, and there is a short, desperate struggle.* **F.** *then forces* **Henry** *backwards over the table and strangles him.* **F.** *stands erect, gazing down at him with wide, staring eyes).*

Waldman   You have killed your master!

F.   *(gasping)* Shall each man have his wife — each beast his mate — and I be alone. I killed him — because he robbed me — of all *she* would have given me. All men hate me — and now — I hate myself. *(looks down at* **Henry**) He is dead who brought me to life, and I — shall be dead soon — and find — God. Rest! Rest! Dead — very soon — soon — rest — rest — *(he groans and moves blindly towards the centre doors. There is a vivid flash of lightning that strikes him and he falls, instantly, shattered. A terrific roll of thunder.* **Waldman** *stands immovable, gazing at* **Henry**'s *dead body).*

End of Play

Prompt Script of *Frankenstein* (1930)

First Performed at the Little Theatre, London
10 February 1930

FRANKENSTEIN
A Play in a Prologue and Three Acts
(Based upon Mrs. Shelley's well known book)
By
Peggy Webling

FRANKENSTEIN

Characters:

Baron Frankenstein
Henry, his son
Dr. Waldman (of the University of Goldstadt, Switzerland)
Victor Moritz
          and
Frankenstein

Baroness Frankenstein
Katrina, her daughter
Emilie Lavenza
Elizabeth

Prologue:

Henry's study in **Dr. Waldman's** house in Goldstadt. A Winter evening. Six months are supposed to elapse.

Act I.   The Same as the Prologue. Morning.

Act II.   Room in the **Baron's** house at Belrive. Afternoon of the same day.

Act III. Hut in the Jura Mountains. Six months later.

Period.
The end of the Eighteenth Century.

FRANKENSTEIN

Prologue

Henry's *study in* **Dr. Waldman's** *house at Goldstadt. A winter evening. A small room lighted by an oil lamp. Centre doors, hidden by long, dark curtains which are slightly open. There is a lounge standing across the corner of the room, with a small table nearby. Big arm chairs by the fire; writing desk, shelves of books. The walls are hung with anatomical drawings. Doors R. and L., both opening away from the audience. It is almost dark when the curtain rises. A flash of lightning through the slit in the curtains over centre doors, followed by a long roll of thunder. The sound of a storm is heard, which gradually dies away as the Prologue proceeds, but there is occasional thunder and lightning to the end. The stage is empty. A loud knocking at the door L., and* **Victor Moritz's** *voice is heard without.*

Victor   Henry! Henry Frankenstein! Henry! Where are you? *(Enter* **Victor**, *wearing a heavy cloak and hat pulled down over his brows. He glances round the room, removes his hat and shakes the water off. As he crosses towards opposite door it is unlocked and* **Henry** *enters, speaking as he does so.)*

Henry   Who is it? Ah, Victor! *(he closes door behind him and advances quickly with out-stretched hand.)* Did you knock before? I am glad you have come before Dr. Waldman.

Victor   Did you expect me on such a night?

Henry   Of all men in the college you are most welcome! *(as they shake hands a gust of wind blows open door at back of stage.* **Henry** *speaks as he goes to shut it)* The wind has blown open the doors. Good God, what a night! *(closes and bolts doors, arranges curtains and turns up lamp a little.)* Take off your wet cloak, Victor. I'll hang it by the stove in my other room. This fire is too small to dry a rag. *(offers to take his friend's cloak and hat)*

Victor   Let me take them into your room. *(goes towards door R.)*

Henry   *(quickly)* No, Victor, no. You can't go into my room. Give it to me — and your hat — *(exit* **Henry** *with cloak and hat. For the few seconds he is absent* **Victor** *stands by the fire, warming his hands and feet. Re-enter* **Henry**. *He has the key of the door in his hand and locks it, putting the key in his pocket)*

Victor   *(carelessly)* Why do you lock your inner door and leave the other open?

Henry   No reason. I expect Dr. Waldman. *(he throws a log on the fire)* Pull up a chair. How the wind howls! I think it's found its way from the lonely Jura Mountains to Goldstadt. Listen! Doesn't it take you back to old Belrive?

*(they sit down. **Victor** lights his pipe. He leans back comfortably in his chair, stretching his feet to the fire. **Henry** is restless and nervous, frequently changing his position and fidgeting. He often stoops forward, clasping his hands on either side of his head)*

Victor   I'm glad that it can't take us back to old Belrive — literally.

Henry   Why are you glad?

Victor   If we suddenly found ourselves in your father's house, or in mine — no smoking all night, or free talk, or late supper, but long evening prayers, after yawning over a good, dull book, or listening to the damned soliloquy that elderly gentlemen call conversation. No disrespect to the Baron, Henry, or my own worthy father.

Henry   *(gloomily)* I don't agree with you. If the wild wind could blow me back to Belrive at this minute, I'd rush out into the night — what's that? Hush! Didn't you hear — ? *(he rises and goes to door R., stooping to listen and signing to the other to be quiet)*

Victor   What on earth is the matter?

Henry   Hush! Listen! *(a pause)* It's all right. It was nothing — my imagination. Nothing! *(he paces up and down the room)*

Victor   What is wrong with you, Henry? You can't sit still for five minutes. You look as nervous and unstrung as a sick girl. Are you ill? Had any bad news? You're over-worked, that's it. *(goes on smoking complacently)* Classes, lectures, reading, writing, and all the rest of the old grind has been too much for your nerves. I know you're the most promising man of your time and we're all proud of you. Old Professor Kempe calls you the new light of natural science. Dr. Waldman is always dinning your achievements in chemistry into our long-suffering ears. The Principal of the University declares ———

Henry   *(impatiently)* Don't talk such nonsense, Victor.

Victor   It's the truth. We all admit it. *(then in a serious tone)* My dear Henry, what is the good of your labours if you half kill yourself? Why do you spend all your days and nights in study? What is your end and aim? Why have you cut yourself adrift from your companions and oldest friend?

Henry   *(stopping a minute to lay his hand on the other's shoulder)* No, no, not that, Victor.

Victor   Yes, yes, Henry. I never see you. Look here! Has a man in the college crossed your threshold for the past three months?

Frankenstein (1930)

Henry   Yes, Dr. Waldman dined with me recently.

Victor   Dr. Waldman! A book-worm like yourself. A grave, learned man, old enough to be your father. *He's* no companion for Henry Frankenstein.

Henry   He understands me. He's the greatest and kindest man I've ever met.

Victor   *(lightly)* Then why do you welcome such a fellow as me? I'm no pedant — no scientist —

Henry   *(sitting on the arm of his friend's chair)* Because we've known each other all our lives, Victor. I love you like a brother. I wish — I wish you'd come to see me more often.

Victor   To speak the truth, when I do come you're so absent-minded, or so absorbed in your own thoughts, that I only feel in the way. Don't apologize. It was just the same when we were boys at Belrive. You wanted to be an alchemist in those days, studying to turn metals into gold, or discover the elixir of life. What fools we are when we're young!

Henry   No, youth is the age of true wisdom.

Victor   Was it true wisdom of you to believe in alchemy, or hunt for the philosopher's stone? No, the wisest step you ever took, my friend, was on the day you gave it up and engaged yourself to our pretty neighbour, Emilie Lavenza.

Henry   *(staring in front of him, sadly)* Yes, that was wise.

Victor   *(inquisitively)* How is the charming Emilie?

Henry   Well — at home.

Victor   Have you seen her lately?

Henry   *(with constraint)* Not for — some months.

Victor   You astonish me. Goldstadt is only a ride from Belrive, and you both love riding.

Henry   I have been absorbed in study. All my time, my thoughts, my energies have been devoted to a certain work. But it is done at last. Victor! I am glad you have come to-night. I am thankful that I sent for you, although I am afraid —

Victor   *(in surprise)* My dear Henry, why *afraid*?

Henry   Because — because this will be the greatest and the most wonderful night in the whole course of my life — or the most terrible and bitter. To-night

	I shall conquer the world of science, or fall into black despair. To-night I shall triumph, or fail, in the most daring and marvellous experiment ever attempted by mortal man.
Victor	Henry!
Henry	Oh, don't think I'm a madman. Don't be frightened. You know me of old. I've got the courage of the devil.
Victor	A devilish courage when your blood is up.
Henry	Yes, but to-night I must be calm and cool as the Jura hills. I must control myself. I must! I must! *(he paces the room again in agitation)*
Victor	What have you done? What do you mean by all this wild talk?
Henry	Stop with me, Victor, and you shall learn. Don't leave me till I tell you to go. You belong to my old life, *(very affectionately)* You come from my home. Swear you'll stand by me whatever happens.
Victor	Of course I'll stand by you. *(a roll of thunder)* My dear boy, where's this courage of the devil you brag about? You're shaking from head to foot, and your pulse — *(**Henry** drags his hand away)*
Henry	*(wildly)* If *you* had waited, and waited, and longed for to-night as I have done — if *you* knew what was hanging in the balance —
Victor	Why don't you tell me? *(a knock at the door L. **Henry** starts violently, then speaks in a loud voice)*
Henry	Who's there? Who is it?
Waldman	*(outside)* Dr. Waldman.
Henry	*(earnestly, as he hurries to open the door)* Don't leave me, Victor. Come in, Dr. Waldman! *(Enter **Waldman**)* I was afraid you had forgotten your promise.
Waldman	Oh, no, but I was reading in my room upstairs and the hour slipped past. I didn't mean to miss our appointment, Henry. Victor Moritz, is it not?
Victor	Yes, sir. *(they shake hands)*
Henry	Will you sit in the arm chair, doctor? Victor, please lock the door. *(**Victor** does so while **Henry** pulls chair forward for **Waldman**)*
Waldman	What a night of storm! The wind and rain have been fighting for mastery and the wind is beaten. Can we not have a little more light, Henry? Does

Frankenstein (1930)

	this mysterious experiment of yours require a dark room and crashes of thunder? *(thunder far away)*
Henry	If you like, sir. *(he turns up the lamp making the stage light.* **Waldman** *and* **Victor** *sit by fire,* **Henry** *at table, facing audience)*
Waldman	*(lighting his pipe)* That is a little more cheerful. *(a pause)* Well, Henry? Your class is seated and admirably attentive.
Henry	Do you remember, sir, supping with me in this room about six months ago? We were all alone.
Waldman	Very well. I'm afraid we talked nearly the whole of the night.
Henry	The sun was rising before I got to sleep. Do you remember all that we said, Dr. Waldman?
Waldman	*(smiling)* No, indeed.
Henry	Not the gist of the talk — the subject?
Waldman	We discussed the origin of life.
Henry	Yes, and the possibility of science, in the far future, being able to discover the secret of creation.
Waldman	*(smiling again)* I recollect leaving that supposition to my junior, Henry. You must forgive the inexperience and modesty of age! *(turns deliberately to* **Victor***)* Have you read Ludenburg's latest treatise, Moritz?
Victor	Not yet, but I have heard ——
Henry	Stay, Victor! *(entreatingly)* Dr. Waldman, I beg you not to attempt to turn me from my purpose. If you disapprove of our former discussion, believe me you will alter your opinion to-night.
Waldman	Our former discussion, my young friend, was futile and fruitless. Wild exaggeration and unsupported tales of marvels have nothing whatever to do with science. Forgive my bluntness. We were both rather foolish on that occasion. Let us forget it. So I wish you'd tell me, Moritz, whether you have heard that Herr Ludenburg's most original treatise is ——
Henry	*(striking the table excitedly)* No, doctor! No! By Heaven, you *shall* hear me.
Waldman	*(resignedly)* Well, well, well! Don't get excited, dear boy.
Henry	*(rapidly)* You know — you both know — how deeply I have devoted myself to natural philosophy, and particularly chemistry, in the most

comprehensive sense of the term. But you do *not* know the years that I have spent in deep and occult study of the secrets of life, before and since I came to Goldstadt. One question haunted me day and night — one problem I would have given the best years of my life to solve — the secret of the principle of life. I have studied physiology and anatomy, birth and death. I understand the natural growth and decay of the human body. I have long lost all sense of restraint and moderation. I have sought my subjects in the hospitals and the grave. ·

Waldman *(smiling slightly)* Well, well, well!

Victor *(to* **Waldman***)* What does he mean by that?

Waldman *(looking at* **Henry** *as if doubting his reason)* God knows.

Henry I tell you I have handled the newly dead. I have spent nights and days in vaults and charnel-houses. I have learned the processes of corruption, the secrets of the flesh, but always before my mind — a light in the darkness — I hoped to discover the cause of generation. At last — at last — *(he rises)* when my strength was nearly gone, when I was haggard and worn with labour — when I had tasted the bitter cup of despair — I saw the flaming of the torch! I had found the secret of giving life. The desire and dream of humanity had burst upon me. It was too much for my heart and brain. It was mine! It was mine! *(drops again into his chair and covers his face with his hands, visibly trembling with excitement)*

Victor My dear Henry! *(wonderingly)*

Waldman *(sternly)* Tell us your meaning in plain words. Master yourself.

Henry *(lifting his head slowly)* I — I'm sorry, doctor. I — I — I'm over-worked and unnerved. What a fool I am! Forgive me. Victor, will you get that little bottle and glass from the shelf yonder — thank you! *(***Victor** *brings them.* **Henry** *vainly tries to pour a dose)* This is too absurd! My hand shakes. Victor, pour it out for me —there — *(he indicates the dose.* **Victor** *pours it and* **Henry** *drinks.)*

Waldman *(looking at bottle)* Be careful how you use this drug.

Henry That is better. I beg your pardon, doctor, for all my wild talk. Let us hear no more of it.

Victor But Henry was telling us of his discovery, doctor.

Henry *(eagerly)* Do you believe in me, Victor?

Victor I — I hardly know what to say.

Frankenstein (1930)

Henry Wait till the end. *Wait*, doctor!

Waldman We must follow you step by step. Describe your work in detail.

Henry That is impossible. I have told you the truth as surely as the sun shines in heaven. I can bestow animation upon lifeless matter.

Waldman No, no, Henry Frankenstein. You ask too much of our faith in you, my poor friend. No, no, no.

Henry Hear me out, Dr. Waldman. My ambition, after this great discovery, was to prove its practical truth. I hesitated for a long time. Then I determined to prepare an object — a form — a body — for the vital experiment.

Waldman *(astounded)* Do you mean a human body?

Henry Yes. I began to dream of the creation of a being like ourselves, the physical man complete.

Waldman *(protestingly)* My friend! My friend!

Henry I set to work. I — *(covers his face for a second)* I can't tell you everything I did. You would think I was a cunning madman. Look! *(holding out his hand)* I'm shaking from head to foot, my mouth is parched, and my head swims at the mere recollection of the awful task. *(in a hoarse whisper)* In a dark cellar beneath the ground I made the Thing I had dreamed of. It was horrible — horrible — but I could not stop. I collected all the gruesome parts from secret haunts of death. I crept, like a murderer, night after night to my frightful labour — *(again overcome, he covers his face with his hands)*

Waldman *(calmly and emphatically)* And at the end you *failed*.

Henry No, I succeeded! The Thing is finished. To-night I shall perfect my work and give it life.

Victor Impossible!

Waldman Oh, Science! What falsehood is spoken in thy name!

Henry An hour ago I used my discovery to animate the senseless body — I'll say no more of that, no more! The secret shall live and die with me. *It* is there, locked in my room. *(points to inner door)* Victor, old schoolfellow, will you come with me? We will bring It here. Will you come?

Victor Yes. What do you want me to do?

Henry Help me. Doctor, wait for us — *(Exit* **Henry***.* **Victor** *is about to follow when he turns and speaks quickly)*

Victor	What do you think, Dr. Waldman? Has Henry Frankenstein gone out of his mind?
Waldman	*(slowly)* God knows what he has done. Go with him! *(as* **Victor** *crosses stage and exits,* **Waldman** *says to himself)* I must see this to the end! *(he rises and stands over the fire, looking frowningly towards the door. A flash of lightning, followed by thunder.* **Waldman** *shudders. Re-enter* **Henry** *and* **Victor***, carrying the inanimate body of* **Frankenstein***, with a big, black cloth thrown over it)*
Henry	There — down upon the lounge — steadily, Victor — *(they place him on the lounge, and* **Victor** *straightens his back with an outward breath)*
Victor	A dead weight! Who is this hidden man? *(makes gesture to pull away drapery)*
Henry	Not yet! *(stopping him)*
Victor	How still! I think he must be insensible. What do you say, doctor? *(looking over his shoulder at* **Waldman***)* I do not want to touch him — how cold it seems to be all of a sudden! *(moves away from the lounge)*
Henry	Dr. Waldman may touch him. Doctor, you have heard Victor's question. Tell him the condition of this man — feel his pulse — *(***Henry** *draws the cloth sufficiently on one side to show a shoulder and arm. A pause.* **Waldman** *lifts the hand to feel his pulse, puts it down again and stoops for a second over him, listening for his breathing. Another pause)*
Waldman	There is no life in this man.
Henry	*(looking from one to the other impressively)* There is no life in this man.
Victor	*(indignantly)* Henry, you have gone too far. It's ghastly. This is a corse. It's horrible.
Henry	No, he is not dead, for he has never lived. You shall look upon the creature I have made with these hands. Draw the cloth from the face, one of you. *(they hesitate)* Victor?
Victor	No — no — I —
Henry	Then Dr. Waldman! *(a slight pause, then* **Waldman** *pulls aside the cloth enough to show the head and shoulders of* **Frankenstein***. He is dressed like* **Henry** *in dark, plain clothes, but* **Henry** *wears a high, black stock, and* **F.**'s *shirt is open, showing his throat and a piece of chest. The men's faces express fear mingled with amazement)*
Waldman	*(gaspingly)* My God!

Frankenstein (1930)

Victor It is the death mask of a strange, inhuman being. Look, doctor! Look at the great lips and the brow! *(gazes confusedly at his friend, then again at F.)*

Waldman *(running his hand down the figure)* This is the physical body of a young, strong man.

Henry Now you see my accomplished labour.

Waldman There is no vital force in it.

Henry *Not yet!* But my secret is at work. The hour of waiting is nearly over. Shall I triumph or shall I fail?

Waldman I warn you, solemnly, against the sin of vain presumption. From God alone is the breath of life. Be warned!

Henry You are too late. He lives!

Waldman No — no — *(he again takes* **F.**'*s wrist.* **Victor** *and* **Henry** *strain forward. The storm is heard very faintly. The doctor lays down the hand and turns to* **Henry***)* You have failed!

Henry *No!* I have succeeded. Look! *(***Henry** *slowly draws drapery off* **F.** *After a slight pause,* **F.** *very slowly clenches and unclenches his hand hanging down at side of lounge. Then stretches his arms over his head and raises himself on one elbow.* **Henry** *utters a wordless exclamation, or groan, but the other men remain speechlessly gazing.* **F.** *stands up, thrusts both hands in front of him, as if groping in the dark, his head sunk on his chest. After a few seconds he lifts his head, in the full light of the lamp, his mouth a little open, eyelids quivering. At last he opens his eyes and stares blankly in front of him.)*

End of Prologue.

———————————————————

FRANKENSTEIN

Act I

The same scene as Prologue. Six months later. A bright summer morning. The curtains drawn away from the centre doors to show a garden flooded with sunshine, arranged to give an impression of distance. The doors closed.
   Enter **Dr. Waldman** *and* **Baron Frankenstein**, *talking as they come.*

Baron   I am glad to have met you, doctor. Very fortunate. Very fortunate.

Waldman   The pleasure is mutual, my dear Baron. (**Waldman** *closes the door L.* **Baron** *holds his hat in his hand. He glances round the room eagerly as he comes in*)

Baron   Henry is not here, I see. Perhaps he is in the other room. (*he turns towards door R.*)

Waldman   (*stopping him*) No, your son isn't at home. He is — er — at a lecture, or at one of the professors' classes. It's no use looking for him elsewhere in the house, Baron. (*he speaks hurriedly and with some confusion*)

Baron   No matter. No matter. I'll wait for him. Don't let me detain you, doctor.

Waldman   You're not detaining me. I've nothing to do.

Baron   (*surprised*) Fortunate man! Nothing to do towards the end of term. In my young days it was the students who had nothing to do and the masters who worked. Times have evidently changed for the better. Why doesn't Henry leave his doors open? (*he goes to centre doors and pulls the handles*) What the devil — (*shakes the doors*)

Waldman   (*mildly*) No, the bolt — allow me — (*he draws back the bolts top and bottom and throws the doors wide*)

Baron   Thanks. That's better. Ugh! It's hot! (*he stands between doors looking out.* **Waldman** *moves away, watching him with a thoughtful expression, perplexed and anxious*) Charming little garden! I drove around the edge of that wood in the distance — (*pointing*) beautiful bit of road, smooth and shady. The prettiest bit of road between Goldstadt and Belrive. (*turns back into the room*) Won't you sit down, Dr. Waldman? (*they sit*) When d'you think my too studious son will return? He doesn't expect me, or I'm sure I should have found him at home.

Waldman   Oh, at any minute. Why do you call Henry your "too studious" son? It's a rare fault in a young man, but I'm afraid he's guilty of it.

Frankenstein (1930)

Baron No? Well, it's not an inheritance from his father. A good boy, doctor, but weak here — weak — *(tapping his forehead)*

Waldman Henry? I don't agree with you. *(smiling)*

Baron Too fond of books and learning. Too serious. Thinks too much. If you want to be happy and live to a jolly, gay old age, don't *think*. It's dangerous. Men who think so much, doctor, are generally too long in the legs, lean and grizzly-bearded.

Waldman *(stroking his own grey beard)* True, my dear Baron.

Baron Look at me. *I'm* not a thinking man. *I'm* not profound.

Waldman No one would ever suspect you of it.

Baron *(failing to see any sarcasm in the reply)* I hope not, thank God. Now, look at Henry. You know what a fine, amiable looking boy he is —

Waldman Ah! *(he leans his head on his hand, tapping his foot softly on the ground)*

Baron An only son, doctor, with a father who has never thwarted him, a mother who adores him, a dear little sister, a beautiful home, and one of the sweetest and best girls in the world waiting to marry him. Is he happy and content? No! He throws it all on one side for the sake of his studies. He's mad on his studies. It's only ten miles to our house — ten miles from door to door — but he hasn't spent a single day with his parents and his sweetheart for six months. Six months! It's a shame, doctor, it's a confounded shame! *(he begins to walk the room in agitation)*

Waldman Don't let it trouble you too much, my friend. No doubt when Henry leaves college —

Baron Hang college! I wish I'd never let him stay on at college. There's our neighbour's son, young Victor Moritz — *he* hasn't forgotten his family.

Waldman Victor Moritz has neither the genius nor application of your son.

Baron I wish my son had the genius for making other people happy and the application to devote himself to his father and mother. Our little Katrina longs for him. There never was a brother half so kind as Henry used to be. She's not like other girls, our little Katrina. She can't run about and play, or dance, or ride, or dream of a sweetheart. *(he speaks very gently and tenderly)* She has always walked with a crutch, a tiny thing, barely to my shoulder.

Waldman Lame, is she? That's a great affliction for you to bear.

Baron	True, true. But somehow Katrina makes one forget it. She's so happy and content. I'm not a poetical, sentimental man, doctor, but sometimes I think, when I look at the child, that she can't belong to us — me and my good wife — although we have watched her grow from a baby nearly to a woman.
Waldman	How do you mean?
Baron	*(very earnestly)* I mean she is a bright and heavenly spirit, innocent, but wise. It seems as if the crutch alone held her to this earth and made her human. Free from that, she would be perfect. Do you smile at a father's fancy?
Waldman	No, no, it is a beautiful thought, Baron.
Baron	Her mother says she couldn't be happy in Heaven itself without Katrina. In this life we both listen for the tap of the little crutch, in the life to come we shall hear the flying footsteps of our child, running to meet us . . . God knows . . . *(he jumps up in a different mood)* But all this talk has nothing to do with Henry. When did you say his confounded lecture would be over?
Waldman	I am not at all certain. Perhaps it would be better not to wait ——
Baron	Not to wait? I haven't driven from Belrive to run back again without him. I've come to take him home, Dr. Waldman.
Waldman	To-day? Now? Impossible!
Baron	Why should it be impossible? Henry is not a prisoner at Goldstadt. *(he laughs a little)* You look positively frightened.
Waldman	*(hurriedly, forcing a smile)* Not at all, but you forget it is term time and he is hard at work.
Baron	What of that? Have you never heard of a young man playing truant?
Waldman	You will not be able to persuade him to go.
Baron	I don't persuade, doctor. I command.
Waldman	I'm afraid he'll disobey your commands — hush! I think I hear your son's step. *(hastily)* Baron, you must be prepared for a change in Henry. Don't be alarmed, but I expect you'll find — hush! Here he is! *(Enter* **Henry** *L. He starts violently and stares at his father. There is a marked alteration in his appearance. He is haggard and pale, his dress neglected, his manner anxious and nervous)*

Frankenstein (1930)

Henry Father!

Baron My — dear — boy! Why, Henry! My son! *(shocked and surprised)*

Henry *(glancing from one to the other)* Dr. Waldman! Father!

Baron Are you pleased to see me, Henry?

Henry Of course I'm very pleased. I — I was only a little — a little surprised. *(they shake hands cordially. The* **Baron** *lays both hands on his son's shoulders)*

Baron Why, what's the matter with you, Henry? Have you been ill? You should have told us. My poor boy!

Waldman *(cheerily)* Oh, he's very well, my dear Baron Only a little tired — he's quite himself — *(he steps behind* **Henry** *and shakes his head at the* **Baron**, *frowning and touching his lips)*

Baron *(bewildered)* But he's not quite himself. He looks as if he'd seen a spectre. (**Waldman** *frowns and shakes his head again.)* Eh? What? Why the devil are you scowling and wagging your head about at me, Dr. Waldman? What have I said?

Waldman Nothing. I wasn't scowling at you.

Baron But you were.

Waldman Oh, no, you're mistaken. I always frown. It's a bad habit of mine.

Baron *(softly)* Damned bad habit. What is wrong with you, Henry?·

Henry *(irritably)* I'm well enough, Father. If I had been ill, of course I should have told you in my letters.

Baron Your mother will break her heart —

Henry My dear mother! Sit down, sir. Don't leave us, Dr. Waldman. What a pleasure to see you, Father! What a pleasure to hear your voice, and feel your hand. *(he presses his own over it for a moment)* How is my mother? And Katrina? And our good old Elizabeth, and Gustave, and John, and all the others at home? *(they sit.* **Waldman** *strolls to the centre doors and stands there, looking out)*

Baron Your mother is well, but Katrina misses you sadly. We believe she cries about it, although she never lets us see her tears.

Henry Poor little Katrina!

Baron	She keeps all your letters and reads them over and over again. She has not been out in her little boat since you left home. I would gladly take her, but it's — 'No, Father, I'll wait for Henry.' She talks to her tame doves about her brother Henry. It's Henry, Henry all the time.
Henry	Go on, Father! I love to hear your voice. It is like a strain of familiar music. *(he sighs and leans back in his chair)*
Baron	*(drily)* Well, the music has been waiting for you patiently, although our good friend yonder wanted me to go away before you came home from your lecture.
Henry	I haven't been to any lecture this morning.
Baron	No?
Henry	No, I was — I was — in my bedroom overhead, reading.
Baron	Dr. Waldman assured me you were not in the house. Doctor! If you had let me go to Henry's other room above stairs I should have found him at once.
Waldman	I'm sorry, but I thought — it would disturb —
Henry	*(returning* **Waldman's** *expressive glance)* He was right, Father. You would have wakened me from a most refreshing sleep.
Baron	Sleep? Why, you said just now you had been reading.
Henry	*(embarrassed)* Did I? At all events, *(turning to* **Waldman***) You* know I mustn't be disturbed when I am reading, — *reading*, doctor.
Baron	Why, the boy's caught the bad habit of frowning and wagging his head. You both of you look so solemn and mysterious. No wonder, reading and sleeping all day! What is the latest study, Henry?
Henry	Hang the latest study! Tell me the news of Belrive. Talk to me of my mother and little Katrina.
Baron	And somebody else, Henry? You haven't asked a single question about Emilie Lavenza.
Henry	*(rising hastily)* Father, don't speak to me of her.
Baron	*(also rising)* What is the trouble, Henry? Can't you tell me the truth? Have you ceased to care for Emilie? Do you still love her?
Henry	*(passionately)* Do I love her? Emilie! Emilie!

Baron	You do? Then you have a strange way of showing your love. Mark my words, the most unselfish and constant of women will not take a man's love on trust if he never shows it. If she were your wife —
Henry	*(interrupting in the same passionate manner)* I would to God she were my wife. She could save me. *(turning fiercely on the* **Baron***)* Why do you come here to torture me? Why do you talk of home and all the peace and happiness I have thrown away? Why do you tell me that I'm unworthy of Emilie Lavenza? Who knows the truth better than I? Father, I'm on the rack! Spare me —
Waldman	*(stepping between them and speaking sternly)* Henry, Henry! Control yourself. Be calm. *(then consolingly)* My dear Baron, you mustn't be alarmed. My young friend is over-wrought — words, words, words!
Henry	*(miserably)* Oh, doctor, this useless, eternal balm of yours on an open wound.
Waldman	*(ignoring him and continuing to the* **Baron***)* Now, if you'll only take my advice and leave me alone with Henry — my dear sir, pray hear me out — I know that I can do him good. Be persuaded. Be reasonable.
Baron	*(hotly) I'm* reasonable enough —
Waldman	Yes, yes, yes, but if you'll only leave me alone with Henry for ten minutes — five minutes — where are your carriage and horses?
Baron	In the stable of old Pastor Clerval, ready for Henry and me to drive back to Belrive.
Henry	I cannot come —
Baron	*(angrily)* You must!
Henry	Father, it is absolutely impossible! *(played very quickly from this speech to the* **Baron***'s exit)*
Baron	You refuse, in spite of my command?
Henry	I refuse.
Waldman	Henry, let me speak to you alone.
Henry	Doctor, it's no use!
Baron	You have no respect for my wishes. You are deaf to your mother's prayers. But don't be mistaken, Henry — *(stepping close to him)* — I *will* know the reason before I go. Dr. Waldman, talk to the headstrong young fool. Teach him his duty if you can.

Waldman	(*almost pushing* **Baron** *out of the door*) Yes, I will, my dear Baron, but in the meantime —
Baron	In the meantime I'll wait for you at the Pastor's house, Henry. Come to me soon, or by Heaven I'll return here and drag you home. Goodbye, Dr. Waldman.
Waldman	Let me have the pleasure of showing you the way, Baron.
Baron	Pleasure! Pleasure! You seem to want the pleasure of kicking me out — (*Exit, talking,* **Waldman** *mildly and the* **Baron** *angrily.* **Henry** *sinks into a chair and buries his face in his hands. After a few seconds re-enter* **Waldman**. *He lays his hand on* **Henry's** *shoulder.* **Henry** *starts and raises his head.*)
Waldman	Come! Come! Why did you betray yourself to your father?
Henry	(*miserably and vaguely*) Why, what did I say?
Waldman	You were nervous, angry, unnatural. You must be more careful —
Henry	(*quickly*) Ah! What's that? Did you hear the handle turn? There's a hand on the door. Who is it? (*a tap at door L.*)
Waldman	Quiet! Who is there?
Victor	(*outside*) May I come in? Victor Moritz.
Henry	It's Victor. Come in, Victor! (*enter* **Victor**)
Victor	(*taking off his hat to* **Waldman**) Good morning, Dr. Waldman. How are you, Henry? (*they shake hands*)
Henry	Alive, Victor. (*he stares in front of him unhappily. The others exchange a troubled glance. A pause.* **Waldman** *draws a chair close to* **Henry**. **Victor** *leans against the table*)
Waldman	(*softly*) Where is — he? (**Henry** *points to door R.*) Alone? (**Henry** *nods*)
Victor	I saw, as I approached the house, that the shutters are closed. Is — *he* in semi-darkness?
Henry	Yes.
Waldman	You kept him all the winter months in the laboratory underground. But since you brought him to your own rooms, a week ago, surely he has seen the sunlight?
Henry	Only through the cracks of the shutters. I forbade him to touch them.

Frankenstein (1930)

Victor Does he obey you?

Henry *(contemptuously)* Does a frightened slave obey? Does a beaten hound obey?

Victor But he is as strong as yourself.

Waldman How have you mastered him?

Henry Don't ask me, doctor. It is better not to know.

Victor But he is your equal in height and —

Henry *(rising, angrily)* Victor, Victor! What is strength of muscle and sinew compared to the cunning of the brain? What is the courage of a wild beast compared to the cruelty of man?

Victor *(recoiling a little)* Have you tortured him?

Henry *(opening and then clenching his out-stretched hand)* Is he not mine — *mine*?

Waldman Can he speak?

Henry Yes. I have taught him, day after day, night after night. He is never out of my thoughts. When I fall asleep, from sheer exhaustion, I meet him in dreams of horror. *(he sits down again in his old attitude of despair)*

Waldman Can he learn from your teaching? Does he understand?

Henry As a child understands, but now and again there is a flash of deeper thought across his narrow mind. He is elemental, unconscious of his own strength, a brute — a beast! You have both seen him and he remembers you.

Victor I cannot bear to look at him. He is strangely like yourself in gesture and movement — his great hands, his face, his body, but a sullen devil looks at me out of his eyes.

Henry *(with a groan)* Spare me, Victor!

Waldman *(with great earnestness)* No one must see him. Your father, above all, must never see him. You must follow the Baron to Pastor Clerval's house and induce him to go back to Belrive at once.

Henry How can I do that? You know how obstinate my father is. He will not leave without me, and how can I leave him and go home?

Waldman But he *must not* come here again — *(loud knock, or blow, on door R.)* What is that?

Peggy Webling and the Story behind Frankenstein

Henry   Ah! It is Frankenstein.

Waldman   *(in surprise)* Frankenstein?

Henry   I call him by my own name. He *is* Frankenstein. *(knock repeated)*

Victor   What does he want?

Henry   He wants to come in here. He has never seen the sun shine as it does to-day.

Waldman   Let him come in.

Henry   Are you not afraid?

Waldman   No, no.

Victor   We are three strong men. *(3 bangs)*

Henry   *(warningly, as he goes to door R.)* Remember, we must keep him beneath our feet. *(he unlocks the door R.* **Waldman** *and* **Victor** *retire to back of stage, watching)* Frankenstein! *(a pause.* **Henry** *speaks again in harsh, commanding tones)* Frankenstein! Come here, I say! Frankenstein! *(Enter* **Frankenstein** *slowly. He is in dark, loose clothes, with his shirt open at the neck. He is bending forward, slightly stumbling, instinctively shielding his eyes from the light with his hands. As he comes into the full stream of sunlight he suddenly crouches on the floor, frightened.)*

Victor   *(whispering)* Look at him, doctor! He moves like a half blind animal.

Waldman   Hush! *(***Henry** *sits, looking at* **F.** *with frowning severity.* **Waldman** *and* **Victor** *move to the other side of the table, farther away.* **F.** *makes an uncouth sound of fear, hiding his face)*

F.   Burn! Burn! Fire *(springs to* **Henry** *and tries to cling to him.* **Henry** *spurns him away.* **F.** *points to window)* Fire!

Henry   Yes, but a good fire — a bright, grand fire. Go! *(threatens to strike him.* **F.** *moves towards the centre doors, frequently looking over his shoulder fearfully at* **Henry.** *At first he bends forward, gazing up into the sky, then slowly stretches out his hands and rubs them in the hot rays, rears himself to his full height, arms lifted over his head, and stands amazed at the brilliance.)*

Waldman   *(as if the words were forced out of him)* Man — devil — what are you?

F.   *(with a long drawn breath)* Oh — great fire! *(he takes a step forward and lays his hands on the glass doors, staring out into the garden, then pulls*

Frankenstein (1930)

	his shirt open so that the heat falls upon his breast) Great — soft — fire! *(another pause, then he suddenly lies down and curls himself up like a dog)*
Henry	*(sharply)* Frankenstein! *(F. does not move)* Frankenstein! *(F. stretches himself at full length to be more comfortable.* **Henry** *advances and stirs him with his foot)* Frankenstein! *(F. pulls himself into a kneeling position and lays his face down on* **Henry's** *foot. Then looks up at him humbly)*
F.	You are — my master!
Henry	Frankenstein, look out of the windows. That is my garden. Say it after me. Garden.
F.	*(in an expressionless tone)* Garden.
Henry	Those are trees, and flowers, and the blue heaven over all.
F.	Heaven — over — all.
Henry	That is the sky, and the great fire is called the sun.
F.	*(quite bewildered)* The sky — the sun — the sun — *(he looks out for a while, then lies down again muttering)* The great fire — the sun — the sun — *(begins to fall asleep)*
Henry	Frankenstein, wake up! Come here and kneel beside me — farther off — your touch is repulsive — *(F. kneels at a little distance)* Frankenstein, what is this? *(puts out his hand)*
F.	*(very slowly)* Your hand.
Henry	*(points to F.'s hand)* And this?
F.	My — hand.
Henry	What is your name?
F.	Frankenstein.
Henry	Do you remember my name? *(F. stares at him dumbly)* What *am* I?
F.	Man. *(mutters the word to himself several times)* Man — man. Master — man. Frankenstein — man. *(gives it up and points to centre doors)* I want — the sun.
Henry	No, you mustn't go into the sun now. You must stop here beside me. Now, listen. Look at me. Look me in the eyes. *(at first F. shrinks almost to the ground and then obeys him)* Tell me your thoughts.
F.	My — thoughts.

Henry	What do you think of me — of us — of this other man? (**Victor** *comes a little nearer*)
F.	(*looking at them fixedly in turn*) You are — big — big — you are — you are — like each other, but I — (*stops helplessly*)
Henry	Well, go on. What else do you want to say?
F.	Are there men like — like — Frankenstein? (*indicating himself*)
Henry	No. (*spoken together*)
Victor	Oh, no!
F.	(*repeating in the same tone*) No! Oh, no! Then — then — (*he clenches both hands beneath his chin, trying to think*)
Henry	What now? (**Victor** *makes an impatient movement*)
Waldman	Silence, Victor!
Henry	What now, Frankenstein?
F.	Why — why — why are there no men — like me?
Henry	I can't tell you. You wouldn't understand.
F.	(*to* **Victor**) Are you — like my master? Do you — do you — (*he lifts his hand clenched and frowns darkly*)
Victor	Does your master hate you?
F.	Yes. Hate — hate — what does that mean?
Henry	How can I answer? (*rising and speaking to* **Waldman**)
Waldman	It is impossible for him to understand. What can you say?
Henry	I don't know, doctor. I don't know! (*he sits on the lounge in an attitude of dejection.* **Waldman** *stands pondering.* **Victor** *watches* F., *who slowly creeps towards* **Henry** *and points to his eyes*)
F.	What is that? Your eyes are wet. (**Henry** *rises with an angry sound and goes to centre doors with* **Victor**. F. *touches his own eyes and looks at his hand. Sits on lounge in* **Henry's** *favourite position, bending forward with his hands clasped between his knees.*) All men — hate me. Hate Frankenstein — hurt Frankenstein — (*suddenly yawns, stretches himself and lies down on the lounge to sleep, muttering incoherently.* **Henry** *returns and stands over him. He slowly stoops and holds his hands over* F.'s *throat*)

Frankenstein (1930)

Waldman	*(quickly and softly)* Henry, what are you doing?
Henry	It would be no sin — no sin — but have I the strength? *(clasps* **F.**'s *throat as if to strangle him.* **Waldman** *and* **Victor** *start forward)*
Waldman	Henry — (**F.** *opens his eyes at the touch and stares at him.* **Henry** *tightens the clutch.* **F.** *gives a guttural gasp, instinctively catches* **Henry**'s *wrists, and there is a second's struggle. Then* **F.** *throws* **Henry** *off. The latter reels back a few steps.* **F.** *stares at him wonderingly)*
Henry	Keep off! His hands are like steel, Dr. Waldman. I think that he would kill —
F.	*(interrupting quickly)* Kill? Kill! *(then in his usual slow way)* What does that mean? *(he repeats his gesture of throwing* **Henry** *off)*
Henry	*(angrily)* Frankenstein, why did you throw me off? Dog! How dare you touch me!
F.	*(stretching out his arms, clenching and unclenching his hands)* I — threw you off! *(passes his hands with great swiftness down* **Henry**'s *arms from his shoulders)* A man — tall — strong — *(he suddenly realizes his own size)* Frankenstein is tall — strong — *(he stands quite erect)*
Henry	*(fiercely)* Down! Crouch upon the ground — or I will make you — (**F.** *crouches, but unwillingly, and covers his mouth with his hands)*
F.	No! No!
Henry	Then lay your face upon my foot — don't touch my hand — (**F.** *obeys him, but not so cringingly as he did before)*
F.	*(points to garden)* Let me go — out there. (**Henry** *turns away)*
Waldman	Not now, Frankenstein. You shall go into the garden when the Sun sets.
F.	The sun sets.
Waldman	When the great fire in the sky is burnt out. To-night.
F.	To-night?
Waldman	Yes, before we go to sleep.
F.	I want to go there — now. *Now!* There is — there is — *(pleadingly)* Tell me!
Waldman	There is beauty in the garden.
F.	Is that — the word? Beauty. Beauty.

Peggy Webling and the Story behind Frankenstein

Waldman Yes, the fresh grass, the wind, the flowers.

F. Are the great — flowers called beauty?

Waldman You mean the trees. It is all beautiful.

F. *(spreading his arms wide)* All — beautiful. All — *(Howls)*

Henry Hush! What's that? *(a knock at the door L.)* Stand back! (**Henry** *lays a hand on* **F.**'s *arm and signals to* **Victor** *to open door*)

Henry See who it is, Victor! (**Victor** *opens the door a little*)

Victor Good heavens! It is — *(he goes out, nearly closing door behind him)*

Henry Be silent, Frankenstein! Stand still.

F. What — is — it? *(Re-enter* **Victor***, closes door and looks in an agitated way at* **Henry** *and* **Waldman***, still grasping the handle)*

Victor *(softly)* Henry! Doctor! It's Emilie Lavenza! She has ridden over from Belrive to see Henry. What shall we do? (**Henry** *is astounded*)

Waldman We must send her to find the Baron — no, stay! Let me think — let me think — *(a second's pause)*

Henry I know. Yes! Frankenstein, go you into the other room and stop there. Do you understand? At once — on the instant — Go!

F. *(cowering and pointing to door L.)* Who is — there?

Henry *(stamping)* Go, I say! (**Waldman** *opens door R.* **F.** *exits quickly, scowling darkly over his shoulder at the men.* **Waldman** *closes door and locks it. Knock)*

Waldman Now, Henry — Victor! (**Victor** *opens the other door. Enter* **Emilie Lavenza**. *She stops short, staring at* **Henry**. *She is a handsome, bright, high-spirited girl of twenty-three, wearing a riding costume and hat. Her manners are frank and unaffected.)*

Victor *(hastily)* This is one of our professors, Emilie. Allow me to present Dr. Waldman — Miss Lavenza.

Waldman I have heard so much of Miss Lavenza that I seem to know her already.

Emilie *(offering her hand in an abstracted way)* I am pleased to meet you, Dr. Waldman. I have come to see Henry.

Henry Yes, I am here.

Frankenstein (1930)

Emilie I knew the Baron was driving into Goldstadt to-day. Was it very bold of me to follow him on horseback, doctor? We are all distressed over Henry's long absence from home, especially his mother and little sister Katrina.

Waldman It was kind and good of you, Miss Lavenza, but at the same time — *(she does not heed him)*

Emilie *(almost inaudibly)* Is this really Henry!

Waldman Moritz and I will leave you together. *(then very seriously, in a fatherly way to* **Emilie***)* Miss Lavenza, let me entreat you, as an old and a true friend of Henry's, to forgive him for his seeming neglect. There is a reason for it that even you would not be able to understand. Trust him and believe him. Henry! *(in a lower voice)* Do not forget the man in your other room. Be careful!

Victor *(expressively to* **Henry***)* If you want us we shall be near at hand. Goodbye! *(he bows to* **Emilie***)*

Waldman Come, Moritz! *(Exit* **Waldman** *and* **Victor**. **Henry** *closes the door after them. He then turns and faces* **Emilie**. *They look at each other eagerly and curiously, as people do after separation)*

Emilie Oh, how changed! *(in a pained voice)*

Henry Oh, how unchanged! *(he goes towards her with out-stretched hands)*

Emilie Are you glad to see me?

Henry Glad? Glad? *(he seizes her hands and presses them passionately to his lips and then tries to clasp her in his arms. She steps back quickly)*

Emilie No, no, Henry —

Henry *(still trying to embrace her)* My darling! My love! My darling!

Emilie *(as she goes into his arms)* Oh, if you must — you must —

Henry *(incoherently as he kisses her)* I have you again — you, you! I've waited for this for months — sweetest — dearest —

Emilie *(gently pressing his face away and looking pityingly into it)* My poor Henry! How pale and worn and old you look. An old man! I was not prepared for this. What *can* have happened to you? Now, let me go. Dear, let me go! *(he releases her. She sits down and he kneels beside her holding her hands)* Why have you deserted us for so long? If I were not the most forgiving and faithful creature in the world I should never speak to you again. I thought you loved me.

Henry	*(again kissing her hands)* I do! I do!
Emilie	Then why haven't you been to see me, or written to me?
Henry	I have written.
Emilie	*(firmly withdrawing her hands)* Twice in six months, empty, formal notes! Who cares for a letter written with obvious effort and constraint? Take them back! It would be better if you had not written at all. *(takes two letters out of her pocket and tosses them on the table.)*
Henry	If you only knew!
Emilie	If I only knew — what? You have mystified your father and mother. Although you ignore all their affection and authority, perhaps *I* shall not plead in vain. *(with winning tenderness, lightly twining her arm round his neck)* Dearest, what is your secret? Why do you look so changed and unhappy? Won't you tell me? Can't you trust me?
Henry	Trust you, Emilie? Against the world!
Emilie	Then tell me, or come back to Belrive with your father and me.
Henry	My father is now on his way home, I hope.
Emilie	Let us ride after him together, you and I.
Henry	*(with an effort)* It is impossible for me to leave Goldstadt to-day.
Emilie	*(coaxingly)* To-morrow then? Promise me to come back to us to-morrow.
Henry	No, no, no. *(drearily)*
Emilie	*(with great tenderness)* Yes, yes, yes! Promise me!
Henry	*(rising and moving away)* I am a phantom-haunted man. *(desperately)* Do you think I would refuse you if I dared to promise? But I'm afraid — *(looking about him wildly)*
Emilie	*(also rising)* Phantom-haunted? Afraid? Of what are you afraid? The very air of this room is full of mystery. You look distraught. You are different from the man I loved. I feel as if I can't breathe here — *(faintly)* Open the doors wide, Henry. Give me a little air! (**Emilie** *stands against the doorpost. He watches her wretchedly)* Ah, how sweet and refreshing! It gives me new life to feel the wind. *(she takes off her hat and pushes her hair back from her forehead. Looks at him again, smiling a little)* I'm afraid we've been much too serious with each other. Don't let us talk about phantoms and misery and cruel letters. I'll forget them. *(points to letters on table)*

Frankenstein (1930)

Henry Emilie, if you knew —

Emilie Well? You said that before. 'Emilie, if you knew!' But you refuse to tell me anything. Never mind! *(fondly)* You shall tell me all about this mystery of yours when we are at Belrive. Then my love will teach you to forget it.

Henry I can never forget.

Emilie *(taking his hand for a minute)* Henry, what is it? Let me try to guess. Where shall I find the clue? In this room? *(drops his hand, looking curiously round)* Do you study here — work here?

Henry Not very often.

Emilie Where then?

Henry In my laboratory.

Emilie *(pointing to door R.)* Is that your laboratory?

Henry *(very emphatically, stepping forward so as to prevent her going to the door)* No, not there.

Emilie *(gaily)* Another mystery! Who is the man Dr. Waldman whispered was in that room?

Henry Did you hear that?

Emilie Yes, and why did he say "Be careful"? *(sudden loud knock on the door R. They both start)* What's that?

Henry Nothing — nothing.

Emilie Nothing? *(knock repeated)* There it is again. *(with sudden suspicion)* Who is the man concealed in that room? Henry, *who* is it?

Henry Don't be frightened. I will speak to him. I will make him be quiet. Stand away from the door — farther! *(he gently pushes her towards the other side of the room)*

Emilie Why, your hand shakes! You are so pale. *(fearfully)* Let me see the hidden man.

Henry No, no. I'll speak to him. (**Henry** *goes to inner door and opens it,* **Emilie** *watching him with anxious curiosity. He speaks in a harsh voice)* Stand back! Be silent! Stand back, I say! *(then with agitation)* No, you shall not come in here. Stop where you are — hands off, Frankenstein! (**Henry** *disappears for a second into inner room)*

Peggy Webling and the Story behind Frankenstein

Emilie (*in amazement*) Frankenstein! (*all to be played very quickly with increasing excitement.* **F.** *is seen to throw* **Henry** *on one side as he enters.* **Emilie** *gives a cry of fear.* **F.** *sees her and stops dead, staring*)

Emilie Henry! Who is this? (*she suddenly clenches both hands over her mouth as if to suppress a scream and gasps out the next words*) I am afraid! Save me — save me — let me go — ! (**Henry** *makes a quick movement towards her, but she eludes him and rushes out of the door at back of stage*)

Henry (*in agitation as she goes*) Emilie — my dear —

F. Who was — that? Went out — ran away — I will follow —

Henry (*wheeling round from the door where he has watched* **Emilie** *go*) You follow a woman! Follow her! No!

F. Was that — a woman! I — will — follow —

Henry No! Back, Frankenstein! You shall not go. Slave! Down — down at my feet! (*he strikes* **F.** *in the face as if in a last, desperate effort to master him.* **F.** *catches his wrist and they stand for a second, both drawn to their full height, eyes staring into eyes*) I am your master — down!

F. My — master! No! (*flings* **Henry** *off*)

Henry Help! Victor! Victor! Waldman! Help! Help! (**Waldman** *and* **Victor** *rush in.* **F.** *speaks to them.*)

F. Let me go!

Henry Stop him, for God's sake! Stand back, you brute! You thing without a soul! You shall not follow her — stand back!

F. You must — let me go —

Henry Curse you to Hell! No! (**Henry** *springs at* **F.**'s *throat, but* **F.** *finally throws him off, and breaks through* **Waldman** *and* **Victor** *spring*)

F. I will go — the woman (*Exit* **F.**, *leaving the others staring after him*).

End of Act I.

FRANKENSTEIN

Act II

*Room in **Baron's** house at Belrive, etc.*

*Curtain rises on empty stage. Enter **Emilie** hurriedly at door L. She is in a state of great agitation and runs on to balcony, leans over rail, eagerly looking down, turns back into room, pulls off and throws down her hat, looks to right and left, then rings bell-cord beside door R., again goes to balcony and back into room.*

Emilie	*(in wild impatience)* Oh, why don't they come? Baroness! Katrina! Katrina! *(as she calls their names she runs toward the little door R., it opens and the **Baroness** enters quickly, followed by **Katrina**)*
Baroness	*(in surprise)* Emilie Lavenza!
Katrina	*(almost at the same second)* Emilie dear!
Emilie	*(seizing the **Baroness's** hands)* Don't send me away! Let me stay here — for Heaven's sake, let me stay! *(**Katrina** comes to her other side she clings to her arm)*
Baroness	What do you mean? What's the matter?
Katrina	Emilie! What is it?
Emilie	*(releasing the **Baroness's** hands and kissing **Katrina** effusively and wildly)* Little Katrina! Let me hold you close — close! *You* will protect me — I am safe with *you* —
Baroness	My child! What on earth is the matter? *(staring at **Emilie** with increased surprise)*
Katrina	*(gently disengaging herself as she speaks)* Sit down, Emilie — have you been to Goldstadt?
Baroness	*(anxiously)* Where is the Baron?
Emilie	I don't know. I didn't see him at Goldstadt.
Katrina	Have you seen Henry? Why doesn't he come home?
Baroness	He is very unkind to stop away from you, Emilie, and his dear little sister.
Emilie	*(as she sinks into a chair, the **Baroness** on one side, **Katrina** on the other)* Yes, I went to Henry this morning, and I saw — oh! I can't tell you — *(gasping and looking at the balcony and at the door L.)*

Katrina	*(repeating the words fearfully)* You went to Henry this morning, and you saw — what?
Emilie	Another Frankenstein! *(the* **Baroness** *and* **Katrina** *draw back from her in amazement)*
Baroness	Another — Frankenstein?
Katrina	What do you *mean*?
Emilie	There was a strange man in Henry's room called by his own name — *(she rises and points with both hands towards the door L., as if she still saw the scene at Goldstadt)* They stood before me — I can see them now — Henry Frankenstein and the other! *He* looked at me — stared at me — and I was filled with horror. I saw — I tell you I was looking on a creature without a soul — a brute beast in the body of a man. I rushed away — I don't know what I did — I found my horse and I galloped all the way from Goldstadt to Belrive. My instinct was to fly — any-how, anywhere — away from him.
Baroness	Who *was* this strange man?
Emilie	I don't know. *(she gives a sudden cry and turns to the balcony)* Has he followed me? Will he come here? What *shall* I do?
Baroness	*(also rising)* Oh, no, no, my child! He isn't here.
Katrina	*(going to* **Emilie** *and drawing her back into the room)* No, no, Emilie. You are safe with us — dearest!
Emilie	*(frowning darkly)* His eyes were like a hunted beast, his mouth was cruel, eager, his hands were horrible, and yet — and yet he looked like Henry.
Katrina	Impossible!
Baroness	No, Emilie!
Emilie	Oh, I can't make you understand — I hated him — feared him — loathed him — but I tell you he looked like Henry. *(spoken quickly)*
Katrina	My dear, good brother! No, no! *(she covers her eyes with one hand, trembling)*
Emilie	Forgive me, Katrina. I'm so unnerved — I'm not myself — dear Baroness, let me stop with you for a little while before I go home. I daren't go out alone. I'm afraid — I'm so terribly afraid — —
Baroness	Of course, my dear, you shall stop as long as you choose.

Frankenstein (1930)

Katrina	Stop with me, dear one! Dear one! (*pressing her cheek to* **Emilie's** *hand*)
Emilie	Yes, I am safe with you and — (*the sound of a carriage approaching*) I shall be calm when — ah! what is that? (*continues speaking as she hurries to balcony*) It must be your Father.
Katrina	Father and Henry. Henry at last! (*she also goes towards balcony*)
Baron	(*outside*) John! Max! Hillo there! John!
Emilie	Yes, and two other men — Dr. Waldman and Victor Moritz.
Katrina	(*stopping short*) Is my brother with them?
Emilie	I don't see him.
Katrina	(*turning sadly away*) No Henry.
Emilie	I do not want to meet your Father and his friends. They will question me about Goldstadt. Let me go to your little sitting room, Katrina. Pray let me go! Come with me.
Baroness	No, I'll come with you, Emilie. Katrina is so anxious for news of her brother. There! (*draws* **Emilie's** *hand through her arm*) Why, you're still shaking! (*to* **Katrina**) Meet your Father, sweetheart. Come and tell us about Henry as soon as you can. Come, Emilie — my dear child — (*Exit* **Baroness** *talking constantly to* **Emilie**.)
Baron	Come in! Come in! Where are you, Baroness? Ah, little Katrina! (*kisses her*)
Victor	(*almost interrupting him*) Is Emilie Lavenza here?
Baron	(*surprised at the question*) Why? Emilie?
Katrina	Yes, she is here.
Victor	(*softly, half to himself*) Thank God!
Baron	Dr. Waldman, this is my daughter Katrina. (**Waldman** *kisses her hand*)
Katrina	(*smiling*) Dr. Waldman. I'm glad to see you, Victor.
Victor	And I to see you, dear Katrina. (*he also kisses her hand*)
Katrina	(*to* **Victor**) Why did you ask so anxiously for Emilie? I wish Henry had come with you.
Baron	Oh, your brother's mad!

Peggy Webling and the Story behind Frankenstein

Katrina	*(protestingly)* Father dear!
Baron	*(throwing down his hat and gloves)* He refused to drive with us, but mounted his own horse and galloped off to the Lavenzas' house. He was riding like the devil. Sit down, Dr. Waldman.
Waldman	Thank you, Baron. *(then quickly to **Victor**)* Go on to the balcony, Moritz, and look for Henry. Give him the signal we arranged at Goldstadt that all is well —
Victor	*(equally quickly)* I will, doctor. (**Victor** *goes to balcony and shows, by the way he leans forward and watches, that he is very eager to see* **Henry**)
Baron	*(to* **Katrina***)* Where is your Mother?
Katrina	She is in my little room with Emilie. Shall I call her?
Baron	No matter. Did you hear me shouting for John and Max? No civility! No promptitude! I must show you my garden and stables presently, doctor. I've got a new little mare — a jewel! She is —
Victor	*(turning towards the room)* Henry is coming! *(he takes out his handkerchief and waves it up and down several times)*
Waldman	*(to* **Baron***)* That is our signal to your son that all is well. (**Henry's** *horse is heard to stop at the front door*)
Baron	*(testily)* He knows that all is well. What do you mean?
Victor	*(bending forward over balcony)* She is here! Emilie is here!
Katrina	Henry at last!
Baron	I said he started riding like the devil. He must have ridden like twenty devils! *(Enter* **Henry** *quickly L, hat and whip in hand, speaking as he enters)*
Henry	Is Emilie here? Is she safe, doctor?
Waldman	Yes —
Henry	I thank God!
Katrina	Henry!
Henry	Little Katrina! *(they embrace affectionately)*
Katrina	So you have come back after all? Poor, tired Henry! *(she puts her hand up to smooth his cheek)*

Frankenstein (1930)

Henry	Have you missed me so much, little Katrina?
Katrina	Yes, so very much — haven't we, Father? I talk about you all day long.
Henry	Well — well *(smoothing her hair)*
Katrina	Why didn't you come home? Your books are here and a quiet room for your studies; your boat is asleep on the water with her sails furled. The garden waits for you. The house is empty without you. Henry! *(points to birds' cage)* you've never seen my tame doves! *(goes to cage)*
Henry	*(tenderly looking at her)* You gentle dove! *(then with renewed anxiety)* But, dear Katrina, tell me, where is Emilie now?
Katrina	She is with mother —
Henry	*(interrupting)* Is she well? What did she say to you? She is quite safe, Katrina? Quite safe?
Katrina	Of course she is quite safe, dear Henry.
Henry	Oh, I'm thankful! The agony of dread — I'm thankful! *(he turns on to the balcony as if unable to control himself.* **Waldman** *and* **Victor** *whisper to each other, unheard, as the* **Baron** *speaks)*
Baron	What is the matter with you, my son? You're at home. You've escaped from your prison at Goldstadt.
Henry	A prison indeed!
Baron	We'll have a glass of wine after our drive.
Waldman	*(nervously)* Thank you, Baron, but perhaps Moritz and I had better go with Henry in search of — of — *(he stops uncertainly)*
Victor	*(with similar hesitation and embarrassment)* Henry's friend — the man from Goldstadt — the stranger — *(to* **Henry***)*
Baron	We want no strangers here. Katrina, go to the stairs, my little heart, and call to Elizabeth to bring us a bottle of wine and some glasses.
Victor	I'll tell her, Katrina.
Katrina	Thank you, Victor.
Baron	*(stopping him)*
Henry	*(ignoring his Father)* Can I go up to your little room, Katrina? I'll greet my dear Mother, and ask her to leave us. I must see Emilie by herself.

Baron	Oh, these moony, abstracted lovers! Won't you have a glass of wine before you go, Henry?
Henry	No, Father. Excuse me, Dr. Waldman. Katrina, take me to Emilie.
Katrina	*(as they go towards door R.)* But you wish to be alone with her?
Henry	After a little while. But I want her to see me first hand in hand with *you*. *(he puts his hand, she takes it. Exit* **Henry** *and* **Katrina** *R.)*
Baron	Well, well, all the more wine for us! *(Enter* **Elizabeth***, carrying a tray)* Set it down, Elizabeth. Set it down.
Elizabeth	If you please, Sir — If you please Sir, there is a man at the door who is asking for you, Baron.
Baron	*(as he passes a glass of wine to* **Waldman***)* Ah, who is it, Elizabeth?
Elizabeth	*(in a frightened voice)* I don't know. All he said was — "Master! Master!" *(glances nervously over her shoulder)*
Waldman	*(with a quick look at* **Victor***)* What is he like?
Elizabeth	*(again glancing over her shoulder)* I don't know. His hair is blown over his face. He is very tall, and big, and — strange.
Waldman	I know who it is!
Baron	*(in surprise)* Do you?
Waldman	Yes, Victor Moritz and I know this man.
Elizabeth	*(in an agitated manner)* Oh, I hear him on the stairs. He has followed me.
Waldman	*(quickly to* **Baron***)* This man is a friend of Henry's. He is rough and uncouth, but — here he is! *(***F.** *appears at door L. He is bare-headed, his hair straggling over his face, his clothes & boots flecked with dust. He stands on the threshold staring at the other men. After a second he takes a step forward, thus enabling* **Elizabeth** *to pass behind him & exit)*
Baron	Good Heavens!
F.	*(gazing round)* Strange — place. *(revolves slowly)*
Waldman	Silence, do as I tell you.
F.	Who is — that? *(points to* **Baron***)*
Baron	Who d'you think I am? I am the master of the house.

F.	You are not — my master. Why are you — so white — so big — are you — an old man?
Waldman	*(to F.)* Be silent! Pray pardon him, my dear Baron —
F.	Where is — the woman?
Waldman	Hush!
Victor	You will never see her again.
F.	Never — never — what does that mean?
Baron	*(looking at F. very curiously)* You haven't told me this surprising young man's name, doctor.
Waldman	*(embarrassed)* His name? It is — it is —
Baron	Yes? *(to F.)* What is your name, sir?
F.	My name? Frankenstein.
Baron	What? Our name? Does he claim to be one of the same family?
Waldman	No, no.
Baron	Where were you born? *(to F.)*
F.	I do — not know.
Baron	You don't know? Who were your Father and Mother?
F.	I do — not know.
Baron	How old are you? *(F. looks blank)* Why did you come here?
F.	*(turning to Waldman and Victor)* I saw you there — where my master lives — I saw — the woman —
Baron	What woman does he mean?
F.	I ran — I ran — far — far *(holds his hands over his eyes as if watching* **Emilie** *disappear in distance)*
Waldman	Did you see us — in the carriage — drive away?
F.	Yes there was — noise — on the road — noise — *(looks at* **Baron** *and imitates plying a whip)* I —
Victor	Where were you?
F.	I ran — white all over me — white —

Peggy Webling and the Story behind Frankenstein

Baron You mean the dust of the road?

Waldman Did you run at the side of the road?

F. Ran so you could not see me — trees all round me — grass — leaves under my feet. I fell — my hands are cut — branches struck me — I tore them off — so! So! Water — I drank — so! *(imitates drinking from his hands)* The great fire burned! Pain! Pain! I did not care *(clutches at his heart, imitating exhaustion)* I ran — I ran — the woman — was gone — I saw my master — my master —

Baron Who *is* your master?

Waldman *(quickly & emphatically interposing)* Do not listen to him, my dear Baron. He has no master — he does not know what he is saying — *(turns to* **F.***)* Silence, Frankenstein!

F. *(unheeding him)* I want — to drink. I want to drink — *(looks about him)*

Baron *(contemptuously pitying him)* I understand him now. Well, Frankenstein, will you drink a glass of wine? Sit down.

Waldman *(authoritatively)* Sit down beside me, Frankenstein — speak no more. Moritz, sit on his other hand. *(***F.*** obeys, staring at* **Baron***. They all drink.* **F.** *tastes his wine and instantly withdraws glass from his lips with an exclamation of disgust)*

Baron *(incredulously)* You don't care for this?

F. No! *(hurls glass out of the window)*

Baron *(rising indignantly)* What the devil —

Waldman *(fiercely)* Frankenstein!

Victor You brute!

F. I want — to drink — to drink — *(notices a bowl of flowers on the table, snatches them out, and throws them on the ground. Drinks the water noisily)*

Waldman Give me that bowl! *(takes bowl as* **F.** *is about to throw it away)* My dear Baron, forgive him, he doesn't understand —

Baron You should beg my pardon, young man! *(***F.*** stares at him, makes a guttural sound of disgust and goes to balcony. He is no longer afraid of the men)*

F. The great fire is — burning — low. *(points down)* Look! Look! — water — Shining water!

Frankenstein (1930)

Baron	Have you never seen a river before?
F.	River? Water.
Baron	Well, the water down there is called a river.
F.	*(excitedly)* water — Sun — shining —
Baron	*(half to himself)* Look at him now! He's a strange creature! I can't understand him — *(he folds his arms and steps closer, watching* **F.** *with growing distrust)*
Victor	*(softly to* **Waldman**) What are we to do, Doctor? Shall I go for Henry?
Waldman	Yes — no! *(goes to* **Baron**) Have you forgotten your promise as we drove from Goldstadt, Baron?
Baron	*(absently, staring at* **F.**) What promise was that?
Waldman	To show me your garden and stables. What of the new mare? I'm longing to see her. Come, Baron! *(puts his hand through the* **Baron's** *arm)* Is she really such a little jewel?
Baron	*(with interest)* A jewel, Doctor! A little beauty!
Waldman	I'll go with the Baron, Moritz. You stay here with Frankenstein.
Baron	No, no, Victor! I don't want to lose sight of Frankenstein. Come with us. *(to* **F.**)
Waldman	*(reassuringly to* **Victor**) Well — very well!
Baron	Come with us.
F.	*(eagerly)* Out there — to the water — and the sun?
Victor	Wherever we choose to take you.
F.	*(excitedly)* Water — sun shining — this way — I show you this way — *(he coolly thrusts* **Baron** *on one side and exits L.)*
Baron	Of all the vulgar young louts —
Waldman	Follow him, Moritz! *(Exit* **Victor** *quickly)* He is ignorant and ill bred, Baron. He means no harm. It's only — only — his boyish, sportive way —
Baron	*(as they go out)* Boyish! Sportive! Those are not my words for damned impertinence. I beg your pardon, Doctor, but upon my life I never met —
Waldman	Neither did I, Baron — *(Exit* **Waldman** *and* **Baron**. *Enter* **Henry** *R., speaking as he opens the door)*

Henry	Dr. Waldman — Victor — we must go out — *(He sees the room is empty and stops dead, looking round. Enter **Emilie** behind him, also very hurriedly)*
Emilie	Henry —
Henry	Emilie, go back — go back to Katrina's room.
Emilie	Why did you rush away from me?
Henry	*(obviously struggling to be calm and ordinary in manner, while he gently pushes toward door R.)* Go back, my dear — go upstairs again —
Emilie	*(resisting and grasping his hands)* No, Henry, I can't bear this — do you know what you've been saying? Do you realize what you told me? Do you understand —
Henry	*(with passionate earnestness, taking her in his arms)* Before God, I have told you the truth.
Emilie	*(pressing away from him to study his face)* Impossible! It is impossible! *(then with sudden pity)* Oh, my poor love! You are over-strained and ill — you don't know what you're saying.
Henry	*(solemnly)* I have told you the truth, Emilie. I swear I have done this thing. My wicked pride conceived this inhuman monster — my devilish power brought it to life —
Emilie	Let me go — *(he releases her and she stands staring at him, as if stupefied)*
Henry	I have turned my world into Hell. Will you *desert* me? Will you drive me to *destruction*? Can't you understand my agony — my shame — my remorse? Emilie! Emilie! My only hope is in you. Love me! Try to forgive me! — pray for me! *(he drops into chair by table, hiding his face)*
Emilie	*(distractedly)* What can I do? What *can* I do? *(puts her hand on his shoulders and stoops over him)* Courage, Henry, courage! I told you at Goldstadt, nothing will change my love. *(he lifts his head, takes one of her hands and crushes it against his lips)* Why did you rush away from me in Katrina's room? You were like a madman.
Henry	*(rising and speaking wildly)* Frankenstein! Frankenstein! That is the answer to all your questions. Where is he now? What is he doing? I live in fear — every sound startles me — my own thoughts appall me.
Emilie	He has gone — he has vanished — let him go.
Henry	You don't know what you say. This brute is not a man —

Frankenstein (1930)

Emilie (*her alarm again awakened*) What will he do? What do you dread?

Henry God knows. Who can foretell.

Emilie (*leaning for support against the table, pressing her hands to her temples*) I can hardly breathe — you frighten me, Henry! Let me go home. I must go home —

Henry (*coming to her*) I can't let you go alone.

Emilie No, no — no, no!

Henry (*entreatingly*) Stay here, my dearest — stay with Katrina — I'll send a message to your home. One of the servants shall —

Emilie (*interrupting*) Not one of the servants. Will you go yourself?

Henry My dearest, I — (*with a gesture of disapproval*)

Emilie To please *me!* Tell my Mother I am well — I am happy — I will be home tomorrow —

Henry Are you indeed happy?

Emilie Not now — but I shall be — we shall both be happy again very soon, my poor Henry.

Henry Very well then. I will go — but before I go (*kisses Hand*)

Emilie I *will* pray for you — Farewell.

Henry Return to Katrina's room — stay with Katrina.

Emilie Yes, even to be near Katrina, will give me peace and courage — good-bye.

Henry God guard you! (*Exit* **Henry**. **Emilie** *gazes sadly after him, then slowly turns to the window and leans her head wearily against the frame with eyes closed. She moves, after a few seconds, glances at the doves' cage & bends down, abstractedly looking at the birds. Her back is to door L. Enter* **Frankenstein**. *He is panting, amazed*)

Emilie You! (*gaspingly*)

F. The — woman! The same — woman — (*she steps back as he advances a little, with an expression of fear*) I saw — you down there — (*points vaguely before him*) in the place — where my master lives. I — threw down my master — my master — (*he imitates the action*)

Emilie (*quickly*) Who are you? What is your name?

F.	Frankenstein. I — saw you — I — followed you —
Emilie	You followed me? Why?
F.	I want *you*! *(throwing out his arms)*
Emilie	*(in breathless alarm)* If you come near me, I will shriek —
F.	*(trying to understand)* Shriek? You will — cry out?
Emilie	Yes.
F.	When I cry out — *(in a hoarse whisper)* my master — stops my mouth *(covers his mouth with his hands)* I — will so stop — yours! *(slowly approaching her)* Come — close to me! Come! Come!
Emilie	*(she moves quickly away from him, in such a way that her back is towards door L.)* No! No!
F.	Woman! Woman! What have you done to me? *(in a tone of agony)* Pain — joy — beauty — come to me — You — Mine!
Katrine	Emilie! *(advances as quickly as she can)* Let her go! *(she boldly lays her hand on his chest. He looks at her in utter amazement. His grasp of* **Emilie** *loosens. She moves away from him, still trembling. His arms drop to his sides.* **Katrina** *still retains her position and speaks calmly and slowly)* I don't know why she looks so frightened. I don't quite understand, but you must not hold her like that again. It is not right. Emilie, come back to my room. *(puts out her hand to* **Emilie**, *but does not turn her eyes from* F.'s *face)* You stop here till I return.
Emilie	Katrine, let us go. *(they turn towards door R.)*
F.	I — want — the woman — *(blankly staring at* **Katrina***)*
Emilie	Katrine, don't leave me! *(to* F.*)* No, no! I hate you. I can't breathe the same air — horrible! horrible!
Katrine	*(to* F.*)* Wait here for me. *(Exit* **Katrine** *and* **Emilie** *R.)*
F.	Hate — horrible! horrible! I — want — the woman! *(he walks backwards & forwards in an agitated state for a few seconds, then stops at the window, looking out. Suddenly turns his face upwards, lifting his hands to point at a bird. Then he glances at the doves, takes up the cage and looks closer, puts it down again in such a position that the audience cannot see inside, opens door, thrusts in his hand and pulls out the artificial bird from where it had been concealed, shuts cage door roughly and takes bird to window. His attention is attracted by something below, so he leans out, crushing the bird on the sill*

Frankenstein (1930)

beneath his two hands. When he looks at it again he does not understand that it is dead, but is puzzled by its quietude and throws it out, saying "Fly!" As it falls he looks down, pointing to it wonderingly. Re-enter **Katrine**, *unheard. She gazes at him from the door, crosses room, and, after a slight hesitation, touches him on the arm. He turns round quickly and stares at her. She does not withdraw her hand. He looks down at it and then again into her face)*

Katrine	Did you come with Henry?
F.	Yes.
Katrine	Then you are very welcome. I am pleased to see you. What is your name?
F.	Frankenstein.
Katrine	Is it truly Frankenstein? You must be my cousin, or my — oh! *(she catches sight of the cage, goes to it and bends down, distressed)* Oh, my doves! My pretty, pretty doves! One of them has gone. Sweetest dove, where is your gentle mate? *(with her face close to cage)*
F.	It has gone — out there.
Katrine	*(rising and going to window beside him)* Did it fly into the blue?
F.	No. It fell down — down — to the water. I saw it — on the water. Still, still!
Katrine	Did it float along the river?
F.	Yes, like — those leaves — on the water — going on and on still — on the water.
Katrine	Then it must be dead. I was so fond of both my doves. *(she leans beside* F. *on the sill. He looks at her shoulder resting against his, then touches her face very carefully)*
F.	What is that? Your eyes are wet. I have seen — my master's eyes like that.
Katrine	They are tears.
F.	Tears?
Katrine	*(very simply)* Yes. I am sorry — unhappy, and I am crying. Have you never cried?
F.	No. *(puzzled for a second, then points to the river again)* I like — to see them — float.
Katrine	The leaves?

263

F.	And — the bird! (**Katrine** *sits down near the cage, resting her crutch on the side of her chair, looking at him thoughtfully. After a few seconds he turns to her, picks up her crutch and examines it curiously*)
Katrine	Please give me back my crutch. *(he takes no notice)* Give me back my crutch. I can't walk without it. *(shakes her head.* **F.** *holds it out to her humbly. She puts her hands forward for him to help her to rise. After a pause, he does so)*
F.	Why — did you do that? I — *(stops helplessly)*
Katrine	I don't know what you mean.
F.	You gave me — your hands. May I feel them — again? *(stretches out his own, palm upwards.* **Katrine** *lays her hands on them for a second)* No one — has ever done that — before. *(she gently withdraws her hands)* My master — will not touch me. Those men — *(points vaguely)* will not touch me. That woman — hates me. Do you hate me?
Katrine	No, no, my poor friend.
F.	Friend? What is that?
Katrine	I am your friend. Why do you look so sad? So strange!
F.	Sad? I do — not know.
Katrine	This is such a beautiful world, with so many kind and good people in it. Look at the flowing river and the drifting clouds. Let us go out of doors.
F.	Out there?
Katrine	Yes, I am always running out of doors.
F.	Can you — run?
Katrine	*(half sadly)* No, I am lame, and I get tired so easily. But I love to feel the soft air and lean over the side of my little boat, touching the water with my fingers. It whispers, "Little Katrine! Little Katrine!"
F.	*(slowly repeating the words in her voice)* Little Katrine! Little Katrine!
Katrine	Will you come with me?
F.	Yes. I — will come.
Katrine	*(laying her finger on her lips as she opens the door R.)* Look! This opens on a narrow staircase, above is my own little room, below is a little door leading to the river bank where my boat is lying. Come!

Frankenstein (1930)

F.	Out there to the shining water, where the leaves float — and the bird.
Katrine	Yes, I will show you the way — it's such a narrow stair — take my hand.
F.	*(as he does so)* little Katrine —
Katrine	This way — *(Exit* **Katrine** *first, her hand stretched behind her, lightly holding his. Exit* **Frankenstein**. *A slight pause, then the voices of men heard outside. Enter* **Baron**, **Waldman**, *and* **Victor**).
Baron	*(Speaks off before entrance, as he comes in)* Of course I'm glad you and Henry came, Doctor, though I admit it was very surprising. The boy refused to leave Goldstadt this morning, and you encouraged him. Do sit down. I want to talk to you. *(they sit, all at a distance from the window)*
Waldman	*(to* **Victor***)* Where is Frankenstein?
Victor	He eluded me when we were left alone in the orchard.
Baron	Let well alone. Perhaps he has run away or followed Henry to the Lavenza's house. This Frankenstein, as you call him, is the man I want to talk about, Dr. Waldman. Do you know him well?
Waldman	I — I know him well, Baron. You mustn't take his roughness ill. He's only ignorant and —
Baron	Only ignorant! My hound has better manners. He took a goblet of wine and threw it out of the window. You saw him do it. I've never met a man before, however ignorant, who hasn't learned where to toss wine. *(indicates his mouth)* But here's the point. There's something strange about him. *(draws his chair close to* **Waldman***)* I wouldn't say so to Henry, for he'd only laugh at me, but my blood runs cold in my body when I look at young Frankenstein.
Waldman	*(forcing a smile)* Really, my dear Baron!
Baron	Truth, sir, truth! He seems to me like an evil thing — no man at all as we know men.
Waldman	Well, Henry must get him away from Belrive.
Baron	I shall tell Henry to have nothing more to do with him. My son is not his keeper.
Waldman	Take my advice, Baron, leave the matter in your son's hands entirely.
Baron	Henry must give me a promise to renounce him.
Waldman	It will be far wiser to trust to his discretion.

Peggy Webling and the Story behind Frankenstein

Victor I'll do *my* best with Henry to take Frankenstein away.

Baron *(looking with surprise from one to the other)* What! Both of you? *(with sudden suspicion)* What are you hiding from me?

Waldman Nothing, my good sir, nothing.

Victor *(boldly)* There is nothing to hide, Baron.

Baron That's a lie — it's a lie, Victor Moritz. You know it is. *(rises)* Who is this man calling himself by my name? Where does he come from? How long has my son been in his power?

Waldman Henry is not in his power.

Baron False again! I see it in your face. Henry and Victor are afraid of him and *you* know the reason, Dr. Waldman.

Waldman I assure you solemnly, Baron —

Baron *(getting very angry)* I'm not a fool. I'm not in my dotage. Why did my son stop away from home for six months and rush here to-day in pursuit of this Frankenstein? Why did you both come with him? What have you done with the man? *(to* **Waldman***)* Where is he now?

Waldman I wish to God I knew.

Baron *(turning appealingly to* **Victor***)* Victor, you're a good, kind fellow. Tell me what you know of Frankenstein. I entreat you to tell me.

Victor *(embarrassed)* Baron, I — I know so little of Frankenstein.

Baron Do you know his people, his home, his character?

Victor No.

Baron Where did you first meet him? *(a pause)* Well?

Victor In Goldstadt. In — in Henry's rooms.

Baron Then he was Henry's friend, not yours, or Dr. Waldman's?

Victor *(more and more troubled)* Yes, he — Henry knew him first.

Baron What did Henry tell you about him?

Victor *(desperately)* Baron, I can't answer this volley of questions. Ask your son himself. *I* am not responsible for this Frankenstein.

Baron Then, Henry is responsible.

Frankenstein (1930)

Victor	*(after an irresolute pause)* Yes.
Baron	Tell me the truth about him.
Victor	How can I tell you? You wouldn't understand —
Baron	*(in a towering rage)* There's one thing I *do* understand. You are all determined to deceive me. Where has Frankenstein gone? I'll find him! Frankenstein! Frankenstein! *(he takes a quick step towards the door L., it opens and **Elizabeth** enters, very white and agitated)* Elizabeth! *(all look at her in surprise, to be played rapidly)*
Elizabeth	Oh, Baron! Baron! Where is my mistress? Something terrible has happened — oh, gentlemen! it's too dreadful — she's gone! She's gone! Our little angel! Let me go to her poor mother — *(she hurries towards door R.)*
Baron	Elizabeth! *(spoken together)*
Waldman	What is the matter?
Elizabeth	*(looking over her shoulder)* I met him at the door. He's bringing her in. Oh, Lord! have mercy —
Waldman	Quick, Moritz, pull out the lounge! — *(**Victor** obeys him. Enter **F.** carrying **Katrina** in his arms. She is drowned. Her dress clings to her figure and water drips from her hair. His eyes are wide with wonder as he looks from one to another. For a second they are too shocked to speak)*
Baron	Oh, God! My child!
F.	*(blankly)* Little Katrina!
Waldman	Put her down here.
Baron	*(as he takes **Katrina** from **F.** and puts her down on lounge, while **F.** only stares)* My little girl! Little Katrina! *(turns to **Elizabeth**, while **Waldman** feels **Katrina**'s pulse, etc.)* Go to my wife. Don't let her come here. Tell Emilie — go to my poor wife! *(exit **Elizabeth**, crying bitterly)*
Victor	Doctor —
Waldman	Silence! *(lays his hand on **Baron**'s shoulder)* My poor friend, your child is — *(stops)*
Victor	Dead?
Waldman	She has been drowned.
Baron	Oh, doctor! Can nothing be done?

Peggy Webling and the Story behind Frankenstein

Waldman   Nothing.

Baron   *(brokenly, bending over lounge)* Our little Katrina! My own loving little girl! *(more brokenly)* I must go to my wife — my poor wife — where is my wife? *(exit* **Baron** *R., blindly)*

Waldman   *(to* **F.***)* Where did you find her? What do you know of this?

F.   *(bewildered)* She took me *(points to door R.)* down there to the boat. I — I — pushed it away from land — on the water. The leaves floated on the water — like the white bird — shining water —

Waldman   Go on! Go on! What then?

F.   *(with appropriate gestures)* I took — her hands. And — lifted her up — and laid her — down upon the water — *(looks at them vaguely)*

Waldman   Go on, Frankenstein.

F.   She held my hands — but I — shook her off. I — wanted to see her — like the bird — on the water. "Oh! Oh!" she cried. Then — I pressed her down — under the water. Beauty — beauty — her hair — her face — under the water —

Waldman   You held her under the water — ah! —

F.   I held her down — long time down. Then — then — I raised her up. She was still — still — like this! *(points to her)*

Victor   You have killed Katrina. *(then in a deep, horrified whisper)* Murderer!

Waldman   Moritz! Remember he doesn't understand.

Victor   He has killed little Katrina!

F.   *(staring at them in turn)* I have — killed little Katrina!

Waldman   Yes, she will never speak to us again.

F.   *(very slowly beginning to realize the truth)* Never — speak again. Never take my hand. She — did not hate me. She — touched — me. *(he creeps nearer the lounge)* Is she — asleep?

Waldman   She is dead.

F.   She looks — the same —

Waldman   No, she is utterly changed. You have killed her.

F.   Changed? I have — killed her? *(raises his voice)* Katrina! Katrina! Look at me! *(wildly appealing to* **Waldman***)* Oh! What — does it all mean? *(laying* *his hand on his heart)* Pain — pain — but not with my master's blows. Help me! Help me, men! *(looking up to heaven)* Is there — no one — in all the world — to help me? Katrina! Katrina! I know — now — what I have done. Sorrow — sorrow — pain — pain — I — I understand— now *(he breaks into a storm of uncontrollable grief and throws himself down over **Katrina**. Silence for a few seconds, the other men watching him in an awe-stricken way. Then **Waldman** beckons **Victor** to come to him)*

Waldman	We must take her away. Henry must not find her here! Can you carry her up to her room?
Victor	Yes, doctor. Will you speak to him, or shall I? *(they both look doubtfully at F., then **Waldman** lays his hand on **Victor's** chest to keep him back)*
Waldman	Leave it to me. Do not say a word, I entreat you. This grief will pass, and then — who knows? Keep still! *(gives **Victor** a warning look and slowly advances to F.)* Frankenstein! *(speaks calmly, but draws back his hand as he is about to touch him)* Now, Frankenstein! Come! Rise to your feet. Rise! *(F. slowly lifts his head and slowly stands up)* She must be taken away. Do not look at her again.
F.	What — am I — to do?
Waldman	Listen to me. When your master comes —
F.	*(in a changed voice)* Where is — my master?
Waldman	He will tell you what to do.
F.	Why did he not — tell me that the shining water could kill?
Waldman	Now, Moritz — carry her to her room. Gently, gently — reverently — *(**Victor** lifts **Katrina** and slowly carries her out at door R.)*
Victor	*(as he exits)* Katrina! Poor, poor little girl!
F.	*(gazing after them in a puzzled way)* Where — has she gone? Let me go with her.
Waldman	Not now, not now! *(F. goes to balcony)*
Henry	*(outside, calling as he approaches)* Waldman! Waldman! *(he enters very quickly L.)*
Waldman	*(advancing to meet him, also very quickly)* Oh, my poor Henry, Katrina — Katrina —
Henry	*(instinctively grasping **Waldman's** hand)* I know! I know! They told me at the door. Where is Frankenstein?

Peggy Webling and the Story behind Frankenstein

Waldman He is here —

Henry My sister's murderer! (*F. rises and turns his back to the audience, facing* **Henry**) His cursed life shall pay for hers —

Waldman (*with great earnestness, coming between them*) Henry! Think! Think! He is not responsible. He doesn't understand — for God's sake control yourself —

Henry (*with stern determination*) He killed my sister. Let me go, Dr. Waldman —

Waldman (*wildly, clinging to* **Henry's** *arm*) No! No! Henry —

Henry (*removing* **Waldman's** *hand by force and speaking more and more quickly, his eyes on* F.) Let me go!

Waldman Not now — not yet! *You* cannot kill him. He is bound to you more closely than a brother. He is yours — you made him —

F. (*with sudden passion*) You — made me! I am yours!

Henry Yes. That is why all men hate you. *We* are born, we grow, we are made by God — but — I a man made you!

F. You made me! Then you can help me. I want the woman — give her to me!

Waldman No, no, he can never do that.

Henry (*to* F.) Fool! She is mine — my wife to be — my own — my mate.

F. Your woman — your mate — not mine? (*striking himself on the breast*)

Henry Never, never yours. Listen to the truth, Frankenstein! No living woman will give herself to you. No woman in the world can ever love *you*! (*he advances to* F. *and they stand, stooping a little towards each other in the same attitude, both forgetting* **Waldman** *who drops back, watching them tensely*)

F. (*becomes more and more fierce, but no quicker in speech*) No woman can — ever love me. I am alone. You made Frankenstein — make — a woman like me, for Frankenstein!

Waldman (*in horror*) What does he mean?

Henry (*answering, but not looking at* **Waldman**) I know what he means.

F. Make me a mate — you *can*, my master.

Henry (*distractedly and feebly*) Never! Never!

Frankenstein (1930)

F.	You *must*, my master. *(in a hoarse, deep voice)* Then I will go away — far away — I will take — my mate — away with me — for ever —
Henry	*(desperately)* If I refuse —
F.	*(clenching his hands)* I will — kill you — I will — kill you first, and then your mate —
Henry	No! No!
F.	I will kill — you first — and then — her!
Henry	*(turning to* **Waldman***)* Oh, my friend! What am I to do? Am I to sacrifice Emilie?
F.	Make me — a mate — and I will go away — for ever. Now choose, my master! Choose! *(towering over* **Henry***)*
Henry	Help me, Waldman!
Waldman	It is for you to choose. Do what is *right*.
F.	If you do not — promise me — I will follow you — I will never leave you — I will — destroy you — choose!!
Henry	Frankenstein — my choice is made — I will do your bidding.
F.	You will make me a woman, another Frankenstein! a mate for me.
Henry	May God forgive me — Yes!
F.	Ah!! You are my Maker, but I am *your* Master. Now *your* Master! *Your* Master! *(throws* **Henry** *down)*

End of Act II.

FRANKENSTEIN

Act III.

Six months later.
A lonely hut in the Jura Mountains. Night. The hut is bare and rough in appearance. A small door up stage R., leading to an inner room, and a second, wide door centre back, leading out of doors. Two narrow, uncurtained windows right and left of this door, through which is seen a view of desolate, mountainous country in bright moonlight. There is no carpet on the floor of the hut; a table on which a lamp stands; several wooden stools; a closed cabinet, a heavy wooden chest; a shelf of books; a brazier in which is a glowing fire; a number of surgeon's tools, measures and charts. Towards the back of the stage, placed crosswise, is a low couch, or bier, on which is lying the form of the female Frankenstein, covered in a long, dark drapery. This drapery must be arranged in such a way that it can be lifted without the audience actually seeing the figure.

When the curtain rises the lamp is turned low, the moonlight falling in a long, silver beam across the head and chest of the figure under its covering. **Henry** *is discovered, sitting on a stool by the brazier, his elbows on his knees, staring thoughtfully into the fire. After a pause* **Waldman** *is seen slowly approaching the centre doors. He knocks and* **Henry** *starts to his feet. Another pause.* **Henry** *goes to doors and throws them open.* **Waldman** *stands silently waiting, he is closely muffled in a cloak and leans on a stick.* **Henry** *reels back, astounded.*

Henry   Great Heaven! what's that? Dr. — Waldman!

Waldman   My dear, dear Henry Frankenstein! *(stretches out both hands)*

Henry   Is it possible? I am afraid to touch you, old friend. You come like a dream of the past, too dear, too wonderful to be real! *(they clasp hands)*

Waldman   Have I found you at last, Henry? It seems like years, instead of months, since you left us all at Belrive. *(although* **Waldman** *smiles affectionately, he is very grave and anxious in voice and manner)*

Henry   *(***Waldman** *enters hut.* **Henry** *closes door.* **Waldman** *takes off his hat, throws back his cloak and looks about him)* Let me take your hand again — the truest, kindest friend man ever had. *(they again clasp hands)* Why have you sought me out, Dr. Waldman? Have you come alone to this desolate place?

Waldman   Victor Moritz brought me to the little village — a mere group of huts — five miles away.

Henry   Good dear, Victor!

Frankenstein (1930)

Waldman I would not let him come any further. I have kept my word to you, Henry, for not a soul except myself knows that you are here. Your friends all think —

Henry Stop, Dr. Waldman! Don't speak of my friends, or my home. Spare me that! *(almost sternly, then affectionately)* Sit down by the fire. The midnight hour is very cold. (**Waldman** *sits and* **Henry** *kneels by the brasier*) You have a great, courageous heart to come to me at my — my — awful work. *(he lays his hand on* **Waldman's** *knee)*

Waldman How long have you been here, my poor Henry?

Henry Three months. When I rushed away from Belrive — you remember? — I tried to hide myself from — from — *him.*

Waldman Frankenstein? (**Henry** *nods*)

Henry It was useless. He followed me like a beast of prey upon the scent. His face haunted me day and night. His voice was always in my ears. On the seashore — in mountain passes — in the depths of the forest — he found me out. *You know* my promise — *you know* what he wanted me to do.

Waldman *(quickly)* You must never do that.

Henry *(in a low voice, drooping his head)* My friend — it is done!

Waldman *(rising & drawing back from him)* Impossible! Impossible! *(as he says this,* **F.'s** *face is seen at window R., the moonlight full upon it, glaring in with a terrible expression of malignity)*

Henry Look there! *(They both turn,* **F.** *passes on and stares in at the other window.* **Waldman** *clutches* **Henry** *by the arm)*

Waldman *(in a terror-stricken whisper)* Is it — Frankenstein?

Henry *(with the calmness of despair)* Yes, it is Frankenstein! *(the moonlight from this point onward begins to be less bright) (after an irresolute pause* **Henry** *rushes to the centre door, throws it open and looks in all directions)* He is gone, lost in the shadows of the rocks. Come here, doctor! (**Waldman** *goes to door*) There is nothing to be seen, but I know that he is lingering near. Day or night he never leaves me.

Waldman *(shivering)* Black clouds are drifting across the moon. *(stretches his hand out)* It rains. There is a storm brewing over the distant hills, another night of hell — God how I hate these storms! *(a slight flash of lightning, followed by a faint rumble of thunder far away).*

Henry Come, Doctor, come! *(he closes door again)* Sit down again by the fire.

Peggy Webling and the Story behind Frankenstein

Waldman This is a miserable hut. *(points to door L.)* What door is that?

Henry It leads to my other room where I sleep — *when* I do sleep.

Waldman Do you not bolt or bar your doors?

Henry *(wearily)* What need? I did so when first I came, but Frankenstein broke in one night when I was lying in the heavy sleep of utter exhaustion. I awoke to find him bending over me — oh, it was terrible! His eyes glared into mine, his hands were moving about my throat, his breath was like icy wind upon my face, I couldn't move, or cry out — I was helpless! Then he dragged me up from my bed and made me come in here — to work!

Waldman To — work?

Henry Yes — on that! *(he points to the recumbent figure. Another slight flash of lightning and distant thunder)* It was on such a night of storm as that at Goldstadt, like this, when I poured my secret elixir into the cold blood of Frankenstein, and he came to life. *Then* I was swept with wild emotion — pride, ambition, triumph! *Now* I am in despair. *(very earnestly)* Do you dare to look upon the work that is nearly done? It but awaits the quickening touch. Do you dare?

Waldman Tell me what I shall see.

Henry A being like Frankenstein, but a woman — his mate. I was upheld at Goldstadt by the false dream of my own greatness. I thought I could control and master the thing of my own creation. But in making — that — I have been overwhelmed by fear and abhorrence of the task. For hours — for days — I have wandered about the mountains, unable to return to this accursed place. I have been afraid to come in — afraid to touch it — afraid of myself — but Frankenstein has always driven me back. His damnable threats against my life — against my love — have conquered my manhood and my soul. Waldman! Waldman! I shall be free tonight! When I give *her* to him — a warm, living, breathing creature — I shall be free! (**F.** *looks in at window R., a flash of lightning showing his face)*

Waldman *(in a hoarse voice, pointing to window)* There — again!

Henry He is waiting. He understands. He knows the only thing there is to be done. Come! Look upon her! (**Henry** *goes to figure and stands behind couch, laying his hands upon the cloth as if to raise it)*

Waldman No! No! Do not raise that cloth. I cannot bear it. I will not look. No, no, Henry!

Frankenstein (1930)

Henry *(lifting the cloth in such a way that neither* **Waldman** *nor the audience can see the face)* What is there to fear in the unliving? What is flesh and blood — even *such* flesh and blood! — without life? What is the gross body compared to the dark spirit of evil that I shall awaken in it? *(he drops the cloth over figure and goes to* **Waldman***, who has covered his face)* Oh, forgive me! Forgive me!

Waldman My poor friend, what have I to forgive? *(they clasp hands)* I would to God that I could help you. *(he suddenly lays both hands on* **Henry's** *shoulders)* You must never, never do this thing.

Henry I must.

Waldman Then you will be lost eternally.

Henry I must.

Waldman Henry, then why do you hesitate? Why do you paint yourself so black? It is too late to undo the past — too late to save Katrina or the happiness of your home — but it is not too late to save your soul.

Henry Do you think for a moment, friend, if I deny Frankenstein his mate that he will spare me? Do you realize the strength of his hate? Listen! *(lowers his voice, after glancing towards the windows)* I have destroyed the principal tools with which I worked, and the diary in which I described my progress every day. Only one sheet of cipher and one thin phial remains — in that locked cabinet. Here is the key hanging round my neck.

Waldman One sheet of cipher and one thin phial in there? Well?

Henry I will show you, but go to the window first and look if you can see — Frankenstein. *(while* **Waldman** *goes to window, peering carefully out,* **Henry** *unlocks cabinet)*

Waldman No. The lightning is playing over the distant sky. The storm is coming nearer and nearer.

Henry Look, Dr. Waldman! *(he holds out a scroll and* **Waldman** *goes close to him, both speaking in earnest voices)* This is the secret formula that no man has ever read but myself. It tells me what to do before I use this — stand back — you must not touch it! *(he takes a glass sphere out of the cabinet, covered by two cloths, one vivid scarlet and the other yellow, and places it on the table; then removes the cloths and glass stopper and takes out a long thin glass phial, half filled with a colourless fluid)* The elixir that gives life — see! — it looks like pure and sparkling water! *(as he holds it up there is a flash of lightning, but not thunder)* See, it flashes into the night and

	draws down the very fire from heaven! Quick! Quick! *(he returns the phial to glass sphere and covers the latter swiftly with red and yellow cloths)* Back — back to your secret hiding place! *(as quickly closes and relocks cabinet, then staggers forward, his hand to his brow)* My head swims. I am as weak as a dying man. *(pours water from a jug on the table and drinks eagerly)* I must go and lie down — I must rest — I must rest — before I end my work! *(points to figure)*
Waldman	*(with momentary fear)* Will you leave me — alone?
Henry	You need not fear, he has no grudge against you, he will not harm you. Sleep! If I could only sleep! *(he groans and exits L. As **Henry** closes the door behind him **Waldman** looks fearfully round: then, after folding his hands and standing erect for a moment as if in silent prayer, goes to the fire and sits down. A pause. **F.**'s face at the window. **Waldman** is looking into the fire and does not see him. Another pause. Then the centre door slowly opens and **F.** enters. He is haggard and wild in appearance and limps painfully. His clothes hang about him in rags and are stained with earth and rain. He closes the door behind him stealthily and looks round. **Waldman** hears him and rises quickly. He sees **F.** and starts back. They stare at each other for a second)*
Waldman	*(in a breathless whisper)* Frankenstein!
F.	*(looking round again)* Where has — he gone — the man —
Waldman	Your master — be quiet! — he is asleep.
F.	*(points to figure)* She will — be mine — tonight — *(he slowly goes to figure and raises the cloth over it in the way **Henry** previously did, while **Waldman** watches him nervously, his right hand plucking at his mouth)* He — will make her — live tonight. She is still — still — *(he drops cloth over figure and draws nearer to **Waldman**, who shrinks back)* Are you — afraid of me?
Waldman	No! I am not afraid, but I — I — *(nervously watching his every movement)*
F.	You hate me. All men hate — Frankenstein. Why do men hate Frankenstein?
Waldman	How can I make you understand? Sit down, Frankenstein. I will talk to you. *(**Waldman** sits on stool by fire. **F.** sits on ground at a short distance)*
F.	*(waving his hand over his head in a flash of lightning)* Fire! Fire! Fire! *(a roll of thunder)*
Waldman	Do you understand why men should hate you? Do you know why your master hates you?

F.	*(brooding)* No. I want — my woman. My master will — give me — the woman — or I will kill him — kill him — so! *(he clenches his hands before him)*
Waldman	No, no, not that!
F.	*(innocently)* I — can kill him —
Waldman	Listen to me. You know that Katrina is dead?
F.	The little thing — Katrina.
Waldman	She is dead.
F.	I know. I know. I wept so — for her — it hurt me — hurt me — shining water could kill *(hides his face in his hands)*
Waldman	Yes, but that pain you went through then awakened your soul. In the depths of pain and sorrow the soul awakes.
F.	Soul? *(with a gleam of intelligence)* My soul? What do you mean?
Waldman	*(very distinctly)* Katrina is dead. Her body will not move again, but her soul is not dead.
F.	Then — then — where is her — soul? Oh, tell me!
Waldman	Her soul is with God.
F.	*(repeats the word slowly, with hands out-stretched as if groping in the dark)* God! Where is — God?
Waldman	I cannot tell you.
F.	Would God — hate me?
Waldman	No. He alone would pity and help you.
F.	He would — take my hand — like the little thing, Katrina. *(he rises and takes a step towards **Waldman** who also rises)* Show me the way — to Him.
Waldman	You must find the way for yourself.
F.	*(looking round helplessly)* I do not know the way. Did the bird's soul fly to God — when it fell down — on the water? Was the bird dead?
Waldman	Yes.
F.	Katrina is dead. Did her — soul fly to God?

Peggy Webling and the Story behind Frankenstein

Waldman Yes. Yes.

F. I must — find the way —

Waldman (*quickly*) Begone! I hear your master's step —

F. (*his face instantly changing to ferocity as he gives a snarl*) Tell — my master — I am there (*points to centre door*) I am — there! Tell my master — (*he makes an emphatic gesture towards the recumbent figure*) The hour has come! (*Exit quickly, passes before the window R. and disappears.* **Waldman** *follows him up to the door, which he closes and stands with his back to it as* **Henry** *enters L*).

Henry (*apprehensively, stopping short*) Frankenstein? (*the action to be gradually intensified from this point to end of act*)

Waldman Yes, he was here. He is waiting.

Henry The hour has come!

Waldman Those were the very words he used. (*leaves door and goes to* **Henry**, *who is staring towards the window*) Could you not go to sleep? (**Henry** *shakes his head without moving*) What are you going to do now? (*a slight pause*)

Henry (*slowly*) End my work. Gain my freedom. (*as* **Henry** *crosses before* **Waldman** *going towards the cabinet, the latter clutches his shoulder*)

Waldman Henry! Henry! You will buy your freedom at too high a price. Listen to the truth before it is too late. Think of the awful possibilities — realize what it will mean to give a woman like himself to Frankenstein. (*they look at each other with a sudden flash of mutual understanding*)

Henry I know!

Waldman (*his horror increasing every minute*) It will mean that she will be his — it will mean that she will bear him children — —

Henry I tell you, Waldman, *I know*.

Waldman Ah! But you have not thought that the children born of Frankenstein, and the unnatural mate of Frankenstein, will be the children of *your* guilty mind — the work of *your* sinful hands! (**Henry** *remains immovable, staring in front of him*) Do you remember the day at Belrive, after Katrina's death, when Frankenstein told you to choose?

Henry (*passionately*) Shall I ever forget?

Frankenstein (1930)

Waldman	I tell you to choose now! Will you do this monstrous thing, people the world with Frankensteins, with all its appalling consequences, or will you refuse before it is too late — too late?
Henry	*(almost triumphantly)* You shall see what I will do! *(he swiftly unlocks and throws open the doors of the cabinet. At that minute* **F.'s** *face appears at the window R., but the others do not see him.* **Henry** *takes out the cloth-covered glass sphere and scroll. He places the sphere on the table and holds out the scroll to* **Waldman***)* Look, Waldman! Without this formula my work could never have been accomplished. *(throws it on table, lifts the sphere, still covered, high in the air in both hands)* Without the secret phial of elixir which this contains I can never give life to that senseless body. It will decay and rot and return to dust! *(lays hand for a second on* **Waldman's** *shoulder)* My friend, I have chosen! *(the centre door opens and* **F.** *stands on the threshold, staring at them, still unperceived)* Look! Look! *(he catches up the scroll, tears it in half and thrusts both halves in the fire, holding them as they burn away. Comprehension of what* **Henry** *is doing dawns in* **F.'s** *face as he stoops forward, eagerly watching.* **Henry** *speaks as the paper burns)* *(He tears off the coverings of the sphere, throwing them aside so that they fall, bright specks of red and yellow, through the air)* Life to the emblem of life! Mystic flame to mystic flame! Fire to fire! *(he takes out the phial and pours the liquid into the brasier. As the drops fall in, flames of as bright and beautiful colour as it is possible to obtain must leap up, while lightning plays over the stage,* **Henry** *saying as this happens)* My secret! Burn! Burn! Burn! Gone for ever! Gone for ever! *(***F.** *springs into the room with a howl of frenzy.* **Henry** *turns to meet him,* **Waldman** *reeling back, unheeded. The two face each other in silence for a few breathing spaces)*
F.	Now — you cannot — give me — *(points wildly to the recumbent figure)*
Henry	No! *(almost as the word is spoken* **F.** *leaps at* **Henry's** *throat, like an animal, and there is a short, desperate struggle.* **F.** *then pins* **Henry** *to the ground and strangles him.* **F.** *stands erect, gazing down at him with wide, staring eyes, dazed for a second.* **Waldman** *throws himself on his knee beside* **Henry***)*
Waldman	You have killed your master.
F.	Killed — my master! Then his soul — his soul — with little Katrina — I am alone — alone *(he gives a deep, long moan)* I must find — my way — to God — alone — alone — where shall I find — Him! He will help me — I must go — into the night! How shall I find — the way — how shall I find the way — *(he moves blindly to the centre door, and stands there for*

	a second, his face raised. Then there is a vivid flash of lightning that strikes him and he falls instantly)
Waldman	*(standing over him until the clap of thunder after the lightning fades away)* He is dead. The guilty work is destroyed, but his soul has returned to its Creator. *(turns and looks tenderly and solemnly down at* **Henry***)* Man! Man! From God alone is the breath of life!

End of Play

APPENDIX 1
EXCERPTS FROM WEBLING LETTERS CONCERNING FRANKENSTEIN

Note: Punctuation and spelling are Webling's

1) 27 FEBRUARY 1921. 124 The Grove, Hammersmith. *Author*: Peggy Webling
Topic: Business, Writing (Matheson Lang and Frankenstein)

... I went to see Mr Lang at the theatre on Tuesday last, and was much encouraged by his still keen interest in the Frankenstein idea; he says certainly go on with it & remembered all about the prologue. I could only see him for a few minutes, as he was making up, but I spent some time with Mrs Lang & she said she would talk to him about the play. So I'm longing to get on with it. ...

2) 17 OCTOBER 1921. 124 The Grove, Hammersmith. *Author*: Peggy Webling
Topic: Writing, Business (writing of Frankenstein, mention of Matheson Lang)

Dearest Jossie. I am so absorbed in Frankenstein I can hardly think of anything else. I have written the Prologue & first act, and all the rest is in my head ready to be written down. It is much more difficult than I imagined and perhaps I shall not be able to pull it off. ... I had a box last week for Mr Lang's new play, "Christopher Sly," a brilliant series of pictures and fine acting, but a thin play...

3) 30 OCTOBER 1921. 124 The Grove, Hammersmith. *Author*: Peggy Webling
Topic: Writing, Business (writing of *Frankenstein*, mention of Matheson Lang)

... I have finished the prologue and first two acts of "Frankenstein;" of course I may be wrong, but *I* think is [sic] is very strong; it was much more difficult to write than I imagined, but I had thought it out so thoroughly that on the last day I worked at the second act—the longest and most important in the play—I could not write the words down fast enough and when it was done I was shaking from head to foot and (as they say in novels) gave way to a burst of emotion! I am now debating whether I will write, or go to see, Mr Lang. ...

4) 9 NOVEMBER 1921. [124 The Grove, Hammersmith] *Author*: Ethel Webling
Topic: Writing (*Frankenstein* finished)

... P. has actually finished F. last night. ...

Appendix 1

5) 11 NOVEMBER 1921. (continuation of 9 November letter).   *Author*: Ethel Webling
Topic: Writing, Business (Ethel's opinion of *Frankenstein*, mention of Matheson Lang)

... P. read us her play last night – it is very fine – it made Rs eyes fill with tears. I long for P. to go & see Lang ... F is a great play – original & deep & strong [end of letter]

6) 30 JULY 1925. 124 The Grove, Hammersmith.   *Author*: Peggy Webling
Topic: Business (mention of Edgar Selwyn)

... By the way, do you see theatrical papers? Or could you find out (without trouble) where Edgar Selwyn is to be found? Lucy tells me he is very well known and popular in the States; I met him years ago, and I think of writing to him about "Frankenstein;" perhaps he has a theatre in New York? Can you suggest where I could find out his address? Is there still a New York Mirror? He would probably advertise in the best stage "trade journal." ...

7) 23 SEPTEMBER 1925. Seaford, Sussex.   *Author*: Peggy Webling
Topic: Business (Mention of Edgar Selwyn, Farquharson, Ruskin Watts)

... My next literary job is to be a shot at a play. (By the way, has Ruskin received my letter about Mr Edgar Selwyn & "Frankenstein"? And has Mr Farquharson's agent in New York sent the Ms.?) ... So I am going to try a comedy myself... [a play of her novel *Comedy Corner*] ... I always have a feeling that *some day* I shall pull off a play that *will* be produced and – perhaps – make a hit.......

8) 8 OCTOBER 1925. 124 The Grove, Hammersmith.   *Author*: Peggy Webling
Topic: Business (mention of Ruskin Watts re: *Frankenstein*)

... I wonder whether Ruskin has done anything about "F." yet? ...

9) 3 NOVEMBER 1925. [124 The Grove]   *Author*: Ethel Webling
Topic: Writing, Business (Peggy beginning new play; mention of Ruskin Watts re: *Frankenstein*)

... P. began her play [*Comedy Corner*]. ... Pity Ruskin did not do as I specially asked to keep letter & see him personally. Cant [*sic*] be helped. She will write. Lovingly E.

10) 7 NOVEMBER 1925. 124 The Grove.   *Author*: Peggy Webling
Topic: Business (mention of Ruskin Watts re: *Frankenstein*, Edgar Selwyn, the Barrymores)

My dearest Jossie, First of all, about "F." Ever so many thanks for your message from Ruskin; knowing the little ways of theatrical people so well I am not surprised at any discourtesy on the part of Edgar Selwyn. I am sorry Ruskin did not do as I suggested – not give up the letter until he had a reasonable chance of seeing the man, but now (if there is still no reply) is it possible for him to call at the theatre, or anywhere else, and try again to see Selwyn himself? If not, what about approaching the Barrymores – or any other leading man you can think of. (All this, of course, if Ruskin cares to have a shot at the business, but if he doesn't, for any reason, just let me know and I will tell you where to forward the typescript). ...

11) 10 DECEMBER 1925. 124 The Grove.   *Author*: Peggy Webling
Topic: Business (mention of Ruskin Watts re: *Frankenstein*, Nigel Playfair)

[at the end of a long Christmas letter] Has Ruskin been able to do anything about Frankenstein? I sent it to Nigel Playfair, but he couldn't do anything with it. I am now writing a play on Comedy Corner.... ...

12) [EARLY 1927] Partial letter. Writers' Club, 10 Norfolk Street, Strand. *Author*: Peggy Webling
Topic: Business (Jossie to send copy of *Frankenstein* typescript)

...will send me the copy you have of "Frankenstein" as soon as you conveniently can. It is the only correct one I have & I want to show it to somebody over here. Will you register it & I will send stamps for the amount. ...

13) 1 MARCH 1927. 39 St. Stephen's Avenue, London W. 12.   *Author*: Peggy Webling
Topic: Business (mention of Ruskin Watts, mislaid ms., Edgar Selwyn, Farquharson)

Dearest Jossie, I am *so* sorry you are worried over "Frankenstein." The facts have slipped your memory. I did *not* give it to you last time you were over, but I sent it to Ruskin, (or rather Mr Farquharson's representative in New York forwarded it for me), with a letter of introduction to Edgar Selwyn. But Ruskin was unable to do anything about it. Now do you recollect? Perhaps Ruskin has the Ms., at all events, I expect he will remember the incident. I am going to type it again, as of course I have a rough copy here, but *if* it turns up, I know you will post it on. ...

14) 4 APRIL 1927. [39 St. Stephen's Avenue]   *Author*: Peggy Webling
Topic: mislaid manuscript

[last sentence of letter] Adieu. Looking forward to news of Frankenstein. Your own Peggles

15) 20 SEPTEMBER 1927. 39 St. Stephen's Avenue.   *Author*: Peggy Webling
Topic: Business (sent copies of *Frankenstein* to Stanley Drewitt and Hamilton Deane)

I have recently typed "F." yet again! Stanley Drewitt still has one copy, & I wanted another for a man named Hamilton Deane, who knew Lucy in the old Haviland days. He has

Appendix 1

lately written & produced in London a version of Bram Stoker's vampire book "Dracula" which is a great success. ...

16) 24 SEPTEMBER 1927. 39 St. Stephen's Avenue. *Author*: Peggy Webling
Topic: manuscript found!

Dearest Jossie, It was indeed a delight to get another letter from you so soon after the last. I hope you received mine in which I begged you not to think anymore of the "Frankenstein" loss – & now it has turned up! I am *very* glad & thank you ever so much for forwarding it at once. The packet has not yet arrived, but we expect it daily. ...

17) 28 SEPTEMBER 1927. [39 St. Stephen's Avenue] *Author*: Peggy Webling
Topic: Business (Deane delighted by *Frankenstein*; Farquharson involved with contract)

Dearest Jossie, We must not hope too much – there's many a slip, etc. – but I am writing a hasty note to tell you that the second man to whom I sent "F." is simply delighted with it & wants to know terms at once, with talk of giving it a provincial production to be followed by London! He has his own company & is the author & producer, as I think I told you, of "Dracula," a piece now running in the West End & to be given (he tells me) at a New York theatre next month. I have now to see Mr Farquharson, as I think of putting the business into his hands. You can imagine how excited I feel – in spite of the "many a slip" truth. I am not telling anybody about it, except yourself, Ethel (of course) & Lucy, so please don't mention it either. This morning I have been to the Author's Society, making some enquiries about copyright, but all is satisfactory on that score. The book ("F") was published in 1818 & Mrs Shelley died in 1851, so the rights are free. I will write again when anything is to be told. Mr Hamilton Deane says it is "deep & moving tragedy" & he has not read any play for years that has "impressed him so much." He wants "the film & world rights." I am just off to Mr Farquharson........

All well at home. Lucy very much more comfortable in her new flat. Ethel has nearly finished her big pictures of the Madonna & Child – I expect you have heard of them from her. Ruth has gone to-day to St. Albans to the shrine of Britain's proto-martyr & St. Emma. Oh, if "F." comes out – wot larks! Dearest love from your Peggles.

18) 16 OCTOBER 1927. 39 St. Stephen's Avenue. *Author*: Peggy Webling
Topic: Business (contract signed with Deane via Farquharson, play in provinces within 6 months, West End production within a year of original production)

Dearest Josie. Hip – Hip – HIP huroar! "Frankenstein" is going to be produced! On Friday I received the signed contract, per my energetic Farquharson, from Hamilton Deane. He is offering very good terms – a royalty on gross box office takings – on a sliding scale, and he has already planked down fifty pounds as a guarantee advance on future royalties. It is to be brought out (the play I mean) within six months in the provinces, & within a year of the date of the original production in a West End

Appendix 1

London theatre. You can imagine *how* pleased I am. I couldn't sleep on Friday night with excitement. I am not to tell the name of the play until the date of production is fixed. It has been a very anxious time, wondering whether it would really be settled. You will have had my letter from the Club while the negotiations were going on. Ever so many thanks to you and Ruskin for returning the copy; it arrived safely. But, after all, it is not that version Mr Deane has accepted, but the one in which "Henry" and "F." are played by different actors. He wants a few slight alterations, chiefly to stress the moral point of the absurdity of man trying to assume the powers of God. At present we have not discussed the literary part of the business at all – Deane & Farquharson have been corresponding on business only, but I think I told you he (Deane) wrote that he considered the play "quite wonderful." It seems too good to be true after seven years of waiting, and typing, & rewriting, and disappointments, & hopes. … Your devoted P(laywright).

19) 18 OCTOBER 1927. 39 St. Stephen's Avenue. *Author*: Ethel Webling
Topic: family comments on *Frankenstein*

Dearest Jossie – You can imagine the interest and excitement over F.

20) 24 NOVEMBER 1927. 25 St. Stephen's Avenue. *Author*: Ruth Webling Torr
Topic: family comments on *Frankenstein*

[last paragraph] Peggy's news about her play is good. We are all looking forward to the spring to go and see the first performance. Will you be over in the spring – I hope so – you must try and make an effort to see the play, I have just read the book.

21) 28 NOVEMBER 1927. 25 St. Stephen's Avenue. *Author*: Lucy Webling McRaye
Topic: play, mention of Hamilton Deane

I *said* the play would bring you over – it is of course our great news, and something to look forward to – wasn't it curious that I should have been on tour with Hamilton Deane, years ago, in "The Only Way"?

22) 7 DECEMBER 1927. Red Lion Hotel, Church Street, Preston. *Author*: Peggy Webling
Topic: Production at Preston, Writing (mention of Matheson Lang, W. E. Holloway; last act not strong enough, will write violent scene between Henry and F.)

Darling Jossie. To-day's the day! I came down to Preston (Lancashire) on Monday, & you can imagine how anxiously I am looking for the first performance, of "F.," which takes place at the Empire Theatre (very big house) this evening. Hamilton Deane can't say enough of the play, although he is quite right in his opinion that the last act isn't strong enough; I am going to re-write it when I return, introducing a violent scene between Henry & F. Mr Deane will make a very intense "F," although he is not the type of

Appendix 1

man *I* imagine, except in height & breadth of shoulders, for he is *very* thin, with a long, hawklike face: he has all new scenery, costumes, and quite a fair company, Henry being played (isn't it odd?) by E.W. Holloway [*sic*: W.E. Holloway], who was Matheson Lang's partner when he produced "Westward Ho!" Mr Deane says he will turn every stone to *make* "F." a success, "pulling and tugging it together when once he has seen how it goes before an audience."

I know your thoughts would be with us if you knew – how strange it seems that you haven't yet heard the production is tonight – I wrote you directly I knew myself last week. Ethel is coming down to-day. Deane assures me, *if* we can make it the hit he believes we can, there will be a *lot* of money in it. I can't realize the day has come; I have thought of "F." so much & put so much emotion into it.

Farewell – I'll write the result & *prospects* whatever they are. Your own Peggles.

23) 9 December 1927. Red Lion Hotel, Church Street, Preston.   *Author*: Peggy Webling *Topic*: Production at Preston, Writing (Hamilton Deane, the cast, calls for author, Dracula, no extensive alterations in writing)

Dearest Jossie. SUCCESS! I know you will be eagerly waiting for the news of "Frankenstein;" (it has been such an anxious, *happy* time & it has had the funny effect of making my hand so shakey – but that will get better).

Oh, if you could have been here on Wednesday night! If you could have heard the call – enthusiastic, determined – for Author; if you could have seen me hurrying all the way from the middle of the circle (where Ethel & I were sitting) to the side of the stage. And Mr Deane led me on & then presented me, from the company & staff, with a wonderful bouquet, so big -- a great sheaf -- that it almost reached to my shoulder! Ethel said I looked *little* on that great stage. Mr Deane thinks, & so do I, we can work this play up into a really great thing – I don't mean by that that it needs extensive alterations, but one can never see some things until a play is actually before an audience. H.D. makes a fine "F;" he plays it with quite extraordinary pathos – & he has only put in *one* sentence & cut out two. He has never produced before, he says, without working over & altering again & again. In fact, he can't praise the play enough. The Prologue *grips* the people, as the Henry – in fact all the men – are very good. You can hear a sort of murmured "Oh!" go through the house when F. first moves; he is made up white – almost gray in colouring – with dark, rather long brown hair, his lips very wide & his eyes – just for the time when he comes to life – look as if they glittered, an effect obtained by a way they have of making up the lids. Afterwards he is dressed like Henry – wigs alike – & they are almost of the same height.......oh, I won't wait to tell you details, for I could go on for a week! I came down on Monday & Ethel came just for the first night, & went home yesterday morning; I go tomorrow. H.D.'s present tour goes on till the end of February, & he will play "F" every week in his repertory. A fortune has been made out of "Dracula" – is it going to be made out of "Frankenstein"? I am going (as I think I told you) to write in a scene in the last act, I *ought* to have thought of it, but I didn't until I saw it (the whole act) rehearsed.

How I wish you were here! Isn't it odd, the man who plays "Victor" reminds me of poor Dirk Daniell? We had always said *he* was to be "Victor."

Farewell – I am so happy – Your own <u>Peggles.</u> *Write soon.*

24)   13 December 1927. 39 St. Stephen's Avenue.   *Author*: Ethel Webling
Topic: family comments on *Frankenstein*

Dearest Jossie – We have been living through a wonderful time. To see F. produced, by such a fine cast, Henry, F., Waldman, Victor, the Baron, little Katrine, could not be better, & the Baroness too -- the servant & Amelia [*sic*] could be bettered but the others just the living characters. It was most thrilling & our Peggy Playwright looked so very attractive as she took the call. Now she is making a few changes & it has come to the day for Xmas letters. ...

25)   15 December 1927. [39 St. Stephen's Avenue]   *Author*: Ethel Webling
Topic: comments on *Frankenstein*

... Naturally we talk [of] F a very great deal and P. & I have talked it over & over & settled the changes she is making, that will strengthen it enormously.

The first night was so thrilling. I left London by the 10.50 train. Peggy met me at Preston & we went and had a poached egg tea, then bought flowers to give our ladies, then went to our Red Lion, changed our dresses & got our seat from H.D.'s manager – such bowing & exchange of good wishes, & down we sat in the middle of the dress circle.

I am too tired to tell you about it tonight but it was a very wonderful night's experience & Peggy looked so small & attractive on the big stage near the big men & scenery, holding the big sheaf of exquisite flowers. You would have felt proud of the play, as she says it is the most thrilling event in literature to have a play produced. We sat talking in her bedroom while she unwired all the flowers & put them in water, lots of violets all together, then put very pale & lovely chrysanthemums. ...

26)   15 January 1928. 39, St. Stephen's Avenue.   *Author*: Peggy Webling
Topic: Writing, Performance schedule (rewrite of last act: demand of F. for a mate, fight with Henry, altered F.'s meeting with Emilie in Act 2)

Dearest Jossie. Time passes so quickly, and my memory is so bad, that I can't remember how much I have told you of the "F." news. Well, I have re-written the last act, introducing the demand of F. (as in the book) for a mate, and Henry's refusal to make one; of course in my version F. is not educated and intelligent, so his demand has to be in a way vague, but I think it loses nothing by that; then comes a fight between Henry and F., in which the latter is overpowered, but not wounded, and it ends as now with his leap from the crag. I have not yet heard what Hamilton Deane thinks of the alteration; I have also quickened and made stronger F.'s meeting with Emilie, in the second act. The following is the tour list – *what place will you come to?* I do not yet know whether "F." will be

Appendix 1

played at the Borough, Stratford, or the King's, Hammersmith, but I hope not, as both those theatres are too near the West End. I hope to go to Bournemouth, to stay with Mrs Heelas for a few days, and that will give me an opportunity to see Deane and find out everything – he is very bad at answering letters. Here's the list: --

Jan. 30 Victoria Theatre, Burnley
Feb 6 Theatre Royal, Bournemouth
       13 Palace Theatre, Westcliff-on-Sea
       20 Grand Theatre, Wolverhampton
       27 Borough Theatre, Stratford
March 5 Grand Theatre, Blackpool
       12 Theatre Royal, Huddersfield
       19 New Theatre, Oxford
       26 Empire Theatre, Swindon
Apr. 2 VACATION
       9 Prince's Theatre, Bradford
       16 Shakespeare Theatre, Liverpool
       23 Grand Theatre, Derby
       30 Grand Opera House, Scarsborough
May 7 Empire Theatre, Sheffield
       14 King's Theatre, Hammersmith
       21 Grand Theatre, Hull
       28 Royal Theatre, Nottingham
June 4, 11, 18 Royal Theatre, Nottingham

So you see it (F.) is going to two of our old reciting strongholds – Bradford & Sheffield. ...

27) 3 FEBRUARY 1928. [39 St. Stephen's Avenue]   *Author*: Ethel Webling
Topic: Writing (working on alterations)

... We talk of F. a great deal. P. still cogitating on the alterations. ...

28) 2 MARCH 1928. 39, St. Stephen's Avenue.   *Author*: Peggy Webling
Topic: Writing (rewrite 3rd act: Henry says he will make a mate for F. but reconsiders; F. will kill Henry and die by lightning; keeps scene with Waldman and F. discussing God)

... There is another revolution in "F."! Mr Deane is playing this week ("Dracula") at the Borough Theatre, Stratford, so I went with Lucy to the matinée, and we saw him afterwards. He reported that the play (I always mean F. by "the" play!) went wonderfully well the previous week at Wolverhampton, but the weakness of the last act is its one *great* weakness, and he had had an idea that he was very diffident of suggesting to me, but when he *did* I instantly saw the possibilities. It is to use the incident of the book, showing Henry's consent to make a mate for F., but realizing that he must not complete the work because of the chance of peopleing (spelling right?) the world with monsters – there's a situation for you! So I am thinking it out and then I shall entirely re-write the last act – except for the little scene (do you remember?) between Waldmand [*sic*] and F. in which the latter tries to understand that it is God alone who can help and pity him, as Deane says that always "gets over" and *he* considers it the most touching thing in the whole play. This new idea ought to make an end as thrilling as the prologue; he says he will spare no expense or trouble to get the production as perfect as possible; F. will kill Henry and die himself by a flash of lightning, thereby carrying out the thought that he comes to life in a storm and ends in a storm – Henry dies by his own wicked act, indirectly, and F. dies by the forces of Nature. This will mean, as you will see, slight alterations all through to lead up to it – my re-writing for the *seventh* time! I also had a talk with Mr Holloway (the Henry), and he says that now Deane is playing the part very finely; he has just got the right "tone." It is all to be finished and tried out at Nottingham as I told you in my last. Are you coming? ...

29) 5 April 1928. [39, St. Stephen's Avenue] *Author*: Peggy Webling
Topic: Cast changes

... Yesterday I saw Mr Holloway (Henry in "F."), who is in town for the company's vacation week. He tells me Deane has engaged a new "Emilia." The last girl was the *very* bad one in the cast, so I hope this means a great improvement. ...

30) 15 April 1928. 39 St. Stephen's Avenue. *Author*: Peggy Webling
Topic: Writing (last act: burning of formula, description of props and effects, violent fight at the end)

... Yes, as you say, "Frankenstein" has obsessed me. Hamilton Deane is at Liverpool now, then Derby, Scarborough, Sheffield, Hammersmith, & I shall have a chance to hear how things are going. He is a good letter writer when he *wishes* to tell me anything, but hard to get at at other times, forgets to answer what I ask him & is vague. You speak of the burning of the formula in the new last act. Did I tell you that the great effect is after that is done? Henry then takes the phial containing his elixir of life out of its hiding place. It is kept in a glass sphere, covered with two vivid silk coverings, & directly these are removed flashes of lightning play about the room. "See!" he says, "how it flashes into the night & calls down the very fire from Heaven!" The elixir itself is a colourless fluid which he pours into the fire, which causes flames of a beautiful colour, while he cries: – "Life to the emblem of life! Mystic fire to real fire! Flame to flame!" At least that is the way it is written, but of course the actual way of producing has to be left to Deane. I am hoping

Appendix 1

for a great improvement in the play from the new girl to play Emilia. Mr Holloway told me he finds Henry a difficult & trying part, as it begins at top notch and keeps it up all through -- & in the new ending he has to finish up with a violent fight! It is as necessary to have a powerful Henry as a strong "F."

31) 13 DECEMBER 1928. 39 St. Stephen's Avenue.   *Author*: Peggy Webling
Topic: Writing (P.W. to New Brighton; 2nd act: switching scenes between F. and Katrine, and F. and Emilie; act closes with quarrel between F. and Henry)

… On Monday I am off to New Brighton for a week of "F." The alterations are made in the second act, the chief one being that the scenes between F. & Katrina & F. & Emilie are transposed, so that all the excitement now comes right at the end, closing (as you will remember) with the quarrel scene between F. & Henry. The girl you saw as Emilie has left the company, so I shall see a new (the third) Emilie. The new novel has had to be put on one side until after Christmas. …

32) 14 DECEMBER 1928. 25 St. Stephen's Avenue, Goldhawk Road.   *Author*: Lucy McRaye
Topic: Peggy's travels re: Frankenstein

… Peggy is going for a week to New Brighton (near Liverpool), she leaves on Monday next. …

33) 17 JANUARY 1929. 39 St. Stephen's Avenue.   *Author*: Peggy Webling
Topic: Business, Writing ('financial' and 'artistic'; a very big possibility)

… Now, I *may* have some big and unexpected news to tell you of "F." very shortly – nothing to do with a possible London production this year – and it is news that will *surprise* you, for it has to do with the artistic side, as well as the financial, of the prospects of the play. It has all been very exciting & not a little agitating, but I do believe it will turn out well. I will only say, that a *very big* possibility – for me – is now hanging in the balance, & yet it is not *all* delightful. Now, are you curious? I'll write at once when things are definite: it may be next week, it may not be for several weeks. …

34) 9 FEBRUARY 1929. 39 St. Stephen's Ave.   *Author*: Peggy Webling
Topic: Business and pleasure (seeing *Frankenstein*; P.W. and Farquharson to see Hamilton Deane)

Next Wednesday I have a party at Westcliff – Ethel, Ruth, Ruthie, Lucy, Mrs Chaple, Alice Shilton and Mr Farquharson, all to see "Frankenstein." I am entertaining the ladies to tea, but Mr F (Farquharson, not Frankenstein) & I are going to see Hamilton Deane.

35) 24 MARCH 1929. Clarendon Hotel, Oxford.   *Author*: Peggy Webling
Topic: Business (Balderston collaboration for America; he saw *Frankenstein* at New Brighton in December, part author of Dracula; contract with P.W. and B.)

Appendix 1

Dearest Jossie. I expect you will be surprised to hear from me at Oxford, but Mr Deane was playing "F." here last night, and I wanted to see him so I came down & return to-day to my lonely home. ... Dearest, I *may* come to U.S.A. & Canada as soon as I can afford it. All depends upon Frankenstein. In the greater matter of my unspeakable loss I have forgotten to tell you it is *practically* settled that a Mr John Balderston – an American who wrote that brilliant play, "Berkeley Square," now running in London – is to collaborate with me in a version of "F." for the American stage. There has been any amount of talk & correspondence between him, Mr Deane & myself. He (John Balderston) came down to New Brighton at Xmas on purpose to see the play, & was so impressed that he kept Deane up till three in the morning discussing it. *But he* declares there must be vital changes to suit America. He is also part author of the U.S.A. version of "Dracula" (which is an enormous financial success there), &, to cut a long story short, I have agreed to let him come in with me. His agent was over from New York & made the contract, which I showed to the Authors' Society, & which Farquharson had altered on all the points with which I could not agree. I have sent B. a copy of the play as it now stands, & he is going to write his version from that showing it to me as he goes on act by act. In about six months he guarantees to finish it & get an American production, or he forfeits the small money he has paid me; if he can't manage this, he pays me a hundred pounds for another nine months option. But I believe he *will* do it. He is a very clever, peculiar man, with an extraordinary sense of the dramatic – a great sense of the theatre – combined with practical skill & artistic feeling. He lives in London, at Knightsbridge – perhaps you know his writing on the New York World? This play of his, "Berkeley Square," is exceedingly fine. When his version of "F." is finished, Mr Deane & I are to settle whether it will be played (or part of it played) in this country. I have stipulated that *here* it is always to be announced as by "Peggy Webling & John Balderston." In U.S.A. it will be (as an advertisement following the huge success of "Dracula") "By John Balderston & Hamilton Deane, adapted from the play by Peggy Webling." It is rather absurd to have Deane's name, but I *had* to give way on that point. So there the matter stands. Mr Balderston has great hopes of America -- play, film rights, "talkies," everything – and we share equally – fifty-fifty – in everything that is made. It has all been very agitating, but I think I have done a wise thing – Ethel highly approved – in closing with Balderston. Deane has tremendous faith in him, & also says he is absolutely straight in business. Of course U.S.A. is the place to make money – if it is to be made at all – with a play. So – who knows?..........

36) 27 May 1929. 39 St. Stephen's Avenue. *Author*: Peggy Webling
Topic: Business (reminder about previous letter re: Balderston)

... Did you ever receive a long letter from me written when I was at Oxford? I told you all about Mr John Balderston & the plans for "Frankenstein" in U.S.A. This week Mr Deane is at the King's Theatre, Hammersmith, but of course he will not be doing "F." as it is too near the West End. ...

Appendix 1

37) 7 June 1929. 39 St. Stephen's Avenue. *Author*: Peggy Webling
Topic: Business (again, reminder about previous Oxford letter re: Balderston)

... I think I asked you before if you received a long letter from me written at Oxford? It told you all about the plans for "Frankenstein." Mr Deane is playing it two nights at Nottingham next week. ...

38) 3 October 1929. 39 St. Stephen's Avenue. *Author*: Peggy Webling
Topic: Business, Writing (Balderston failed to complete his version by deadline, 9 month extension; P.W. hopes for London production, plans a change in 2nd act)

[3rd paragraph] I have been very occupied and worried over various business, chiefly "Frankenstein." Mr Balderston, the American, has not been able to complete his version for the United States as he agreed to do, and now he is a member of the Prime Minister's party, representing the American Press, so I have consented to extend the time and he still declares he will sell the play within nine months – according to our contract – but in the meantime I have confident (fairly confident) hopes that Hamilton Deane will produce mine in London. Neither he nor I like Balderston's desired alterations. I went down to Chester for one night last week on purpose to talk it all over with Deane, and I have arranged to make an alteration he wants in the second act, and *then* we shall see! The play went tremendously in Birmingham, the business increased every night and the papers were most enthusiastic. We have a new "Henry." You will remember seeing Holloway, but the fresh man is a great improvement on him, good as he was. It is an actor named Malcolm Russell, about thirty, of wide experience, and he plays the part in a most "creepy" way, as if Henry were on the brink of madness. There is also a new Emilie (the fifth) but she isn't good. Of course Deane will have a very good actress if he comes to town. I treated Lucy to a week at Leicester, when Deane was there, and we went to see all his plays, and the Frankenstein audience was more enthusiastic than any other.

Review attached for Birmingham production (typed out by Peggy):

Prince of Wales Theatre. Birmingham.[*Birmingham Evening Despatch*, 27 August 1929, p. 3] Frankenstein, which Mr Hamilton [*sic*] and his Company brought to the Prince of Wales Theatre this week, is to the ordinary thriller as a Poe story is to a nursery rhyme. The play is so steeped in horror, so gruesome in its workings on the imagination, that it might well have been written by that great master of horrible phantasy. Actually it is founded on ancient legend and made into a play by Peggy Webling from the story by Mrs Shelley the poet's wife. Frankenstein is no robot. He is a creature of flesh and blood, hideously fashioned by the hand of man, given life by the will of man. He is horrible in his soulless strength, pitiable in his groping ignorance.

There is no denying the power of this play, and there is no denying the power with which it is acted. Mr Hamilton Deane, with high skill, succeeds in being a man and yet no man; a figure of horror and pathos. . . . . Acting of such full-blooded nature is rarely seen in the theatre to-day.

39) 19 October 1929. Parkstone Heights, Parkstone, Dorset. *Author*: Peggy Webling
Topic: Business, Writing (Balderston in America, will finish version and sell in 9 months; P.W. made alterations in Act 2)

… "Frankenstein" is at Warrington, Lancashire, this week; next, at Liverpool; then Deane gives it for a whole week at Burnley. I think I told you Mr Balderston is now in America, & declares he will have his version ready & sold within nine months. I have made some alterations (slight) in the second act which Deane says are "most excellent." …

40) 25 November 1929. 39, St. Stephen's Avenue. *Author*: Peggy Webling
Topic: London Production, Business, Writing (Peggy's version used in London; Balderston's unfinished)

… Now for the thrilling news: – Frankenstein is to be produced next year, on Monday, February 10, at the Little Theatre, John Street, Adelphi. It will be *my* version, as Mr Balderston has not written his & neither Mr Deane nor I cared for his ideas. He (Deane) tells me he is going to have new dresses, furniture & scenery. You can imagine how pleased I am – if only Ethel were here! …

41) 2 December 1929. 39, St. Stephen's Avenue. *Author*: Peggy Webling
Topic: London Production

… I'm longing to hear what you think of "F." in London. I shan't sleep for a week before the first night. It will be two years next week since it was produced at Preston. …

42) 10 December 1929. 39, St. Stephen's Avenue. *Author*: Peggy Webling
Topic: London Production, Business (publicity man hired; no word from Balderston; Berkeley Square produced in New York)

… My other letter was to tell you the thrilling news of the production of Frankenstein on the 10th of February at the Little Theatre. I don't think you ever went there, did you? It is in John Street, Adelphi, a few minutes' walk from Charing Cross District Railway. Mr Deane tells me he is having new furniture, dresses and scenery. He has already engaged a publicity man, named Stanley Hale. I could not sleep the first night after I heard the great thing is coming at last – and Ethel won't be there! It was Frankenstein's second birthday the other day. I hear Mr Balderston has brought out his "Berkeley Square" in New York; if ever you have a chance to see it – do! It's a brilliant play. But neither Mr Deane nor I have had a word from him about the American version of "F." …

43) 31 December 1929. 39, St. Stephen's Avenue. *Author*: Peggy Webling
Topic: Business (Balderston and American production)

… If Mr John Balderston does as well as he expects with "F." I may come over. It is now decided to my great satisfaction (did I tell you?) that he has nothing whatever to do with

Appendix 1

the play in this country. He wanted Deane to postpone till his version was ready! Thank Heaven Deane said "No!" & so it is settled. ...

44) 5 JANUARY 1930. 39, St. Stephen's Avenue.   *Author*: Peggy Webling
Topic: London Production preparations

Dearest Jossie, Just a hasty letter to tell you the preliminary announcements of "F." have appeared in all the London papers – I enclosed a few to show you how the campaign is started. Mr Deane's press agent is a young man named Stanley Hale, who is coming to see me one day next week, as he has had no opportunity of seeing the play and I have to "post" him in what to say about it. There will be only one change in the men of the company; the part of "Henry" is to be played by an actor who is beginning to be very well known in London, named Hallett [*sic*]; he is a tall man, as big as Hamilton Deane. "Emilie" is to be played (I hear) by a beautiful girl – the fifth since the play was first produced – and the Baroness by another new member, while Miss Grimshaw (whom you saw as the Baroness) will be "Elizabeth," the servant. Of course little Miss Patrick remains the "Katrina;" she is going to wear white, not blue as she did at Reading when you were there. That's all the news I have at present. ... [I] made an endeavour to catch up with my correspondence – already it is coming in a good deal over "F.," applications for parts, etc. Did I tell you Mr Deane wants me to collaborate with him in writing a play? He has a book that he thinks (and so do I) will make a fine drama *if* we can do it. [*Reprieve* by Halbert J. Boyd] The author is willing and I begin to see how to tackle it – nuf said at present. ...

45) 8 JANUARY 1930. 39, St. Stephen's Avenue.   *Author*: Peggy Webling
Topic: London production preparations, Business ('Frankenstein of *my* existence – John Balderston' extending agreement)

... You will have had my last letter with the latest news of "F." I hear that Mr Deane's new furniture (for the piece) is very handsome. To-day I am having his publicity man, H. S. Hale, at the club to meet my (for the sake of friendship) publicity man, Jimmie Spence. Yesterday I went to see Mr Farquharson to hear the latest request of the Frankenstein of *my* existence – John Balderston. He wishes our agreement (for the American version and production) to be pushed on six months, which means he has to the end of this year in which to do his play and get somebody to take it. I have consented, as he agrees to pay another advance, and my own version meantime can go on in this country. ("Let soap so!" as one of Leonard Merrick's characters says.) ...

46) 12 JANUARY 1930. 39, St. Stephen's Avenue.   *Author*:
Peggy Webling
*Topic: Lo*ndon production preparations

... The night of Frankenstein approaches, and I hardly dare to think of it! Mr Deane will be playing in the provinces up to the Saturday before the 10th, so, if he is not too far from

Appendix 1

town, I shall try to go and see the new members of the cast before the London opening. I have been very busy lately, for I have a good many engagements at the club, and in connection with "F.," to say nothing of family affairs, house-cleaning, etc., etc. etc., for there always seems so much to do. I have had letters about parts in the play.... ...

47) 21 JANUARY 1930. 39, St. Stephen's Avenue.   *Author*: Peggy Webling
Topic: London production preparations, dress

... I have bought my dress for February 10th! It is very pretty and good, a ring velvet, black ground, flecked with a moony sort of blue shade, and I have also got an evening cloak of ring velvet, with a big collar – all black. I shall wear black shoes with sparkling buckles and light stockings to match the peculiar blue of the dress. Lucy and I got the things yesterday at Kensington. We are going to have a taxi on the night, and I am going to hire another taxi to bring Maysie, Leo, Phil and Pom. How I wish you could be here!

48) 28 JANUARY 1930. 39, St. Stephen's Avenue.   *Author*: Peggy Webling
Topic: London production preparations

... Two weeks today I shall have seen my press notices – that is, the daily papers! I have met my new "Henry," an actor named Henry Hallett [*sic*], who has now gone down to Barrow-in-Furness, to rehearse with Deane's company. He (Mr Hallett) is a tall, thin man, very like Deane, but younger, and he is greatly interested in the part, and considers the play "a very strong, interesting drama." He has acted all sorts of parts, and (he tells me) is never out of work. The new Emilie (whom he knows) is reported to be a beautiful girl, with very fair hair – she is evidently not going to wear a wig – and Deane writes me he is sending his stage manager with scenery, etc. to town in the middle of next week. The Dress Rehearsal is on Sunday, the 9th, and of course I am going. I'll write you a note on the day after the production, *sure*. ...

49) 6 FEBRUARY 1930. The Writers' Club, 10 Norfolk Street, Strand.   *Author*: Peggy Webling
Topic: London production preparation

Dearest Jossie, Here I am, in the very flush & rush of the week before "F." appears, & I am trying to enjoy every minute of it – always with the nearly-a-year old longing for my Ethel in my mind. The Little Theatre is being re-decorated, as it is some time since it was open. The box office is in full swing – that is to say, it's *ready* for anybody who comes along. There are big bills outside & the enclosed cards in heaps. I have had fifteen seats given to me – ten for my party, Lucy, Louis, Ruth, Ruthie, Leo, Maysie, Phil, Pom, Lily & myself; two for Mr Farquharson, two for the Wilsons, & one for Mr Spence. We are going to have one taxi for the St. Stephen's crowd & another for the Bates pair & the Chaples. Leo has (very kindly) done a red chalk drawing of me that Mr Hale (Deane's publicity man) is getting into a good weekly, & the Bookman is paying for me to be photographed by the best photographer in London – Hoppé, to whom I am going tomorrow. Wot larks!

Appendix 1

Lucy says she has "'ad 'er 'air cut & put off the 'ospital;" Ruthie is borrowing a *pink satin* evening cloak; Maysie has a gorgeous ditto & frock -- if only, only you & Rosie and my darling could be there!

50) 10 FEBRUARY 1930. Cable. *Author*: Josephine Webling-Watts.

Webling 39 St. Stephen's Ave W. 12. London
Darling, best wishes, love, success for the night of nights. With you in thought always, am writing – J.

51) 13 February 1930. 39, St. Stephen's Avenue. *Author*: Peggy Webling
Topic: First-hand impressions of the premiere

My dearest Jossie,
 I think we have done the trick! "F." was received most enthusiastically on Monday evening, and the Press is considered by the managers of the theatre and Mr Deane's publicity man as "very good indeed." I haven't seen H.D. himself since the opening night.
 Oh, my dear Jossie, what a night it was! Let me begin at the beginning. Like Mrs Bagnett, I felt (in spite of the scorn of the family) that I must get the washing off my mind! So I did it in the morning, thinking all the time (I needn't tell you) of THE PLAY—and you –and my darling Ethel – and everbody [sic] I love. Then I had dinner with Luce, got home, arranged the boxes of sweets I was taking for the ladies in my party, had tea, and began to dress a good hour and a half before starting! I was ready, in consequence, twenty minutes too soon, so I sat quietly by the gas fire in my room, trying to be quite still and send good thoughts to everybody concerned in the production. I confess, I couldn't help crying when I thought of how Ethel had looked forward to this night – but I feel she knows about it. Then in came Louis, in his overcoat with a white silk muffler, like a man, smiling and radiant. We looked out of the window until the car arrived; in we got, picked up Ruth, Luce and Ruthie and off we went. Then through the crowded, strange, familiar streets, through the park, along The Strand, down Adam Street to John Street. The theatre looks so charming, as it has just been entirely re-decorated in pale cream, with small blue medallions, the seats being a dark, rich red. I had ten seats at the back of the stalls – the only place they could give me ten together. We sat in this order – back row, Ruthie, Phil Chaple, Ruth, Lily, Louis; front row, Maysie, Pom Chaple, Peggy, Luce, Leo. We were all in evening dress and I had a few most lovely carnations, and Rosie sent me a bouquet of tulips. The stalls were filling fast, nearly all men, as we had *all* the best, dramatic critics in London there, a very difficult, sophisticated audience. But the play went well from the start, not the hint of a laugh in the wrong place, and really *prolonged* applause at Deane's first exit in the first act, and again when he went out with Katrina. It went without a hitch, and the effects, scenery, etc. are very fine indeed. Mr Hallatt was extremely nervous – the night before, at the Dress Rehearsal, he had been in such a bad state of nerves that I was dreadfully worried – but he got through without prompting and they all say he will improve. After the second act I went behind, escorted by Mr Cavanah, straight to Deane's room. He was sitting on his

trunk, doing nothing – just resting. I said: "Well, Mr Deane, what do you think?" "I think we're *all right*," he answered: "We've turned the corner." At that minute along came the boy – "Third act!" "Come with me," said Deane. "I want you to stand on the prompt side and leave it to me whether you take a call or not. Will you?" "Certainly," said I. But just as we were going to cross the stage, the assitant [sic] stage manager snapped his fingers amd [sic] said: "She's going up!" (meaning the curtain) So I couldn't get to the side he meant, but waited with Mr Greene, Mr Lomath and Miss Patrick. The stage hands do the thunder and final flash of lightning most wonderfully and the side of the hut falls in as it is struck – a much more finished effect than when you saw it – you never heard such a crash and flash and rush of excitement. Then the curtain began to go up and down, the first twice on H.D. and Mr Hallatt, then Deane alone five times, then (as there were mingled shouts of "Speech!" and "Author!") he made a capital, witty little speech to this effect: "Ladies and gentlemen. I thank you most sincerely for the very kind way you have received this – this – weird little play. That is the case for the defence. The case for the prosecution you will hear tomorrow—" there was a great laugh from the men in the house — "But the verdict, after all, is in your hands. Thanks again – most awfully –" Then, after another call, he came to the back and nodded to me and took my hand and led me forward. They said I looked so small, as he is so huge. He stepped behind me. I bowed, they shouted "Speech!" so I just thanked them, turned to Deane, and we smiled and down came the curtain finally. Not one of those hard-headed old cirtics [sic] went out until the end of it all. They have (that is, the thirteen London dalies [sic]) given us long, important notices. Deane gets unstinted praise, my part is somewhat severely criticised, but you must remember I suffer (as a playwright) by this perpetual comparison with Dracula, which is (in spite of it's [sic] cleverness) a fifth rate play, considered as a literary work. I mean, it has been so drummed into people that they *will* look upon "F." as a thing exactly in the Dracula style.

They are perfectly delighted at the theatre with our Press, for they say it is "a box office Press." (You know what *that* means!) I haven't been to the theatre at night since, but I called in one afternoon and met Mr Henry Miller, one of the proprietors, and he was elated with the notices. I have asked Rosie to forward them to you. The two best critics in London speak well of me, "R.L.S." saying "Miss Peggy Webling's remarkably fresh and original version," and E.A. Baughan that I "have done my work well." Also, if I hadn't written the part as I did (even to giving all the business) Deane could not have made the sensational success he has done. I had no idea I should have had so much to do – heaps of letters, seeing people, helping Mr Hale – oh, it's all *fun*, but agitating.

Many, many thanks, darling, for your lovely cable – or wireless – I was so pleased to get it. I had twelve telegrams and three letters at the theatre.

This is but a scrappy letter, but I'll write again and let you know the *business* prospects at the end of the week. ...

<u>I'VE GOT A PLAY RUNNING IN LONDON, I HAVE!</u> Your own Peggles.

52) 23 FEBRUARY 1930. 39, St. Stephen's Avenue.   *Author*: Peggy Webling
Topic: Business, Writing (Liveright, Balderston negotiations; critics' notices)

Appendix 1

Your hustling New York pressmen have anticipated my news! Mr Liveright has *not bought* "F.," for I should not dream of selling it – even if he had wished to do so – but I hope the arrangements with him with [*sic*: will] be concluded within the new [*sic*: next] few weeks – perhaps sooner. It is a long story, but the last chapters have taken place very quickly. John Balderston, having resigned all claims – or rather all wishes to collaborate in the play – since the production, has been concentrating his energies on U.S.A. Liveright's representative has been to see "F." twice, cables have been exchanged, and now Mr Balderston has had a definite offer, and, as I said above, we are only waiting for Mr Farquharson to draw up an agreement between him (Mr B.) and myself. We are getting wonderfully good terms from Liveright, and it is understood that Mr Balderston shall do his version (of course founded on mine) in time for production within a year, Liveright paying a sum down for the option. You can imagine how thrilled I am over it. Who knows? Balderston (who *should* know, as he has pulled off two immense successes – "Dracula" and his own play "Berkeley Square") thinks we may have a production that will mean a little fortune – it might run on for years in all parts of the States. It seems like a dream, doesn't it? I have got *my* play running in London, and Deane says it is absolutely right for this country, and now I look to Balderston to pull off the big money deal.

Well, we've had an enormous Press – every daily and weekly, and pictures in many of the papers. Artistically, as I explained in my last, I have suffered from Deane's reputation as a producer of "thrillers," but all the critics have had to acknowledge that it *is* a striking and exciting play, and Deane has had amazingly good notices from them *all*, and (after all) *I* gave him the opportunity. The best papers – The Times, the Daily News, and Punch – have praised my work. Punch gives us as funny a picture as I have seen for years. I am sending it to you. Isn't it comic? I burst out laughing when I saw it at a railway station. The business is going up steadily, and Deane has engaged the publicity man to continue working, so we are all doing everything we can. How I wish – wish you could step into the Little Theatre one night! I can hardly believe it even now! ...

53) 16 March 1930. 39, St. Stephen's Avenue.   *Author*: Peggy Webling
Topic: London production, Business (Liveright), Other versions of F.

... At last I enclose a programme of "F." It is still running, in spite of terribly bad theatrical business in London. I only seem to have realized lately how horrible a play I have written! Four people have screamed and had to be taken out since we started, and there is a nurse in attendance every night! The play goes smoothly now, Mr Hallatt has improved enormously, he has a beautiful voice and is very powerful. Mr Russell (who was not in the company when you went to Reading), gives a very fine performance; he is the youngest man in the company, but he can look old and has a delicate, intense face that reminds one a little of Henry Irving. I've never seen thunder and lightning – or rather heard thunder and seen lightning – as they can do it at the Little Theatre, and the final flash is the biggest and brightest that can be given on the stage. As you will see, there is no orchestra. Miss Hirstfield is a fine pianiste, and dresses in a dress of the period of the play with a white wig. She plays her second piece, before the Prologue, in a quite dark house and it is very effective. Last week I signed a lengthy document with Mr Liveright, and Mr Balderston tells me he (Mr L.) will be in London by the end of the present week, so I expect he will see the play on Saturday night. Mr Deane tells me he intends to send out a company in this country if he (D.) decides to go to U.S.A., but I do not think he will. He seems to dread the work of playing such a heavy part eight times in the big American theatres. However, Balderston has evidently set his heart on having him, so I suppose he will be offered big money and may be tempted to go. The other day I was introduced, at the theatre, to a man Deane would like to get to play "F." (if he himself ever goes out of the cast.) He is a young fellow, very tall and big, but he has just signed a year's contract with another manager. One can only "wait and see." I have had no end of letters since the play came out. One man wrote and told me he and a friend had written a version of "Frankenstein" three years ago, and he would like to discuss our different ideas – he had taken a party to the Little and liked *my* version – and (he kindly added) "as there is no question of copyright, you can be sure I shall make no claim on you" !!!! Another man wrote to ask me "the real name of Miss Shelley's novel, as his library had never heard of a book of the same name as my play." A woman wrote to say she "liked to keep up to date with literary matters," so would I come and see her. Another lady thought I might like to send her a trifle (she suggested twenty five pounds) to help her along in the world. Another wished to show me some very beautiful lingerie – no obligation to buy – if she might send her "fitter" to me. ...and one lecturer (where I took the chair at a Club in Lancaster Gate) said my play "was the talk of the town" !!!'! Wot larks!

I am not sending the press notices after all, there are such a heap of them, but I've already sent Punch, the Bookman, and others. Wasn't Punch lovely? . . . I hope to come over if "F." makes the money for me. . . . Who knows? If Mr Balderston is right – and he thinks it ought to equal Dracula – we *may* make a fortune. Well, I should like to do that for many reasons, it would be such a joke.

54) 4 April 1930. 39, St. Stephen's Avenue. *Author*: Peggy Webling
Topic: End of London production, 200th performance, autumn tour, business (Balderston and Liveright)

... Have I told you that "F." is to be withdrawn from the Little Theatre after the performance on Saturday, April 12th? It will have run nine weeks – Mr Deane originally wanted four weeks – and that has enabled him to book (or begin to book) a special tour of all the big cities and towns in the autumn; he will send out a company even if he himself goes to New York. That is still under discussion between him, Balderston and Liveright. I hear there are alarums and excursions, but I have nothing to do with *that*; also I have had some absurd clippings from American papers, for Liveright appears to be an impulsive gentleman who talks to everybody. But he's shrewd and (if all is well and Balderston makes his alterations) the play will certainly be tried out in the early autumn. It was the two hundredth performance on Wednesday night this week, and the play went particularly well – seven calls at the fall of the curtain and cheers. (I mean of course two hundred altogether counting from the production at Preston in 1927). I gave Deane one

Appendix 1

of Ethel's miniatures (Joseph Jefferson) as a souvenir and he is simply delighted with it; I also gave little presents to all the original members of the cast. ...

Yes, let's go to Vancouver together – if I come. I cannot settle until I see whether "F." catches on in America, as I can't afford to spend my small capital on the trip. ...

I'm glad you were amused with the man who said I need not fear he would make claims on me for writing "F." Now another one has turned up! It is a composer (I gather), who has written to Mr Deane to say he (the man) has composed a grand opera (!) on the book, (F.) ...

55) 13 APRIL 1930. 39, St. Stephen's Avenue.   *Author*: Peggy Webling
Topic: Final London performance, possible productions in Germany/Scandinavia, provincial tours

... Last night Frankenstein made his last bow to a London audience. Ruth, Ruthie and I were there, and the play went splendidly as it always does. I think if Mr Deane had cared to go on through the bad Lent time, it would have had a longer run, but he is not content unless he makes a *big* salary for himself over and above his expenses and the ordinary return for his money. He had to make a speech last night and the curtain went up, at the end, nine or ten times. Well, I have thoroughly enjoyed the run – and I shan't be happy till I get another play out! ...we have had applications from Germany and Scandinavia for copies of "F.", so there may be a chance of production abroad, and I have to type at least one myself, as no typist could possibly make out either Mr Deane's copy or mine. "F." is at the Grand Theatre, Croydon, for a week, starting on Easter Monday, then the company goes to Derby (F. one night), Scarborough a week (F. one night), then Blackpool for a month (F. one week,) then Nottingham for a month (F. one week). This will bring Mr Deane up to his summer vacation, and in the autumn he begins the tour with "F." only. If he goes to America the tour will go on just the same, as he has made all his contracts with provincial managers for "an actor of equal standing" to play the chief part if he himself is not able to do so. ...

56) 27 APRIL 1930. 39, St. Stephen's Avenue.   *Author*: Peggy Webling
Topic: Provincial tour, Business (New York and Balderston's version, $1000 advance from Liveright, possible travel to US), earlier versions of Frankenstein

... Mr Deane began his grand tour at the Grand Theatre, Croydon, this week, and wrote me after Monday night to say there was a splendid house. I could not get over to see him. You will not see my "F." in New York, but Balderston's version; I have heard nothing from him for weeks, but I hope he is getting on with it. We (he and I) have received Mr Liveright's "advance" money—a thousand dollars, and that is all I have to tell you so far. I have written two acts of the new play for Deane's consideration. ... *One* play (from a money standpoint) is worth more than half a dozen books, and is *much* more thrilling and interesting. I have made no fortune as yet, but I'm better off than I've ever been before, and if the autumn tour of "F." and America pan out as we hope – well, as far as one can make plans ahead, these are mine. By Christmas we *ought* to know whether "F." is going to be (as Liveright and Balderston foretell) a big winner in America; if it is, I will come next year, either in the very early spring and stay till (say) August, or later in the year and spend the winter in Vancouver, returning home in time for the summer in England. As you know, I want to buy myself an annuity, then I shall be safe for the future, and I dream of also buying one for Lucy (not a word to her or anybody about this) and doing one or two other little things that will mean a goodly sum; then I shall be free to spend on a trip over the sea. ... P. S. ... Yes, there have been many versions of "F." in dramatic form, but not for some time. We had a play-bill on view at the Little Theatre (at least, Mr Deane had), of the very first, when the Monster was played by the well known actor Cooke, and Mrs Shelley professed herself delighted with his performance. The latest was by Stephen Phillips, but it was (I believe) in one act, and Henry Ainley played the big part; one of the papers said it was not a patch on mine. I think I told you one man wrote to tell me he had made an opera of the theme, and had I infringed his copyright, or had he infringed mine! And another man said he and a friend had written a play three years ago. I answered them both, of course, but I have heard nothing farther. As you know, there can be no infringement of copyright (on this book) unless there is plagiarism. So I am safe in this country, but America is another matter.* I shall be glad when I hear that the U.S.A. production is well in hand – I mean, Liveright's. By the way, Mr Deane has decided not to go to the States to play the part, although they offered him very big money. Personally I am glad, as I should not like the big Autumn tour here to have another man as "F."

* I mean, how can one keep one's eye on plays in a country as big as the U.S.A.?

57) 13 May 1930. 39, St. Stephen's Avenue. *Author*: Peggy Webling
Topic: Another version of Frankenstein; Liveright has a big mouth

... I cannot think that the version of "F." you speak of, that is being acted by Philip Greenwood's company, is a coincidence, as Mr Liveright (rather foolishly Mr Deane and I think) has been talking about the play to all sorts of people in the States. I do hope you have not told Mr Greenwood anything about the way I have worked out the story — I do not mean that he would *purposely* talk about it to another author, but you know how all actors chatter over plays and the least said the better. I expect you thought of this, but if you did not, please don't tell him anything more of it. I shall not mention it (this new version) to anybody here, and I do not think it can possibly hurt us. ...

58) 1 August 1930. 39, St Stephen's Avenue. *Author*: Peggy Webling
Topic: Play versions, autumn tour

... Then, haven't you my news of "Frankenstein"? There is a fortnight's delay in the production, and I may as well tell you definitely you will not see *my* play in N.Y., but a version of it through the eyes (or rather, pens) of Mr John Balderston, and three other gentlemen in the States! Lyn Harding promises to make a great "monster" – there has

Appendix 1

been any amount of correspondence, cables, and agitation, chiefly because Liveright does not like Balderston's chief alterations – at which I do *not* grieve! But they're going to "boom it big," and I do hope we make some money. Deane starts his Autumn tour, with "F." only, on Monday next at Manchester. He then plays four weeks in the London suburbs, then a week at Birmingham, then he takes a month's vacation, and goes on again. ...

59) 5 March 1931. 39, St. Stephen's Avenue. *Author*: Peggy Webling
Topic: Business (Balderston renews 6-month option)

... My good news is that Mr Balderston has again taken up a six months' option on "Frankenstein," and I'm sure he wouldn't part with his good money a second time unless he felt very confident of getting it back out of the play. ...

APPENDIX 2
EXCERPT FROM *THE STORY OF A PEN* BY PEGGY WEBLING, 1941

Note: Original pagination in the margin, with a vertical line at the point where the page number changes in that line; punctuation and spelling as written by Webling

p. 110 Chapter XV

AN ADVENTURE IN THE MACABRE

"It was a dreary night of November when the pale and haggard student bent over the horrible monster of his creation."

This is the impressive opening, after a few unimportant chapters, of that remarkable novel Frankenstein, by Mary Wollstonecraft Shelley.

It was written in 1816 and published two years later. Mary Shelley was only nineteen at the time, living with her husband on the Lake of Geneva.

We had a fourpence ha'penny copy of the book on our shelves at home when I was a girl. It was bound in paper, with a crude coloured drawing on the cover of the haunted student facing the gigantic being he had made.

I did not read the eerie tale until I was grown up. Then I could not leave it, although it is a somewhat wearisome book, written in stilted language, but redeemed by the obvious sincerity of the writer and her belief in the true horror of her conception.

I had not thought of it for years. Indeed, many of the incidents and characters had passed entirely out of my memory.

One day I was walking along High Holborn, westward bound, meditating (as I so often do) on the possibility of writing another play. Suddenly Frankenstein flashed into my mind to be almost as quickly dismissed.

p. 111 The difficulties of representing the Monster seriously on the stage appeared insurmountable, especially as Mary Shelley's story is supposed to cover a long period of years and its scenes are laid in all parts of the world, ending at the North Pole.

By the time I had walked along Oxford Street, however, the idea of such a play had returned and taken possession of me.

I was glad to leave the streets, at Marble Arch, for the comparative quietude of Hyde Park. I can hardly recall now how I worked out the plot, it was altered

Appendix 2

so much afterwards, for the play was fated to be written six times before I had done with it.

Nevertheless, I never materially changed my conception of the way the Monster could be adapted for the stage. Mrs. Shelley develops his mentality in an amazing way and does not dwell upon the dual nature of being both as innocent as a child and as brutal as a wild animal, nor does she touch upon any problems of sex.

The hideous and revolting appearance of the creature was the only thing about him that I found it necessary to modify. The actor who ultimately played the part was strange enough, at times terrifying and inhuman, and it says much for his extraordinary performance that he aroused compassion in his audiences, as I meant that he should.

p. 112
I do not remember actually writing Frankenstein – the play was in a prologue and three acts – until reaching the end of the second act. Fortunately, I was alone, for it had such an effect upon me that I could not restrain a burst of violent emotion.

This was caused by the drowning of a character named Katrine (she is not to be found in the book), followed by the realisation by Frankenstein of a death for which he is guilty. I should say that while the monster was never given a name by Mary Shelley, it was necessary in a play for him to be known by the same name as the student who was his creator.

They were supposed to resemble each other, and for men to address him as "Monster" would have been ridiculous. One critic was severe with me on this point (he said I had fallen into "the vulgar error of confusing the two characters") but I really do not see how it could have been avoided.

When the first version was finished I wrote to several leading London actors whom I knew. The usual correspondence followed and the play, like a curse, came home to roost. I am not easily baffled, but I admit many disappointments chilled my enthusiasm.

p. 113
I re-wrote the whole thing with a slight return of the original emotion. One offer of production, I am thankful to say, | did not materialise. A certain young actor, then on the crest of the wave, persuaded me to alter the play so that the two parts, creature and creator, could be taken by the same man, on the lines of The Corsican Brothers, The Lyons Mail, and other old successes.

I realised it could not be done effectively, so Frankenstein was once again hidden in a drawer and (as novelists say) time rolled on.

The amazing success and long run in London of a play founded on Bram Stoker's lurid novel, Dracula, (in spite of a Press unique in condemnation) drew my attention to the man who had dramatized, produced, acted the chief part and ventured his money in putting it on at the Little Theatre – Hamilton Deane.

My youngest sister, as it happened, had played with Mr. Deane when they were both beginners, and it was she who advised me "to try him with Frankenstein."

Appendix 2

I shall not forget the day when he wrote to me with an offer of production. To use the trite phrase, it seemed too good to be true.

Hamilton Deane was then on tour with his capital company, while Dracula was still doing big business in town with another actor, Sam Livesay, as Dr. Van Helzing, [sic] the principal character.

Terms were quickly settled with Mr. Deane. He had an option on the play for six months and I received an advance on royalties of fifty pounds.

p. 114

It was about four months later that Frankenstein was announced "the first time on any stage" at the Empire Theatre, Preston, Lancashire.

An opening night and a call for "Author!" are the greatest professional thrills in a writer's life. To hear one's dialogue spoken on the stage for the first time gives one – or it gave me – a peculiar sensation of mingled pleasure, excitement and unreality.

It vividly recalled for a minute, at the first rehearsal I attended, the old days when my sisters and I were touring with "April Jest" in our funny little entertainment in Canada.

The Empire is a big theatre (it is now turned into a Cinema) and the Preston audiences were enthusiastic and demonstrative.

I sat in a box the night before the production, and, when I heard the noise in the pit and gallery at the situations in Dracula, I felt extremely nervous, for there were many quiet moments in my play. At the same time, if it got hold of such a crowd at all, I thought it might work them up to a high state of excitement.

Hamilton Deane played Frankenstein (the Monster) and W. E. Holloway was cast for the student whom I called Henry Frankenstein, Mary Shelley's name of Victor being one that I dislike. The part of Katrine, the lame girl who was drowned in the second act, was in the hands of Dora Mary Patrick, who played it with a beautiful and touching simplicity.

p. 115

The house was packed on the opening night. My sister Ethel and I sat in the middle of the first circle. My nervousness had vanished, | or reached a point when it was numbed into indifference.

The Dress Rehearsal had been "rough" and I relied (as in the days of Westward Ho!) on the old superstition that it meant a smooth first night.

I think our anxiety (I am speaking of Hamilton Deane and myself) will be understood by anyone who can appreciate the difficulties of writing and acting such a theme and character as Frankenstein.

Unless it could be done with sincerity and unwavering gravity it would have been impossible to make an audience take it seriously. The word "thriller" had never occurred to me when I wrote it, for the strange and imaginative tale had impressed me as an illustration of a continually recurring and great truth; the truth that a wicked deed, even a monstrous thought, thrown out into the world may become an instrument of destruction.

Also, the innocent Katrine, being the only person who neither hates nor fears the Monster, I meant to be a symbol of compassion, pitying the evil thing

Appendix 2

and awaking in him, even though the girl herself dies by his hand, a sorrow that approaches humanity.

That the play was looked upon as simply as adventure in the macabre does not distract – I think – from its purpose. Katrine's death was always received in the provinces, and afterwards in London, with silent attention. A few people told me that I had | conveyed to their minds the impression that I have tried to express in the above sentence, and for the others – they liked it as a "thriller".

p. 116

I am only echoing the London Press when I say that Hamilton Deane played his part with extraordinary power and originality. An actor of many years and wide experience in this country and America, I do not believe that anyone who saw his Frankenstein is likely to forget it. More than one old playgoer compared it to Irving's Mathias in The Bells.

His "pace", to use a stage term, was perfect, and he never failed to grip the audience. It was a long, sustained effort, a part of few words and entirely depending on self-control and terror in abeyance.

I wish Mary Shelley could have seen him – six feet three in height; uncouth; lithe as an animal; haggard and strange in facial expression; violent in gesture; intelligence very slowly dawning; hate and vengeance and desire, loneliness and despair taking possession of his dark, passionate heart.

* * *

Frankenstein had been running for several weeks before I fully realised that the third act was *no good*. That fatal third act! All Hamilton Deane's skill could not save it. A night came when we both admitted that future success depended on a drastic change.

p. 117

I had come down from London to see how things were going. We discussed it after the performance, and when I went back to my hotel I could not help giving way to a fit of deep depression. I could not sleep that night.

Indeed, I spent many nights and many days haunted by Frankenstein, little suspecting the worries and anxieties still in store for me.

A big success seemed to be within my grasp, but I could not close my hand upon it. Then Hamilton Deane had an idea – it ought to have occurred to *me* – and I immediately saw what to do. It meant a third act entirely different from the original one, much better and stronger.

This was written and rehearsed in time for production at the Theatre Royal, Nottingham, a place where Mr. Deane was particularly popular. I was more than gratified at the result of the change, and returned home still haunted – pleasantly now – by old man Frankenstein.

The play must have been running on tour something over a year before any further anxieties disturbed my peace. Then John Balderston appeared upon the scene!

Appendix 2

Now, John Balderston is an exceedingly clever American Journalist, and author (with J. C. Squire) of one of the best plays of our time, Berkeley Square.

p. 118

I yield to no one in my admiration of Berkeley Square. Unfortunately Mr. Balderston, having successfully collaborated with Hamilton Deane in a version of Dracula for America, thought he could improve Frankenstein.

He had great ideas as to increasing the horror and dramatic possibilities – until he tried to put them on paper. Of course his futile attempts to re-write the play took place with my consent.

Alas! Nothing came of it beyond wearisome correspondence and a hopeless manuscript of which not a line could be used. This would-be part Author then turned his attention to a production of my play in the United States. We were to receive equal shares, fifty fifty, if he succeeded.

Again the wearisome correspondence started with the addition, this time, of letters from possible and impossible theatrical managers, and cables from New York and Hollywood.

My friend and agent, John Farquharson, stood up to the attack with courage and patience. He had to calm me when I became agitated; he had to argue with Balderston (who was then in London); he had to answer no end of communications and try to stem the torrent of cables that people who did not have to pay for them thought it necessary to pour over the sea.

p. 119

This went on for months and months. Then Hamilton Deane brought the play to London and it was produced at the Little Theatre, John Street, Adelphi.

It was a Jolly First Night. The notices of the play were of a kind that the manager of the theatre called "a box office press". Hamilton Deane made a striking personal success.

Horace Thoroughgood called the play A Triumph of Terror. The Rev. Clarence May preached on it in his Church in Windmill Street, Piccadilly. Punch favoured us with an extremely comic caricature of the Monster being severely taken to task by the student (played in London by Henry Hallatt): – "Now, Frankenstein, you haven't brushed your hair or washed your hands since I created you!" James Agate devoted his weekly broadcast to the Little Theatre thriller.

Those would have been happy days for me if I had not been living in the dark shadow of a great personal sorrow: –

> "The day of days was not the day;
> That went before, or was postponed;
> The night Death took our lamp away
> Was not the night on which we groan'd."

There was a lull in the correspondence and cables from the United States until Frankenstein had been running about a month in London, then it all started again with redoubled fury. We had been looking forward to an American

Appendix 2

p. 120

production when a sudden change of policy took place. The possibility of a film made the Balderston | army of friends and advisers, agents and managers turn their attention to Hollywood. The Universal Picture Corporation of America was approached. I expect it was through Brandt and Brandt, one of the most "live" of agencies in New York.

We were made an exceedingly good offer and immediately accepted it. Our money in advance reached five figures (in dollars), and we were also to receive a royalty on every show given. It was a small royalty, but when one considers that the film was the biggest success the company had had for two years and ran in all parts of the world for two years and a half (it was revived afterwards and again did remarkably well) it will be seen that this pen of mine at last had made a little fortune.

Hamilton Deane was offered the chief part in the film – he was on tour again playing Frankenstein at all the big places in England – but did not accept. Boris Karloff was then chosen for the Monster, and the late Colin Clive went from London to the States on purpose to play the Student.

I was in Canada, at the beautiful city of Vancouver, British Columbia, when the film was first shown at Hollywood, having been produced by a man on the crest of the wave, James Whale.

p. 121

American slang, as we all know, is as expressive as it is | astounding. I thought it could not surprise me until I received the first verdict on the film in a Cinema Journal. Splashed over the front page were the words: –

"Frankenstein! A sock in Wash!!" And on the next page: –

"Frankenstein! A wow in Cleve!!!" And after this extremely effective way of recording success in Washington and Cleveland, the paper proceeded on milder lines:–

> "Frankenstein shivers the dollars into the box office in the Bean City!"
> "Frankenstein beats all records in the Saints City."
> "Frankenstein keeps the doors open till two in the morning in New York!"
> "See Frankenstein if YOU DARE in Chicago!"

And so on, playing "to capacity" at every picture house where it was shown.

Later on, when I was in San Francisco, I was amused to see the film advertised outside one cinema by a gigantic mechanical figure with glowing red eyes, and at another by a huge hand writing our old London slogan in flaming colours high up over the building: – "A Triumph of Terror."

p. 122

The film was released in London during my absence in Canada. I first saw it at the chief picture house in Vancouver [*sic*: Seattle]. So long a | queue of people was waiting at the doors that the local representative of Universal Picture Corporation could only manage to find me a seat in the gallery.

(A cheerful gentleman, this local representative: "I don't care what happens anywhere s'long as the box office don't go hooey!" said he).

Appendix 2

I went to California before returning home. It is a most lovely State, and Hollywood an amazing place. The roads seemed to me as crowded as London or Paris. Indeed one might have been in any big city until raising one's eyes to the beautiful surrounding hills, with their white houses and perfect gardens, groves of peach blossoms, fields ablaze with the fire of the poinsettia and the bloom of roses, vineyards of low, crowded bushes, and rich orchards of avocado pears and orange trees in flower and fruit.

I motored to Hollywood and beyond the Cinema City to Santa Monica, and other famous beaches, where people were swimming and sun-bathing in the clear, light air of March. Had I had time, the name of Frankenstein would have been an Open Sesame! to the great studios and wonders of the most artificial – most modern – most thrilling world of the Film.

I sailed home from New York, after ten months holiday thanks to Frankenstein, and so ended my adventure in the macabre.

* * *

APPENDIX 3
CONTRACTS

Note: These contracts are held in the Webling Archive.

Appendix 3

Memorandum of Agreement between Peggy Webling and John L. Balderston, 24 February 1930

MEMORANDUM OF AGREEMENT made this 24th day of February 1930 B E T W E E N PEGGY WEBLING of 39 St. Stephen's Avenue, Goldhawk Road, London W.12. (hereinafter referred to as the Playwright) and JOHN L. BALDERSTON of 38 Trevor Square, London S.W.7. (hereinafter referred to as the Adaptor).

WHEREBY it is mutually agreed as follows concerning the play by the Playwright entitled :

FRANKENSTEIN

hereinafter referred to as the old play all rights in which shall remain the property of the Playwright.

1. Subject to the stipulations hereinafter set forth the Playwright hereby grants to the Adaptor the exclusive right to make an adaptation of the old play, said adaptation hereinafter referred to as the new play.

2. The Adaptor agrees to make an adaptation of the old play and to endeavour to place it in the United States of America within twelve months (12) of the date of this agreement and he shall pay to the Playwright the sum of five hundred dollars ($500) as option money for the said period of twelve months such sum to be paid within one month of the date of this agreement and to be regarded as an advance on account of royalties accruing to the Playwright for the rights granted by her in this agreement.

3. Should a new play fail to be produced for a run in the United States within twelve (12) months of the date of this agreement, or the option fail to be renewed by payment by the Adaptor to the Playwright of an additional $250 for six months or $500 for one year, the said various sums of $500, $250 and/or $500 shall not be returnable by the Playwright but all rights hereby granted shall revert to her but if the new play is produced in America within the time stated the terms of such production shall be governed by the Minimum Basic Agreement now in force for all sales of dramatic work in the United States except that the Adaptor shall better the terms of the Basic Agreement so far as he is able.

4. All performing rights in the new play shall be excluded from Great Britain and Ireland except by the consent in writing of the Playwright.

5. All monies and royalties accruing from the grant or sale of rights and licences of every kind whatsoever in the said new play that comes under the term copyright, Great Britain and Ireland Rights only excepted, shall be divided in the proportions of Fifty per cent to the Playwright and fifty per cent to the Adaptor.

6. The new play may be announced in America as "By the authors of DRACULA" or "By John Balderston and Hamilton Deane" as they please, followed in either event by the words "adapted from the play by Peggy Webling" and the new play shall be registered by the Adaptor at the Library of Congress, Washington under the joint names of John Balderston and Peggy Webling.

7. It is understood that in the event of a sale to America one half of all proceeds from the motion picture rights would be granted to the American manager, in which event the remaining half proceeds would be divided fifty per cent to the Playwright and fifty per cent to the Adaptor, followed by five per cent (5%) from each party to Mr. Hamilton Deane.

8. The Playwright shall be free to refuse to have her name associated with the new play without any prejudice as to share of royalties accruing to her.

9. If and when the old play is used which would only be outside the United States of America, the Playwright alone shall have the right to make terms and receive all monies accruing therefrom but in all cases where the new play or a part or parts thereof are used the monies therefrom shall be divided equally as aforesaid and all contracts shall be signed by both the parties hereto.

Appendix 3

10. The business negotiations for the said play shall be conducted through Brandt & Brandt, 101 Park Avenue, New York, the agents for the Adaptor and John Farquharson, 8 Halsey House, Red Lion Square, London W.C.1., as agents for the playwright. They shall prepare contracts for the said play subject to the approval of the adaptor and the playwright and shall collect all sums due under said contract and be entitled to deduct therefrom 10% commission dividing the remainder in such manner as stipulated in this agreement within one week from the receipt of all sums collected from performances of said play throughout the world in all languages and from all other rights of the said play.

IN WITNESS WHEREOF the parties hereto have set their hands on the day and year hereinbefore first written.

John L Balderston

Appendix 3

Contract Agreement between Peggy Webling, John L. Balderston and Horace B. Liveright, 26 February 1930

THIS AGREEMENT, made and entered into this 26th day of February, 1930, by and between HORACE LIVERIGHT of New York, New York, party of the first part, hereinafter referred to as the Manager, and JOHN L. BALDERSTON and Peggy Webling of London, England, parties of the second part, hereinafter referred to as the Authors;

WITNESSETH:

WHEREAS, the Authors are the Authors and/or Proprietors of a certain play or dramatic composition provisionally entitled FRANKENSTEIN; and

WHEREAS, the said Manager has signed the Minimum Basic Agreement and is in good standing with the Dramatists Guild of the Authors League of America, Inc. of which Guild the Authors are members; and

WHEREAS, the Manager desires to obtain an exclusive lease to produce and present the said play in the United States of America and the Dominion of Canada, AND MEXICO provided for in said Minimum Basic Agreement, and the Authors wish to grant such lease; and

NOW THEREFORE, in consideration of the premises and the sum of One Dollar and other good and valuable considerations, the receipt whereof is hereby acknowledged, it is mutually agreed as follows:

FIRST: The Authors hereby warrant that they are the Authors and/or proprietors of said play and have a right to execute this lease.

SECOND: The said Author, John L. Balderston, agrees to revise and adapt the said play in accordance with his own ideas and to deliver a manuscript of said revision to said Manager. Whenever the word "play" is used in this agreement it shall be considered as meaning the said revised and adapted version by John L. Balderston as delivered to the said Manager.

THIRD: The Authors hereby lease to the Manager the sole and exclusive right of presentation on the regular speaking stage in the United States of America and Dominion of Canada, of the play now entitled FRANKENSTEIN on the covenants and conditions stated herein, and in the Minimum Basic Agreement between the Dramatists Guild of the Authors League of America, Inc., and the Manager, which is made a part hereof, and which shall constitute the agreement as to all terms and/or conditions not specifically referred to herein. Where no specific period of time or percentage of interest is referred to herein, it is agreed that the Authors are entitled to the minimum terms that are provided for in the said Minimum Basic Agreement.

FOURTH: The Manager agrees to produce the play on or before the 1st day of February, 1931. The Manager agrees, upon the signing of this contract, to pay the Authors through their duly authorized agents BRANDT & BRANDT DRAMATIC DEPARTMENT, INC., 101 Park Avenue, New York City, the sum of One Thousand ($1,000.) Dollars, (Five Hundred Dollars for the first option of six months and Five Hundred Dollars for the second option lasting until February 1, 1931), the receipt of which sum is hereby acknowledged, as an advance upon royalties accruing as provided herein. It is further understood that if the said play is not produced on or before February 1, 1931, all rights in and to the said play and all rights granted to the Manager by this contract shall cease and determine and shall revert to the Authors forthwith.

FIFTH: It is understood that no rights of any description whatsoever and no options are granted on any rights in the British Isles, and that all rights in and to the said play in the British Isles AND TALKING PICTURES are specifically reserved by the Authors, except such motion picture rights in the British Isles as the Manager may become entitled to under this agreement by giving the number of performances required to entitle him to such rights.

Advance royalties on options for all other foreign rights as provided in Section Twelfth-G of the Minimum Basic Agreement shall be One Thousand ($1,000) Dollars.

SIXTH: Royalties shall be on the following percentage basis: Seven and one-half (7½%) on the first Eight Thousand ($8,000) Dollars of gross weekly box-office

313

Appendix 3

receipts; Ten (10%) percent on the next Two Thousand ($2,000) Dollars of gross weekly box-office receipts; Twelve and one-half (12½%) percent of all gross box-office receipts in excess of Ten Thousand ($10,000) Dollars.

SEVENTH: It is understood, however, that in the event that the Manager, instead of producing the play himself, shall sublease it to another management for production in any towns in which it shall play not more than four (4) consecutive nights, and only in such towns, then instead of the royalty provided for above, the Manager shall pay a flat royalty of Four Hundred ($400) Dollars per week and a proportionate amount for each part of the week during which the said play is so presented.

EIGHTH: All net profits, royalties and/or sums received from the following, in the event the Manager becomes entitled to a share therein as provided in Section Twelfth (Conditions) of the Minimum Basic Agreement, and so long as he is entitled thereto, shall be divided so that the Manager shall receive the following percentage:

  Stock and Superstock rights...................Fifty percent (50%)
  Radio rights, TELEVISION.....................Fifty percent (50%)
  Little Theatres, Chautauqua, Repertoire Production
    and Tent Shows..........Fifty Percent (50%)
  Amateur rights...............................Fifty percent (50%)
  Foreign language rights in the United States (It is understood that the British Isles are excluded from the Manager's percentage of such rights as are granted herein)..........................Fifty percent (50%)
  Condensed and Tabloid Versions, Adaptations, etc...Fifty percent (50%)
  Motion picture, talking motion picture and
    television rights............Fifty percent (50%)

In the event that the Manager shall produce under his own direction in foreign countries, the stipulated royalties shall be payable. In the event he shall not so produce, the Manager shall be entitled to receive the following:

Australian, New Zealand and/or South African rights (See Section Twelfth-D
   of Minimum Basic Agreement)........Fifty percent (50%)

Rights in Foreign Countries..........................Fifty percent (50%)
  (See Section Twelfth-G)

NINTH: The said John L. Balderston does hereby designate BRANDT & BRANDT DRAMATIC DEPARTMENT INC, as his Agent and does hereby authorize and direct said Manager to pay all moneys and send all statements to be paid and delivered to John L. Balderston, pursuant to this agreement, by said Manager to said Agent, and to accept the receipt of said agent as full evidence and satisfaction of such payments; and in return for the services rendered in negotiating the proposition culminating in this agreement and for other services rendered and to be rendered in the handling of the said play, the said BRANDT & BRANDT DRAMATIC DEPARTMENT INC. shall be entitled to deduct and receive the following; from John L. Balderston a fee of Ten (10%) percent of all moneys received by him under this agreement, and from the Authors and the Manager jointly a fee of Ten (10%) percent of any and all sums of money which may be collected or received by or in behalf of the said Manager and said Authors under any and all agreements for the production and representation of the said play in any form, (with the exception of the performing rights on the regular speaking stage in the United States and Canada) including stock, stock repertoire, by amateurs, in motion pictures (and in respect to the sale of the motion picture rights it is agreed that such sale shall be subject to the conditions of paragraph K, Section Twelfth of the Minimum Basic Agreement) and in foreign countries as provided for in this contract. Said agent shall pay to the parties concerned the respective shares of the compensation due to each of them after deducting the said fee of said Agent as herein provided for. It is understood that the said fee due said BRANDT & BRANDT DRAMATIC DEPARTMENT INC. shall be a continuing interest and shall not be revocable at the will of the said Authors or the said Manager as long as the said BRANDT & BRANDT DRAMATIC DEPARTMENT INC. perform the said services honestly.

TENTH: This agreement is binding upon the parties hereto and their respective successors in interest.

IN WITNESS WHEREOF, the parties hereto have hereunto set their hands and seals the day and year first above written.

Notwithstanding anything set forth in Clause Ninth hereto all royalties and other monies whatsoever that may be and become due to the two authors are divided equally between them and the share belonging to Peggy Webling shall be sent by Messrs Brandt without any deduction of commission or fee whatsoever to her Agent, John Farquharson, of 8 Halsey House, Red Lion Square, London, W.C.1, who alone shall be entitled to ten per cent commission on said royalties and monies.

Horace Liveright

Peggy Webling

John L. Balderston

P.W.

JLB

Appendix 3

Appendix 3

Office of the
General Manager

IN ADDITION TO CONTRACT – FRANKENSTEIN – DATED FEB. 26, 1930.

In the event the manager shall have produced the play as agreed in Section Eleventh of the said Minimum Basic Agreement and shall have faithfully performed all other terms and conditions of this agreement of contract, he shall have, for the period of one year following the first production of the play as provided for in the said Minimum Basic Agreement an option to acquire a lease for the sole and exclusive rights of producing a musical comedy version of the said play, in all territory for which the manager has the rights to produce or to have the said play produced including the territory outside of the United States and Canada except the British Isles, upon the payment of advance royalty of One Thousand ($1,000.00) Dollars: The royalty to be paid to the authors shall be mutually agreed upon but in no event greater than two (2%) percent of the gross weekly box office receipts. The musical comedy shall be produced within six (6) months after the manager shall take up the said option otherwise the rights to present the said play as a musical comedy shall revert to the authors.

BIBLIOGRAPHY

General bibliography

Archives and manuscripts

Billy Rose Theatre Division, New York Public Library for the Performing Arts. John L. Balderston Papers, *T-Mss 1954-02, Box 1.
British Library, Manuscript Division, Lord Chamberlain's Plays. Frankenstein, by Peggy Webling, LCP 1927/47.
Essex Record Office, UK, Sage Collection 105, 'Weblin of Barking'.
United States Library of Congress, Manuscript Division. Frankenstein: A Play in a Prologue and Three Acts, by Peggy Webling, Registration number Du86282, 7 September 1928.
Catalogue of Copyright Entries, no. 9, 1928, 4458.
Mander and Mitchenson Collection. Theatre Collection, University of Bristol:
  MM-2-TH-LO-LIT-7-57 Assorted press cuttings and reviews (A scene from "Frankenstein," the new scientific thriller at the Little. Left to right: Henry Hallatt, Hamilton Deane, Malcolm Russell, and Desmond Greene) [original in *Theatre World*, March 1930]
  MM-2-TH-LO-LIT-7-55. Hamilton Deane as Frankenstein and Dora Mary Patrick as Katrine, Little Theatre 1930
James B. Pond Papers (1863–ca. 1940s), Clements Library, University of Michigan, https://quod.lib.umich.edu/c/clementsead/umich-wcl-M-3073pon?id=navbarbrowselink;view=text (accessed 26 September 2022).
University of Toronto, Thomas Fisher Rare Book Collection. Cover of Frankenstein, G. Routledge and Sons, 1882.
Westminster City Archives, London. Hamilton Deane Papers, Finding Number 2992:
  2992/HD/32 (System ID 2992/4/2) – Scrapbook of provincial newspaper reviews of Frankenstein at the Little Theatre, London (Title Page: Press Cuttings for Frankenstein)
  2292/HD/164 (System ID 2992/13/12) – Prompt Copy of script Peggy Webling adaptation of Frankenstein (prologue and three acts, including an alternative Act II, 108 typed pages with annotations)

Electronic and online databases

Ancestry.com, https://www.ancestry.com/:
  Arriving Passenger and Crew Lists [including Castle Garden and Ellis Island], 1820–1957
  British Censuses, 1901, 1911
  Church of England Parish Registers. London Metropolitan Archives, London
  Ireland, Civil Registration Marriages Index, 1845–1958
  Ireland, Select Births and Baptisms, 1620–1911
  London City Directories, 1736-1943. London Metropolitan Archives
  1939 England and Wales Register. The National Archives, Kew
  UK and Ireland, Incoming Passenger Lists, 1878–1960
  UK and Ireland, Outward Passenger Lists, 1890–1960
The British Newspaper Archive, https://www.britishnewspaperarchive.co.uk/

Bibliography

COVE (Collaborative Organization for Virtual Education, a scholar-driven open access platform), https://editions.covecollective.org/chronologies/launch-atalanta
Familysearch.org, https://www.familysearch.org/en/:
  England Marriages, 1538–1973
Find My Past, https://www.findmypast.co.uk/:
  British Census, 1921
Hathi Trust Digital Library, https://babel.hathitrust.org
Internet Movie Database (IMDb), https://www.imdb.com/
Library and Archives Canada, Passenger Lists, 1865-1922, https://www.bac-lac.gc.ca/eng/discover/immigration/immigration-records/passenger-lists/passenger-lists-1865-1922/Pages/introduction.aspx
Newspapers.com, https://www.newspapers.com/
Romantic Circles edition of Frankenstein:https://romantic-circles.org/editions/frankenstein

Other sources

Ammer, Christine. *The Facts on File Dictionary of Clichés*. 4th edn. New York: Facts on File, Inc., 2006.
Balderston, John L. 'Analysis of "Frankenstein" by Peggy Webling'. John L. Balderston Papers, *T-Mss 1954-02, Box 1, folder 13, item 2, Billy Rose Theatre Division, New York Public Library for the Performing Arts.
Balderston, John L. 'Analysis Mary Shelley's Novel "Frankenstein"'. John L. Balderston Papers, 1915–1950, *T-Mss 1954-002, Box 1, folder 13, item 1, Billy Rose Theatre Division, New York Public Library for the Performing Arts.
Balderston, John L. 'Incomplete Sketch (Autobiography)'. John L. Balderston Papers, 1915–1950, *T-Mss 1954-02, Box 1, folder 7, Billy Rose Theatre Division, New York Public Library for the Performing Arts.
Bligh, N. M. 'The Little Theatre'. *Theatre World* 58, no. 446 (1962): 45–9.
Brereton, Austin. *The Life of Henry Irving*. 2 vols. London: Longmans, Green and Co., 1908.
Chalk, Penny. 'Adaptation as an Intertextual Mode of Practice: British Nineteenth-Century Literature and the Hollywood Studio Era'. PhD thesis, University of Portsmouth, 2018.
Chemers, Michael. *The Monster in Theatre History*. London: Routledge, 2018.
Columbia University Catalogue, 1912/1913. Columbia University Archives, Catalogue of the Officers and Students of Columbia College, https://babel.hathitrust.org/cgi/pt?id=nnc2.ark:/13960/t4gm8wq6j&view=1up&seq=361 (accessed 31 January 2023).
Columbia University Catalogue, 1913/1914. Columbia University Archives, Catalogue of the Officers and Students of Columbia College, https://babel.hathitrust.org/cgi/pt?id=nnc2.ark:/13960/t55d9hm8d&view=1up&seq=362 (accessed 31 January 2023).
Cosby, Brian H. *John Flavel: Puritan Life and Thought in Stuart England*. Lanham, MD: Lexington Books, 2014.
Cox, Jeffrey, ed. *Seven Gothic Dramas 1789–1825*. Athens, OH: Ohio University Press, 1992.
Dawley, J. Searle, director. *Frankenstein*. Produced by The Edison Company, 1910. c. 13 minutes. Available at the US Library of Congress, https://www.loc.gov/item/2017600664/ (accessed 14 June 2023).
The Edison Kinetogram, London, I, no. 1 (15 April 1910): 1–5.
'Esther Tincom's Sampler'. National Museum of American History, Behring Center, Smithsonian Institution, https://americanhistory.si.edu/collections/search/object/nmah_646290 (accessed 26 October 2023).
Fisch, Audrey. *Frankenstein: Icon of Modern Culture*. Hastings: Helm Information, 2009.
Flavel, John. Pneumatologia: A Treatise on the Soul of Man. In *The Whole Works of the Reverend Mr. John Flavel*, vol. 1, 283–383. Glasgow: John Orr, Bookseller, 1754.

Forry, Steven Earl. '"The Foulest Toadstool": Reviving Frankenstein in the Twentieth Century'. In *The Fantastic in World Literature and the Arts: Selected Essays from the Fifth International Conference on the Fantastic in the Arts*, edited by Donald E. Morse, 182–208. New York, Westport, CT and London: Greenwood, 1987.

Forry, Steven Earl. *Hideous Progenies: Dramatizations of Frankenstein from Mary Shelley to the Present*. Philadelphia, PA: University of Pennsylvania Press, 1990.

Fratelli d'Alessandri. 'Robert Wiedemann Barrett Browning; Elizabeth Barrett Browning'. 19 June 1860. National Portrait Gallery, NPG P1094, https://www.npg.org.uk/collections/search/portrait/mw111433/Robert-Wiedemann-Barrett-Browning-Elizabeth-Barrett-Browning?LinkID=mp83905&role=art&rNo=1 (accessed 30 October 2022).

'The Free Christian Church'. *The British Millennial Harbinger*, vol. VI, Third Series. London: Arthur Hall and Co., 1853, 540–4.

Friedman, Lester D., and Allison B. Kavey. *Monstrous Progeny: A History of the Frankenstein Narratives*. New Brunswick: Rutgers University Press, 2016.

Fytton, Francis. 'The Legacy of T. P. O'Connor'. *The Irish Monthly* 83 (1954): 169–73.

Gilbert, Sandra M., and Susan Gubar. *The Madwoman in the Attic*. New Haven: Yale University Press, 1979.

Gill, Stephen. *Wordsworth and the Victorians*. London: Oxford University Press, 2001.

Glut, Donald F. *The Frankenstein Legend: A Tribute to Mary Shelley and Boris Karloff*. Metuchen, NJ: The Scarecrow Press, 1973.

Goble, Alan, ed. *The Complete Index to Literary Sources in Film*. London, Melbourne, Munich and New Providence, NJ: Bowker–Saur, 1999.

Hand, Richard J., and Michael Wilson. *London's Grand Guignol and the Theatre of Horror*. Exeter: University of Exeter Press, 2007.

Hardie, Martin. 'George Henry Boughton'. In *Dictionary of National Biography*, edited by Sidney Lee, 197–8. Supplement II, vol. 1. London: Oxford University Press, 1912.

Hawkins, Ella. 'Solving Mysteries in the SBT Archives: Ethel Webling and Herbert Beerbohm Tree'. https://www.shakespeare.org.uk/explore-shakespeare/blogs/solving-mysteries-sbt-archives-ethel-webling-and-herbert-beerbohm-tree/ (accessed 31 October 2022).

Hawkins, Ella. 'Julius Caesar, Ethel Webling and Herbert Beerbohm Tree'. YouTube video, https://www.youtube.com/watch?v=QNBuImo3CY0 (accessed 31 October 2022).

Helmreich, Anne. 'Forum: Eminent Victorians, Marcus Huish (1843–1921)'. *Victorian Review* 37, no. 1 (2011): 26–30.

Heringman, Noah. 'Science and Human Animality in Mary Shelley's Frankenstein'. *The Wordsworth Circle* 50, no. 1 (Winter 2019): 127–45.

Hinings, Jessica. 'Pfeiffer [née Davis], Emily Jane'. 23 September 2004. *Oxford Dictionary of National Biography*. https://doi-org.ezproxy.uwtsd.ac.uk/10.1093/ref:odnb/22084 (accessed 30 October 2022).

Hitchcock, Susan Tyler. *Frankenstein: A Cultural History*. New York: W. W. Norton & Company, 2007.

Holmes, Richard. *Age of Wonder*. New York: Pantheon Books, 2008.

Homans, Margaret. *Bearing the Word: Language and Female Experience in Nineteenth-Century Women's Writing*. Chicago: University of Chicago Press, 1986.

Horton, Robert. *Frankenstein*. London and New York: Wallflower Press, 2014.

Keller, Betty. *Pauline: A Biography of Pauline Johnson*. Vancouver: Douglas & McIntyre, 1981.

Kent, Charles. 'Taylor, Tom'. In *Dictionary of National Biography*, edited by Sidney Lee, 472–4. Vol. 55. Stow–Taylor, London: Smith, Elder & Co., 1898.

Ketterer, David. *Frankenstein's Creation: The Book, The Monster, and Human Reality*. Victoria: English Literary Monograph Series, 1979.

Kirk, R. E. G., and Ernest F. Kirk, eds. *Returns of Aliens Dwelling in the City and Suburbs of London, Part I, 1523–1571*. Vol. X. Aberdeen: Publications of the Huguenot Society of London, 1900.

Bibliography

Ludlam, Harry. *A Biography of Dracula: The Life Story of Bram Stoker*. London: The Fireside Press, 1962.

Mank, Gregory William. *It's Alive: The Classic Cinema Saga of Frankenstein*. San Diego and New York: A. S. Barnes & Company, Inc., 1981.

Marsh, Joss. 'Mimi and the Matinée Idol: Martin-Harvey, Sydney Carton, and the Staging of *A Tale of Two Cities*, 1860–1939'. In *Charles Dickens, A Tale of Two Cities and the French Revolution*, edited by Colin Jones, Josephine McDonagh and Jon Mee, 126–45. Basingstoke: Palgrave Macmillan, 2009.

Mellor, Anne. *Mary Shelley: Her Life, Her Fiction, Her Monsters*. London: Routledge, 1989.

Merle, Jean-Toussaint, and Antony Béraud. *Frankenstein, ou le monstre et le magicien*. Paris: Bezou Libraire, 1826. https://gallica.bnf.fr/ark:/12148/bpt6k311832c.texteImage#.

Moore, Jeanie Grant. 'Lucy Webling (Lucy Betty MacRaye) (1877–1952) and Peggy Webling (Arthur Weston) (1871–1949)'. In *Dictionary of Literary Biography: Late Victorian and Edwardian Women Poets*, edited by William B. Thesing, vol. 240, 321–31. Detroit: Gale Group, 2001.

Murray, Paul. 'Hamilton Deane (1879–1958)'. *The Green Book: Writings on Irish Gothic, Supernatural and Fantastic Literature* 20 (Samhain 2022): 89–95.

O'Hagan, Lauren. 'Guest post: The birthday book: Tracing an absent presence'. 15 March 2017. Special Collections and Archives / Casgliadau Arbennig ac Archifau Showcasing Research Resources / Hyrwyddo Adnoddau Ymchwil, Cardiff University, https://scolarcardiff.wordpress.com/2017/03/15/birthday-book/ (accessed 31 October 2022).

'Pamphlet Wars: Arguments on Paper from the Age of Revolutions'. No. 4, 'Vox Populi, Vox Dei, A Providence Gazette Extraordinary. August 24, 1765'. John Carter Brown Library, https://www.brown.edu/Facilities/John_Carter_Brown_Library/exhibitions/pamphletWars/pages/crisis.html

Park, Sowon. 'The First Professional: The Women Writers' Suffrage League'. *Modern Language Quarterly* 57, no. 2 (1997): 185–200.

Park, Sowon. 'Women Writers' Suffrage League'. *The Literary Encyclopedia*, 2002, https://escholarship.org/content/qt9rg5g6t3/qt9rg5g6t3_noSplash_ac8968ef86fd89b8017e3f7730021bd7.pdf (accessed 18 October 2022).

Poovey, Mary. *The Proper Lady and the Woman Writer*. Chicago: University of Chicago Press, 1984.

Prioleau, Betsy. *Diamonds and Deadlines: A Tale of Greed, Deceit, and a Female Tycoon in the Gilded Age*. New York: Abrams Press, 2022.

Quinn, James. 'Brooke, Stopford Augustus'. In *Dictionary of Irish Biography*. DOI: https://doi.org/10.3318/dib.000993.v1. Originally published October 2009 as part of the *Dictionary of Irish Biography*, last revised October 2009.

Rose, Marilyn J. 'Johnson, Emily Pauline'. In *Dictionary of Canadian Biography*. Vol. 14: University of Toronto / Université Laval, 2003–, http://www.biographi.ca/en/bio/johnson_emily_pauline_14E.html (accessed 12 January 2023).

Royal Academy Exhibition Catalogue, 1889. https://www.royalacademy.org.uk/art-artists/exhibition-catalogue/ra-sec-vol121-1889 (accessed 11 January 2023).

Royal Academy Exhibition Catalogue, 1892. https://www.royalacademy.org.uk/art-artists/exhibition-catalogue/ra-sec-vol124-1892 (accessed 11 January 2023).

Ruskin, John. *Arrows of the Chace: Being a Collection of Scattered Letters Published Chiefly in the Daily Newspapers, 1840–1880*. 2 vols. Vol. 2. Boston: Dana Estes & Company, no date (c. 1900).

Sharp, Robert. 'Playfair, Sir Nigel Ross'. 23 September 2004. *Oxford Dictionary of National Biography*. https://doi.org/10.1093/ref:odnb/35540; https://doi-org.ezproxy.uwtsd.ac.uk/10.1093/ref:odnb/35540 (accessed 8 June 2023).

Bibliography

Skal, David J. *Hollywood Gothic: The Tangled Web of Dracula from Novel to Stage to Screen*. New York: W. W. Norton & Co., 1991.
Skal, David J. *The Monster Show: A Cultural History of Horror*. New York: Farrar, Straus and Giroux, 1993, rev. 2001.
Skal, David J. *Screams of Reason: Mad Science and Modern Culture*. New York: W. W. Norton and Company, 1998.
Skal, David J. *Something in the Blood: The Untold Story of Bram Stoker, the Man who Wrote Dracula*. New York/London: The Liveright Publishing Company, 2016.
Soister, John T. *Of Gods and Monsters: A Critical Guide to Universal Studios Science Fiction, Horror and Mystery Films, 1929–1939*. Jefferson, NC/London: McFarland and Co., 1999, repr. 2005.
Sparks, Muriel. *Child of Light: A Reassessment of Mary Wollstonecraft Shelley*. Hadleigh Essex: Tower Bridge, 1951.
Taves, Brian. *Robert Florey: The French Expressionist*. Duncan, CK: Bearmanor Media, 2014.
Vlasapolos, Anca. 'Frankenstein's Hidden Skeleton: The Psycho-Politics of Oppression'. *Science Fiction Studies* 10, no. 2 (July 1983): 125–36.
Wearing, J. P. *The London Stage, 1890–1899: A Calendar of Productions, Performers and Personnel*. 2nd ed. Lanham, MD and Plymouth: Rowman & Littlefield, 2014.
Webling-Watts, Josephine. 'John Ruskin'. Radio Lecture by Josephine Webling Watts, 30 April 1929.
Webling, Lucy, and Peggy Webling. *Poems and Stories*. Toronto: R. G. McLean, 1896.
Webling, Peggy. 'An English Actor's Ghost Story'. *Brantford Expositor*, 2 January 1891, 7.
Webling, Peggy. 'GO! A Canadian Trotting Tale'. *The Sun*, 1 August 1893, 1.
Webling, Peggy (under pseudonym Arthur Weston). *An April Jest*, 1893.
Webling, Peggy. *Blue Jay*. London: William Heinemann, 1906.
Webling, Peggy. *The Story of Virginia Perfect*. London: Methuen & Co., Ltd., 1909.
Webling, Peggy. *A Spirit of Mirth*. London: Methuen & Co., Ltd., 1910.
Webling, Peggy. *Felix Christie*. London: Methuen & Co., Ltd., 1912.
Webling, Peggy. *The Pearl Stringer*. London: Methuen & Co., Ltd., 1913.
Webling, Peggy. *Westward Ho!*, 1912–1913.
Webling, Peggy. *A Sketch of John Ruskin*. London: Self-published, 1914.
Webling, Peggy. *Edgar Chirrup*. London: Methuen & Co., Ltd., 1915.
Webling, Peggy. *Boundary House*. London: Hutchinson & Co., 1916.
Webling, Peggy. *Guests of the Heart*. London: Self-published, 1917.
Webling, Peggy. *In Our Street*. London: Hutchinson & Co., 1918.
Webling, Peggy. *Saints and Their Stories*. London: Nisbet & Co. Ltd., 1919.
Webling, Peggy. *The Scent Shop*. London: Hutchinson & Co., 1919.
Webling, Peggy. *Verses to Men*. London: Self-published, 1919.
Webling, Peggy. *Comedy Corner*. London: Hutchinson & Co., 1920.
Webling, Peggy. *The Fruitless Orchard*. London: Hutchinson & Co., 1921.
Webling, Peggy. *Peggy: The Story of One Score Years and Ten*. London: Hutchinson & Co., 1924.
Webling, Peggy. *The Amber Merchant*. London: Hutchinson & Co., 1925.
Webling, Peggy. 'Some Queer Trades of London'. In *Wonderful London*, 3 vols, edited by Arthur St John Adcock, 598. Vol. 2. London: Fleetway House, 1926.
Webling, Peggy. 'The Real Pumblechook'. *The Dickensian* 22, no. 3 (July–September 1926): 157–8.
Webling, Peggy. *Anna Maria*. London: Hutchinson & Co., 1927.
Webling, Peggy. *Strange Enchantment*. London: Hutchinson & Co., 1929.
Webling, Peggy. *The Rhyme of Little Mark*. London: Self-published, 1936.
Webling, Peggy. *Opal Screens*. London: Hutchinson & Co., 1937.
Webling, Peggy. *Young Laetitia*. London: Hutchinson & Co., 1939.

Bibliography

Sources from the Webling archive

Books by Peggy Webling

The Story of a Pen: A Book for Would-be Writers, by Peggy Webling (unpublished, 1941)
A Spirit of Mirth, by Peggy Webling. London: Methuen & Co. Ltd, 1910 (dedication page to 'The Beloved Five – Ethel, Josephine, Ruth, Rosalind, and Lucy')
Verses to Men, self-published, 1919 (copy no. 1, inscribed to W. H. Spence)

Plays by Peggy Webling

Plays Produced with copies in Webling archive

Westward Ho!, Act III (later added in Webling's hand: Peggy Webling Graham House. 123 Ladbroke Grove. London. W.11.) (produced by Matheson Lang in 1912–1913)
Frankenstein, A Play in a Prologue and Three Acts [registered 16 January 1923 by the Incorporated Society of Authors, Playwrights and Composers] (same actor plays Henry and Frankenstein)
Frankenstein, Act I and Act II, (124 The Grove W.6) (different actors play Henry and Frankenstein; converted back from same actor version)
Frankenstein, Prologue 1927 and 1930 (39, St. Stephen's Avenue. London W.12) (in Webling's hand: 'Produced at the Empire Theatre, Preston, on December 7, 1927, by Mr Hamilton Deane. Produced at the Little Theatre London, on February 10, 1930, by Mr Hamilton Deane')
Reprieve, A Play in Three Acts and an Ending By Peggy Webling. Founded on the Novel of the same name by Halbert J. Boyd. [produced by Hamilton Deane in 1931]

Unpublished play manuscripts in Webling archive

The Stream (before 1908, later revised)
Magwitch (between 1932 and 1935?) [based on Dickens' *Great Expectations*]
Rossetti's Wife, with P. W. Chaple (1933-1934) [about Dante Gabriel Rossetti and Elizabeth Siddal]
Torn Manuscript (1938?) [about John Ruskin, Effie Gray and John Everett Millais]
Mansfield Park (after 1939) [based on Jane Austen's novel]
Abominable Snowmen, with Hamilton Deane (1939-1940)

Letters

Tom Taylor (Lavender Sweep, Wandsworth) to Mrs Webling, 19 February 1880
Ellen Terry to Miss Lucy Webling, 25 May 1893 (copy; original in collection of Lindsay Dorney)
R. J. Webling to Herrick Torr, 1 September 1912
R. J. Webling to Josephine Webling Watts (undated; *c.* 1913?)
Peggy to Josephine, 7 February 1913
Peggy to Josephine, 13 June 1913
Peggy to Josephine, 29 July 1913
R. J. Webling to Josephine, 17 January 1914
Peggy to Josephine, 25 November 1917

Bibliography

Peggy to Josephine, 25 May 1918
Peggy to Josephine, 16 November 1918
Peggy to Josephine, 21 October 1919
Peggy to Josephine, 7 January 1920
Peggy to Josephine, 1 February 1920
Peggy to Josephine, 13 February 1920
Peggy to Josephine, 26 March 1920
Peggy to Josephine, 2 July 1920
Peggy to Josephine, 28 July 1920
Peggy to Josephine, 18 February 1921
Peggy to Josephine, 17 October 1921
Ethel Webling to Josephine, 9 November 1921
Ethel Webling to Josephine, 11 November 1921
Peggy to Josephine, 2 September 1923
Peggy to Josephine, 30 July 1925
Peggy to Josephine, 23 September 1925
Ethel Webling to Josephine, 3 November 1925
Peggy to Josephine, 7 November 1925
Peggy to Josephine, 10 December 1925
Peggy to Josephine, 25 April 1926
Peggy to Josephine, 12 November 1926
Peggy to Josephine, undated, but probably February 1927
Peggy to Josephine, 1 March 1927
Peggy to Josephine, 20 September 1927
Peggy to Josephine, 24 September 1927
Peggy to Josephine, 28 September 1927
Peggy to Josephine, 16 October 1927
Peggy to Josephine, 7 December 1927
Peggy to Josephine, 9 December 1927
Peggy to Josephine, 15 January 1928
Peggy to Josephine, 2 March 1928
Peggy to Josephine, 13 December 1928
Peggy to Josephine, 17 January 1929
Peggy to Josephine, 24 March 1929
Peggy to Josephine, 3 October 1929
Peggy to Josephine, 19 October 1929
Peggy to Josephine, 25 November 1929
Peggy to Josephine, 10 December 1929
Peggy to Josephine, 31 December 1929
Peggy to Josephine, 5 January 1930
Peggy to Josephine, 8 January 1930
Peggy to Josephine, 21 January 1930
Peggy to Josephine, 28 January 1930
Peggy to Josephine, 6 February 1930
Peggy to Josephine, 13 February 1930
Peggy to Josephine, 23 February 1930
Peggy to Josephine, 16 March 1930
Peggy to Josephine, 4 April 1930
Peggy to Josephine, 13 Apr 1930.

Bibliography

Peggy to Josephine, 27 April 1930
Peggy to Josephine, 13 May 1930
Peggy to Josephine, 1 August 1930
Peggy to Josephine, 5 March 1931
Peggy to Josephine, 13 January 1934
Lucy McRaye to Josephine, 23 November 1935
Peggy to Josephine, 11 August 1939
Peggy to Josephine, 25 June 1940
Peggy to Josephine, 20 August 1940
Peggy to Josephine, 7 October 1940
Peggy to Josephine, 16 Mar 1941

Birth, marriage and death records

Postcard with birthdates dated 1906, in Maria Webling's and Ethel Webling's hands
Birth Registration: Margaret Webling, General Record Office (UK), 1871, District of Long Acre, County of Middlesex, No. 467, Jan–Feb–March Quarter, 5b 179
Marriage Registration: Robert James Webling and Maria Webling, General Record Office (UK), 1858, St Pancras District, No. 135, Oct–Nov–Dec Quarter, 1b 245
Death Registration: Ethel Webling, General Record Office (UK), 1929, Kensington, No. 380, Jan–March Quarter, 1a 409
Death Registration: Peggy otherwise Margaret Webling, General Record Office (UK), 1949, Camberwell, No. 158, Jul–Aug–Sep Quarter, 5c 174
Will of Margaret Webling, proved London 15 September 1949

Contracts

Memorandum of Agreement between Peggy Webling and John Balderston, dated 24 Feb 1930
Agreement between Peggy Webling, John Balderston and Horace Liveright, dated 26 February 1930, with Addition to Contract, dated 26 February 1930

Art and miniatures by Ethel Webling

Silverpoint Drawing of John Ruskin as frontispiece for *A Sketch of John Ruskin* by Peggy Webling
Elizabeth Barrett Browning and her son Pen, from a Fratelli d'Alessandri photograph taken 1860, watercolour on ivory
Ethel Webling, self-portrait, *c.* 1890, watercolour on ivory
Lucy Webling, *c.* 1900, watercolour on ivory
Peggy Webling, *c.* 1892, watercolour on ivory
Robert James Webling, *c.* 1880, watercolour on ivory
In the collection of Lindsay Dorney:
Rosalind Webling, *c.* 1895, watercolour on ivory
In the collection of Elmer French, Jr./Timothy French:
Josephine Webling, ca. 1878, watercolour on ivory
Maria Webling, *c.* 1880, watercolour on ivory
Peggy Webling, *c.* 1882, watercolour on ivory

Bibliography

Miscellaneous ephemera

Research of D'Arcy Webling on the Webling name and history
Peggy Webling's Autograph Birthday Book
'Peggy's Paper or Unch and Udy', 1887
Lucy and Peggy Webling, *Poems and Stories*, Inscription pages on inside cover: 'Toronto August 1896' (copy; original in the collection of Lindsay Dorney)

Newspaper clippings

Review of Frankenstein, with cartoon, in *Punch*, 19 February 1930, 219
'Women Love Thrillers', *Daily News and Westminster Gazette*, 27 February 1930, 2

Notes for lectures

Josephine Webling Watts, 'Personal Recollections of the closing-in of the Victorian Era', Lecture given at Plandome, Long Island, NY, 1 p.m., 7 October 1925
Josephine Webling Watts, 'John Ruskin', Radio Lecture, 30 April 1929

Photographs

'The Sisters Webling. Rosalind, Josephine, Peggy', c. 1880
'The Misses Webling' (Rosalind, Josephine, Peggy and Lucy), c. 1884
'The Misses Webling, Lilliputian Fair 1882'
Lucy Webling as Little Lord Fauntleroy, 1888
Peggy Webling as Dick and Lucy Webling as Little Lord Fauntleroy, 1888
Pauline Johnson, Rosalind, Peggy, Josephine and Lucy Webling, A.A. Watts, 1 July 1892
'Britannia' (Rosalind, Peggy and Lucy Webling), c. 1895
'Peggy Webling, Novelist', Hulton & Co., Ltd, dated 25 July 1920

Play, recital and other programmes

Programme, *Beauty and the Beast*, 24 January 1879
Programme, 'Dramatic Recital' by 'The Sisters Webling', 5 July 1879
Programme, 'Dramatic Recital by the Misses Webling, Josephine, Rosalind and Peggy (Age 8 years)', 29 October 1879
'Programme of Recital given in presence of Their Royal Highnesses The Prince and Princess of Wales', 23 June 1882
Programme, 'The Misses Webling's Dramatic Recital', Steinway Hall, June 30 1885
Programme, *The Real Little Lord Fauntleroy* (Horace Lingard's Company), 30 Aug 1888
Programme, *Becket*, 29 May 1893, Royal Lyceum Theatre (copy; original in the collection of Lindsay Dorney)
Programme, *The Ambassador*, St James's Theatre, London, 2 June 1898
Programme, *The Only Way*, Prince's Theatre, Bristol, 19 June 1899
Programme, *The Only Way*, Theatre Royal, Merthyr, 17 July 1899
Programme, 'Concert Followed by a Debate', RMS *Adriatic*, 26 Mar 1915 (Suffrage Debate)
Programme, 'Frankenstein, by Peggy Webling. From Mrs. Shelley's Wonderful Story', Monday, 11 June 1928 'for Six Nights', Theatre Royal, Nottingham

Bibliography

Programme, 'Frankenstein' [10 February–12 April 1930] Cover: Little Theatre John Street, Adelphi, Strand, 'Hamilton Deane presents "Frankenstein", Every evening at 8.30, Matinees Wednesday and Saturday at 2.30'; Inside Cover: Little Theatre, John Street, Adelphi, Strand. 'Hamilton Deane presents *An Adventure in the Macabre:* "FRANKENSTEIN" By Peggy Webling'

Programme, 'Hamilton Deane and his company in "REPRIEVE" by Peggy Webling. Founded on the Novel of the same name by Halbert J. Boyd', 20 July 1931, for Six Nights at 7.45, Theatre Royal, Nottingham

Play flyer for *Dracula*, 27 July 1931, Theatre Royal, Nottingham

INDEX

Adcock, Arthur St John   35, 43
An Adventure in the Macabre   59, 303, 306, 309
   not Webling's title   75 n.35
Ainley, Henry   59, 78–9, 301
Albertus Magnus   70
Alexander, George   15
The Ambassador   15, 16 n.38, 46
Alice in Wonderland. See Carroll, Lewis
Armitage and Leigh Company   48
Ashford, Harry   30
The Athenaeum   39
Austen, Jane   32
Authors Society. *See* Society of Authors, UK

Balderston, John L.
   Berkeley Square   49, 56–8, 291, 293, 298, 307
   Bride of Frankenstein   103
   Dracula adaptation   3, 49–50, 49 n.76, 54, 56–7, 58 n.133, 63, 65, 97, 290–1, 298–9, 307
   early life   54–5 (*see also* Columbia University)
   Frankenstein
      adaptation of   1–2, 4, 56–7, 59, 63–5, 80 n.59, 81 n.63, 95, 97–101, 107, 290–3, 307
      agreements with Peggy Webling   57–9, 63, 294, 297–302, 311–12
      contract with Universal Pictures   3, 65–7, 308
      and Hollywood   65, 67, 308
      lawsuit against Universal Pictures   67, 103 n.101
      New York production attempt   57–9, 63–5, 290–302
   and Hamilton Deane   49–50, 54, 56–8, 62–5
   and Harold Freedman (agent)   56–7, 62 n.166, 64 n.184, 65
   and Horace Liveright   3, 49, 56, 63–5, 313–16 (*see also* Liveright, Horace)
   and J. C. Squire   49, 56, 307 (*see also* Balderston, John L., *Berkeley Square*)
   newspaper work   55–6 (*see also New York World*)
      reporter for Tutankhamen   55
   other plays   56 n.116
Baughan, E. A.   61–2, 297
Beauty and the Beast   13
Bennett, William   35 n.143
Benson, Frank   79 n.57
Birmingham Gazette   58 n.140

Bligh, N. M.   49 n.72
Blow, Sydney   39, 43
The Bookman   28 n.104, 33, 35, 60, 295, 299
Booth, Edwin   24
Borough Theatre, Stratford   52, 288
Borthwick, A. T.   49 n.73
Boughton, George, R. A.   16
Boyd, Halbert J.
   Reprieve   36–7, 294
Brereton, Austin   20 n.63
Bride of Frankenstein   3, 75, 103
British Library   3 n.3, 4, 75 n.37, 80, 88, 93
Britton, Hutin   30
Brockell, Gillian   23 n.79
Brooke, Stopford   13–14
Browning, Elizabeth Barrett   19 n.60
Browning, Robert   19, 69 n.6
Browning, Tod
   Dracula (film)   65
Burnett, Frances Hodgson   20–1
   Editha's Burglar   21
   Nixie   21
   The Real Little Lord Fauntleroy   15, 20

Canterbury Tales   13
Carpenter, Ernest   29
Carroll, Lewis (Charles Lutwidge Dodgson)   13
   Alice in Wonderland   20
Catt, Carrie Chapman   23 n.79
Chalk, Penny   80 n.59
Chaple, P. W.   37, 295–6
Chemers, Michael   69 n.6
Chesterton, G. K.   60
Christian, Bertram   28, 35 n.141
City of Westminster Archives. *See* Westminster City Archives
Cline, Louis   65
Columbia University   55. *See also* Balderston, John L., early life
Cooke, T. P.   59 n.152, 69, 73, 76 n.42, 301
Cornwallis-West, Patsy   20
Cosby, Brian H.   98 n.87
Cox, Jeffrey   70 n.12, 71 n.18, 72, 74 nn.31, 32

Daily Express   61 n.161
Daily News   17 n.52, 20 n.63, 33 n.133, 49 n.73, 59 n.147, 61, 62 n.165, 298
Daily News and Leader   33

Index

Daily News and Westminster Gazette 40
Daily Telegraph 28 nn.104, 106, 33 n.133, 35, 52, 59 n.147, 64 n.182
Dangerfield, Fred 33 n.137
Dawley, J. Searle
   Frankenstein 1910 (*Edison Film*) 3, 68, 77–9, 82, 83 n.65
Deane, Hamilton
   Abominable Snowmen 37–8
   acting career
      in America and Canada 46–8
      in English provincial repertory 46–8
      Fixing Sister 47
      The Only Way (Haviland–Coleridge Company) 46, 47, 47 n.59, 53, 285, 304
      The Whip 47, 64
   as actor-manager 48–9
   birth 46
   and Dora Mary Patrick 48, 49 n.68
   Dracula production 2–3, 44, *48*, 48–52, 58, 284, 286, 288
      and Florence Balcombe Stoker 48
      London production 49–50, 304–5
      nurse on duty 49
      New York production 49–50
      provincial performances 3, *48*, 49–50
      reviews 49
      writing *Dracula* playscript 38, 44, 48–9
   Frankenstein production
      contacted by Peggy Webling 2, 44
      contract with Peggy Webling 45, 50
      first performance 2–4, 50–2, 75, 87, 90, 107, 109, 285–7, 305
      London production 2, 44, 52, 58–62, *60*, 64, 69, 75–6, 80, *80*, *82*, 85–6, *85*, *86*, *88*, 93, 95–7, 100, 107, 221–80, 284–5, 290, 293–300, 307–8
      first performance in London 2, 9, 58–62, 221, 293–7, 307
      nurse on duty 49 n.73, 298
      New York production attempt 2–3, 57–9, 63–5, 290–302
      not a commission 2, 44
      not written as companion piece to *Dracula* 2, 44
      possible star in New York production 64, 299, 301
      provincial performances 2–3, 50–2, *55*, 56, 58, 300, 302
      reviews 3, 51–3, 58–9, 61–2, *62*, 79, 80 n.59, 96 n.82, 292
      revisions 2–4, 50–4, 56, 58, 69, 80 n.59, 82 n.64, 90–1, 93–5
   Hamilton Deane Papers 4, 95

and Horace Liveright 3, 49, 54, 56, 64–5, 301
   (*see also* Liveright: Horace)
and John Balderston 49–50, 54, 56–8, 62–5, 97, 290–1, 307
and Peggy Webling 2–4, 44–5, 50–3, 57–9, 61, 64, 86–7, 90, 95, 100, 107, 283–301, 304–7
   Reprieve 36–7, 64, 294
de Hamel, Herbert 37 n.158
De Morgan, Evelyn Pickering 16 n,46
De Morgan, William 16 n.46
Derby Daily Telegraph 31 n.122, 48 n.62, 49 nn.68, 71, 57
Dickens, Charles 13, 23, 33, 43, 46, 75
   The Dickensian 43
   Great Expectations 44 n.47
   A Tale of Two Cities 46
   Tiny Tim 75
Donovan, Kathryn Kiningham 19 n.56
Doppelgänger 59, 68, 76–7, 79
Dorney, Lindsay 14 n.32, 20 n.67, 26 n.89
Douglas, Dicky 28
Dracula (novel) 44, 48, 284, 304
Dracula (play) 2–3, 38, 44, *48*, 48–52, 54, 56–8, 61, 63, 65, 97–8, 284, 286, 288, 290–1, 297–9, 304–5, 307. See also Deane, Hamilton, *Dracula* production; *Dracula* (novel)
Dracula (Universal film) 65, 97
Drewitt, Stanley 44, 283–4
Dryden, Vaughan 61

The Edison Kinetogram 77
Edwards, George W. 14, 26
Eliot, George (Mary Ann Evans) 32
Elliott and Fry 15
Ellis, Wilfrid F. P. 35 n.143
Empire Theatre, Preston, Lancashire 3, 50, 75, 90, 285, 305
The Era 14 n.30, 15 nn.36–37, 17 n.51, 20 n.71, 28, 44 n.43, 46 nn.50–52, 57, 48 n.64, 52 n.92, 53 n.103, 96 n.81
Evening News (London) 61 n.161

Faragoh, Francis E. 101 n.98
Farjeon, Herbert 9
Farquharson, John 43–5, *45*, 57, 59, 64 n.176, 282–5, 290–1, 294–5, 298, 307.
   See also Webling, Peggy, agent John Farquharson
Faust/Dr Faustus 20, 70
Fields, 'Happy' Fanny 28
Fisch, Audrey 1 n.1, 69 n.6, 74–5, 77 nn.44–45, 47, 77 n.49, 78 nn.51–53, 80 n.59
Flavel, John 98 n.87

Index

Folger Shakespeare Library 16 n.40
Forry, Steven 44, 66 n.199, 69 n.6, 70 nn.9, 13, 15, 71 n.17, 72 nn.23–26, 75 nn.33, 35, 80 n.59, 81 n.63, 85, 90 n.75, 93 n.77, 97 n.85, 98 nn.86–87, 89–90, 100 n.97
Frankenstein (film) 66–7, 100–2
Frankenstein (general) 1–5, 22, 37–8, 44, 67
Frankenstein (novel). *See* Shelley, Mary
Frankenstein by Peggy Webling. *See* Webling's *Frankenstein*
Fratelli d'Alessandri 19 n.60
Freedman, Harold 56–7, 62 n.166, 64 n.184, 65. *See also* Balderston, John L., Harold Freedman (agent)
Friedman, Lester and Kavey, Allison 44, 69 n.6, 90 n.75
Fytton, Francis 25 n.84

The Garrick Club 16 n.40, 24 n.83
Gilbert, Sandra M. and Gubar, Susan 68 n.2
Gill, Stephen 14 n.28
Glut, Donald F. 38 n.162, 67 nn.205–206
Goble, Alan 33 n.137
Goldwyn, Samuel 42 n.30
Grace, Kathleen 82
Grand Guignol 49. *See also* Levy, José; Little Theatre, London
Grand Theatre, Derby 49, 288
Greene, Desmond 80, 297
Grimshaw, May 294

Hale, Stanley 59, 75 n.35, 293–5, 297
Hallatt, Henry 59, 61, 80, 82, 88, 93, 102, 296–8, 307. *See also* Webling's *Frankenstein*, Cast of Characters, Henry Frankenstein
Hamilton, Cicely 31 n.123
Hand, Richard J. 49 n.72
Hannon, John 26, 28
Hatton, Bessie 31 n.123
Haviland, William 16, 46, 47
Haviland-Coleridge Company
  The Only Way 44, 46, 47, 283
Hawkins, Ella 16 n.40
Helmreich, Anne 16 n.47
Hepworth, Cecil M. 33
Heringman, Noah 73 n.30
Hinings, Jessica 19 n.59
Hitchcock, Susan Tyler 69 n.6
Holloway, W. E. 285–6, 289–90, 292, 305
Holmes, Oliver Wendell, Sr. 19
Holmes, Richard 83 n.67
Homans, Margaret 68 n.2
Hoppé, Edward 60, 295
Horton, Robert 100 n.98
Huish, Marcus 16

Incorporated Society of Authors, Playwrights and Composers. *See* Society of Authors, UK
Irving, Henry 2, 16, 20, 29, 48, 298, 306

The Jackdaw of Rheims 28
James, Henry
  The Sense of the Past 56
Johnson, Pauline (Tekahionwake) 16, 21–2, 24, 25
  The White Wampum 21 n.74, 25
Jones, Colin 46 n.50

Karloff, Boris 1, 5, 100–3, 308
Kavey, Allison. *See* Friedman, Lester and Kavey, Allison
Kerr, John
  The Monster and the Magician 3, 69–70, 72, 74
Ketterer, John 68 n.5
King Edward VII 2, 20
Kingsley, Charles
  Heroes 20
  Westward Ho! 29–30, 36–7, 40, 286, 305

Laemmle, Carl, Jr. 65, 97
Lang, Matheson 29–30, 36, 40–1, 79, 281–2, 285–6
Langbridge, Frederick 46
Langtry, Lily 2, 20
Lear, Edward 17, 20
Leslie, Mrs Frank (Miriam Follin) 23
Levy, José 49. *See also* Grand Guignol
Library of Congress 3–4, 53, 56, 63, 65, 75, 77, 97, 107, 165
Lingard, Horace 15 n.36
Little Lord Fauntleroy (character) 2, 14–15, 20, 23
Little Theatre, London 2–3, 9, 37, 49, 58–9, 60, 75, 80, 82, 85, 86, 86, 88, 93, 96 n.82, 102, 107, 293, 295, 298–9, 301, 304, 307. *See also Dracula* (play); Grand Guignol; Levy, José
Liveright, Horace 3–4, 49, 54, 56, 62–5, 97, 297–302, 313–16. *See also* Balderston, John L., and Horace Liveright; Deane, Hamilton, and Horace Liveright; Webling, Peggy: and Horace Liveright
Lomath, Stuart 48, 297
Lord Chamberlain's Office/Plays 3–4, 49, 75 n.37
Ludlam, Harry 48 n.64
Lyceum Theatre, London 20, 29, 48
Lyceum Theatre, Sheffield 75 n.35, 76

M. A. P. (*Mostly About People*) 26, 28–9
McCarthy, Charlotte 13, 16
McCarthy, Justin, M. P. 13
McDonagh, Josephine 46 n.50
McLeay, Franklin 26
McRaye, Louis Drummond 4, 14, 38, 57, 60, 67
McRaye, Lucy Betty. *See* Webling, Lucy

329

Index

McRaye, Lucy Webling. *See* Webling, Lucy
McRaye, Walter   16, 21 n.74
Mank, Gregory William   38 n.162, 67 nn.205–206, 102 n.100
Marsh, Joss   46 n.50
Martin-Harvey, John   46 nn.50, 52
Mayer, Louis B.   42 n.30
Mee, Jon   46 n.50
Mégroz, R. L.   37 n.158
Mellor, Anne   71
Merle and Béraud
   Frankenstein, ou le monstre et le magicien   3, 69, 73
Metro Pictures   42 n.30
Metro-Goldwyn-Mayer   42 n.30
Milner, Henry
   Frankenstein, or the Man and the Monster   3, 69–70, 72–4, 101
Moore, Jeanie Grant   33 n.132, 35 n.147
The Morning Leader   26, 28, 35 n.141, 78
The Morning Post   21 n.72, 28 n.106, 59 n.147, 60 n.152, 79
Murray, Paul   48, 49 nn.69–70

The Nation and Athenaeum   62
New York Public Library
   John L. Balderston Papers   4, 50 n.76, 55 nn.113–114, 56 n.116, 95 n.80, 103 nn.101–102
New York Times   38 n.162, 63 n.174, 67 n.206
New York World   24 n.80, 55–6, 291
Nixie. *See* Burnett, Frances Hodgson, *Nixie*; Webling, Lucy, as Nixie
Nosferatu (film)   48

O'Connor, T. P.   25–6
O'Hagan, Lauren   11 n.16
Ogle, Charles   3. *See also* Dawley, J. Searle
Orpheum Theatre, Seattle   66

Page, Henry   20, 50
Park, Sowon   31 n.123
Patrick, Dora Mary   48–9, *85*, *86*, 294, 297, 305
Peake, Richard Brinsley
   Presumption; or, The Fate of Frankenstein   3, 59, 69–74, 76 n.42, 92–3
Pfeiffer, Emily Davis   19
Phillips, Stephen
   Aylmer's Secret   3, 59 n.152, 75 n.34, 78–9, 301
Plato's *Timaeus*   5
Playfair, Sir Nigel Ross   43, 283
Pond, Major J. B.   23 n.78, 26
Poynter, Sir Edward   16
Prince Albert   11
Prioleau, Betty   24 n.79

Pulitzer, Joseph   55
Punch   17 n.53, 28 n.106, 36, 39 n.3, 61–2, 298–9, 307

Queen Alexandra   2, 20
Queen Victoria   11
Quinn, James   14 n.28

Reynolds's News   61 n.161, *88*
Robins, Elizabeth   31–2
Rose, Marilyn J.   21 n.74
Rossetti, Dante Gabriel   37
Rossetti, William   37 n.158
Ruskin, John   2, 14, 16–20, *19*, *22*, 35, 38
Russell, Malcolm   *80*, 292, 298

St Clair, William   70
St Martin's Theatre, London   56
Salt, Titus, Jr.   20
Selwyn, Edgar   42–3, 282–3
Severn, Joan   17
Shakespeare, William   11 n.16, 13, 16 n.40, 18
   The Comedy of Errors   78
   Julius Caesar   16 n.40
   Love's Labour's Lost   13, 17
   The Merchant of Venice   30 n.120, 79 n.57
   A Midsummer Night's Dream   18 n.55
   Twelfth Night   16 n.40
Sharp, Robert   43 n.33
Shaw, Henry G.   46 n.51
Shelley, Mary
   Frankenstein   1–3, 22, 38 n.162, 40, *41*, 44, 50, 59 n.152, 66 n.199, 67–71, 73, 75, 76 n.41, 83, 93–4, 98, 100–1, 103, 284, 292, 299, 301, 303–6
Shelley, Percy Bysshe   20
Siddal, Elizabeth   37
Skal, David   44, 48 n.66, 49 nn.73, 75, 56 nn.118, 120–1, 57 n.131, 58 n.132, 62 nn.166–167, 63 nn.168–170, 172, 64 nn.179, 184, 65, 66 nn.198–199, 67 nn.204, 206, 69 n.6, 76 nn.41–42, 100 n.98, 101
The Sketch   78
Slade, Felix   16
Slade School of Fine Art   16
Smiley, Joseph
   Life Without Soul (1915 film)   77
Society of Authors, UK   37 n.156, 42, 44, 57, 75 n.36, 90 n.73, 284, 291
Soister, John T.   38 n.162
Sparks, Muriel   68 n.5
Spence, Jimmie   294–5
Spence, W. H.   35
Squire, John C.   49, 56, 307. *See also* Balderston, John L., and J. C. Squire

Index

Steele, Flora Annie 31 n.123
Steinway Hall, London 2, 15 n.35, 17–18, *18*
Stoker, Bram 44, 48. *See also Dracula* (novel)
Stoker, Florence Balcombe 48, 49 n.76. *See also* Deane, Hamilton, *Dracula* production, and Florence Balcombe Stoker
Street, George 49
Sunday Graphic 61 n.161
Sutherland, Lucie 79 n.57

Taves, Brian 69 n.6, 81 n.63
Taylor, Tom 17–18
Terry, Ellen 2, 16 n.40, 20, 23 n.78
Theatre Royal, Nottingham 37, 53, *55*, 306
Tilley, Vesta 26
The Times, London 17, 29, 33, 59, 61–2, 298
Townsend, Stephen 21
Tree, Herbert Beerbohm 2, 16, 24
Tristan and Iseult (play) 29
Tutankhamen 55. *See also* Balderston, John L., newspaper work, reporter for Tutankhamen
Twain, Mark (Samuel Langhorne Clemens) 19, 23 n.78

Universal Picture Corporation 1, 3–4, 65–7, 75, 81 n.63, 97, 100, 103, 308
Universal Studios. *See* Universal Picture Corporation
University College London 16
Urlin, Ethel 30

Victor of Aveyron 73
Vlasopolos, Anca 68 n.5

Watts, Alfred Allen 22, 24, *24*
Watts, Josephine Webling. *See* Webling, Josephine
Watts, Pamela 18 n.56
Watts, Patricia 18 n.56
Watts, Ruskin 42 n.25, 43–4, 282–3
Wearing, J. P. 25 n.87
Webling, Emilie 21 n.73, 22
Webling, Ethel 4, 9 n.2, *12*, 13–14, 16, 19, 24, 28, 33 n.136, 39, 41, 43 n.35, 51, 57, 60, 281–2, 284–8, 290–1, 293, 295–6, 300, 305
Webling, Hastings 21 n.73
Webling, Henry 10–11
Webling, Josephine (Josephine Webling Watts, Mrs A. A. Watts) 2, 5, 10–11, *12*, 13–15, *15*, 16 n.46, 17–20, *18*, 21–4, *21*, *22*, *24* , 30–2, 33 n.136, 39–43, *45*, 50, 56, 60, 63, 65, 79, 296
Webling, Lucy (Lucy Webling McRaye, Lucy Betty McRaye) 2, 4, *12*, 13–15, *15*, 16 n.40, 20–4, 23–24, 25–7, *27*, 33, 37 n.158, 38, 42–4, 46, 52, 66, 282–5, 288, 290, 292, 295–6, 301
  in *The Ambassador* 15, 46
  as Little Lord Fauntlerory 2, 14–15, 20, *23*, 42, 44
  as Nixie 21
  in *The Only Way* 44, 46
Webling, Maria (mother) 1, 9–11, 17–19, 23, 43
Webling, Maria Astle (grandmother) 11
Webling, Mary *12*, 13
Webling, Peggy
  agent John Farquharson 43–5, 57, 59, 64 n.176, 282–5, 290–1, 294–5, 298, 307
  ancestors and London roots 10–11, 10 n.7
  autograph birthday book 4, 11, 14
  birth 1, 9, *12*
  in Canada 2, 21–2, 24, *24*, *27*
  contract with Balderston and Horace Liveright 4, 64, 313–16
  contract with John Balderston 4, 57–8, 63, 95, 97, 290–2, 311–12
  contract with Universal Pictures Corporation 3–4, 66–7, 66 n.199
  death of sister Ethel 57, 60, 293, 295–6
  as Dick in Little Lord Fauntleroy 20, *23*
  early life 9–11, 13–14, 16–17
  and Ellen Terry 20
  as feminist and suffragist 30–2, 35 (*see also* Webling, Peggy, Published Works Cited, *Verses to Men*; Womens' Social and Political Union; Women's Suffrage Movement; Women Writers' Suffrage League)
  Frankenstein (*see* Webling's *Frankenstein*)
  and Hamilton Deane 2–4, 44–5, 50–3, 57–9, 61, 64, 86–7, 90, 95, 100, 107, 283–301, 304–8
  did not know him before *Frankenstein* 2, 44
  and Horace Liveright 3–4, 63–5, 297–302, 313–16
  and John Balderston 3–4, 54, 56–9, 62–7, 80 n.59, 81 n.63, 95, 97–100, 290–4, 297–302, 306–8, 310–12
  and John Ruskin 2, 16–19, *19*, 35, 38
    letters from Ruskin 18, 35, 38
    meets Ruskin 16–17
    Ruskin writes testimonial 2, 17
    visits to Brantwood 19
  as journalist 2, 26, 28
  as model at the Slade School 16
  as Moth in *Love's Labour's Lost* 13, 16
  in New York City 23–4
  as novelist 28–9, *34*
  and Pauline Johnson 21–2, *24*, 25

331

Index

in peacock feathers   20, *21*
performs for royalty   20, *22*
as playwright   1–2, 9, 29–30, 33, 36–8, 40–3, 51, 53, 61, 64–5, 75
published works cited
  The Amber Merchant   33 n.135, 42
  Anna Maria   43
  Blue Jay   28
  Boundary House (film)   33, 38
  Boundary House (novel)   33, 38, 68 n.4
  Comedy Corner   39, 43, 282–3
  Edgar Chirrup   33
  'An English Actor's Ghost Story'   22
  Felix Christie   29 n.109
  The Fruitless Orchard   40 n.17
  Guests of the Heart   35
  Opal Screens   33 n.136
  The Pearl Stringer   29 n.109, 33 n.135
  Peggy: The Story of One Score Years and Ten   13, 18, 35, 42
  Poems and Stories (with Lucy Webling)   25 n.86, 26, 33
  'Queer Trades of London'   43
  'The Real Pumblechook'   43
  Reprieve (dramatic adaptation)   36–7, 64, 294
  The Rhyme of Little Mark   35
  Saints and Their Stories   35
  The Scent Shop   33 n.135, 35
  A Sketch of John Ruskin   17 n.48, 19, *19*, 35
  A Spirit of Mirth   13 n.27, 28 n.100, 29 n.109
  The Story of Virginia Perfect   28, 29 n.109, 32 n.126
  Strange Enchantment   33 n.136
  Verses to Men   35–6
  Westward Ho! (dramatic adaptation)   29–30, 36–7, 40 n.9, 286, 305
  Young Laetitia   33
recitals and performances   13, *17*, 17–20, *22*, 23–4, *27*
as Silverstar Queen of the Fairies   13
unpublished works cited
  Abominable Snowmen   37–8
  Rossetti's Wife   37
  The Story of a Pen   4, 32, 38, 303–9
  The Stream   37
visit to Hollywood   309
Writers' Club   30, 33, 283, 295 (*see also* Writers' Club, London)
Webling Sisters (Misses Webling)   2, 13–15, 17, *18*, 20, *21*, *22*, 23, *27*
Webling's *Frankenstein*
  cast of characters
    Baron Frankenstein   81–2, 102, 287
    Baroness Frankenstein   59, 82, 287, 294
    Dr Waldman   53, 76–7, *80*, 80–92, 94–9, 102–3, 287–9
    Elizabeth (the maid)   *60*, 294
    Emilie Lavenza   52, 54, 59, 75, 81–7, *82*, 91, 94, 287, 290, 294–5
    Frankenstein   50–4, 76–7, 79–98, *80*, *85*, *86*, *88*, *93*, 101–3, 287–90, 304–7
    Henry Frankenstein   45, 50–3, 59, 75, 79–87, *80*, *82*, *88*, 89–92, *93*, 94–8, 101–2, 287, 290, 294–6, 304–5, 307
    Katrina / Katrine Frankenstein   41 n.19, 51, 54, 61, 75, 79, 82–7, *85*, *86*, 91–5, 102–3, 287–90, 292, 294–6, 304–6
    Victor Moritz   75, *80*, 80–82, 87–9, 95, 287
  Empire Theatre, Preston, Lancashire (*see* Empire Theatre, Preston, Lancashire)
  Little Theatre, London (*see* Little Theatre, London)
  1923 version   68 n.3, 69, 75–6, 79–85, 80 n.61, 83 n.66, 87, 90, 91 n.76, 95–6
  1927 version   3, 68 n.3, 69, 75–6, 79, 80 n.51, 82, 83 n.66, 85, 87, 90, 91 n.76, 95–6, 107, 109–64
  1928 version   3–4, 53, 56, 66 n.199, 68 n.3, 69, 75, 79, 82 n.64, 90 n.75, 91, 93, 95–7, 107, 165–220
  1930 Prompt Script   3–4, 68 n.3, 69, 75, 79, 82 n.64, 95–6, 107, 221–80
  playbills   55, *60*, *76*
  Webling's revisions to *Frankenstein*   2–4, 50–4, 56, 58, 69, 80 n.59, 82 n.64, 90–1, 93–5
Westminster City Archives
  Hamilton Deane Papers   3–4, 59, 75 n.39, *82*, *86*, 95
Weston, Arthur (pseudonym of Peggy Webling)   25
Whale, James
  Bride of Frankenstein   3, 75, 103
  Frankenstein   1, 3–4, 75, 81 n.63, 97, 98 n.86, 100–3, 308
Whitney, Mrs. Lucius   24
Wilde, Oscar   2, 20, 23
Wilde, Willie   23
Wills, Freeman   46
Wilson, Michael   49 n.72
Winter Gardens Theatre, New Brighton, Merseyside   54
Women Writers' Suffrage League   30–2
Women's Social and Political Union   30–1, *31*
Women's Suffrage Movement   14, 23 n.79, 30–2, 35
  Great Procession 18 June 1910   32
Wordsworth, William   14 n.28
Writer's Club, London   30–1, 33, 283, 295